THE COMPLETE KNIGHT'S CROSS

— VOLUME ONE —

THE YEARS OF VICTORY 1939–1941

KEVIN BRAZIER

FONTHILL

For Mr Keep, my history teacher who inspired me so much

Fonthill Media Language Policy

Fonthill Media publishes in the international English language market. One language edition is published worldwide. As there are minor differences in spelling and presentation, especially with regard to American English and British English, a policy is necessary to define which form of English to use. The Fonthill Policy is to use the form of English native to the author. Kevin Brazier was born and educated in Loughton, Essex; therefore British English has been adopted in this publication.

Fonthill Media Limited
Fonthill Media LLC
www.fonthillmedia.com
office@fonthillmedia.com

First published in the United Kingdom and the United States of America 2021

British Library Cataloguing in Publication Data:
A catalogue record for this book is available from the British Library

ISBN 978-1-78155-781-5

Typeset in 10pt on 13pt Sabon
Printed and bound in England

Acknowledgements

My initial thanks must go to Fonthill Media, and to Jay Slater in particular for commissioning me to write this book. Also, thanks go to my friends who have helped and supported me through this project: Christine McIntyre, Wytzia Raspe, Antia Motmans, and Ronny and Patricia Colson. Thanks also to Tom Johnson, BEM, whose help is always welcome.

I must thank Lance Renetzke, Thomas Rückert, Mike 'Lutz' Passmore, and Tony 'Horst' Dudmann, for their knowledge of the German Army; Hugo Langendries, for tracking down some much needed books for me; and Siggi Drepper and Jill Sugden, for translating German text. Special thanks to Mark Green, whose help in tracking down the last resting places of so many Knight's Cross holders has been invaluable.

I must thank the staff of the many museums and cemeteries I have been in contact with, either on the phone or in person.

Thanks also to Nathan Dudenbostel, for info on his relative, Wolfgang Luehrs, and for letting me use a photo of him.

Special thanks to my late friend Joe Dever, for reformatting all my photos for the book.

Finally, Josh Greenland for his editing and putting up with my constant last-minute changes.

Due to space, I am unable to include a complete chronological list of Knight's Cross holders, but I will be happy to supply this to anyone who wants it, email me at kib1856@yahoo.co.uk or find me on Facebook: Kevin Brazier Author.

Contents

Glossary

Abwehr:	German Intelligence Department
Alpini:	mountain
Ardennes offensive:	last major German attack in the West
Arzt:	doctor
Assault gun:	tracked armoured fighting vehicle with a fixed gun
Assistenzarzt (equal in rank to *Leutnant*):	assistant doctor
Barbarossa:	the invasion of Russia
Batallionführer (equal to *Hauptmann*):	battalion leader
Bau-Pionier:	construction troops
Berchtesgaden:	Hitler's hilltop retreat.
Bf 110:	twin-engined heavy fighter
Blitzkrieg:	lightning war
Bolshevism:	a communism form of government formed in Russia
Brandenburg/Brandenburger:	commando unit, sometimes dressed in enemy uniform
Bundesmarine:	post-war German Navy
Bundeswehr:	post-war West German Government
Campaign in the West:	refers to the invasion of Belgium, Holland, France, and Luxembourg
Claymore:	a double-edged broadsword
Condor Legion:	German forces used in the Spanish Civil War
Conducător:	leader

Cupola:	fortified domed firing position
Destroyer wing:	heavy fighter unit
Do 215:	twin-engined medium bomber/ night fighter
Ersatz:	replacement
Fallschirmjäger:	paratrooper
Feldmeister (equal to *Leutnant*):	foreman
Fieseler Storch:	single-engined light reconnaissance aircraft
Fliegerkorps:	flying corps
Flugplatz:	airfield/airport
Freiherr von:	baron of (noble family title)
Freikorps:	right-wing nationalist
Freiwilligen:	volunteer
Friedhof:	cemetery
Fw 190:	single-engine fighter, also used for ground attack
Gebirgsjäger:	mountain troops
Gestapo:	secret police
Handelsmarine:	merchant navy
He 111:	twin-engined bomber
Heer:	army
Jagd-Panzer IV:	assault gun armed with a 75-mm anti-tank gun
Jäger:	hunter, also used to indicate a mountain unit
Ju 87 'Stuka':	dive bomber
Ju 88:	twin-engined bomber/night fighter
Kaiserlichemarine:	Imperial Navy
Kampfgruppe:	a battlegroup made of several other units
K-Boat Flotilla:	Klein boat, a small craft unit
Kirchhof:	churchyard
Kirkegard:	cemetery
Krieg:	war
Kriegsmarine:	War Navy
L-boat:	landing or assault boat
Luftflotte:	air fleet
Luftwaffe:	German Air Force
Marine-Schreiber:	navy clerk
Marsch Company/Battalion:	*ad hoc* or temporary unit

Matilda tank:	British infantry tank with very think armour
M-Boat:	minesweeping boat
Me 163:	single-engined jet fighter
Me 262:	twin-engined jet fighter
Nord:	north
Oberarzt (equal in rank to *Oberleutnant*):	senior doctor
Oberbaustab:	Construction HQ Staff
Oberfeldarzt (equal in rank to *Oberleutnant*):	senior field doctor
Oberfernschreibmeister:	senior telegraph operator
Oberfeuerwerker:	blacksmith or metal worker
Oberschirrmeister:	over harness master
Oberstabsarzt (equal in rank to *Hauptmann*):	senior staff doctor
Ost:	east
P-38 'Lightning':	twin-engined US fighter
P-51 'Mustang':	single-engined US fighter
Pak:	anti-tank gun or unit
Panzerfaust:	handheld anti-tank weapon
Pour le Mérite:	Imperial Germany's highest award up until 1918, commonly known as the Blue Max
Putsch:	Push
R-Boat:	patrol boat
Reich:	empire
Reichswald:	large forest on Germany's border with Holland
Reichswehr:	Army allowed Germany under the Treaty of Versailles, limited to 100,000 men
Ritter:	knight, title awarded by royal decree
Sanitäts:	medic
S-boat:	fast torpedo boat, called E-boats by the British, possibly 'E' for enemy boat
Schnelle:	fast
Sea Lion:	German code name for the planned to invasion of Britain
Section:	group of about eight men
Sonderkommando:	unit that took part in the killing of Partisans, Jews, and civilians

Sortie:	a patrol made by aircraft
Spiess:	senior NCO responsible for the welfare of the men
Stab:	staff
Stabsarzt (equal in rank to *Leutnant*):	staff doctor
Strafing:	low-level attack made by aircraft
Sturm:	assault
Sturmovik:	heavily armoured Russian twin-engined fighter
Swordfish:	biplane with three crew
T-Boat:	torpedo boat
U-*Jäger*:	submarine chaser
Verband:	*ad hoc* or improvised unit
Volk:	people
Volkssturm:	People's Army, mostly consisting of young buys and old men
VP-boat (*Vorpostenboot*):	heavily armed coastal patrol boat
Waffen-SS:	armed-SS. When used as a prefix to a rank/unit, it indicates a non-Germanic SS volunteer or unit
Wehrmacht:	Germany's military forces
Werfer (thrower):	rocket artillery
Westwall:	German defensive position on its border with France, more commonly known as the Siegfried Line

Acronyms and Abbreviations

aka	also known as
AKCR	Association of Knight's Cross Recipients
AOK	Army Over Commando
APC	Armoured Personal Carrier
BEF	British Expeditionary Force
CO	Commanding Officer
CWGC	Commonwealth War Graves Commission

FA	*Flieger Abteilung* (Flying Section)
FA(A)	*Flieger Abteilung Artillerie* (Flying Section Artillery)
FFA	*Feldflieger Abteilung* (Field Aviation Unit)
GC	George Cross
GD	*Grossdeutschland*
GG	General Göring
GWC	German War Cemetery
HG	Hermann Göring
HMAS	His Majesty's Australian Ship
HMCS	His Majesty's Canadian Ship
HMS	His Majesty's Ship
HQ	Headquarters
JG	*Jagdgeschwader* (Fighter Wing)
LAH	*Leibstandarte* Adolf Hitler
LSI	Landing Ship Infantry
LST	Landing Ship Tank
MI6	British Secret Service
MTB	Motor Torpedo Boat
MV	Merchant Vessel
NCO	Non-Commissioned Officer
NKVD	Russian security police
OBdl	Reconnaissance Group Command of the Luftwaffe
OKH	*Oberkommando der Heer* (Supreme Command of the Army)
OKL	*Oberkommando der Luftwaffe* (Supreme Command of the Air Force)
OKM	*Oberkommando der Kriegsmarine* (Supreme Command of the Navy)
OKW	*Oberkommando der Wehrmacht* (Supreme Command of the Armed Forces)
POW	Prisoner of War
RAAF	Royal Australian Air Force
RAF	Royal Air Force
SD	Security Police
SOE	Special Operations Executive
US	United States

Comparative Ranks

The Army

German/Other	English
Fähnrich/SS-Standartenjunker/Fahnenjunker	Officer Cadet
Feldwebel/Wachtmeister/ SS-*Oberscharführer*	Staff Sergeant
Gefreiter/SS-Sturmmann	Lance Corporal
General/*General de corp de armată* (Romania)	General
Generalfeldmarschall/Airmarschall	Field Marshal
Generalleutnant/SS-Obergruppenführer/ SA-*Obergruppenführer/Generale di Divisions* (Italian)/*General de diviszie* (Romanian)/ *Altábornagy* (Hungarian)	Lieutenant-General
Generalmajor/SS-Gruppenführer/ *Generale di Brigata* (Italian)/ *General de Brigadă* (Romanian)	Major-General
Generaloberst/SS-Oberstgruppenführer/ *Generale di Corpo* (Italian)/ *General de armată* (Romanian)	None
Grenadier/Pioneer/Jäger/Flieger/ SS-*Schutze*/SS-*Mann*/SS-*Grenadier*/SS-*Kanonier/* *Volkssturmmann*	Private
Hauptfeldwebel/SS-Stabsscharführer	Company Sergeant Major
Hauptgefreiter	None
Hauptmann/Rittmeister/SS-Hauptsturmführer/ *Stabsintendant* (a rank for officials)	Captain
Leutnant/SS-Untersturmführer	Second Lieutenant
Major/SS-Sturmbannführer/*Maior* (Romanian)	Major
Oberfähnrich/SS-Standartenoberjunker	None
Oberfeldwebel/Oberwachtmeister/ SS-*Hauptscharführer*	Warrant Officer Class 2
Obergefreiter/SS-Rottenführer	Corporal
Obergrenadier/SS-Oberschtze	None
Oberleutnant/SS-Obersturmführer	First Lieutenant
Oberst/SS-Standartenführer/ SS-*Oberführer/* *Colonel* (Romanian)	Colonel
Oberstleutnant/SS-Obersturmbannführer	Lieutenant-Colonel
SS-*Brigadeführer*	Brigadier
Stabsfeldwebel/Stabswachtmeister/ SS-*Sturmscharführer*	Warrant Officer Class 1
*Stabsgefreiter/SS-Stabsrottenführer**	Corporal

Unterfeldwebel/SS-Scharführer	Sergeant
Unteroffizier/Oberjäger/SS-Unterscharführer	Corporal

* These ranks did not officially exist, but have been used in many written records of the period.

The Navy

Admiral	Admiral
Bootsmannsmaat	Petty Officer 2nd Class
Fähnrich zur See	Officer Cadet
Fregattenkapitän (Frigate)/*Korvettenkapitän* (Corvette)/*Capitano di Corvetta* (Italian)/ *Capitano di Fregata* (Italian)	Commander
Generaladmiral	None
Grossadmiral	Admiral of the Fleet
Kapitän zur See	Captain
Kapitänleutnant	Lieutenant-Commander
Kommodore	Commodore
Konteradmiral/Contraadmiral (Romanian)	Rear-Admiral
Leutnant zur See	Sub-Lieutenant
Matrose	Seaman
Matrosengefreiter	Seaman 1st Class
Oberbootsmannsmaat	Petty Officer 1st Class
Oberfähnrich zur See	None
Oberleutnant zur See	Lieutenant
Obermaat	Petty Officer 3rd Class
Obermaschinist	Chief Machinist
Oberstabsgefreiter	Seaman 2nd Class
Obersteuermann	Chief Helmsman
Seekadett	Midshipman
Stabsoberfeldwebel	Senior Sergeant-Major
Stabsobermaschinist	Senior Chief Machinist
Stabsobersteuermann	Senior Chief Helmsman
Vizeadmiral	Vice-Admiral

Introduction

This book is about bravery, nothing else. I say this because, when I told a friend I was writing it, he asked me 'Why are you writing a Nazi book?' My response was to ask whether he thought that only the Allied soldiers were brave. To quote Karl Wegner from the 914 Regiment of the 352nd Grenadier Division: '... we were young men fighting for our country. Yes, it was an evil government, but we had known no other'.

This is the fourth book in my series of *The Complete*. It tells the story of the 7,364 men who were awarded the Knight's Cross. Volume One focuses on the awards from 1939–41 (numbers 1–1267) and is subtitled 'The Years of Victory'. Volume Two explores the years 1942–43 (numbers 1268–3685) and is subtitled 'The Years of Stalemate'. Volume Three surveys 1944–45 (numbers 3686–7364) and is subtitled 'The Years of Defeat'. They are listed in the order of the date of award.

Like my last book, *The Complete Blue Max*, you may notice this book is not in exactly the same format as the first two; this is due in part to the fact that the Knight's Cross was not always awarded for a signal act of bravery but also for reaching a level of achievement or for successful military leadership. Additionally, many holders have no known graves, and the unknown whereabouts of their medals makes doing such a list pointless.

The Knight's Cross was awarded a total of 7,364 times (including all the disputed awards). The Oak Leaves were awarded 890 times, and on four occasions, they were awarded at the same time as the Knight's Cross—to Wilhelm Crinius (1897), Bodo Spranz (3281), Isoroku Yamamoto (2824), and Mineichi Koga (4446) (the last two being political awards made by Hitler after the deaths of the recipients). The Swords were awarded 160 times; the Diamonds were awarded twenty-seven times; and the Golden Oak Leaves, Swords and Diamonds only once, to Hans-Ulrich Rudel (1273). Likewise, the Grand Cross was only awarded once, to Hermann Göring (1).

Disputed Awards

There are a number of disputed awards, and they fall into four main categories, the first being those awarded under the Dönitz-Decree, which approved all bestowals of the Knight's Cross and its higher grades that had been received by the OKW up until the surrender became effective; in 1988, these awards were deemed illegal by the Deutsche Dienststelle (WASt). The second category were those awards that were unlawfully presented by field commanders without authorisation during the closing weeks of the war (Sepp Dietrich claims to have been authorised by Hitler to award the Knight's Cross in May 1944. This is questionable and there is no documentation to confirm it). Third were the recommended awards where the paperwork was started but not finished by the end of the war; the Association of Knight's Cross Recipients (AKCR), headed by Walther-Peer Fellgiebel (3162), looked into many of these cases and decided whether the awards were justified—if so, they were assigned a date. The fourth category concerned those 'recipients' who claimed to have been awarded it without any real evidence. Additionally, there was Günther Nowak (6706), who did not exist but was awarded the Knight's Cross, and Walter Lippelt (7259), who may not have existed. The most interesting case is Heinrich Scherhorn (6786), who was awarded it as a POW working for the Russians. All of these have been included, and I leave it up to the reader to decide upon them. One interesting case is that of Fritz-Adolf Geisendorf; he was unlawfully presented the Knight's Cross in January 1944 by *Generaloberst* Josef Harpe (772), but unlike the other 'unlawfully' presented awards, Geisendorf does not appear on any Knight's Cross list (although there are photos of him wearing it), for this reason he is not included.

A Note on Place Names

The Soviet Union is referred to as Russia throughout as the German soldiers knew it as *Russland*. Names used when referring to cities, towns, etc. during the war may, of course, be in a different country after it. For example, a soldier who was killed in Kiev, Soviet Union, is buried in Kiev, Ukraine.

Final Note

Every effort has been made to check facts, dates, and names; however, errors are unavoidable, and the responsibility of this is entirely mine. Should you find any errors or indeed have any new information, I would be grateful if you could let me know. I can be contacted at kib1856@yahoo.co.uk or found on Facebook—search Kevin Brazier author.

A Short History of the Medal

The Knight's Cross of the Iron Cross owes its origins to the *Pour le Mérite* (Blue Max). An imperial award dating back to 1740, it was only awarded to officers and was not awarded posthumously. At the start of the Second World War, Hitler reintroduced the Iron Cross 1st and 2nd Class (which date back to 1813 but were reissued in 1870 and 1914) and the Grand Cross of the Iron Cross. Having served in the First World War, he wanted to bridge the gap between the Iron Cross 1st Class and the Grand Gross, which in the First World War was only for senior commanders, so Hitler introduced the Knight's Cross on 1 September 1939. The new award could now be given to all ranks and would also be awarded posthumously. The Knight's Cross measures 48.8 mm and weighs approximately 28 grams. It was suspended around the neck from a 45-mm-wide striped ribbon, which was black, white, red, white, and black.

The Knight's Cross could be awarded for extreme battlefield bravery or successful military leadership. It could also be awarded for reaching a certain level of achievement in battle: fighter pilots were awarded it for shooting down twenty-six enemy aircraft—though, as the war went on, this figure was increased—and U-boat commanders were required to sink 100,000 tons of shipping (but there were exceptions in both cases).

The Knight's Cross could not be awarded until the recipient had been awarded the Iron Cross 1st and 2nd Class; however, all three awards could be, and sometimes were, awarded on the same day, especially during the early stages of the war. The Oak Leaves (OL) to the Knight's Cross (which were also awarded for the Blue Max) were introduced on 3 June 1940 and were worn above the Knight's Cross. As the war went on, it was necessary to introduce further awards, and the Swords (S) were introduced on 21 June 1941; these were worn under the Oak Leaves, but still above the Knight's Cross. On the same day, the Diamonds (D) were introduced; these were placed on the Oak Leaves themselves. One more award was introduced on 29 December 1944: the Golden Oak Leaves, Swords and Diamonds (GOLSD).

To bridge the gap between the Iron Cross 1st Class and the Knight's Cross, Hitler introduced the German Cross (awarded in silver and gold) on 28 September 1941. This award was, however, often presented after the awarding of the Knight's Cross and, indeed, not every Knight's Cross holder was awarded it—although most were.

On 3 March 1945, Hitler banned the award of the Knight's Cross for successful military leadership. However, this message was either ignored or, due to the military situation, was not received; this is evidenced by a number of high-ranking officers still being presented with it after this date.

In 1957, the *Bundeswehr* government of West Germany reintroduced all of the classes of the Iron Cross and Knight's Cross apart from the Grand Gross. The new awards differ only in that the Swastika has been replaced with the Oak Leaves cluster, and the date 1939 has been replaced with 1957. To date, none have been awarded. Also, at this time, living veterans were allowed to wear their wartime awards, though the Swastika has been replaced with the Oak Leaves cluster—the 1939 date was retained.

A quick note on other awards mentioned in the text. The Wound Badge, unsurprisingly, was for being wounded, and it came in three grades: Black for one or two wounds; Silver for three to five wounds, or one wound resulting in the loss of a hand, eye, or causing deafness; and Gold for five or more wounds, or one wound resulting in total disability, permanent blindness, or loss of manhood. The Close Combat Clasp was awarded for continuous days in combat; it also came in three grades: Bronze for fifteen days, Silver for twenty-five days, and Gold for fifty days. Gold recipients were meant to be relieved from combat duties; however, some men still chose to stay on at the front after its award. The Tank Destruction Badge was awarded for the single-handed destruction of an enemy tank. The Silver award was for a single tank and the Gold for five tanks.

1

1939

1. *Generalfeldmarschall* Hermann GÖRING—'The Iron Man'

The son of Dr Heinrich Göring, governor of German South West Africa, Hermann Göring was born in Rosenheim, Upper Bavaria, on 12 January 1893. He was a rebellious and undisciplined child, so he was sent to the military academy at Karlsruhe; from there, he went to Lichterfelde, an army cadet college for future officers. On graduating, with the highest honours that a cadet could achieve, he received praise from the Kaiser himself and was commissioned into the Prinz Wilhelm Regiment Nr. 112. He had a passion for mountain climbing and did not shrink from the danger, believing nothing bad could happen to him.

At the outbreak of war, his regiment was straight into action as it was stationed at Mühlhausen in Alsace-Lorraine, on the wrong side of the Rhine. When the regiment was moved to the Vosges region, he contracted rheumatic fever. While in hospital, he was visited by his friend Bruno Loerzer, who had served in the same regiment with him but was now a pilot with the German Army Air Service. Loerzer's visit gave Göring much to think about, specifically a potential return to the cold and the mud. He wrote to his CO requesting a transfer to the Freiburg flying school, and after receiving no response after two weeks of waiting, he obtained the papers and signed them himself. He spent the next two weeks flying with Loerzer and getting all the training he could. However, his transfer was refused and he was ordered to rejoin his unit; this situation posed a serious problem as he was open to charges of desertion and forging papers. He immediately telegraphed his godfather, *Ritter* von Epstein, who moved in high circles, and suddenly Crown Prince Friedrich Wilhelm intervened, asking that Göring be posted to the German Fifth Army Field Air Detachment. The charges were reduced to one of lateness, and he was given a medical certificate saying that he was unfit for front-line duty. It should be remembered here that he was not trying to get out of the fighting, he just wanted to fight in the air.

In the autumn of 1914, he completed his training and then joined Bruno Loerzer at FFA 25. They flew together as often as possible and soon made a reputation for carrying out the most dangerous missions. In March 1915, they were awarded the Iron Cross 2nd Class. In May, they were sent to carry out a reconnaissance of the French fortresses of Verdun, a task that many others had tried and failed. For three days, they flew over the Verdun area, taking pictures so detailed that General Erich von Falkenhayn asked to see them personally. High Command was so impressed with the results that Crown Prince Wilhelm exercised his royal prerogative and awarded them both the Iron Cross 1st Class in the field. In June 1915, Göring was posted to Freiburg for pilot training, passing out in October and being sent to FA 25. On 16 November, while flying an Albatros, he shot down his first enemy aircraft, a Maurice Farman over Tahure.

In 1916, Göring was posted to *Kek* Stennay, flying Fokker E.IIIs, and then to *Kek* Metz in March, where he shot down a Caudron on the 14th; on 30 July, he shot down another Caudron over Memang. On 9 July, he went back to FA 25 and again to *Kek* Metz on 7 September. He was posted to *Jasta* 7 in early October before swiftly moving, on 20 October, to *Jasta* 5. While on patrol on 2 November, he came across a Handley-Page bomber, and as he closed in on it, he came under fire; returning fire, he killed one of the enemy gunners, before coming under fire from an escorting Sopwith, from which he was hit in the thigh. Losing consciousness momentarily, he came to as he was plummeting towards the ground, managing to regain control and landing next to an emergency hospital just inside the German lines; within a very short time, he was being operated on.

At the beginning of February 1917, he was posted to *Jasta* 26, now under the command of his friend Bruno Loerzer, and by the end of the month, he had brought his score to six downed aircraft. On 10 May, he shot down a DH.4 of 55 Squadron over Le Pavé, and one week later, he was given command of *Jasta* 27, a unit that had yet to score its first kill after three months of existence. On 16 July, he shot down an S.E.5a (victory No. 9) and was in turn brought down by the same pilot, both men claiming a 'kill'. On 21 September, he shot down the Bristol Fighter flown by Lieutenant R. L. Curtis (who had fifteen victories) and Lieutenant D. P. F. Uniacke (who had thirteen victories). His scoring was much slower at this time due to the responsibility of command, and it took until the end of October to bring his own tally to fifteen kills. On 27 October, Göring was awarded the Military Karl Friedrich Merit Order, the Knight's Cross with Swords of the Royal Hohenzollern House Order, and the Knight's Cross 2nd Class with Swords of the Baden Order of the Zahringer Lion. His final kill of the year occurred on 7 November—a DH.4 north-west of Poelcappelle—however, much confusion surrounds this claim as only one British aircraft was reported lost on this date—an AWFK VIII two-seater.

It was not until 21 February 1918 that he scored again, an S.E.5a from 60 Squadron, followed by an R.E.8 on 7 April from 48 Squadron. On 2 June 1918, he was awarded the *Pour le Mérite* by the Kaiser, and by the end of the month, he had brought down three more aircraft, bringing his tally to twenty-one. On 9 July, he was given command of JG 1, the 'Richthofen' Wing, with promotion to *Oberleutnant*; his only victory while leading this unit was on 18 July. From then on, he did very little flying, either deciding or being ordered to take a more administrative role due to the lack of experienced officers.

On 9 August 1918, the order to cease all further air operation came and he was ordered to fly his aircraft to an Allied airfield; knowing full well the Allies wanted the latest Fokkers, he ordered his pilots to set fire to the planes on landing. After fighting in the post-war revolution with the rank of *Hauptmann*, he went to Denmark in a flight advisory capacity, but returned to Germany in the early 1920s.

Göring joined the Nazi Party in 1922 and was appointed commander of the SA in 1923.In November 1923, he was involved in the *Beer Hall Putsch*. Ludendorff, Hitler, and Göring marched in front of a large column with Ulrich Graf carrying a swastika flag before them, shots were fired and Göring was hit in the hip and thighs. As a result of his wounds, he was given two shots of morphine a day for a month.

In 1925, he went into a sanatorium three times to be cured of his morphine addiction, which he did by willpower alone. In 1928, he was elected to the Reichstag and became its president in 1932. When Hitler was appointed chancellor in January 1933, Göring became Reich minister, Reich commissioner for aviation, and acting Prussian minister of the interior; later the same year, he was appointed minister president of Prussia. He was promoted to general in May 1933, but from April, his old wounds started to give him problems and he was back on painkillers. In March 1934, he was named as Hitler's successor. March 1935 saw him appointed general of the Luftwaffe, with the rank of *Generalleutnant*, and he was soon after promoted to *Oberstgeneral*.

In April 1935, he was appointed Reich Commissioner for Resources, which allowed him to channel resources into the Luftwaffe. In October 1936, he was appointed as the person responsible for the 'Four-Year Plan', which was to make the Reich independent from imports. Göring appointed himself commander-in-chief of the Luftwaffe in June 1937. Throughout 1937, he tried many weight cures, though this only weakened him, and he was still being treated for his addiction to pills. He received yet another promotion in February 1938, this time to *Reichsmarschall*. On 30 September 1939, he was awarded the Knight's Cross of the Iron Cross.

Published in 1940, his authorised biography is called *Hermann Göring: The Man and his Work*. On 19 July 1940, after the fall of France, he was promoted to *Reichsmarschall* and was awarded the Grand Cross of the Iron Cross, the only person to be awarded it. He was now at the height of his power.

From the Battle of Britain onwards, his influence started to decline, and his Luftwaffe was unable to dominate the skies as he had promised the Führer. In 1941, his paratroopers suffered heavy losses in the Battle of Crete. He became known throughout Germany as '*Meier*' due to his boast that no enemy plane would ever fly over the Reich—by now a common occurrence. The Führer lost even more faith in him after the fall of Stalingrad in 1943, as Göring had promised he could resupply the city from the air; Göring was, by now, completely unable to stop the bombing of German cites. Reproached by Hitler, he feared being relieved from the command of the Luftwaffe, and mood swings became a common aspect of his persona.

In April 1945, Göring sent Hitler his famous telegram stating that he would assume overall leadership of the Reich if he (Hitler) was unable to act freely. Two days later, Göring was relieved of all offices and Hitler ordered his arrest. He was to be shot after Hitler's death, but the SS guard was unsure of this and telephoned *Feldmarschall* Kesselring, who forbade it and told the guard to leave Göring to himself. On 8 May, he fell into the hands of the Americans. Sent to trail at Nuremberg in 1946 and found guilty of war crimes, he killed himself with poison on 15 October 1946. His ashes were scattered in the River Isar, near Munich.

2. *Grossadmiral* Erich RAEDER

Raeder was born in Wandsbek on 24 April 1876. His father was a headmaster. He joined the *Kaiserliche Marine* in 1894 and became chief-of-staff for Franz von Hipper in 1912. Raeder was also the captain of the Kaiser's private yacht in the years leading up to the First World War. He took part in the raids on Yarmouth and Hartlepool, as well as the bombardment of Lowestoft. He also took part in the Battle of Dogger Bank in 1915 and the Battle of Jutland in 1916.

After the war, Raeder was involved in the Beer Hall Putsch in 1920; due to this, he was marginalised in the navy and transferred to the naval archives, where he studied naval history for two years. While there, he wrote a number of studies about naval warfare, which resulted in him being awarded an honorary doctorate by Kiel University. Raeder was promoted to *Konteradmiral* in 1922 and *Vizeadmiral* in 1925. In October 1928, Raeder was promoted again, this time to admiral, and he was made commander-in-chief of the *Reichsmarine*. Although he disliked the Nazi Party, he supported Hitler's attempt at rebuilding the *Kriegsmarine* in the 1930s, while disagreeing strongly on most other matters. Raeder was promoted to *Generaladmiral* on 20 April 1936, just before his sixtieth birthday.

Raeder was promoted again in 1939 to *Grossadmiral*, becoming the first person to hold that rank since Alfred von Tirpitz. He was awarded the Knight's Cross on 30 September 1939. Raeder suggested invading Norway in order to secure sheltered docks as well as provide direct exits to the North Sea. This would also secure the transport route for the iron ore from Sweden, but this plan was opposed by the Naval Staff. The British needed to stop this supply and an invasion was ordered on 12 March 1940 but cancelled due to peace in Finland; however, Hitler rightly believed that the British would try again and ordered his own invasion of Norway.

Raeder was also against the invasion of Britain, and he believed that the war at sea could be conducted far more successfully by increasing the number of U-boats, S-boats, and R-boats. He favoured a focus on the Mediterranean Theatre, capturing Malta, Gibraltar, and the Canary Islands. He suggested that Rommel be sent to Egypt to capture the Suez Canal. All this, he believed, would knock Britain out of the war. He was also against the war with the Soviet Union; Raeder thought Hitler was so fixed on wiping out the Soviet regime that he did not realise that a global strategy could have easily tipped the balance in Germany's favour.

A series of failed operations (particularly the Battle of the Barents Sea) combined with the outstanding success of the U-boats now under the command of Dönitz led to his demotion to admiral inspector of the *Kriegsmarine* in January 1943. Raeder offered his resignation as an apology and formally resigned in May 1943. Suspected of being involved in the 20 July plot, Raeder cleared himself by going to Rastenburg to personally assure Hitler of his loyalty.

After the war, Raeder was tried and sentenced to life at the Nuremberg Trials for waging an aggressive war, a charge resulting from his plan to invade Norway. His defence was that Germany was compelled to attack Norway to forestall a British invasion and therefore her action was pre-emptive. The plea was rejected and he was sentenced to life.

The sentence was later reduced, and due to ill health, Raeder was released on 26 September 1955. He settled down in Lippstadt and wrote his autobiography called *Mein Leben*. Erich Raeder died on 6 November 1960 and is buried in Nordfriedhof, Feld XE, Grave 338, Kiel, Schleswig-Holstein.

3. *Generaloberst* Fedor von BOCK—'Holy Fire of Küstrin' or 'The Dying One'

Von Bock was born on 3 December 1880 in Küstrin. Von Bock's family were Prussian aristocrats whose military heritage stretched back to his great-grandfather who served under Frederick the Great. At the age of eight, he was sent to Berlin to study at Potsdam, where the education emphasised Prussian militarism; during his time at Potsdam, he quickly became adept in academic subjects such as mathematics, history, and languages (speaking French fluently, with a passable knowledge of English and Russian). From an early age, he developed an unquestioned loyalty to the state and a dedication to military professionalism. At the age of seventeen, von Bock became an officer cadet, being commissioned *Leutnant* in the 5th Foot Guards in 1898.

In 1905, he married Mally von Reichenbach, with whom he had a daughter two years later. Von Bock attended the War Academy in Berlin in 1908 with the rank *Oberleutnant*, and he joined the General Staff two years later as a *Hauptmann*. When the First World War broke out, von Bock was still with the General Staff, but in January and February 1916, he commanded a battalion of the 4th Foot Guards. This was only short-lived as he was soon back on the General Staff on the Western Front, with whom he was promoted to *Major* in December 1916. He ended the war on the General Staff, being awarded the *Pour le Mérite* on 1 April 1918. Two days before the Armistice, von Bock met with Wilhelm II in an unsuccessful attempt to persuade the Kaiser to return to Berlin to crush the mutiny at Kiel.

After the war, he stayed in the army. The tall, thin, narrow-shouldered von Bock was described as arrogant, ambitious, and opinionated, and he approached military bearing with an unbending demeanour. While not a brilliant theoretician, von Bock was a highly determined officer. As one of the highest-ranking officers in the Reichswehr, being promoted to *Oberstleutnant* in 1920. He often addressed graduating cadets, and the theme was always the greatest glory that could become a soldier was to die for the Fatherland; this attitude earnt him the nickname 'Holy Fire of Küstrin' and 'The Dying One'.

In the 1920s, von Bock was a member of a secret group known as *Sondergruppe R*, selected by Hans von Seeckt in charge of helping Germany to evade Part V of the Treaty of Versailles, which limited the army to 100,000 men. In 1925, von Bock was promoted to *Oberst*, and by 1929, he was a *Generalmajor*. He was promoted to *Generalleutnant* in 1931. Hitler appointed him commander of the Third Army Group with the rank of *General* on 1 March 1935. Von Bock personally despised Nazism and remained a monarchist, frequently visiting the former Kaiser's estate. General von Bock commanded the occupation of Austria in March 1938 and then the invasion of Czechoslovakia. He replaced von Rundstedt as commander of Army Group North later the same year. In September 1939, he led Army Group North to victory in the brief Polish campaign, for which he was awarded the Knight's Cross on 30 September 1939. Then he was transferred to the Western Front to command Army Group B for the invasion of France. Von Bock's army was originally intended to lead the main assault into the Netherlands and Belgium, but after the adoption of the Manstein plan, his armies gave up most of their armour and his role was to entice the British and French into Belgium while the armour broke through to the south. Von Bock's troops still managed to capture Paris, where he took the salute on the Champs-Élysées. For this, he was promoted to *Generalfeldmarschall* on 18 July 1940. He spent most of the rest of the summer between his HQ in Paris and his home in Berlin.

On 2 February 1941, von Bock met with Hitler and questioned if the Russians could be forced to make peace even if the Red Army was defeated. Hitler assured him that Germany's resources were more than sufficient. Von Bock's Army Group Centre would lead the assault on Russia; the original assault plan was to follow Napoleon's route north of the Pripyat Marshes straight to Moscow, but against von Bock's advice, Hitler altered the plan and made him go via Minsk and Smolensk to destroy the Russian armies there, in great encirclement battles. He even had to drive towards Leningrad to help Army Group North destroy the armies there before he was allowed to continue his drive on Moscow, but it was late September before this could happen, which meant that he failed to capture Moscow before the onset of winter. On 13 December, the Russian Army counteroffensive began. Von Bock was relieved of his command on the 18th, officially due to a stomach complaint, but in fact he was one of forty high-ranking officers to lose their commands for failing to capture Moscow.

When von Reichenau died from a heart attack in January 1942, von Bock was given command of Army Group South and tasked with the capture of the oil fields to the south of Stalingrad. On 28 June 1942, von Bock's army group drove deep into the Russian lines, splitting the front on either side of Kursk and reaching the Don River on 5 July. Von Bock then wanted to destroy the Russian forces before extending his flank into the void created by the speed of his offensive, but Hitler ordered him to push on to Stalingrad. After a number of disagreements on this matter, Hitler relieved him of command and retired him permanently.

Von Bock felt that he was made a scapegoat for the problems of Stalingrad. He was approached to join the plot against Hitler but refused. With the Russian Army moving in on Berlin in 1945, he was informed that Dönitz was trying to form a new government in Hamburg. On 4 May 1945, von Bock started immediately to make his way to Hamburg with his wife and daughter, but less than a week before the end of the war, his car was attacked by a British fighter-bomber, killing all three inside. He was the only one of Hitler's *Feldmarschalls* to be killed in action. He is buried in St Katharina Friedhof, Grave 23, Lensahn, Schleswig-Holstein.

4. *Generaloberst* Walter von BRAUCHITSCH

Von Brauchitsch was born on 4 October 1881. He was commissioned *Leutnant* in the Prussian Guard in 1900, and by the start of the First World War, he was appointed to the General Staff with the rank of *Hauptmann*, where he spent most of this time during the war. By the war's end, he was a *Major*.

In 1933, when Hitler came to power and began expanding the military, von Brauchitsch was named chief of the East Prussian Military District. In 1937, he became commander of the Fourth Army Group. Personally, he disliked much of the Nazi system, but he did welcome the rearmament and he was dazzled by Hitler's personality. Von Brauchitsch was appointed commander of the army in February 1938 with the rank of *Generaloberst*; he was the replacement for *General* Werner von Fritsch, who had been dismissed. He resented the growing power of the SS, believing they were attempting to take over as the official German armed forces. Like General Beck, Brauchitsch opposed the annexation of Austria and Czechoslovakia, but he took no action when Beck tried to persuade the whole General Staff to resign if Hitler proceeded with plans to invade Czechoslovakia.

In September 1938, a group of officers began plotting against Hitler and repeatedly tried to persuade him to lead the coup, but the only assurance he gave them was 'I myself won't do anything, but I won't stop anyone else from acting.' His Knight's Cross was awarded to him on 30 September 1939.

In early November 1939, Brauchitsch and Franz Halder considered overthrowing Hitler after he fixed 'X-day', the invasion of France, for 12 November. Brauchitsch agreed to read a memorandum recommending against launching an attack on the West that autumn, saying that the morale in the army was worse than it was in 1918. Flying into a tremendous rage, Hitler accused the General Staff and Brauchitsch personally of disloyalty, cowardice, sabotage, and defeatism. Hitler then called a meeting of the General Staff to declare that he would smash the West within a year. However, following heavy snowfall, 'X-day' was postponed until further notice. Brauchitsch would never again challenge Hitler.

On 19 July 1940, Brauchitsch was promoted to *Generalfeldmarschall* and took a key role in the Blitzkrieg in the West, making modifications to the original plan to overrun France. Had Operation Sea Lion succeeded, Hitler intended to put Brauchitsch in charge of Britain.

In 1941, Brauchitsch had a serious heart attack and was relieved of his command on 10 December. He spent the last three years of the war in the Brdy Mountains, south-west of Prague. After the war, he was arrested and charged with war crimes, but died in Hamburg in 1948 before the trial started. He is buried in Waldfriedhof, Salzgitter, Lower Saxony.

5. *Generaloberst* Wilhelm KEITEL 'Lakeitel'

Keitel was born on 22 September 1882 in Helmscherode. He joined the army in 1901 as an officer cadet, and by the start of the First World War, he was a *Hauptmann* in the artillery. He was wounded in September 1914 and, upon his recovery, was posted to the General Staff in 1915. After the war, he stayed on in the army, rising to *Oberst* by 1931. He suffered a heart attack and double pneumonia in 1932. By 1935, he had been promoted to *Generalmajor*.

In 1938 he was appointed chief of the OKW, a post he held until the end of the war. He planned many of the Wehrmacht's campaigns, although he also advised against invading France and Operation Barbarossa, although he backed down in the face of Hitler and offered his resignation, which was refused. After the fall of Poland, Keitel was awarded the Knight's Cross on 30 September 1939, though this was unusual for a non-field commander. He was promoted to *Generalfeldmarschall* after the fall of France. Keitel realised that Germany could not win the Battle of Britain, and after the initial success of Barbarossa, his authority was undermined in Hitler's eyes. In 1942, when Hitler wanted to fire *Feldmarschall* Wilhelm List, Keitel confronted Hitler, but he spurned Keitel's pleading. This was Keitel's last act of defiance, and he never again questioned one of Hitler's orders. He was dubbed 'Lakeitel', a play on his name and the word 'Lakai', which means lackey.

Keitel played an important part in foiling the 20 July plot to kill Hitler in 1944. He then sat on the 'Court of Honour' that handed over many officers to the people's court for their part in the plot.

After the war, Keitel was arrested and charged with war crimes, and he testified that he knew many of Hitler's orders were illegal but claimed he was merely following orders in conformity to 'the leader principle'. He was found guilty, and as his signature was on orders that called for the killing of soldiers and political prisoners, he was sentenced to death. He requested to be shot, but to underline the criminal nature of his acts, he was hanged. In the six weeks from sentencing to be hanged, Keitel wrote his memoirs, which were edited by Walter Görlitz under the title *The Memories of Feldmarschall Wilhelm Keitel; Chief of the German High Command 1938–1945*. Keitel's last words were 'I call upon the Almighty to have mercy on the German people. More than two million German soldiers went to their deaths for the fatherland before me. I now follow my sons. Everything for Germany.' His ashes were scattered in the River Isar, near Munich, but his name is on the family plot at Bad Gandersheim Friedhof, Lower Saxony.

6. *Generaloberst* Wilhelm LIST

List was born in Oberkirchberg near Ulm on 14 May 1880. He joined the army as a cadet in 1898 and was promoted to *Leutnant* in 1900. By the start of the First World War, List was a *Hauptmann* on the General Staff, where he would remain throughout the war. After the war, he stayed on in the army as an administrator until 1932, when he took command of the 14th Division with the rank of *Generalleutnant*.

In 1938, he was made responsible for integrating the Austrian Army into the Wehrmacht. In 1939, he commanded the 14th Army in the Polish campaign, with his army linking up with Guderian's XIX Panzer Corps on 17 September to complete the encirclement of the Polish Army. For this, he was awarded the Knight's Cross on 30 September 1939.

For the French campaign, he commanded the 12th Army in the breakthrough at Sedan. His contribution to victory was considerable, and he was rewarded with promotion to *Generalfeldmarschall* on 19 July 1940. In 1941, List's XII Army was ready to invade Greece, and on its conclusion, he was appointed supreme commander in the south-east. It was while here that he was involved in reprisal killing of hostages in retaliation for partisan activity.

In July 1942, he was moved to the Russian Front to command Army Group B. List was a planner rather than a Blitzkrieg enthusiast. By refusing to commit his exhausted troops to further operations, he drew the wrath of Hitler, who sacked him in September. He took no further part in the war but was arrested at the end by the Allies and charged with war crimes relating to his action in the Balkans. Sentenced to life, he was released in 1953. He died on 17 August 1971 and is buried in Waldfriedhof, Plot 71, Row W, Grave 13, Munich.

7. *Generaloberst* Gerd von RUNDSTEDT

Von Rundstedt was born on 12 December 1875 in Aschersleben. He served in the First World War as a staff officer, being awarded the Iron Cross 1st and 2nd Class (1914). By the time the Nazis came to power in 1933, he was a *General*. At his own request, von Rundstedt was retired in 1938 but was recalled in August 1939 to command Army Group North for the invasion of Poland. For his part in the campaign, he was awarded the Iron Cross 1st and 2nd Class (1939) and the Knight's Cross on 30 September 1939. In May 1940, he commanded the Panzer groups that smashed their way to the Channel coast. In Russia, he commanded Army Group South, where his forty-two divisions overran vast areas of territory, but once the winter set in, they found themselves fighting a series of defensive battles. In December 1941, von Rundstedt asked for permission to withdraw and was sacked.

Recalled again in March 1942, he was appointed supreme commander west. In the months preceding the invasion, he differed over tactics with his immediate subordinate, Rommel. When the invasion started on 6 June 1944, Keitel telephoned him to ask what could be done and von Rundstedt replied: 'Make peace, you idiots!' He was awarded the Oak Leaves on 1 July and was sacked on 6 July, probably as result of what he said to Keitel. Recalled again in September 1944, he was reappointed supreme commander west and was responsible with Model for the Allied defeat at Arnhem. He did not take part in the planning or execution of the Ardennes offensive, in which he had no faith. Awarded the Swords on 18 February 1945, he was dismissed for the last time in March 1945. He was taken prisoner by the Allies but was one of the few that were not tried for war crimes. No lover of the Nazis, he often referred to Hitler as 'That Bohemian corporal'. Von Rundstedt died on 24 February 1953 and is buried in Stadtfriedhof, Abt A II, Stöckener Strasse 68, Stöcken, Lower Saxony.

8. *General* Johannes BLASKOWITZ

Blaskowitz was born on 10 July 1883 in Paterswalde. He served in the First World War, being awarded the Iron Cross 1st and 2nd Class (1914). As a *General* in Poland, he commanded the 8th Army under von Rundstedt and negotiated the surrender. He was awarded the Iron Cross 1st and 2nd Class on 11 and 21 September 1939 and the Knight's Cross on 30 September 1939. He was made military commander of Poland but was horrified by the excesses committed by the Party and the SS. Blaskowitz protested to Brauchitsch and, as a result, was side-lined for the next four years. By 1943, he commanded an army corps occupying France; he missed out on promotions but managed to steer clear of the bomb plotters. In 1944, he was given command of Army Group G, responsible for southern France. His forces bore the brunt of the Allied landings and, with only two inferior armies and poor communications, could only retreat. He was sacked by Hitler when his armoured counterattack failed in September 1944.

He was awarded the Oak Leaves on 29 October 1944. During the winter, he organised the defence of the Vosges sector, and in January 1945, he was given command of Army Group H in the Netherlands. Blaskowitz managed to pull his motley troops together and to offer bitter resistance to the end. The Swords were awarded to him on 25 April 1945.

He was tried as a lesser war criminal but committed suicide in prison on 5 February 1948 by throwing himself off a balcony; it was unlikely that he would have been convicted. He is buried in the village cemetery, Bommelsen, Bomlitz, Northern Germany.

9. *General* Albert KESSELRING—'Uncle or Smiling Albert'

Kesselring was born on 30 November 1885 in Marksteft. He served in the artillery during the First World War and was awarded the Iron Cross 1st and 2nd Class (1914). During the Polish campaign, Kesselring commanded *Luftflotte* I, where his aircraft supported von Bock's army group. For this, he was awarded the Iron Cross 1st and 2nd Class (1939), as well as the Knight's Cross on 30 September 1939. For the campaign in the west, he commanded *Luftflotte* II, again supporting von Bock's army, but he was unable to make good Göring's promise to destroy the BEF. Promoted to *Generalfeldmarschall* in July 1940, he was one of the few to be enthusiastic about Operation Sea Lion.

After the failure to destroy the RAF, Kesselring was moved with *Luftflotte* II to the east for the invasion of Russia, again supporting von Bock. In December 1941, he was appointed supreme commander south, with command over all German forces in southern Europe, including the Africa Corps. However, his primary task was to supply the men in Africa, to deal with Malta, and to keep open the sea routes in the Mediterranean. He was awarded the Oak Leaves on 25 February 1942 and the Swords on 18 July 1942. Often at loggerheads with Rommel over his constant demands for air support, once when on a visit to the desert, his HQ came under air attack, much to the delight of Rommel's staff—even more so when Kesselring jumped into a slit trench that had been used for kitchen waste.

Active command of ground troops came in July 1943, when Italy surrendered and the Allies invaded the mainland. Initially, he had two armies and he conducted the brilliant series of defensive battles up the leg of Italy that so effectively slowed the Allied advance. For this, he was awarded the Diamonds on 19 July 1944. In October 1944, Kesselring's car was involved in an accident, which kept him away from the front for three months. His last command was as supreme commander west, but it was far too late to make any difference. Tried as a war criminal by the British for the shooting of partisans by men under his command, his main opponent, US General Mark Clark, said in Kesselring's defence that he did no wrong and that he (Clark) would have acted in the same way. Sentenced to death, which was reprieved, he was released in 1952 due to ill health. He was known by his men as Uncle Albert, but as Smiling Albert by the Allies. His autobiography, *A Soldier's Record*, was published in 1954. He died on 16 July 1960 and is buried in Bergfriedhof, Miesbach, Bavaria.

10. *General* Günther (aka Hans) von KLUGE—'Clever Hans'

Von Kluge was born on 30 October 1882 in Posen. He served on the General Stuff during the First World War, being awarded the Iron Cross 1st and 2nd Class (1914). In 1918, he was seriously wounded. At the start of the Second World War, he was in command of 4th Army under von Bock and took part in the Polish campaign. For this, he was awarded the Iron Cross 1st and 2nd Class (1939) and the Knight's Cross on 30 September 1939. On 10 May 1940, his 4th Army forced its way across the Meuse and through to the Channel coast. He was promoted to *Generalfeldmarschall* in July 1940. In 1941, he took his army into Russia and advanced all the way to Moscow before being bogged down in December. Von Kluge replaced von Bock during the winter of 1941–42. He was approached by the resistance, and although in general agreement, he declined to act against the head of state to whom he had sworn loyalty. 'Clever Hans' as he was known by his follow officers was awarded the Oak Leaves on 18 January 1943 and the Swords on 29 October 1943. By now, von Kluge agreed to act with the plotters but was injured in a car crash in November 1943 and was out of action for six months.

Recovered, he was sent to Normandy in July to stop the Allies expanding their bridgehead, he took over from von Rundstedt full of eagerness until he realised, after conference with Rommel, that the situation was hopeless. When von Kluge's HQ went out of contact for a whole day in August, Hitler suspected he was meeting with the Allies to discuss surrender. On 17 August, Model arrived at his HQ with a letter relieving him of command and orders for him to report to Berlin. Realising he had no chance, von Kluge took poison on 19 August 1944 while on his way back to Germany. He was buried in Böhne Friedhof, Rathenow, but the tomb was removed after the war. Von Kluge's name appears on his wife's grave at Stadtfriedhof, Überlingen, Baden-Württemberg. His brother, Wolfgang, was also awarded the Knight's Cross.

11. *General* Georg von KÜCHLER

Von Küchler was born on 30 May 1881 in Philippsruhe Castle in Hanau. He fought in the artillery during the First World War. At the start of the Second World War, he was given command of 3rd Army, and his men captured Danzig. He was awarded the Knight's Cross on 30 September 1939. In the West, he commanded the 18th Army, which invaded the Netherlands and Belgium. In France, his forces tried in vain to cut of the BEF from the English Channel at Dunkirk.

Von Küchler commanded Army Group North in Russia, and at the siege of Leningrad, he launched massive bombardments on the city. He was promoted to *Generalfeldmarschall* on 30 June 1942. In January 1944, when the Russians broke the siege, he was sacked for demanding a withdrawal to the Luga River. After the war, he was tried for war crimes by the Americans for the treatment of partisans in Russia. Sentenced to twenty years, he was released in 1953 due to ill health and old age. He died on 25 May 1968 and is buried in Alter Friedhof, Feld 2-I-H-29, Darmstadt, Hesse.

12. *General* Alexander LÖHR

Löhr was born on 20 May 1885 in Drobeta-Turnu Severin, Romania. He served in the Austro-Hungarian Army during the First World War. In 1934, Löhr was made commander of the Austrian Air Force, a position he held until 1938 when Austria and Germany were joined by the 'Political Union', becoming commander of the Luftwaffe in Austria. As *General*, he commanded *Luftflotte* 4 in the East and carried out the bombing of Warsaw in 1939 and Belgrade in 1941. He was awarded the Iron Cross 1st and 2nd Class, which was followed by the Knight's Cross on 30 September 1939.

From July to December 1942, he was commander of the 12th Army, and from January 1942 to August 1943, he was commander-in-chief of the south-east. Löhr was also commander-in-chief of Army Group E, overseeing the Dodecanese Campaign. Awarded the Oak Leaves on 20 January 1945, he surrendered to Slovenian Partisans on 9 May 1945. He was tried for war crimes, specifically the bombing of Belgrade, and shot by firing squad on 26 February 1947; he has no known grave.

13. *General* Walter von REICHENAU

Von Reichenau was born on 8 October 1884 in Karlsruhe. He fought in the First World War and was awarded the Iron Cross 1st and 2nd Class (1914). He commanded the 10th Army during the 1939 Polish campaign as a *Generaloberst*. For his part in this campaign, he was awarded the Iron Cross 1st and 2nd Class (1939), which was followed by the Knight's Cross on 30 September 1939. Von Reichenau then commanded the 6th Army for the attack on Belgium and France, and in July 1940, Hitler promoted him to *Generalfeldmarschall*.

During the 1941 invasion of Russia, he again commanded 6th Army, capturing Kiev and Kharkov. He inspected every Russian tank he came across, and according to Staff General Paul Jordan, on seeing the T-34, he said: 'If the Russians ever produce it on an assembly line, we will have lost the war'. In October 1941, he issued an order to his men that they should treat all Jews as partisans, thus paving the way for mass executions. In January 1942, he suffered a cerebral haemorrhage, and it was decided to fly him back to Germany, but the aircraft had to make an emergency landing. Von Reichenau died of a heart attack on 17 January 1942 and is buried in the Invaliden Friedhof, Feld F, Plot 2, Grave 3 (headstone removed), Scharnhorstrasse, Berlin.

14. *Kapitänleutnant* Günther PRIEN—'The Bull of Scapa Flow'

Prien was born on 16 January 1908 in Osterfeld. He joined the *Handelsmarine* in 1923 and passed his master's license in 1932. Later, he was posted to *U-26* and took part in the Spanish Civil War. He commissioned *U-47* on 17 December 1938 and was promoted *Kapitänleutnant* on 1 February 1939. On

5 September 1939, Prien scored the second U-boat kill of the war when he sank the British ship *Bosnia*.

On 14 October, Prien risked shallow water, unknown shoals, and currents to penetrate Scapa Flow, the Royal Navy's primary base. He made two attacks on the 29,150-ton *Royal Oak*, which sank, and he returned home to instant fame. He was awarded the Knight's Cross personally by Hitler on 18 October 1939, becoming first combat soldier to be awarded it. His success earnt him the name 'The Bull of Scapa Flow'.

He scored a hit on the British cruiser *Norfolk* on 28 November, but she did not sink. Then, on 5 December, *U-47* spotted convoy OB 46 with twelve merchant ships and three destroyers; Prien attacked, sinking the 8,795-ton British steamer *Navasota*. Two more ships followed these to the bottom before *U-47* had to return to base. During 1940, Prien sank twenty-seven ships, including the 15,501-ton British *Arandora Star* and the 13,056-ton tanker *San Fernando*. Prien was awarded the Oak Leaves on 20 October 1940, only the fifth person to receive them.

On 26 February 1941, *U-47* sank three ships and damaged the British MV *Diala*. Not long after being promoted to *Korvettenkapitän*, while attacking convoy OB 293, on 7 March 1941 and damaging the MV *Terji Viken*, *U-47* was sank with all hands by HMS *Wolverine*. Günther Prien was one of the most successful U-boat commanders; in just fourteen months, he had sunk thirty-one ships (a total of 192,223 tons) and damaged nine ships (a further addition of 55,968 tons).

15. *General* Heinz GUDERIAN—'Fast Heinz'

Guderian was born on 17 June 1888 in Kulm. He served in the First World War as a signals specialist and on the general staff, being awarded the Iron Cross 1st and 2nd Class (1914). During the 1920s, he developed his ideas for the Blitzkrieg, but his superiors were not impressed until Hitler saw for himself when they were demonstrated to him in 1933. For the Polish campaign, Guderian commanded the largely motorised XIX Corps, which he led all the way to Brest-Litovisk. For this, he was awarded the Iron Cross 1st and 2nd Class (1939); the Knight's Cross followed on 27 October 1939. In the West on 10 May 1940, he led three Panzer Divisions in the breakthrough and dash to the Channel coast, often ignoring orders to stop. He finished the campaign with the advance to the Swiss border, cutting France in half. Promoted to *Oberstgeneral* in July 1940, he had nothing to do until the following year.

In Russia, he commanded the 2nd Panzer Group, comprising five armoured divisions and three motorised infantry divisions. He smashed through and drove to the Dnieper in just fifteen days and went on to Moscow. He was awarded the Oak Leaves on 17 July 1941. Although his troops reached the outskirts of the city, the Russian counterattack forced him on to the defensive. He demanded of Hitler that he be allowed to move back to better positions, and when he quarrelled with von Kluge, he was relieved of his command. Not until March 1943 did he work again, being appointed inspector-general of Armoured Forces. In this role, he was frequently and forcefully presented his views, often out with success. After the 20 July bomb plot, he was appointed chief of the General Staff but was dismissed by Hitler in March 1945. Known as 'Fast Heinz' due to his lighting advances, he was another of the few generals not to face war crimes. Guderian is author of *Panzer Leader* and *Achtung Panzer!* One of his quotes was 'If the tanks succeed, then victory follows'. He died on 14 May 1954 and is buried in Stadtfriedhof, Hildesheimerstrasse, Goslar, Lower Saxony. His son, Heinz Günther Guderian, was also awarded the Knight's Cross.

16. *General* Franz HALDER

Halder was born on 30 June 1884 in Würzburg. He served on the General Staff during the First World War and was awarded the Iron Cross 1st and 2nd Class (1914). Between the wars, he served on the General Staff, and by 1938, he was a *General.* Halder participated in the planning for the invasion of Poland and was awarded the Iron Cross 1st and 2nd Class (1939), which was followed by the Knight's Cross on 27 October 1939.

Promoted to *Oberstgeneral* in July 1940, he worked on the 1941 invasion plan for the Soviet Union. During 1942, he had several disagreements with Hitler over the running of the war and was fired on 24 September 1942. After the 20 July bomb plot in 1944, Halder, although not involved, was arrested, and as Hitler considered him a possible threat to himself, he was sent into imprisonment. On 31 January 1945, he was officially dismissed from the army, but along with 140 others, he was liberated and turned over to the US Army in May. He is the author of *Hitler as Warlord* and *The Halder Diaries*. Halder died on 2 April 1972 and is buried in the village cemetery, Blumenstrasse 20, Oberhausen, near Weilheim, North Rhine-Westphalia.

17. *General* Erich HOEPNER—'The Old Cavalryman'

Hoepner was born on 14 September 1886 in Frankfurt an der Oder. He fought in the First World War as a cavalry *Rittmeister* and was awarded the Iron Cross 1st and 2nd Class (1914). As *Generalleutnant*, he took command of XVI Panzer Corps in 1938. For his part in the Polish campaign, he was awarded the Iron Cross 1st and 2nd Class (1939), followed by the Knight's Cross on 27 October 1939. He also took part in the campaign in the West.

In 1941, he was promoted to *Generaloberst* and given command of 4th Panzer Group for the attack on Russia. His tanks drove almost all the way to Moscow before getting bogged down in the winter. On 5 December 1941, he refused to obey Hitler's no retreat order and pulled back in the face of a massive Russian counterattack. In January 1942, Hitler dismissed him from the army with the loss of his pension. Hoepner instituted a lawsuit against the Reich over his pension and won. Involved in the 20 July plot to kill Hitler, he was arrested and tortured by the Gestapo. Hoepner was hanged in Berlin on 8 August 1944; he has no known grave.

18. *General* Hermann HOTH—'Papa Hoth'

Hoth was born in Neuruppin on 12 April 1885. He served in the First World War, being awarded the Iron Cross 1st and 2nd Class (1914). As *Generalleutnant* and in command of XV Motorised Corps, he took part in the Polish campaign, being awarded the Iron Cross 1st and 2nd Class (1939) in September and the Knight's Cross on 27 October 1939. Hoth faced success again during the Western campaign and was promoted to *General* in July 1940.

In 1941, he commanded the 3rd Panzer Group in Russia, capturing Minsk and Vitebsk, and on 17 July 1941, he was awarded the Oak Leaves. In June 1942, he took over the 4th Panzer Army in the south and advanced as far as the Don River. However, in November, the Russian offensive began and smashed through the German lines, trapping the 6th Army in Stalingrad. He was unable to relieve the 6th Army after the Russians renewed their offensive on 25 December. In July 1943, Hoth took part in the Battle of Kursk, making a significant penetration before coming to a halt at Prokhorovka. He was awarded the Swords on 15 September 1943. More Soviet counterattacks forced the German Army back and Hoth was relieved of his command. He was recalled in April 1945 to command the defence of the Harz Mountains, a position he held until the end of the war. Sentenced to fifteen years for war crimes, he was released in 1954. Hoth died on 25 January 1971 and is buried in Feldstrasse Friedhof, Section 11, Grave 23–24, Goslar, Lower Saxony.

19. *General* Adolf STRAUSS

Strauss was born in Schermcke on 6 September 1879. He served in the First World War, being awarded the Iron Cross 1st and 2nd Class (1914). By 1934, he was a *Generalmajor*. Promoted to *General*, he commanded II Corps in the Polish campaign of 1939. He was awarded the Iron Cross 1st and 2nd Class (1939), which was followed by the Knight's Cross on 27 October 1939. On 30 May 1940, he was appointed supreme commander of IX Army in France.

Strauss then moved to the east for Operation Barbarossa with Army Group Centre, where he stayed until January 1943, stepping down on health grounds.

After his recovery, he was appointed commandant of the fortified eastern area. After the war, he was held by the British until May 1949. Strauss died on 20 March 1973 in Lübeck, Schleswig-Holstein.

20. *Generalleutnant* Kurt von BRIESEN

Von Briesen was born in Anklam on 3 May 1886. He fought in the First World War, during which he was wounded. He was awarded the Iron Cross 1st and 2nd Class (1914). He led the 30th Infantry Division as *Generalleutnant* in Poland in 1939. For his part in the campaign, he was awarded the Iron Cross 1st and 2nd Class (1939), followed by the Knight's Cross on 27 October 1939. He again led the 30th Division in the France campaign of 1940. Promoted to *General*, he was appointed to command LII Army Corps. He was killed in action by Russian aircraft on 20 November 1941 and is buried in the German War Cemetery (as unknown), Kharkov, Ukraine.

21. *Generalleutnant* Friedrich OLBRICHT

Olbricht was born on 4 October 1888 in Leisnig. He fought in the First World War with Infantry Regiment Nr. 4. He was not a committed Nazi and distanced himself from them. At the start of the Second World War, he was in command of the 24th Infantry Division, which he led from the front in the Polish campaign, creating an improvised motorised unit by loading men into his own staff car and rushing ahead to secure bridges. For this, he was awarded the Knight's Cross on 27 October 1939.

He became involved in Operation Valkyrie, and on 20 July 1944, he was arrested in his HQ. He was shot by firing squad the same day. Initially buried in full uniform and medals in Alter St-Matthäus Friedhof, Grossgorschenstrasse, Berlin, on 4 August 1944, he was dishonourably discharged from the army on Himmler's orders, and his body was exhumed, cremated, and his ashes scattered.

22. *Generalleutnant* Georg-Hans REINHARDT

Reinhardt was born in Bautzen on 1 March 1887. He fought during the First World War as an infantryman. In the 1939 Polish campaign, he commanded the 4th Panzer Division, which broke through the defences near Częstochowa. The division then advanced to the outskirts of Warsaw by 8 September—it was the first German force to reach the city. He was awarded the Knight's Cross on 27 October 1939. In the Battle for France, he commanded the XLI Panzer Corps, which broke through and reached the sea in May.

In 1941, his corps was deployed on the Eastern Front for the invasion of the Soviet Union, and his corps led the advance to Leningrad. In October, he was given command of III Panzer Army and joined the attack on Moscow. Reinhardt was awarded the Oak Leaves on 17 February 1942 for his defensive operations during the winter. From 1942 until June 1944, III Panzer Army held its ground, defeating most Soviet attacks and only giving limited ground. For this, he was awarded the Swords on 26 May 1944. Having now been given command of Army Group Centre, he was unable to stop the massive Russian attacks and was relieved from duty in January 1945.

After the war, he was arrested and tried for war crimes. He was found guilty and sentenced to fifteen years but was released in 1952. He died on 22 November 1963 and is buried in Tegernsee Friedhof, Seestrasse 13, Bavaria.

23. *Generalmajor* Hans JESCHONNEK

Jeschonnek was born on 9 April 1899 in Hohensalza, Posen. Commissioned as a *Leutnant* in 1914, he joined the German Army Air Service, and by 1917, he had shot down two enemy aircraft. During the 1930s, he worked for the ministry responsible for building aeroplanes banned by the Treaty of Versailles. He became chief of the Luftwaffe operations staff on 1 February 1938 and was promoted to *Oberst* in November.

Jeschonnek was promoted to *Generalmajor* on 14 August 1939 and was awarded the Knight's Cross for his part in the Polish campaign on 27 October 1939. Promoted to *General* on 19 August 1940, he suggested that London's residential suburbs be bombed to break the will of the people, but Hitler refused. Despite the failure in the Battle of Britain, Jeschonnek was promoted to *Generaloberst* on 1 March 1942.

When, as part of Operation Crossbow, Allied bombers attacked Peenemünde, he erroneously ordered Berlin's air defences to fire on 200 German fighters that had mistakenly gathered near the capital. Jeschonnek shot himself at the Wolf's Lair on 19 August 1943. He was buried with full military honours in Städtischer Friedhof, Stubenrauch Strasse, Tempelhof, Berlin.

24. *Generalmajor* Ludwig KÜBLER—'Latschen-Nurmi'

Kübler was born in Munich on 2 September 1889. He joined the army in July 1908, and from 1909 to 1910, he attended war school, being placed fifth out of 166. He was commissioned as a *Leutnant* on 23 October. At the start of the First World War, he commanded a machine-gun platoon, and on 24 September 1914, he was severely injured by shell fragments in the face, leaving him with a large scar. Kübler rejoined his regiment before his wound had healed, was awarded the Iron Cross 1st and 2nd Class (1914), and was made adjutant of the regiment, a position he held until August 1918 when he was given command of a battalion with the rank of *Hauptmann*. After the war, he stayed on in the army and held a staff position until 1935, when he was made commander of the Mountain Brigade.

He was awarded the Knight's Cross on 27 October 1939 for his part in the Polish campaign. On 1 December 1939, he was promoted to *Generalleutnant* and was earmarked to lead the cancelled conquest of Gibraltar. In 1941, during Operation Barbarossa, he was on the southern front, but his performance did not meet Hitler's expectations and he was moved to the leadership reserve. He did not get another command until 1943. In 1944, he was appointed commander of LXXXXVII Army Corps in Yugoslavia, fighting the partisans. He was wounded and captured shortly before the end of the war. Sentenced to death for his part in the partisan war, he was hanged on 18 August 1947 in Ljubljana and has no known grave. His name is on the family plot at Westfriedhof, Munich.

25. *Oberst* August SCHMIDT

Schmidt was born in Fürth on 3 November 1892. He entered the army in 1911 and fought in the First World War, being awarded the Iron Cross 1st and 2nd Class (1914), as well as the Wound Badge in Black.

During the Second World War, he took part in the Polish Campaign, the invasion of France, and Operation Barbarossa. He was awarded the Iron Cross 1st and 2nd Class (1939), and on 27 October 1939, he was awarded the Knight's Cross. He commanded Infantry Regiment 50 from 31 January to 1 March 1942 and 10th Panzergrenadier Division from May 1942 to September 1944, being awarded the Oak Leaves on 23 January 1944 with the rank of *Generalleutnant*. On 15 September 1944, he took over command of LXXII Army Corps, a position he held until 22 January 1945. Schmidt was captured by Soviet forces in April 1945 and held until 1955. He died on 17 January 1972 and is buried in Waldfriedhof, Plot 426, Row 1, Grave 530, Munich.

26. *Oberleutnant* Dietrich STEINHARDT

Steinhardt was born on 26 April 1911 in Glaubitz. He was a company commander in I Battalion, Motorised Infantry Regiment 51, when he awarded the Knight's Cross on 27 October 1939; along with Stolz, he was the first junior officer to be awarded it. Steinhardt was killed in action near Lowat, Russia, on 15 April 1942, and he has no known grave.

27. *Leutnant* Josef STOLZ

Stolz was born on 19 May 1915 in Wiener Neustadt. He was a platoon leader in III Battalion, Motorised Infantry Regiment 51, when he was awarded the Knight's Cross on 27 October 1939; along with Steinhardt, he was the first junior officer to be awarded it. Stolz was killed in action at Bjeloy, Russia, on 24 June 1941, and he has no known grave.

2

1940

28. *Kapitänleutnant* Herbert Emil SCHULTZE—'Daddy'

Schultze was born in Kiel on 24 June 1909. When the war started, he was in command of *U-48*, and on 11 September 1939, he sank the British merchant ship *Firby*. Immediately afterwards, he sent the message: 'Transmit to Mr. Churchill. I have sunk the British steamer *Firby*. Save the crew, if you please'. He did the same after sinking the British ship *Royal Sceptre*, thus saving many of their crew.

Schultze sank sixteen ships in his first four patrols, totalling 109,074 tons. But he was taken ill and forced to hand over command of the boat. On his recovery, he once again took command of *U-48*. On his next patrol, he only sank two ships; however, he regained his form on his next patrol, sinking five ships and torpedoing another. In his last patrol, he sank a further five ships. He was awarded the Knight's Cross on 1 March 1940 and the Oak Leaves on 12 June 1941. 'Daddy', as he became known by his crew, sank twenty-eight ships (a total of 183,432 tons). He died on 3 June 1987 in London, but he is buried in a German war cemetery at Wilhelmshaven, Lower Saxony. At his funeral, Otto Kretschmer said of him: 'Deeply respected by friends and foe, revered by his crew, Schultze was an exemplary naval officer in the best tradition'.

29. *Oberst* Robert FUCHS

Fuchs was born on 11 May 1895 in Berlin. He fought in the First World War, being awarded the Iron Cross 1st and 2nd Class (1914). Fuchs was a *Kommodore* in Bomber Wing 26 when he was awarded the Knight's Cross on 6 April 1940. He died on 15 January 1977 and is buried in Stadtfriedhof, Göttingen, Lower Saxony.

30. *Vizeadmiral* Otto SCHNIEWIND

Schniewind was born on 14 December 1887 in Saarlouis. He fought in the navy during the First World War, being awarded the Iron Cross 1st and 2nd Class (1914). He took part in the invasion of Norway and was awarded the Knight's Cross on 20 April 1940.

On 30 July 1944, Schniewind was relieved of his command and took no further part in the war. After the war, he was tried for war crimes relating to Norway but was acquitted. Schniewind died on 26 March 1964 in Linz am Rhine, Rhineland-Palatinate.

31. *Konteradmiral* Karl DÖNITZ—'The Great Lion'

Dönitz was born in Grünau near Berlin on 6 September 1891. He joined the Imperial Navy in 1910 and was serving on the light cruiser *Breslau* when the First World War started. Together with the *Goeben*, the *Breslau* broke through the Allied blockade and reached Istanbul. Dönitz stayed in Turkey until 1916 when he returned to Germany, being awarded the Iron Cross 1st and 2nd Class (1914). He was transferred to the U-boat service as a watch officer before taking command of *UC-25* in March 1918. He sank the *Cyclops* in the port of Augusta, and on his next patrol, he sank three more ships.

On his return, he was given command of *UB-68*, with which he attacked a convoy heading to Malta, sinking one ship and then being chased by destroyers. While manoeuvring for a second attack, the boat suddenly stood on its head. In Dönitz's words: 'The battery overflowed, the light went out and we plunged into the depths. I gave the order to blow tanks, stop engines and rudder hard to port in an effort to end the submarine's descent. We levelled out at 100 meters. The boat turned upwards and we shot onto the surface. I climbed up the conning tower and discovered that we were in the middle of the convoy. We were fired on from all sides. The boat sank after a number of hits and the crew were picked up by the British destroyer *Snapdragon*. Six men went down with the ship. Dönitz was released in July 1919 and joined the navy as commander of a torpedo boat.

By the late 1930s, he was a commander and qualified staff officer, during which time he wrote several studies on submarine warfare. While commanding the cruiser *Emden* as *Korvettenkapitän* in 1935, he was given the job of building up the U-boat arm from scratch. He achieved a great deal in a short period, but his demands for a large force were not met. His superior, Raeder, and the Nazi hierarchy were more interested in the prestige of large battleships. Thus, at the beginning of the war, Germany had fifty-seven U-boats, of which only twenty-six were fit for long-range operations.

Their success, however, was out of all proportion to their numbers, and Dönitz proved an inspiring leader who was looked on as almost a father by the U-boat crews. He developed the concept of mass attack on convoys, the so-called 'Wolf Pack'. On 21 April 1940, he was awarded the Knight's Cross. On 30 January 1943, Dönitz was named commander-in-chief of the navy and was promoted to *Grossadmiral*. He was awarded the Oak Leaves on 6 April 1943.

The U-boat war was the longest struggle of the Second World War, lasting from the first days of the war until its very end. A total 1,099 U-boats were put into service, as well as four from foreign shipyards and ten captured boats. Of these, 863 saw action and 630 were lost at sea. All told, they sunk 148 warships, damaged another forty-eight, and sank 2,779 merchant ships (a total of 14,119,413 tons). The number of damaged ships cannot be determined. According to official figures, of the 39,000 sailors who served in U-boats, 27,182 lost their lives (including Dönitz's son), but the true figure may be much higher.

After Hitler's suicide, Dönitz became the new Führer—albeit for just twenty-six days. Dönitz was arrested and charged with preparations for a war of aggression and was sentenced to ten years imprisonment; he was released in 1956. In 1958, he published his memoirs: *Ten Years and Twenty Days*. Karl Dönitz died on 24 December 1980, mourned by his men who called him 'The Great Lion', respected by his enemies, and forgotten in his own country. He is buried in Waldfriedhof, Feld L5, Aumühle near Hamburg.

32. *General* Nikolaus von FALKENHORST (born von JASTRZEMBSKI)

Von Falkenhorst was born on 17 January 1885 in Breslau. He fought in the First World War and was awarded the Iron Cross 1st and 2nd Class (1914). During the Polish campaign, von Falkenhorst commanded XXI Army Group. On 20 February 1940, Hitler informed von Falkenhorst he was to be overall commander of the invasion of Norway and was to present a plan by 5 p.m. the same day. With no time to consult military maps, he picked up a copy of the Baedeker tourist guide and planned the attack from it—the plan was approved.

Apart from the large loss to the German Navy, the plan was a success and von Falkenhorst was awarded the Knight's Cross on 30 April 1940. He was to remain in Norway as commander of the garrison and ordered his men to treat the locals with consideration. There is one story that when a Norwegian lady complained about having her jam stolen by a German soldier, she was invite to see him shot. Von Falkenhorst was dismissed from his post on 18 December 1944 for opposing certain radical policies. He held no more commands after this. Tried for war crimes, namely passing on the 'Commando Order' in which captured saboteurs to be shot as spies, von Falkenhorst was sentenced to death. His sentence was commuted to life, but he was released in 1953 due to ill health. Von Falkenhorst died from a heart attack on 18 June 1968 and is buried in Stadtfriedhof, Holzminden, Lower Saxony. His son-in-law, Erich Dethleffsen, was also awarded the Knight's Cross.

33. *Generaloberst* Erhard MILCH

Milch was born on 30 March 1892 in Wilhelmshaven. He fought in the First World War, being awarded the Iron Cross 1st and 2nd Class (1914). Milch commanded *Luftflotte* 5 during the Norwegian campaign and was awarded the Knight's Cross on 4 May 1940.

He spent the remainder of the war involved in aircraft production. Milch was captured by the US Army in May 1945 and tried for war crimes. He was sentenced to life but was released in 1954. Milch died on 25 January 1972 and is buried in Zentralfriedhof, Feld 18 S Nr. 10a, 10b, 10c, Lüneburg, Lower Saxony.

34. *Generalleutnant* Hans GEISLER

Geisler was born on 19 April 1891 in Hanover. He fought in the First World War and was awarded the Iron Cross 1st and 2nd Class (1914). Geisler was *Kommandierender General* of X Fliegerkorps when he was awarded the Knight's Cross on 4 May 1940. He died on 25 June 1966 in Freiburg im Breisgau, Baden-Württemberg.

35. *Major* Martin HARLINGHAUSEN

Harlinghausen was born on 17 January 1902 in Rheda. A bomber pilot, he operated against Allied shipping. He was awarded the Iron 1st and 2nd Class (1939) in early 1940. For sinking 100,000 tons of shipping, Harlinghausen was awarded the Knight's Cross on 4 May 1940. When he moved to the Mediterranean Theatre, he sank another 27,000 tons of shipping and was awarded the Oak Leaves on 30 January 1941.

Appointed leader of the Luftwaffe for the Atlantic in March 1941, he was held responsible for the loss of the battleship *Bismarck*. Sent back to the Mediterranean in July 1942, he remained there until June 1943 when disagreements with his superiors led to him being dismissed. In December 1944, he was appointed chief of *Luftwaffen* Command West, a post he held until the end of the war. Harlinghausen died on 23 March 1986 and is buried in Stadtfriedhof, Gütersloh, Friedhofstrasse 44, North Rhine-Westphalia.

36. *Oberst* Martin FIEBIG

Fiebig was born on 7 May 1891 in Rösnitz. He fought in the First World War in the infantry and as a bomber pilot. He was awarded the Iron Cross 1st and 2nd Class (1914). Fiebig was a *Kommodore* in Bomber Wing 4 during the campaign in the West, but he was shot down over the Netherlands. He was awarded the Iron Cross 1st and 2nd Class (1939). The Knight's Cross followed on 8 May 1940.

Fiebig also took part in the Balkans campaign and was involved in the bombing of Belgrade. During the relief of Stalingrad, he commanded VIII *Fliegerkorps* and was awarded the Oak Leaves on 23 December 1942. He was executed for war crimes in Belgrade on 23 October 1947 and has no known grave.

37. *Hauptmann* Paul-Werner HOZZEL

Hozzel was born on 16 October 1910 in Hamburg. He took part in the Polish campaign as a Stuka pilot and was awarded the Iron Cross 2nd Class. He also took part in the campaign in the West and the attack on Norway. He was awarded the Iron Cross 1st Class on 5 May 1940 and the Knight's Cross three days later. He was the first Stuka pilot to be awarded it.

Hozzel took part in the invasion of Russia, and his unit was involved in supporting the attack on Stalingrad. He was awarded the Oak Leaves on 14 April 1943. He ended the war in a staff post. Hozzel died on 7 January 1997 and is buried in Beiertheim Friedhof, Karlsruhe, Baden-Württemberg.

38. *Oberleutnant* Elmar SCHAEFER

Schaefer was born in Bonn on 28 May 1913. He was a pilot in Dive Bomber Wing 1 when he was awarded the Knight's Cross on 8 May 1940. Schaefer died on 16 April 1983 and is believed to be buried in Burgfriedhof, Bonn.

39. *Leutnant* Werner BAUMBACH

Baumbach was born on 27 December 1916 in Cloppenburg. As a bomber pilot, he took part in the Polish campaign and was awarded the Iron Cross 2nd Class for his part in an attack on an airfield near Warsaw. Switching to the Ju 88 bomber, Baumbach was employed in anti-shipping raids, attacking British convoys during the Norwegian campaign. He was awarded the Iron Cross 1st Class on 4 May 1940. Baumbach sunk over 300,000 tons of shipping, more than some of the U-boat aces. For this, he was awarded the Knight's Cross on 8 May 1940.

After the fall of France, he fought in the Battle of Britain. On one occasion, he was so badly shot up that he only just made it back to the Netherlands, crash landing his bomber. After his recovery Baumbach's unit was posted to Norway were he continued his attacks on Allied shipping. He was awarded the Oak Leaves on 14 July 1941 and the Swords on 17 August 1942. Moved to the Mediterranean area, he found that his unit faced a total lack of organisation due mostly to bureaucratic incompetence. Baumbach fired off complains to the chief-of-staff, and Göring ensured things were put right, but punished Baumbach for bypassing the correct channels by posting him to an admin job researching new radio-controlled bombs. When tasked with a plan to use 'manned' V-1 rockets, Baumbach went directly to Hitler to have the idea dropped. Later, when asked by Hitler for his opinion of the conduct of the air war, he gave a full and critically frank answer. This time, Göring simply ignored his comments. Baumbach was killed in an aircraft crash in Argentina on 20 October 1953, but he is buried in Bethen Friedhof, Cloppenburg, Lower Saxony.

40. *Leutnant* Martin MÖBUS

Möbus was born on 9 May 1917 in Zeisdorf. A close support pilot, he flew over 800 missions and was credited with sinking several ships, destroying over sixty tanks, 600 other vehicles, eighteen anti-aircraft guns, and five armoured trains. Möbus was awarded the Iron Cross 2nd Class in September 1939 and the 1st Class on 3 May 1940. He was awarded the Knight's Cross on 8 May 1940 and the Oak Leaves on 27 April 1944. Möbus was killed in a car crash on 2 June 1944 and is buried in the German War Cemetery, Tomb 5, Table 7, Rovaniemi Norvajärvi, Finland.

41. *Unteroffizier* Gerhard GRENZEL

Grenzel was born on 13 May 1915 in Brandenburg. He was a pilot in Dive Bomber Wing 1 when he was awarded the Knight's Cross on 8 May 1940, the first NCO to be awarded it. Grenzel was killed in action over Malta on 10 January 1944 and has no known grave.

42. *Generaladmiral* Alfred SAALWÄCHTER

Saalwächter was born on 10 January 1883 in Neusalz. He fought in the navy during the First World War, being awarded the Iron Cross 1st and 2nd Class (1914). Saalwächter was responsible for operations in the North Sea at the start of the Second World War. He was given tactical command of the invasion of Norway and was awarded the Knight's Cross on 9 May 1940.

After the fall of Norway, he was put in command of operations in the North Sea and the English Channel, but he was replaced in September 1942. Saalwächter resigned from active service on 30 November 1942. He was imprisoned by the Russians in June 1945 and tried and shot on 6 December 1945 in Moscow. He has no known grave. In 1994, he was exonerated by a Russian court.

43. *Generalleutnant* Eduard DIETL

Dietl was born on 21 July 1890 in Bad Aibling. He fought in the First World War, being wounded four times and awarded the Iron Cross 1st and 2nd Class (1914). Dietl commanded the 3rd Mountain Division in the attack on Norway. He was awarded the Knight's Cross on 9 May 1940 and the Oak Leaves on 19 July 1940, and he was the first person to be awarded them.

He continued to command in Finland and Eastern Europe until 23 June 1944, when his aircraft crashed near Hartberg, Austria, killing him along with Karl Eglseer, Thomas-Emil Von Wickede, and Franz Rossi. Dietl was awarded the Swords on 1 July 1944. He is buried in Nordfriedhof, Plot 114, Row 1, Grave 34, Munich.

44. *Generalleutnant* Richard PELLENGAHR

Pellengahr was born on 19 August 1883 in Wiedenbrück. He fought in the First World War, being awarded the Iron Cross 1st and 2nd Class (1914). Pellengahr was awarded the Knight's Cross on 9 May 1940. He died on 9 October 1964 and is buried in Sennefriedhof, Bielefeld, North Rhine-Westphalia.

45. *Generalmajor* Erwin ENGELBRECHT

Engelbrecht was born on 12 November 1891 in Wildpark. He fought in the First World War and was awarded the Iron Cross 1st and 2nd Class (1914). By 1939, he was a *General*. In 1940, he was aboard the cruiser *Blücher* when she was sunk off the coast of Norway, but Engelbrecht managed to swam ashore. For his leadership in Norway, he was awarded the Knight's Cross on 9 May 1940.

His 163rd Infantry Division was allowed to cross Sweden to join the Finnish forces at Karelia. Later, Engelbrecht was assigned to special forces. He died on 8 April 1964 and is buried in Pasing Friedhof, Feld 2, Row 1, Grave 28, Munich.

46. *Oberst* Hermann FISCHER

Fisher was born on 19 February 1894 in Ostheim. He fought in the First World War and was awarded the Iron Cross 1st and 2nd Class (1914). During the Second World War, he was awarded the Iron Cross 1st (April 1940) and 2nd Class (May 1940). The Knight's Cross was awarded to him on 9 May 1940. Fisher died on 12 March 1968 and is buried in Südfriedhof, Abt 111, Brace 136, Bonn.

47. *Korvettenkapitän* Werner HARTMANN

Hartmann was born on 11 December 1902 in Silstedt. In May 1936, he commissioned Germany's first high-seas boat, *U-26*. Günther Prien was one of his watch officers. On his first combat patrol with *U-37*, he sank eight ships, including the British 10,184-ton steamer *Yorkshire*. He ended his next patrol with another eight sinking pennants. In April 1940, he sank four more ships and torpedoed a *Glasgow*-class cruiser, but this was not confirmed. He was awarded the Knight's Cross on 9 April 1940.

Dönitz moved him to his staff in April, and six months later, he was given command of 2nd U-Boat Training Division in Gotenhafen. In December, he was appointed officer in charge of tactical training and commander of the 27th U-Boat Flotilla. On 3 November 1942, Hartmann commissioned *U-198* and took it into the South Atlantic, returning 200 days later having sunk seven ships. In 1944, he was named commander of U-Boats Mediterranean and awarded the Oak Leaves on 5 November.

On 14 February 1945, he assumed command of the 6th Marine Grenadier Regiment, guarding the North Baltic Canal. Hartmann sunk twenty-five ships (a total of 111,645 tons). He died on 26 April 1963 in Ussel, Hesse.

48. *Major* Walter KLEIN

Klein was born on 31 March 1890 in Drespe. He was a commander of III Battalion, Infantry Regiment 193, when he was awarded the Knight's Cross on 9 May 1940. Klein was killed in an avalanche on 22 March 1941 and is buried in the German War Cemetery, Block 3, Row 6, Grave 10, Bergen-Solheim, Norway.

49. *Kapitän zur See* Erich BEY—'Achmed'

Bey was born in Hamburg on 28 March 1898. He fought in the First World War, being awarded the Iron Cross 2nd Class (1914). He was awarded the

Iron Cross 1st and 2nd Class (1939) in late 1939. Bey took part in the Battle of Narvik, where he sank one British ship and rammed another. For his action, Bey was awarded the Knight's Cross on 9 May 1940. Bey commanded the destroyer force escorting the *Scharnhorst*, *Gneisenau*, and *Prinz Eugen* during the Channel Dash in 1942.

On 26 December 1943, he was commanding the *Scharnhorst* when she was tasked to attack convoy JW55B off the coast of Norway, but the British knew she was coming and sent the battleship HMS *Duke of York* and the cruisers HMS *Jamaica*, *Belfast*, *Norfolk*, and *Sheffield*. The *Scharnhorst* was sunk, and of her 1,968 men on-board, only thirty-six were saved; Bey was not among them.

50. *Oberleutnant* Waldemar GERLACH

Gerlach was born on 23 February 1913 in Eitra. He was a company commander in Machine-Gun Battalion 13 when he was awarded the Knight's Cross on 9 May 1940. Gerlach died on 21 July 1995 and is buried in Hauptfriedhof, Tannenkeckerweg 6, Kassel, Hesse.

51. *Oberleutnant* Leopold MATTHESS

Matthess was born on 12 October 1912 in Müllheim. He was a company commander in Machine-Gun Battalion 13 when he was awarded the Knight's Cross on 9 May 1940. Matthess died on 29 October 1976 and is believed to be buried in Südfriedhof, Wiesbaden, Hesse.

52. *Hauptmann* Walter KOCH

Koch was born in Bonn on 10 September 1910. He joined *Fallschirmjäger* Regiment 1 in 1938 and oversaw the formation of the 'Koch' Parachute Battalion. His battalion was key in the capture of the Belgian Fort Eben-Emael and the four bridges over the Albert Canal in 1940. For this, Koch was awarded the Knight's Cross on 10 May 1940.

Koch fought in Crete in 1941, where he was seriously wounded in the head near Hill 107. In March 1942, he commanded *Fallschirmjäger* Regiment 5 in Tunisia, where he stopped the execution of British paratroopers in defiance of the 'Commando Order'. In January 1943, his regiment was incorporated into the Hermann Göring Panzer Division. Koch became ill in April 1943 and had to be transferred to a German hospital. He joined the officer reserve in August 1943, but he was involved in a serious accident in Berlin and died of his injuries on 27 October 1943. He is buried in Nordfriedhof, Abt 16, Grave 7–8, Bonn. Many in his regiment believe he was murdered because of his criticism of the 'Commando Order'.

53. *Oberleutnant* Rudolf WITZIG

Witzig was born on 14 August 1916 in Röhlinghausen. He was CO of the Koch Parachute Assault Battalion's Pioneer Platoon. Wigzig's greatest feat was the capture of the Belgian Fort Eben-Emael on 10 May 1940, on the same day he was awarded the Iron Cross 1st and 2nd Class and the Knight's Cross; he was also promoted to *Hauptmann*. Badly wounded in Crete in 1941, he was given command of Corps Parachute Pioneer Battalion in May 1942 and promoted to *Major* in August. With this unit, he fought in Tunisia, and the defensive successes in the northern sector of the front are closely linked to him.

During June and July 1944, his unit knocked-out twenty-seven enemy tanks near Kumele. Witzig was awarded the Oak Leaves on 25 November 1944, and on 16 December, he took over command of *Fallschirmjäger* Regiment 16, with which he went into captivity on 8 May 1945. Witzig died on 3 October 2001 in Oberschleissheim, Munich.

54. *Hauptmann* Peter INGENHOVEN

Ingenhoven was born on 16 December 1894 in Düsseldorf. He was deputy group commander in Fighter Wing 103 when he was awarded the Knight's Cross on 11 May 1940. Ingenhoven was killed in action on 1 November 1942 and is buried at Beljajewo/Welish, Russia; his remains are awaiting transfer to a German war cemetery.

55. *Generalleutnant* Kurt STUDENT

Student was born on 12 May 1890 in Birkholz. He was a fighter pilot in the First World War, credited with shooting down six enemy aircraft, and was awarded the Iron Cross 1st and 2nd Class (1914). In 1924, he headed the Air Technical Branch and became involved in glider courses. This was a means to train pilots for the new air force banned under the Treaty of Versailles. He undoubtedly got the idea for airborne troops at this time. Promoted to *Generalmajor* in 1938, he formed a highly secret parachute battalion, which was expanded into a division the following year. The division did not take part in the Polish campaign in order to preserve its secrecy. Its first use was in the attack on Oslo and Stavanger in Norway. He was awarded the Iron Cross 1st and 2nd Class (1939) on 20 September 1939.

The invasion of 'Fortress Holland' was the heyday of the German parachute arm, landing all over the Netherlands and Belgium, including Dordrecht, Moerdijk, Rotterdam, the Albert Canal, and the Fort Eben-Emael. Student was wounded at Rotterdam by a stray German bullet, and he was awarded the Knight's Cross on 12 May 1940. He led the XI Air Corps in the Balkans, and on 3 May 1941, he stood next to List at the victory parade in Athens. In Crete, his men suffered their worst casualties—some 6,500. Despite this, they still managed to overcome the Allies. Student was not allowed to land himself until the danger was over. Many of his key commanders were killed or wounded. He tried in vain to convince Hitler to allow an airborne drop to capture Malta. Although the parachute arm was greatly increased, they were airborne in name only. Student was awarded the Oak Leaves on 27 September 1943. He commanded the 1st Parachute Army in September 1944, fighting against the Allied airborne invasion of the Netherlands. In October, he was appointed commander of Army Group 'H', with control over all forces in the Northern Netherlands. One of the few German generals not to face war crimes charges, he lived an honourable retirement. In 1962, his former enemies, the New Zealand Veterans Association, named Student their vice-president. He died on 1 July 1978 and is buried in Nordfriedhof, Abt 16, Grave 7–8, Bonn.

56. *Oberleutnant* Gustav ALTMANN

Altmann was born in Britz on 13 April 1912. He was commissioned into *Fallschirmjäger* Regiment 1 on 1 September 1939. He was then promoted to *Oberleutnant* in April and given command of Assault Group Stahl. On 10 May 1940, Altmann parachuted into Belgium, captured the Veldwezelt Bridge over the Albert Canal, and held it until reinforcements arrived; for this, he was awarded the Iron Cross 1st and 2nd Class (1939) and the Knight's Cross on 12 May 1940. He was also promoted to *Hauptmann*.

Altmann was captured by the British during the invasion of Crete in 1941 and did not return home until after the war. He died on 20 February 1981 and is buried in Kassel, Hesse.

57. *Oberarzt* Rolf JÄGER

Jäger was born on 1 November 1912 in Klein. He transferred into the 'Koch' Parachute Assault Battalion in February 1940 and took part in the attack on the Albert Canal bridges. Immediately after landing, he set about treating the wounded. Jäger and his assistants recovered seven bodies and treated twenty-four wounded, under heavy fire; for this, he was awarded the Iron Cross 2nd Class on 12 May, and the 1st Class and the Knight's Cross on 13 May 1940.

During the invasion of Crete, Jäger—now as battalion medical officer—once again gave his all in caring for the wounded. He also served as medical officer in Russia and in Italy at Anzio/Nettuno. He was taken prisoner by the British on 8 May 1945. He died on 6 January 1984 and is buried in Stadtfriedhof, Kuhlestrasse, Hagen, North Rhine-Westphalia.

58. *Oberleutnant* Walter KIESS

Kiess was born on 9 October 1914 in Suhl. He was serving in 'Koch' Parachute Assault Battalion when he was awarded the Knight's Cross on 12 May 1940. Kiess died on 24 June 1995 and is buried in Bad Langenbrücken Friedhof, Bad Schönborn, Baden-Württemberg.

59. *Leutnant* Egon DELICA

Delica was born in Stettin on 4 January 1915. He served as an observer during the Polish campaign and was promoted to *Leutnant* on 28 December 1939. He dropped into Belgian Fort Eben-Emael; his men captured Works 18, destroyed Works 11, and repulsed a counterattack. On the morning of 11 May, he linked up with soldiers of the 51st Army. Delica was awarded the Knight's Cross on 12 May 1940.

He was wounded in Russia with *Fallschirmjäger* Regiment 5 in 1942. After his recovery, he was sent back to Russia and fought in the Crimea and was wounded again in April 1943. On 1 January 1945, he took command of *Fallschirmjäger* Regiment 19's II Battalion. Delica was captured in the Reichswald on 12 February 1945. He died on 26 April 1999 in Pullach, Bavaria.

60. *Leutnant* Joachim MEISSNER

Meissner was born on 15 October 1911 in Freystadt. On mobilisation in 1939, he joined Pioneer Battalion 8 but transferred to the parachute arm in January 1940. He was promoted to *Leutnant* in March and joined the Koch Parachute Assault (Glider) Battalion. He landed near the Canne Bridge in Belgium only to find it destroyed, and after his CO had been wounded, Meissner took over and occupied the village of Eben-Emael, which he defended against heavy attacks until relieved; for this, he was awarded Iron Cross 1st and 2nd Class, and on 12 May 1940, he received the Knight's Cross. On 16 May, he was promoted to *Oberleutnant* for bravery in the face of the enemy.

Meissner took part in the Corinth Canal drop in Greece and Crete with *Fallschirmjäger* Regiment 2, and he fought in Russia at the Mius River and the Volkhov. Moved to the West, he was killed in action on 25 July 1944. He is buried in the German War Cemetery, Block 4, Row 40, Grave 1552, Marigny, Normandy, France.

61. *Leutnant* Gerhard SCHACHT

Schacht was born in Berlin on 6 April 1916. He led Assault Group 'Beton' in storming the Vroenhoven Bridge over the Albert Canal, Belgium, in May 1940. The enemy holding the bridge were overwhelmed, with 300 prisoners taken. For this, Schacht was awarded the Iron Cross 1st and 2nd Class, and he was awarded the Knight's Cross on 12 May 1940. He was also promoted to *Oberleutnant*.

Schacht was an operation officer during the 1941 Crete campaign. Promoted to *Hauptmann* on 25 February 1942, he became chief-of-staff of the Ramcke Parachute Brigade in Africa. Sent to the Air Warfare Academy in April 1943, he spent the rest of the war in staff positions. Schacht died on 7 February 1972 and is believed to be buried in Hauptfriedhof, Am Gottesacker 25, Dortmund, North Rhine-Westphalia.

62. *Leutnant* Martin SCHÄCHTER

Schächter was born in Petershagen on 14 March 1914. After joining the parachute arm, he became a company commander in *Fallschirmjäger* Regiment 1 with the rank of *Leutnant* on 1 January 1939. In March 1940, he was assigned to the Koch Assault (Glider) Battalion's Pioneer Company. On 10 May 1940, his men were to capture the bridge over the Albert Canal, but on landing, they found the bridge already blown. Schächter was badly wounded in the head and leg during the mopping up of the bridgehead, which was successfully carried out. He was awarded the Knight's Cross on 12 May 1940.

Recovered from his wounds and promoted to *Oberleutnant*, he took part in the invasion of Crete in 1941 as Meindl's ordnance officer. Schächter was again badly wounded and considered no longer fit for front-line duty. He spent the remainder of the war in staff positions. Schächter was captured in the Rühr Pocket in 1945. He died on 19 August 2007 in Bad Pyrmont, Lower Saxony.

63. *Feldwebel* Helmut ARPKE

Arpke was born on 20 March 1917 in Graudenz. He took part in the Polish campaign with *Fallschirmjäger* Regiment 1 and was promoted to *Feldwebel* on 1 May 1940. Attached to Assault Group 'Stahl', on 10 May 1940, Arpke parachuted into Belgium to capture the Veldwezelt Bridge over the Albert Canal. His squad cut the fuses under heavy fire and put a machine-gun bunker out of action on the west bank of the canal. Then he and his men captured all the barricades on and in front of the bridge. For this, he was awarded the Iron Cross 1st and 2nd Class on 12 May 1940 and the Knight's Cross on 13 May 1940.

Promoted to *Leutnant* on 17 June 1941, he took part in the invasion of Crete. In late autumn of 1941, *Fallschirmjäger* Regiment 1 was sent to Russia, taking part in the bitter fighting at Yakolevka and Zhaikovska. Arpke was known as 'the man who always knew a way out'. He was killed in action on 16 January 1942. He is buried at Schajkowka, Russia, and his remains are currently awaiting transfer to a German war cemetery.

64. *Generalleutnant* Hans Graf von SPONECK

Graf von Sponeck was born on 12 February 1888 in Düsseldorf. He fought in the First World War and was awarded the Iron Cross 1st and 2nd Class (1914). Von Sponeck led the failed attempt to capture The Hague, and he was almost taken prisoner himself. Despite this, he was awarded the Knight's Cross on 14 May 1940. He commanded the 22nd Infantry Division in the invasion of Russia, sticking toward the Crimea. Von Sponeck's unit was responsible for the mass killing of Jewish prisoners of war and Russian civilians during their drive to the Crimea and while stationed there. When the Russians retook the Crimea, Von Sponeck requested to be allowed to retreat to save his men. This was refused three times. In the end, he took the decision to retreat anyway. For this, he was relieved of his command and sent for court-martial.

Found guilty of disobeying his orders, he was sentenced to death, but Hitler commuted this to life. After the 20 July bomb plot, which Von Sponeck had nothing to do with, he was arrested again and shot. After the war, his remains were exhumed; he is now buried in the German War Cemetery, Dahn, Rhineland-Palatinate.

65. *General* Ewald von KLEIST

Von Kleist was born on 8 August 1881 in Braunfels an der Lahn. He fought at Tannenberg in 1914 as a *Hauptmann* in the cavalry, and he later joined the General Staff on the Western Front, being awarded the Iron Cross 1st and 2nd Class (1914). He fought with the *Freikorps* and was accepted into the *Reichswehr* before becoming a *Generalmajor* on the staff. In 1933, under Hitler, he was promoted to *Generalleutnant* and given command of the 8th Division. He was promoted again in 1936 to *General* but retired in 1938. Reinstated in 1939, he commanded XXII Motorised Corps in Poland. Von Kleist was awarded the Iron Cross 1st and 2nd Class (1939).

In France, he commanded '*Panzergruppe* Kleist', the largest mechanised formation ever at that time. Von Kleist was in overall command of the breakthrough in 1940. For this, he was awarded the Knight's Cross on 15 May 1940 and promoted to *Generaloberst*. He led the panzers in the Balkans in early 1941. In the initial attack on the Soviet Union, he led his tanks to the south of the Pripet Marches, and by the end of the year, he commanded I Panzer Army. He was awarded the Oak Leaves on 17 February 1942 and replaced List as commander of Army Group 'A' by the end of the year. Awarded the Swords on 30 March 1944 as a sweetener for being sacked after saving his army group from encirclement, he took no further part in the war. Captured in 1945 by US forces, he was tried for war crimes by the Russians. One of the charges was 'alienating through friendship & generosity the peoples of the Soviet Union'. He died in a Russian POW camp on 13 November 1954 and has no known grave.

66. *Oberstleutnant* Fritz IWAND

Iwand was born on 15 June 1898 in Hünern. He was commander of I Battalion, Rifle Regiment 10, when he was awarded the Knight's Cross on 15 May 1940. Iwand was killed in action on 27 July 1941 and is buried at Tschernorutsche, Russia; his remains are awaiting transfer to a German war cemetery.

67. *Oberleutnant* Otto ZIERACH

Zierach was born in Eberswalde on 26 January 1907. He joined *Fallschirmjäger* Regiment 1 as an *Oberleutnant* in April 1938 and was made chief-of-staff of the Koch Parachute Assault Battalion in 1940. For the planning and his part in the assault on 'Fortress Holland', Zierach was awarded the Knight's Cross 15 May 1940, as well as being promoted to *Hauptmann*.

He took part in the invasion of Crete as a special duties officer. He served in several staff positions until seeing action in Normandy with II Parachute Corps. Zierach became a POW on 8 May 1945, but he was soon released. He died on 12 August 1976 in Nachrodt, North Rhine-Westphalia.

68. *Leutnant* Helmut RINGLER

Ringler was born in Wollstein on 4 October 1915. He joined the Koch Parachute Assault Battalion as a *Leutnant* and took part in the attack on 'Fortress Holland' with Assault Group 'Stahl'. As part of the second wave, he landed in the midst of heavy fighting. Ringler assembled his men and overpowered the enemy manning a trench directly in front of them. He found two weapons containers and was then able to eliminate the enemy with flanking fire and relieve the hard-pressed assault group. Ringler distinguished himself and turned up wherever the situation was in doubt and held the captured positions until relieved. For this, he was awarded the Iron Cross 2nd Class on 12 May, the 1st Class on 13 May, and the Knight's Cross on 15 May 1940.

As a result of wounds suffered in the Netherlands, he was no longer fit for combat duty and was posted to the officer reserve. Ringler returned to action when given command of II Battalion, *Fallschirmjäger* Regiment 2, in the West. He died on 22 June 1962 in Bonn.

69. *Kapitänleutnant* Hans BARTELS

Bartels was born on 5 July 1910 in Frankfurt am Main. He was commander of the mine sweeper *M-1* when he was awarded the Knight's Cross on 16 May 1940. Bartels was killed in an accident on 31 July 1945. He is buried in the German War Cemetery (Neuwerk Friedhof), Block 2, Row 11, Grave 9, Rendsburg, Schleswig-Holstein.

70. *Kapitänleutnant* Otto SCHUHART

Schuhart was born in Hamburg on 1 April 1909. He took command of *U-29* from Fischer and sunk his first ship on 8 September 1939, the 10,176-ton British tanker *Regent Tiger*. On the 13th, he sank a small steamer, and the 8,431-ton tanker *British Influence* followed the next day. Then, on 17 September, he sighted the 22,500-ton British aircraft carrier *Courageous*; Schuhart sent her to the bottom with four torpedoes. This was the first British warship to be sunk in the war. He was heavily depth-charged after the attack.

On 3 March 1940, a small merchant ship was sunk by a mine laid by *U-29*. The next day, Schuhart sank the 6,717-ton *Pacific Reliance* and the 3,072-ton *Thurston*. He was awarded the Knight's Cross on 16 May 1940. In June and July, he sank four ships, including the 8,999-ton *Athellaird*. The last ship he sank was the 6,223-ton *Eurymedon* on 25 September 1940. Schuhart's last post was in the Naval Academy. He died on 10 March 1990 and is buried in Hoppenlau Friedhof, Stuttgart, Baden-Württemberg.

71. *Major* Martin VETTER

Vetter was born on 20 April 1905 in Yabim. He was a group commander in Bomber Wing 26 when he was awarded the Knight's Cross on 16 May 1940. Vetter died on 25 September 1982 in Himmelpforten, Lower Saxony.

72. *Oberleutnant* Albrecht KUNTZE

Kuntze was born on 25 December 1912 in Magdeburg. He was a pilot in Bomber Wing 26 when he was awarded the Knight's Cross on 16 May 1940. Kuntze died of wounds at Ingelheim, Rhineland, on 5 July 1943 and has no known grave.

73. *Oberleutnant* zur See Hermann OPDENHOFF

Opdenhoff was born on 9 January 1915 in Falkenberg. He was commander of torpedo boat *S-31* when he was awarded the Knight's Cross on 16 May 1940. Opdenhoff was killed in action off the coast of Texel, the Netherlands, on 21 March 1945, and he has no known grave.

74. *General* Hugo SPERRLE

Sperrle was born on 8 February 1885 in Ludwigsburg. He fought in the First World War as an observer and was awarded the Iron Cross 1st and 2nd Class (1914). Sperrle was the first commander of the Condor Legion in Spain. At the start of the Second World War, he commanded *Luftflotte* 3, which first saw action in the campaign in the West. For this, Sperrle was awarded the Knight's Cross on 17 May 1940. During the Battle of Britain, his aircraft played a major role in bombing airfields and later the cities of England, up until the autumn of 1941.

Eventually, Sperrle took command of all German air forces in Western Europe, but was dismissed in August 1944. Captured by the Allies, he was changed with war crimes but was acquitted. Sperrle died on 2 April 1953 and is buried in the German War Cemetery, Obermeitingen, Bavaria.

75. *Generalmajor* Wolfram Freiherr von RICHTHOFEN

Von Richthofen (cousin of the famous Richthofen brothers) was born on 10 October 1895 in Gut Barzdorf. He fought in the infantry and as a pilot during the First World War, shooting down eight enemy aircraft, and he was awarded the Iron Cross 2nd Class (1914). He served with the Condor Legion in Spain. Von Richthofen commanded VIII Air Corps in Poland and France, being awarded the Knight's Cross on 17 May 1940.

Von Richthofen continued in front-line service during the Battle of Britain. He also saw service in the Balkans campaign and the invasion of Russia, for which he was awarded the Oak Leaves on 17 July 1941. Moved to the Mediterranean area after the fall of Stalingrad, von Richthofen served there until ill health forced him to step down in late 1944. He was taken prisoner by the Americans in May 1945 and died from a brain tumour on 12 July 1945 while still a POW. He is buried in Bad Ischl Friedhof, Austria.

76. *Oberst* Hans KREYSING

Kreysing was born on 17 August 1890 in Göttingen. He fought in the First World War, being awarded the Iron Cross 1st and 2nd Class (1914). Kreysing also fought in Poland and was awarded the Iron Cross 1st and 2nd Class (1939). After the fall of France, he was awarded the Knight's Cross on 18 May 1940.

The Oak Leaves were awarded on 20 January 1943 and the Swords followed on 13 April 1944. Kreysing died on 14 April 1969 in Oldenburg, Lower Saxony.

77. *Oberstleutnant* Dietrich von CHOLTITZ—'Wrecker of Cities'

Von Choltitz was born on 9 November 1894 in Wiesegräflich. He fought in the First World War and was awarded the Iron Cross 1st and 2nd Class (1914). Von Choltitz took part in the capture (by air) of Rotterdam, for which he was awarded the Knight's Cross on 18 May 1940. He commanded Infantry Regiment 16 during the attack on Russia and saw much action in the Crimea during 1942.

From March 1944, he served in Italy, and from June 1944, he served on the Western Front, becoming governor of Paris on 7 August. Despite being known as the 'Wrecker of Cities' (a reference to his destructions of cities on the Eastern Front), he refused Hitler's order to burn Paris and was known (by some) as the 'Saviour of Paris'. Von Choltitz surrendered his forces to French General Philippe Leclerc de Hautecloque on 25 August and was held until 1947. Von Choltitz died after a long illness on 5 November 1966 and is buried in Stadtfriedhof, Feld 8. Baden Baden, Baden-Württemberg.

78. *Hauptmann* Otto WEISS—'The Lion of Kalinin'

Weiss was born on 25 September 1907 in Breslau. He fought in Poland as a ground-attack pilot and was awarded the Iron Cross 1st and 2nd Class. In France, his wing attacked a French column of some fifty tanks and 150 vehicles, destroying forty tanks. For this, Weiss was awarded the Knight's Cross on 18 May 1940. He was the first ground-attack pilot to be awarded it.

He fought in the Battle of Britain and Yugoslavia before taking part in the invasion of Russia in 1941. Weiss was awarded the Oak Leaves on 31 December 1941 for his part in the fighting at Vyazma-Briansk and Kalinin. In June 1942, he was tasked with experimenting with anti-tank warfare from the air. Promoted to *Oberst* in November 1943, he was posted to the staff of *Luftflotte* 6, where he remained until the end of the war. Weiss died following a long illness on 19 August 1955 and is buried in Südfriedhof, Kiel, Schleswig-Holstein.

79. *Generalleutnant* Friedrich KIRCHNER

Kirchner was born on 26 March 1885 in Zöbigker. He fought in the First World War and was awarded the Iron Cross 1st and 2nd Class (1914). Kirchner fought in Poland, being awarded the Iron Cross 1st and 2nd Class (1939). In France, he led the 1st Panzer Division and was injured when a German vehicle drove over his legs. Kirchner was awarded the Knight's Cross on 20 May 1940 for his part in the French campaign.

On 15 November 1941, he took command of LVII Army Corps, later renamed LVII Panzer Corps, which he commanded until the end of the war. Kirchner was awarded the Oak Leaves on 12 February 1944 and the Swords on 26 January 1945. He died on 6 April 1960 and is buried in Zentralfriedhof, Fulda, Hesse.

80. *Oberstleutnant* Hans MIKOSCH

Mikosch was born on 7 January 1898 in Kattowitz. He fought in the First World War and was awarded the Iron Cross 1st and 2nd Class (1914). He took part in the Polish campaign of 1939, and was awarded the Iron Cross 2nd Class

(1939), and the French campaign of 1940, being awarded the Iron Cross 1st Class (1939) on 14 May; he received the Knight's Cross on 21 May 1940.

Mikosch also took part in the invasion of Russia and saw action at Stalingrad. He was awarded the Oak Leaves on 6 March 1943. Mikosch died on 18 January 1993 and is believed to be buried in Hunsheim Friedhof, Reichshof, North Rhine-Westphalia.

81. *Oberfeldwebel* Josef PORTSTEFFEN

Portsteffen was born on 4 October 1913 in Paderborn. He was a platoon leader in Motorised Pioneer Battalion 51 when he was awarded the Knight's Cross on 21 May 1940. Portsteffen died on 21 June 1974 and is buried in Community Friedhof, Lippstadt, North Rhine-Westphalia.

82. *Oberst* Bruno BRÄUER

Bräuer was born on 4 February 1893 in Willmannsdorf. He fought in the First World War, being awarded the Iron Cross 1st and 2nd Class (1914). On 23 November 1938, he took command of *Fallschirmjäger* Regiment 1 and was promoted to *Oberst* on 1 January 1939. He was awarded the Iron Cross 1st and 2nd Class (1939) in the Polish campaign. He dropped into the Netherlands and took part in the fighting around Dordrecht and Tweede Tool, being awarded the Knight's Cross on 24 May 1940 for 'heroic personal actions in the employment and command of his regiment'.

He led the East Group in the invasion of Crete. From February 1943 until May 1944, Bräuer commanded Fortress Crete, then, on account of illness, he was assigned to command reserve. He was taken prisoner by the British on 10 May 1945 and handed over to the Greeks, who executed him on 20 May 1947 for war crimes in Crete. Ironically, he was known as the most humane commander of Crete. Bräuer is buried in the German War Cemetery, Block 3, Grave 851, Hill 107, Maleme, Crete.

83. *Oberst* Gerhard CONRAD

Conrad was born on 21 April 1895 in Pregelmühle. He fought in the First World War and was awarded the Iron Cross 1st and 2nd Class (1914). Conrad was a commodore in Fighter Wing 2 when he was awarded the Knight's Cross on 24 May 1940. He died on 28 May 1982 in Ruhpolding, Bavaria.

84. *Oberstleutnant* Gustav WILKE

Wilke was born on 6 March 1898 in Deutsch Eyau. He was a group commander in Fighter Wing 11 when he was awarded the Knight's Cross on 24 May 1940. Wilke died on 13 March 1977 and is buried in Waldfriedhof, Oberstdorf, Bavaria.

85. *Major* Heinrich TRETTNER

Trettner was born on 19 September 1907 in Minden. He was adjutant to *Oberst* Wolfram von Richthofen in the Condor Legion and was awarded the Spanish Cross in Gold. Promoted to *Major* in August 1939, he served under Student and together they worked out all of the operations for the Western Campaign. For this, he was awarded the Iron Cross 1st and 2nd Class on 12 May 1940 and the Knight's Cross on 24 May.

In September 1942, he became chief-of staff of XI *Fliegerkorps*, and at his own request, he was given the job of forming the 4th Parachute Division in October 1943. Trettner led his division at Anzio-Nettuno and was awarded the Oak Leaves on 17 September 1944. He was taken prisoner by the British on 3 May 1945. Trettner died on 18 September 2006 in Mönchengladbach, North Rhine-Westphalia. He was the last living general of the Wehrmacht.

86. *Major* Erich WALTHER

Walther was born on 5 August 1903 in Girden bei Falkenberg. He dropped into 'Fortress Holland' with *Fallschirmjäger* Regiment 1, landing near Dordrecht. Walther was awarded the Iron Cross 1st and 2nd Class in April and the Knight's Cross on 24 May 1940. From 27 May, he fought in Norway, supporting the 3rd Infantry Division. In Crete, he fought in the Heraklion area, and on 29 May 1941, he marched into the city at the head of the *Fallschirmjäger*.

He saw action in Russia near Leningrad and was promoted to *Oberst*. In Sicily, he commanded *Fallschirmjäger* Regiment 4, fighting at the Simeto Bridge. At Cassino, his regiment defended the much fought-over hills. He was awarded the Oak Leaves on 2 March 1944. He fought at Nimwegen and Arnhem in the Netherlands, and subsequently took command of the Hermann Göring 2nd Parachute *Panzergrenadier* Division in East Prussia. Promoted to *Generalmajor* in January 1945 and awarded the Swords on 1 February, he was taken prisoner by the Russians on 8 May 1945 and died at Buchenwald, near Weimar, Thuringia, on 26 December 1947. He has no known grave.

87. *Hauptmann* Fritz PRAGER

Prager was born on 17 December 1905 in Wolfenbüttel. He took command of *Fallschirmjäger* Regiment 1's II Battalion in January 1939 and led it in the Polish campaign, capturing Wola Gułowska airfield. For this, he was awarded the Iron Cross 2nd Class on 13 October 1939. In April 1940, Prager underwent an operation for cancer, but this did not stop him from jumping into the Netherlands in May 1940. He led his men in storming the Moerdijk Bridge and was badly wounded taking a number of enemy bunkers, but he remained with his battalion until relieved by the 9th Panzer Division. For this, he was awarded the Iron Cross 1st Class on 10 May and the Knight's Cross on 24 May 1940.

He later took part in the operation to relieve the mountain infantry in Narvik. He was promoted to *Major* on 19 June 1940 and given command of III Battalion, *Fallschirmjäger* Regiment 3, on 1 July. Prager died from cancer on 3 December 1940 and is buried in the German War Cemetery (Taucher Friedhof), Grave 5, Bautzen, Saxony.

88. *Hauptmann* Karl-Lothar SCHULZ

Schulz was born on 30 April 1907 in Königsberg. On 1 January 1940, *Hauptmann* Schulz took command of III Battalion, *Fallschirmjäger* Regiment 1. In the French campaign, his regiment captured Rotterdam airport, which was used for the landing of reinforcements. For this, he was awarded the Iron Cross 1st and 2nd Class on 12 May and the Knight's Cross on 24 May 1940. Promoted to *Major* on 19 July 1940, his next drop was Crete in 1941, landing near Heraklion. He led his men into the city but was forced to retire due to lack of ammunition, but he held on to positions near the city.

On 29 September 1941, Schulz led his battalion in the Leningrad area, fighting at the River Neva. He subsequently assumed command of *Fallschirmjäger* Regiment 1, which he led on his next tour of Russia. Following the Allied landings in Italy, he saw action at Tarent. He distinguished himself at Anzio-Nettuno, at Cassino, and during the fighting withdrawal to Bologna, being awarded the Oak Leaves on 20 April and the Swords on 18 November 1944. He died on 26 September 1972 and is buried in Südfriedhof, Wiesbaden, Hesse.

89. *Oberleutnant* Horst KERFIN

Kerfin was born on 21 March 1913 in Insterburg, Russia. He saw action in Poland with *Fallschirmjäger* Regiment 3, being awarded the Iron Cross 2nd

Class. He fought in the Netherlands with *Fallschirmjäger* Regiment 1. His battalion was tasked with capturing Rotterdam's Waalhaven airport. Kerfin jumped near Feyenoord, stormed through the village, and commandeered a streetcar, which they drove to the Maas Island in the south-east part of the city. His platoon silenced the anti-aircraft guns, crossed the Willems Bridge, and established a bridgehead, which they held until reinforced. For this, he was awarded the Knight's Cross on 24 May 1940.

Kerfin was killed in action on 22 January 1943 and is buried at Saborje/ Demidov, Russia; his remains are awaiting transfer to a German war cemetery.

90. *Oberleutnant* Herbert SCHMIDT

Schmidt was born on 3 October 1912 in Feste Courbiére, West Prussia. He was promoted to *Oberleutnant* on 1 October 1939 and led a company of *Fallschirmjäger* Regiment 1 during Operation Weserübung. His men dropped into Norway on 14 April 1940, landing south of Dombas. For five days, he prevented the British from linking up with Norwegian forces. Schmidt and his remaining thirty-eight men were taken prisoner by the Norwegians, but they were soon freed. For this action, he was awarded the Iron Cross 1st and 2nd Class and the Knight's Cross on 24 (some sources say 29) May 1940.

Still not fully recovered from his wounds, Schmidt joined the staff of the inspector-general of the Luftwaffe. He later became chief-of-staff to 1st Luftwaffe Field Division and the 2nd Parachute Division. On 6 June 1944, while driving from Vannes to Pontivy in Brittany, Schmidt was shot dead by French partisans. He is buried in the German War Cemetery, Crypt 1, Grave Chamber 122, Mont-de-Huisnes, Normandy, France.

91. *Oberleutnant* Alfred SCHWARZMANN

Schwarzmann was born in Fürth on 23 March 1912. He won three gold medals and two bronze for gymnastics in the 1939 Olympics. Schwarzmann joined *Fallschirmjäger* Regiment 1 with the rank of *Oberleutnant* in April 1940. He jumped into the Netherlands on 10 May 1940 and held a key enemy position on the coast, during the course of which he was wounded by a bullet through the lung. For this action, Schwarzmann was awarded the Knight's Cross on 24 May 1940, but he seems to have been awarded the Iron Cross 1st and 2nd Class on the 25th. Some sources say the Knight's Cross was awarded on the 29th. It is likely that the awarding of the Knight's Cross was for propaganda as it was thought his lung wound was fatal.

In Crete, he saw action in near Heraklion, and in 1941–42, he led a company of *Fallschirmjäger* Regiment 3 in Russia as a *Hauptmann*. On 15 March 1943, he was made commander of the HQ of 7th Air Division and, later, 1st Parachute Division. He was forced back into hospital by his old wound in March 1944 and promoted to *Major* in April 1945. Schwarzmann was captured by the British but was released in October 1945. In the 1952 Olympics, he won silver medal for gymnastic. Jack Günthard, the Swiss winner of the gold, said of him: 'The victory should have gone to Alfred—but he was German'. Schwarzmann died on 11 March 2000 and is buried in Hauptfriedhof, Goslar, Lower Saxony.

92. *Leutnant* Wolfgang Lebrecht Graf von BLÜCHER (-FINCKEN added later)

Von Blücher was born on 31 January 1917 in Altengottern. He joined *Fallschirmjäger* Regiment 1 in December 1939 and fought in Norway, being awarded the Iron Cross 2nd Class. He jumped into the Netherlands near Tweede Tool and became involved in street fighting in Dordrecht. He stormed a nest of bunkers, for which he was awarded both the Iron Cross 1st Class and the Knight's Cross on 24 May 1940.

The invasion of Crete in 1941 saw him fighting his way into Heraklion airport and capturing a hill at the eastern end of the field. He and his two brothers were killed on 21 May 1941. Blücher is buried in the German War Cemetery, Block 1, Grave 457, Hill 107, Maleme, Crete.

93. *Leutnant* Cord TIETJEN

Tietjen was born on 10 November 1914 in Danzig-Langfuhr. In January 1939, he joined *Fallschirmjäger* Regiment 1 and he took part in the Polish campaign. On 7 May 1940, he was promoted to *Leutnant*. Tietjen took part in the attack on 'Fortress Holland', landing on the south side of the Maas Bridge near Dordrecht. He and his men stormed across the bridge, capturing the earth bunkers and dykes, Tietjen being wounded during this action. For his part, he was awarded the Iron Cross 1st and 2nd Class on 22 May 1940 and the Knight's Cross on 24 May.

Promoted to *Oberleutnant*, he took command of a company in the 7th Parachute Pioneer Battalion, with which he jumped into Crete. Tietjen was captured on Crete and not released until February 1947. He died on 18 June 2005 in Arnsberg, North Rhine-Westphalia.

94. *Feldwebel* Helmut Gustav GÖRTZ

Görtz was born in Schleusenau on 7 August 1911. He joined *Fallschirmjäger* Regiment 1 and took part in the Polish campaign and Norway, being awarded the Iron Cross 2nd Class. The 1st Class came to him for his part in 'Fortress Holland' on 18 May 1940. During bitter fighting around Dordrecht, his commander was killed, and Görtz and several comrades advanced to the east end of the bridge and halted an enemy attack. He held the bridge until reinforced. For this action, Görtz was awarded the Knight's Cross on 24 May 1940.

In the winter of 1941, he fought at the Neva River, and in the regiment's second tour in Russia, he saw action in the Promklevo area. Görtz was present when the Russians tried to break through towards Baldusch on 4 March 1943 and took part in the counterattack towards Aleshenka. On 26 October 1943, he was named an officer candidate. He was transferred to Italy with his regiment on 9 July 1943 and took part in defensive fighting as a platoon leader, with the rank of *Oberleutnant*. He was recommended for the Oak Leaves in 1945 but was not awarded them. Görtz died on 3 May 1979 and is believed to be buried in Städtischer Friedhof, Dinslaken, North Rhine-Westphalia.

95. *General* Ernst BUSCH

Busch was born on 6 July 1885 in Essen. He commanded a battalion in the First World War and was awarded the Iron Cross 1st and 2nd Class (1914), as well as the *Pour le Mérite* in October 1918. It took him until 1930 to become a battalion commander again, this time with the rank of *Major*. By 1937, he was a *Generalleutnant*, and in 1938, he was promoted to *General*. Busch led his corps with distinction in Poland and was awarded the Iron Cross 1st and 2nd Class (1939). He commanded the 16th Army in France and captured Verdun in a matter of hours. He was awarded the Knight's Cross on 26 May 1940 and was promoted to *Generaloberst*.

During 1941 and 1942, his army fought on the Baltic front, and for his loyalty, he was promoted to *Generalfeldmarschall* in February 1943. Busch was awarded the Oak Leaves on 21 August 1943 and given command of Army Group Centre in November. Now promoted above his capacity, he was unable to hinder the Russian breakthrough in the summer of 1944 and was sacked in June 1944. Recalled in 1945, he was made commander of all forces in the West. He presided over the surrender with Montgomery but was left in command of German units in North Germany. Brought to England as a POW, he died of a heart attack on 17 July 1945 and is buried in the German War Cemetery, Block 6, Row 10, Grave 112, Camp Road, Cannock Chase, Staffordshire, England.

96. *Oberst* Kurt HEYSER

Heyser was born on 27 August 1894 in Braunschweig. He fought in the First World War, being awarded the Iron Cross 1st and 2nd Class (1914). Heyser took part in the campaign in the West as commander of Infantry Regiment 47 and was awarded the Iron Cross 1st and 2nd Class (1939). He was awarded the Knight's Cross on 26 May 1940. He fought in Russia but was captured by US forces in May 1945. Heyser died on 20 April 1974 and is buried in Riensberg Friedhof, Feld P, Grave 79, Bremen.

97. *Oberst* Ludwig WOLFF

Wolff was born on 3 April 1893 in Chemnitz. He fought in the First World War and was awarded the Iron Cross 1st and 2nd Class (1914). Wolff also took part in the Polish and French campaigns, commanding Infantry Regiment 192. He was awarded the Iron Cross 2nd Class (1939) on 13 May, the 1st Class (1939) on 18 May, and the Knight's Cross on 26 May 1940.

Wolff fought in Russia where he commanded the 22nd Infantry Division; he was awarded the Oak Leaves on 22 June 1940. He was captured by US forces in May 1945 and held until 1947. Wolff died on 9 November 1968 and is buried in Hauptfriedhof, Mannheim, Baden-Württemberg.

98. *Oberstleutnant* Werner EHRIG

Ehrig was born on 22 April 1897 in Eibenstock. He fought in the First World War and was awarded the Iron Cross 1st and 2nd Class (1914). Ehrig was chief of operations in 22nd Infantry Division when he was awarded the Iron Cross 1st and 2nd Class (1939) on 14 May and the Knight's Cross on 26 May 1940. He died on 31 January 1981 and is buried in Parkfriedhof, Sandkrugerstrasse 26, Oldenburg, Lower Saxony.

99. *Major* Friedrich-Gustav JÄGER—'Fritz'

Jäger was born on 25 September 1895 in Kirchberg. He fought in the First World War, was wounded six times, and was awarded the Iron Cross 1st and 2nd Class (1914). He fought in Poland and France, and he was awarded the Knight's Cross on 26 May 1940. Jäger also took part in the invasion of Russia and was wounded eight times at Stalingrad but was only flown out when he became ill with epidemic typhus.

Jäger became commander of the Panzer reserve troops in Stettin and Kalisch. Involved in the 20 July plot to kill Hitler (although he would have preferred to see him stand trial), Jäger was arrested, tried, and hanged on 21 August 1944, he has no known grave.

100. *Hauptmann* Gustav ALVERMANN

Alvermann was born on 9 October 1897 in Ilster. He fought in the First World War, being awarded the Iron Cross 1st and 2nd Class (1914). Alvermann was a company commander in Infantry Regiment 47 when he was awarded the Knight's Cross on 26 May 1940. He was killed in action on 7 June 1942 and is buried in the German War Cemetery, Black 10 (as unknown), Sebastopol, Ukraine.

101. *Oberleutnant* Alfred GERMER

Germer was born on 7 June 1914 in Strasbourg. He was a company commander in Pioneer Battalion 171 when he was awarded the Knight's Cross on 26 May 1940. Germer was posted missing on 3 January 1945 near Elbing, Poland.

102. *Oberfeldarzt* Werner WISCHHUSEN

Wischhusen was born on 6 December 1889 in Osterwieck. He was a doctor in 22nd Infantry Division when he was awarded the Knight's Cross on 26 May 1940. Wischhusen died on 8 October 1969 and is buried in Hauptfriedhof, Baden Baden, Baden-Württemberg.

103. *Unteroffizier* Walter KALKHOFF

Kalkhoff was born on 19 February 1913 in Siegburg-Mühldorf. He was a section leader in Motorised Infantry Regiment 67 when he was awarded the Knight's Cross on 26 May 1940. Kalkhoff died on 9 February 1960 in Winterscheid, Rhineland-Palatinate.

104. *Generalmajor* Erwin ROMMEL—'The Desert Fox'

Rommel was born on 15 November 1891 in Heidenheim. He fought in the First World War, was wounded, and was awarded the Iron Cross 1st and

2nd Class (1914), as well as the *Pour le Mérite*. He published a book on infantry tactics in 1937 called *Infantry Attacks*, which impressed Hitler. For most of 1939, Rommel commanded Hitler's HQ troops, and as a result, he asked and was given command of the 7th Panzer Division for the coming French campaign. Leading from the front and often out of touch with his staff, he narrowly avoided capture on a number of occasions. His division stormed across the River Meuse on 10 May 1940. By the 21st, he had reached Arras where the British counterattacked with Matilda tanks. Rommel had to personally direct the fire of 88-mm guns to stop the attack. He was awarded the Iron Cross 1st Class and 2nd Class (1939) (17 and 21 May), the Knight's Cross followed on 27 May 1940. On 28 May, he captured Lille, trapping half the French First Army. His division was halted for rest, but on 5 June, he drove for the River Seine to secure the bridges near Rouen, advancing 62 miles in two days, only to find the bridges blown. On 10 June, he reached the coast near Dieppe, sending his 'Am at coast' signal to the German HQ. On 15 June, he stared his advance to Cherbourg, which he captured on the 18th.

In early 1941, he was sent to the Western Desert with just two divisions to stop the Italian collapse, and within weeks, the situation had completely changed. He chased the British from Cyrenaica back over the Egyptian border. He was awarded the Oak Leaves on 20 March 1941 and the Swords on 20 January 1942. After the capture of Tobruk in June, he was promoted to *Generalfeldmarschall*. But the end was in sight in the material sense. Defeated at Alam-el-Halfa and El Alamein, Rommel was down to a handful of tanks as the long retreat to Tunisia started. Trapped between Montgomery and Patton, he was removed from Africa on health grounds and awarded the Diamonds on 11 March 1943.

For a short time, he was commander of Army Group 'E' in Greece and then Army Group 'B' in northern Italy, but in November 1943, he was sent to the West to study the defences on the Atlantic Wall. He differed with von Rundstedt over the defensive emphasis, wanting to keep the Panzers well to the front while von Rundstedt and the OKW wanted them as a mobile reserve. Rommel was now put in charge of the beach defences and had millions of mines laid, as well as thousands of tank traps and obstacles on the beaches and the countryside—the so called 'Rommel's asparagus'. When the invasion came, he was absent from the front but rushed back to Normandy, but he was unable to turn the tide against the Allies. On 17 July 1944, he was almost killed when his car was attacked by British fighters, ending his active career.

Towards the end, he had certainly been contacted by the plotters but was against the assassination attempt, believing that Hitler should be arrested. When the plot failed on 20 July 1944, it did not take long for Rommel's name to be connected to it. As a national hero, he was given the choice of suicide and safety and honour for his family or arrest and trial. Rommel took poison just outside the town of Herrlingen, near Ulm, on 14 October 1944. He was given a state funeral at Herrlingen Friedhof, Blaustein, Baden-Württemberg. At the time of his death, Rommel was working on another book, most likely to be called *Panzer Attacks*. Forever known as the 'Desert Fox' to the British, to his men, he was 'The General of the Highway'.

105. *General* Ulrich GRAUERT

Grauert was born on 6 March 1889 in Berlin. He fought in the First World War and was awarded the Iron Cross 1st and 2nd Class (1914). Grauert was commander of *Fliegerkorps* I when he was awarded the Knight's Cross on 29 May 1940. He was killed in action when his Ju 52 transport aircraft was shot down on 15 May 1941. Grauert is buried in the WWI German War Cemetery, Block 6, Grave 784, Nampcel, near Noyon, Picardy, France.

106. *Generalleutnant* Bruno LOERZER

Loerzer was born in Berlin on 22 January 1891. At seventeen years old, he joined the army as a cadet in Infantry Regiment 112 (Prince Wilhelm). He was later accepted to military school, and after graduating in 1913, he rejoined his regiment with the rank of *Leutnant*. It was while serving with this regiment that he met Hermann Göring and they were to become inseparable. He soon became tired of the infantry and applied for the German Army Air Service; being accepted, he started his flying training in August 1914. Graduating in October, he was posted to FA 25 as a reconnaissance pilot, and he was soon joined by Göring as his observer. They flew many missions together and were both awarded the Iron Cross 2nd Class (1914) on 7 March 1915. But by the end of June, Loerzer was bored of observation missions and asked to be transferred to a fighter unit; he was sent to FA 60 and from there to FA(A) 203.

On completion of his training, he was posted to *Kek* Jametz, where on 21 March 1916, he shot down his first enemy aircraft, a Farman. On 31 March, he shot down his second and in late 1916 was posted to *Jasta* 5 and from there to *Jasta* 17. On 18 January 1917, he was given command of *Jasta* 26 but his score began to increase slowly, shooting down two in March, one in April, and another two in August. Things started to pick up in September when he shot down five, followed by eight in October. By the end of 1917, he had been awarded the Iron Cross 1st Class (1914) and the Knight's Cross with Swords of the Royal Hohenzollern House Order. With his tally at twenty-three, Loerzer was awarded the *Pour le Mérite* on 12 March 1918 and was given command of *Jagdgeschwader* III nine days later. He was now flying the new

Fokker DVII, usually with *Jasta* 26 and his younger brother, Fritz. Loerzer shot down eleven enemy aircraft between 23 March and 29 August, bringing his tally to thirty-four. Then he shot down five enemy aircraft in the first five days of September, plus two on the 16th, one on the 22nd, and two more on the 26th. He flew a distinctive black and white striped aircraft throughout his career. On 10 October 1918, he was promoted to *Hauptmann*. By the war's end, he had shot down forty-four enemy aircraft.

During the Second World War, he was promoted to *Generalleutnant* of the Luftwaffe, and on 29 May 1940, he was awarded the Knight's Cross of the Iron Cross. Promoted to *Generaloberst*, it is clear that his friendship with Göring had influence on the decision.

Loerzer died on 23 September 1960. He is buried in Ohlsdorf Friedhof, Fuhlsbüttler Strasse, Hamburg.

107. *Hauptmann* Werner MÖLDERS—'Daddy'

Mölders was born on 18 March 1913 in Gelsenkirchen. He fought with the Condor Legion in Spain, becoming the leading ace with fourteen aircraft to his credit. Mölders's first victory of the Second World War came in September 1939 when he shot down a French fighter. For this, he was awarded the Iron Cross 2nd Class. The Iron Cross 1st Class was awarded after his seventh victory. On 27 May 1940, Mölders shot down his twentieth enemy aircraft, for which he was awarded the Knight's Cross two days later. Then, on 5 June 1940, Mölders was shot down by the French ace René Pomier Layrargues and subsequently captured. After the fall of France, he was released.

On his first patrol over England on 28 July 1940, Mölders was badly shot up and wounded in the legs; he only just managed to get his fighter home. He scored well during the Battle of Britain, being awarded the Oak Leaves on 21 September 1940 with forty confirmed victories. By October, he became the first pilot to reach fifty victories, and with his score at seventy-two, he was awarded the Swords on 22 June 1941. A few weeks later, he became the first pilot to surpass Baron von Richthofen's eighty victories and the first pilot to shoot down 100 enemy aircraft. For this, Mölders became the first recipient of the Diamonds on 15 July 1941.

Banned from flying any more combat missions, Mölders was made inspector of fighters. Despite Göring's orders, he did shoot down a few enemy aircraft on the Russian Front, but these had to remain unconfirmed to conform to his flying ban. Then, on 22 November 1941, Mölders was on his way back to Germany in a He 111 bomber, which crashed on landing during a thunderstorm at Breslau; Mölders was killed instantly. He is buried in the Invaliden Friedhof, Feld F, Plot 7, Grave 16 (next to Stutterheim and Udet), Scharnhorstrasse, Berlin.

108. *Oberleutnant* Hermann (or Hermann-Albert) SCHRADER

Schrader was born on 10 February 1913 in Beverstedt. He fought in the campaign in the West as a company commander in Infantry Regiment 16 and was awarded the Knight's Cross on 29 May 1940. Schrader took part in the invasion of Russia and was killed in action on 14 June 1942. He is buried in the German War Cemetery, Block 10 (as unknown), Sebastopol, Ukraine.

109. *Oberleutnant* Hellmuth SCHREIBER-VOLKENING

Schreiber-Volkening was born on 22 November 1911 in Pea Radja, Indonesia. He was a company commander in Infantry Regiment 16 when he was awarded the Knight's Cross on 29 May 1940. Schreiber-Volkening was killed in action on 9 August 1942 in Russia. He has no known grave.

110. *Feldwebel* August GRAUTING

Grauting was born on 23 July 1908 in Assel. He was a platoon leader in Infantry Regiment 16 when he was awarded the Knight's Cross on 29 May 1940. Grauting was killed in action on 4 July 1941 and is believed to be buried in the German War Cemetery (as unknown), Chisinau, Moldova.

111. *Kapitänleutnant* Erich GRUNDMANN

Grundmann was born on 2 June 1906 in Kiel. He was flotilla engineer in R-Boat Flotilla 1 when he was awarded the Knight's Cross on 31 May 1940. Grundmann died on 7 September 1973 and is buried in Niederbachem Friedhof, Mehlemer Stresse, Wachtberg, North Rhine-Westphalia.

112. *Stabsobersteuermann* Arthur GODENAU

Godenau was born on 19 January 1903 in Netzort. He was commander of *R-17* in R-Boat Flotilla 1 when he was awarded the Knight's Cross on 31 May 1940. Godenau died on 16 February 1983 and is buried in Nordfriedhof, Laboe, Schleswig-Holstein.

113. *Stabsobersteuermann* Karl RIXECKER

Rixecker was born on 18 November 1906 in Merchweiler. He was commander of *R-23* in R-Boat Flotilla 1 when he was awarded the Iron Cross 2nd Class in October 1939 and the 1st Class in April 1940. Rixecker was awarded the Knight's Cross on 31 May 1940. He died on 22 September 1959 and is buried in Alter Friedhof, Wetzlar, Hesse.

114. *Generalleutnant* Werner KEMPF

Kempf was born on 9 March 1886 in Königsberg. He fought in the First World War and was awarded the Iron Cross 1st and 2nd Class (1914). In 1939, he led the 6th Panzer Division in Poland, for which he was awarded the Iron Cross 1st and 2nd Class (1939). For his part in the French campaign, Kempf was awarded the Knight's Cross on 3 June 1940.

From 5 May 1942, he commanded the XXXXVIII Panzer Corps in Russia and was awarded the Oak Leaves on 10 August 1942. Kempf fought at Kursk and later commanded the Wehrmacht in the Baltic. He was taken into captivity in May 1945 and released in 1947. Kempf died on 6 January 1964 and is buried in Stadtfriedhof, Bad Harzburg, Lower Saxony.

115. *Generalleutnant* Adolf-Friedrich KUNTZEN

Kuntzen was born on 26 July 1889 in Magdeburg. He fought in the First World War, being awarded the Iron Cross 1st and 2nd Class (1914). Kuntzen was awarded the Knight's Cross after the fall of France on 3 June 1940 as commander of the 8th Panzer Division.

In 1941, he was appointed commander of LVII Army Corps. Kuntzen was then given command of LXXXI Army Corps in May 1942 and was in this post on D-Day in France. He was transferred to the reserve list on 14 September and retired in December 1944. Kuntzen died on 10 July 1964 and is believed to be buried in Stadtfriedhof, Hanover.

116. *Generalleutnant* Rudolf SCHMIDT

Schmidt was born on 12 May 1886 in Berlin. He fought in the First World War and was awarded the Iron Cross 1st and 2nd Class (1914). He led the 1st Panzer Division in Poland, for which he was awarded the Iron Cross 1st and

2nd Class (1939). In France, he led XXXIX Panzer Corps and was awarded the Knight's Cross on 3 June 1940 for his efforts.

Awarded the Oak Leaves on 10 July 1941, he replaced Guderian (who was sacked) as commander of II Panzer Army on 25 December 1941. Schmidt was held in high regard until his brother, Hans-Thilo Schmidt, was arrested. He had been selling secrets, including the Enigma machine, to the French before the war. On his person were letters written by Rudolf criticising Hitler's conduction of the war. Rudolf was acquitted at his court-martial and transferred to the reserve in September 1943; he never commanded again. Taken as a POW by the Russians at the end of the war, he was not released until 1955. Schmidt died on 7 April 1957 and is buried in Hauptfriedhof, Krefeld, North Rhine-Westphalia.

117. *Generalleutnant* Rudolf VEIEL

Veiel was born on 10 December 1883 in Stuttgart. He fought in the First World War and was awarded the Iron Cross 1st and 2nd Class (1914). He commanded the 2nd Panzer Division in Poland and France, was awarded the Iron Cross 1st and 2nd Class (1939), and, on 3 June 1940, he received the Knight's Cross.

Veiel took part in the Balkan and Greek campaigns as well as the invasion of Russia in June 1941. He would remain on the Russian Front until recalled to become commander of Battle Group V in Stuttgart in September 1943. Veiel was relieved of his command due to complicity over the 20 July bomb plot, but he was not charged. He was taken prisoner by US forces in May 1945 and released in 1947. Veiel died on 19 March 1956 and is buried in Pragerfriedhof, Abt 34, Row 11, Grave 1, Stuttgart, Baden-Württemberg.

118. *Oberst* Hermann BREITH

Breith was born on 7 May 1892 in Pirmasens. He fought in the First World War and was awarded the Iron Cross 1st and 2nd Class (1914). Breith was awarded the Iron Cross 1st and 2nd Class (1939) after the fall of Poland. He was commander of 5th Panzer Brigade when he was awarded the Knight's Cross on 3 June 1940.

Breith was awarded the Oak Leaves on 31 January 1942 as commander of 3rd Panzer Division and the Swords on 21 February 1944 as commander of III Panzer Corps. He was also awarded the Wound Badge in Gold. Breith died on 3 September 1964 and is buried in Niederbachem Friedhof, Mehlemer Stresse, Wachtberg, North Rhine-Westphalia.

119. *Oberst* Wolfgang FISCHER

Fischer was born in Carolath on 11 December 1888. He fought in the First World War, being awarded the Iron Cross 1st and 2nd Class (1914). During the Polish campaign, he commanded Infantry Regiment 69 and was awarded the Iron Cross 1st and 2nd Class (1939). In France, he was CO of the 10th Rifle Brigade, which he led on a series of raids into the enemy rear. For this, he was awarded the Knight's Cross on 3 June 1940.

In Russia, he was promoted to *Generalmajor* in August 1941, and on 22 April 1942, he was awarded the German Cross in Gold. Sent to Tunisia with the rank of *Generalleutnant* in November 1942, he fought in the defensive battles there. It was largely due to him that the Germans won the 'race to Tunis'. He was awarded the Oak Leaves on 9 December 1942. Fischer was killed in action on 1 February 1943 and he is buried in the German War Cemetery, Courtyard NAS Ossario 2A, Panel 2, Bordj-Cedria, Tunisia.

120. *Oberst* Johann von RAVENSTEIN—'Hans'

Von Ravenstein was born on 1 January 1889 in Strzelin. He fought in the First World War and was awarded the Iron Cross 1st and 2nd Class (1914), as well as the *Pour le Mérite*. He led a battalion in the western campaign with an aggressive style of command. For this, he was awarded the Iron Cross 1st and 2nd Class (1939), and the Knight's Cross followed on 3 June 1940.

He was given command of the 21st Panzer Division on 20 May 1941 and sent to Africa with it. Von Ravenstein was captured by the British on 29 November 1941. He died on 26 March 1962 and is believed to be buried in Nordfriedhof, Blütenstrasse 55, Duisburg, North Rhine-Westphalia.

121. *Oberst* Karl ROTHENBURG

Rothenburg was born on 8 June 1894 in Fürstenwalde. He fought in the First World War and was awarded the Iron Cross 1st and 2nd Class (1914), as well as the *Pour le Mérite*. He fought in Poland and France as commander of Panzer Regiment 25, part of 7th Panzer Division, he was awarded the Iron Cross 1st and 2nd Class (1939), and on 3 June 1940, he was awarded the Knight's Cross. Rothenburg was killed in action at Minsk, Russia, on 28 June 1941 and has no known grave.

122. *Oberst* Paul-Hermann WERNER

Werner was born on 19 March 1893 in Stade. He fought in the First World War and was awarded the Iron Cross 1st and 2nd Class (1914). Werner took part in the Polish and French campaigns as commander of Panzer Regiment 31. He was awarded the Iron Cross 1st and 2nd Class (1939), and on 3 June 1940, he received the Knight's Cross. Werner drowned in the Atlantic off the coast of Brest on 30 June 1940. His body was not recovered.

123. *Oberstleutnant* Hermann BALCK

Balck was born on 7 December 1897 in Danzig. He fought in the First World War, being wounded five times. He was awarded the Iron Cross 1st and 2nd Class (1914). In the invasion of France, he commanded Rifle Regiment 1, part of the 1st Panzer Division. His men were among the first to across the Meuse at Sedan and storm the heights above the river on the west bank. He was awarded the Iron Cross 1st and 2nd Class (1939) in May 1940 and the Knight's Cross in the field on 3 June 1940. Next he took part in the Balkans campaign.

Balck did not see combat again until May 1942 in Russia, where he was again under Guderian taking over the 11th Panzer Division, which destroyed ninety-one tanks in a single day. Later, he commanded XLVIII Panzer Corps during the battles around Lemberg. His last command in Russia was 4th Panzer Army. He was awarded the Oak Leaves on 20 December 1942, the Swords on 4 March 1943, and the Diamonds on 31 August 1944. In September 1944, he took over Army Group 'G', holding the Lorraine area while preparations for the Ardennes offensive were completed. In 1945, he was sent back to the Eastern Front in Hungary to command the 6th Army, fighting a series of rear-guard actions back to Austria. After the war, he was charged with ordering the execution of an artillery officer in November 1944. Balck had the man shot after he was found drunk and having no idea where his guns were on the eve of an operation. He was sentenced to three years but was released after eighteen months. Balck died on 29 November 1982 and is buried in Hasefriedhof, Abt 2-wall grave location 68, Osnabrück, Lower Saxony.

124. *Oberleutnant* Gerhard ETZOLD

Etzold was a born on 17 March 1910 in Seelingstädt. He was platoon leader in Motorcycle Battalion 8 when he was awarded the Knight's Cross on 3 June 1940. Etzold died of wounds on 6 May 1941 and is buried at Donetsk, Ukraine; his remains are awaiting transfer to a German war cemetery.

125. *Feldwebel* Walter RUBARTH

Rubarth was born on 7 July 1913 in Polle. He was a platoon leader in Motorised Pioneer Battalion 49 when he was awarded the Knight's Cross on 3 June 1940. Rubarth died of wounds Selkaovka, Russia, on 26 October 1941; he has no known grave.

126. *Oberst* Werner-Albrecht Freiherr von und zu GILSA

Freiherr von und zu Gilsa was born on 4 March 1889 in Berlin. He fought in the First World War and was awarded the Iron Cross 1st and 2nd Class (1914). After the Polish campaign, he was awarded the Iron Cross 1st and 2nd Class (1939). In 1940, his regiment succeeded in taking Charleville with intact bridges, contributing to the German advance. For this, *Freiherr* von und zu Gilsa was awarded the Knight's Cross on 5 June 1940.

From 1 April 1941 to 4 April 1943, he commanded the 216th Infantry Division, which fought at Suchinitschi during the Russian winter of 1941–42. For this, he was awarded the Oak Leaves on 24 January 1942. From 11 June 1944 until 23 November 1944, he commanded LXXXIX Army Corps, and on 8 November 1944m he was appointed military commander of Dresden, where he opened the Wehrmacht hospitals and food warehouses to the civilian population. He was also a confidant of the conspirators in the 20 July bomb plot. Captured by the Russians, he killed himself on 5 May 1945 at Litoměřice, Czechoslovakia. He has no known grave.

127. *Oberst* Hans JORDAN

Jordan was born on 27 December 1892 in Scheuern. He fought in the First World War, being awarded the Iron Cross 1st and 2nd Class (1914). Jordan fought in France as commander of Infantry Regiment 49 and was awarded the Iron Cross 1st and 2nd Class (1939) in May 1940. The Knight's Cross followed on 5 June 1940.

He took part in the invasion of Russia and was awarded the Oak Leaves on 16 January 1942 while still commanding Infantry Regiment 49. Jordan was awarded the Swords on 20 April 1944 and given command of IX Army on 20 May 1944. He was unable to stop the Russian offensive in June 1944 and Badruysk was encircled. Hitler blamed Jordan for this and relieved him of command. Jordan died on 20 April 1975 and is buried in Stadtfriedhof, Rastatt, Baden-Württemberg.

128. *Oberstleutnant* Günther SCHUBERT

Schubert was born on 1 November 1896 in Iaşi, Romania. He was commander of I Battalion, Infantry Regiment 49, when he was awarded the Knight's Cross on 5 June 1940. Schubert was killed in action near Toropec, Russia, on 30 August 1941. He has no known grave.

129. *Major* Friedrich FILINGER

Filinger was born on 23 May 1891 in Dresden. He was commander of III Battalion, Artillery Regiment 8, when he was awarded the Knight's Cross on 5 June 1940. Filinger died on 21 August 1984 in Wörtsee-Steinebach, Bavaria.

130. *Oberleutnant* Ernst-Friedrich LANGENSTRASS

Langenstrass was born on 16 January 1914 in Schneidersfelde. He fought in France and was awarded the Iron Cross 1st and 2nd Class, most likely in May 1940, and the Knight's Cross on 5 June 1940. Langenstrass died on 22 September 2010 and is buried in Nussdorf am Inn Friedhof, Bavaria.

131. *General* Curt HAASE

Haase was born on 15 December 1881 in Honnef. He fought in the First World War and was awarded the Iron Cross 1st and 2nd Class (1914). He commanded the III Army Corps in Poland and France, being awarded the Knight's Cross on 8 June 1940.

Haase was relieved of his command in November 1940 and placed on the reserve list. In early 1941, he was given command of XV Army, which he led until December 1942 when he was again placed on the reserve list. Haase died from advanced heart disease on 8 February 1943 and is buried in the Invaliden Friedhof, Feld C, Plot 3, Grave 17, Scharnhorstrasse, Berlin.

132. *Oberstleutnant* Friedrich WEBER

Weber was born on 31 March 1892 in Château-Salins. He was commander of Motorised Grenadier Regiment 41 when he was awarded the Knight's Cross on 8 June 1940. Weber died on 2 September 1974 in Deggendorf, Bavaria.

133. *Feldwebel* Kurt HOFFMANN

Hoffmann was born on 22 May 1914 in Bindow. He was a platoon leader in Motorised Pioneer Battalion 28 when he was awarded the Knight's Cross on 8 June 1940. Hoffmann was killed in action near Primorsky, Russia, on 20 March 1942 and has no known grave.

134. *Admiral* Rolf CARLS

Carls was born on 29 May 1885 in Rostock. He fought in the First World War and was awarded the Iron Cross 1st and 2nd Class (1914). Carls was the chief-of-staff of Marine Group Command East when he was awarded the Knight's Cross on 14 June 1940. He was killed in a bombing raid on 24 April 1945 in Bad Oldesloe, Schleswig-Holstein.

135. *Vizeadmiral* Günther LÜTJENS—'Pee Ontgens'

Lütjens was born on 25 May 1889 in Wiesbaden. He fought in the navy during the First World War, being awarded the Iron Cross 1st and 2nd Class (1914). For his command of destroyer operations in the North Sea, Lütjens was awarded the Iron Cross 1st and 2nd Class (1939), after the Polish campaign. In April 1940, Lütjens was given temporary command of the entire German surface fleet for the invasion of Denmark and Norway. For this, he was awarded the Knight's Cross on 14 June 1940.

In the aftermath of the campaign, he was given full command of the surface fleet. Once the Battle of Brittan was effectively lost, he turned his attention to blockading Britain. In May 1941, Lütjens took command of a task force consisting of the battleship *Bismarck* and the heavy cruiser *Prinz Eugen*. In the Battle of the Denmark Straits, the battle cruiser HMS *Hood* was sunk—there were only three survivors. Three days later, on 27 May 1941, the *Bismarck* was sunk by British warships; Lütjens when down with his ship. In 1967, the German Navy named a destroyer after him to recognise his long service.

136. *Konteradmiral* Hubert SCHMUNDT

Schmundt was born on 19 September 1888 in Świdnica. He fought in the navy during First World War, being awarded the Iron Cross 1st and 2nd Class (1914). After the fall of Poland in 1939, Schmundt was awarded the Iron Cross 2nd Class (1939) in October and the 1st Class (1939) in April 1940.

He commanded the Bergen group of warships in the Norwegian campaign, for which he was awarded the Knight's Cross on 14 June 1940. Schmundt was appointed *Admiral* commanding Northen Norway 1941–1942 and commander of German forces in the Baltic 1943–44. He was dismissed in April 1944 and taken prisoner by the British in 1945, not being released until 1947. Schmundt died on 17 October 1984 in Bad Soden, Hesse.

137. *Major* Fritz-Kurt DOENCH

Doench was born on 19 May 1904 in Wittenberg. He was a group commander in Bomber Wing 30 when he was awarded the Knight's Cross on 14 June 1940. Doench was killed in an accident on 14 June 1942 and is buried in the German War Cemetery, Block 16, Grave 250, Cassino, Italy.

138. *Hauptmann* Wilhelm BALTHASAR

Balthaser was born on 2 February 1914 in Fulda. He fought in the Condor Legion in Spain during the Spanish Civil War, shooting down seven enemy aircraft. Balthasar's unit missed the attack on Poland, but in May 1940, he shot down fourteen French/Belgian fighters, bringing his total to twenty-one. He was awarded the Knight's Cross on 14 June 1940. He ended the campaign with twenty-three victories.

On 4 September 1940, he was seriously wounded in the leg over Canterbury but managed to get home. Balthasar was still on crutches when he returned to flying fourteen days later. He shot down five more fighters before returning to hospital in November 1940. Between 22 and 27 June 1941, he shot down nine RAF aircraft, including five Bristol Blenheims on the 23rd. For this, he was awarded the Oak Leaves on 2 July 1941. With his score at forty-seven, Balthasar was shot down and killed, his Bf 109 crashing near Saint-Omer. He is buried in the WWI German War Cemetery, Block 2, Grave 78 (with his father, who was killed in the First World War), Illies, on the N41, south-west of Lille, France.

139. *Hauptmann* Arved CRÜGER

Crüger was born on 25 June 1911 in Pillau (present-day Baltiysk). He was awarded the Iron Cross 2nd Class in March and the 1st Class in May 1940. A bomber pilot, Crüger was awarded the Knight's Cross on 14 June 1940 for his leadership during anti-shipping raids against the British Home Fleet. On 29 March 1941, his group attacked the British aircraft carrier HMS *Formidable*, claiming three hits. He spent some time on the Russian Front before returning to the Mediterranean Sea to join in attacks on Malta. Crüger was reported missing in action on 22 March 1942, when it is believed he was shot down by anti-aircraft fire from British warships.

140. *Hauptmann* Claus HINKELBEIN

Hinkelbein was born on 28 December 1909 in Ludwigsburg. He was a group commander in Bomber Wing 30 when he was awarded the Knight's Cross on 14 June 1940. Hinkelbein died on 28 April 1967 and is believed to be buried in Bad Salzuflen Friedhof, North Rhine-Westphalia.

141. *Oberleutnant* Horst HARRAS

Harras was born on 22 March 1915 in Berlin. He was a platoon leader in Flak Regiment 18 when he was awarded the Knight's Cross on 14 June 1940. Harras died on 26 October 1999 and is buried in Evangelischer Friedhof, Bergisch Gladback, North Rhine-Westphalia.

142. *Oberleutnant* Franz WIETING

Wieting was born on 26 June 1911 in Kiel. He was a squadron leader in Bomber Wing 30 when he was awarded the Knight's Cross on 14 June 1940. Wieting was killed in action on 29 June 1941 and is buried in the German War Cemetery, Prilep, Macedonia.

143. *Generalleutnant* Herbert LOCH

Loch was born on 5 August 1886 in Idar-Oberstein. He fought in the First World War and was awarded the Iron Cross 1st and 2nd Class (1914). Loch was commander of 17th Infantry Division when he was awarded the Knight's Cross on 16 June 1940. He died on 28 October 1975 and is believed to be buried in Landau Friedhof, Rhineland-Palatinate.

144. *Oberst* Franz LANDGRAF

Landgraf was born on 16 July 1888 in Munich. He fought in the First World War and was awarded the Iron Cross 1st and 2nd Class. Landgraf was commander of 4th Panzer Brigade when he was awarded the Knight's Cross on 16 June 1940. Landgraf was killed in action at Stuttgart on 19 April 1944 and has no known grave.

145. *Oberst* Wilhelm Ralf SODAN

Sodan was born on 7 July 1880 in Regensburg. He was commander of Infantry Regiment 338 when he was awarded the Knight's Cross on 16 June 1940. Sodan killed himself on 18 April 1945 and is buried in the German War Cemetery, Drachhausen, Brandenburg.

146. *Oberstleutnant* Anton GRASSER

Grasser was born on 3 November 1891 in Bossendorf. He fought in the First World War and was awarded the Iron Cross 1st and 2nd Class (1914). Grasser also fought in France in 1940 and was awarded the Iron Cross 1st and 2nd Class (1939), as well as the Knight's Cross on 16 June 1940.

Grasser spent the rest of the war on the Eastern Front and was awarded the Oak Leaves on 5 December 1943. He was captured in 1945 and released in 1947. Grasser died on 3 November 1976 in Stuttgart, Baden-Württemberg.

147. *Oberstleutnant* Heinrich NICKEL

Nickel was born on 5 December 1894 in Wesel. He fought in the First World War and was awarded the Iron Cross 1st and 2nd Class (1914). Nickel took part in the attack on Poland in 1939 and was awarded the Iron Cross 1st and 2nd Class (1939). He also fought in France where he was awarded the Knight's Cross on 16 June 1940.

Nickel would spend the rest of the war on the Eastern Front, where, on 8 August 1944, he was awarded the Oak Leaves. He was captured in May 1945 and released in 1948. Nickel died on 2 January 1979 and is buried in the Old Cemetery, Lingen, Lower Saxony.

148. *Oberstleutnant* Friedrich SIEBERG

Sieberg was born on 15 February 1896 in Schwerte. He was commander of Panzer Regiment 10 when he was awarded the Knight's Cross on 16 June 1940. Sieberg died of wounds on 3 November 1943 and is believed to be buried in the German War Cemetery (as unknown), Kirovograd, Ukraine.

149. *Major* Friedrich-Wilhelm JÜRGEN

Jürgen was born on 2 October 1895 in Damerow. He was commander of II Battalion, Rifle Regiment 2, when he was awarded the Knight's Cross on 16 June 1940. Jürgen died in Russian hands near Stalingrad on 16 October 1954 and has no known grave.

150. *Major* Rudolf ZÜRN

Zürn was born on 4 March 1895 in Hamburg. He fought in the First World War, being awarded the Iron Cross 1st and 2nd Class (1914). Zürn was commander of II Battalion, Infantry Regiment 65, when he was awarded the Knight's Cross on 16 June 1940. He died of wounds on 15 October 1941 and is buried in the German War Cemetery, Block G, Row 6, Grave 27, Bucharest, Romania

151. *Unteroffizier* Hermann Ritter von INGRAM

Ritter von Ingram was born on 3 November 1903 in Vienna. He was a section leader in Infantry Regiment 309 when he was awarded the Knight's Cross on 16 June 1940. Von Ingram died on 22 April 1995 and is buried in Petersfriedhof, Salzburg, Austria.

152. *Kapitänleutnant* Heinz BIRNBACHER

Birnbacher was born on 26 May 1910 in Villach, Austria-Hungary. He was commander of S-Boat Flotilla 1 when he was awarded the Knight's Cross on 17 June 1940. Birnbacher died on 5 December 1991 in Villach, Austria.

153. *Oberstleutnant* Johannes de BOER

De Boer was born on 5 September 1897 in Altona. He fought in the First World War and was awarded the Iron Cross 2nd Class (1914). De Boer was commander of Artillery Regiment 22 when he was awarded the Knight's Cross on 19 June 1940. He was captured by the British in Norway in May 1945. De Boer died on 14 March 1986 and is believed to be buried in Ohlsdorf Friedhof, Fuhlsbüttler Strasse, Hamburg.

154. *Oberleutnant* Otto SCHULZ

Schulz was born on 29 May 1915 in Duisburg-Beeck. He was a company commander in Infantry Regiment 125 when he was awarded the Knight's Cross on 19 June 1940. Schulz was killed in action on 6 April 1941 and has no known grave.

155. *Feldwebel* Willi SCHULTZ

Schultz was born on 18 August 1916 in Gollnow (Goleniów). He was a pilot in Bomber Wing 30 when he was awarded the Knight's Cross on 19 June 1940. Schultz was killed in action near Amsterdam on 19 November 1940 and has no known grave.

156. *Oberst* Johannes FINK

Fink was born on 28 March 1895 in Pfullingen. He fought in the First World War, for which he was awarded the Iron Cross 1st and 2nd Class (1914). Fink was a *Kommodore* in Bomber Wing 2 when he was awarded the Knight's Cross on 20 June 1940. He died on 1 June 1981 and is buried in Pfullingen Friedhof, Baden-Württemberg.

157. *Oberst* Alois WINDISCH

Windisch was born on 3 February 1892 in Bad Fischau. He fought in the First World War. Windisch took part in the attack on Poland and Norway, for which he was awarded the Knight's Cross on 20 June 1940. In 1945, he was captured by the Russians, who handed him over to Yugoslavia; he was not released until 1953. Windisch died on 28 December 1958 and is buried in Städtischer Friedhof, Wiener Neustadt, Austria.

158. *Oberstleutnant* August SORKO

Sorko was born on 9 August 1891 in Klagenfurt. He was commander of II Battalion, *Jäger* Regiment 137, when he was awarded the Knight's Cross on 20 June 1940. Sorko was killed in action at Winnyzja, Russia, on 19 July 1941 and has no known grave.

159. *Oberstleutnant* Adolf WOLF

Wolf was born on 23 May 1899 in Braunschweig. He fought in the First World War, being awarded the Iron Cross 1st and 2nd Class (1914). Wolf was commander of I Battalion, Flak Regiment 64, when he was awarded the Knight's Cross on 20 June 1940. He died on 11 March 1973 and is buried in Stadtfriedhof, Bayreuth, Bavaria.

160. *Major* Oskar DINORT

Dinort was born on 23 June 1901 in Berlin. He commanded Dive Bomber Wing 2 in Poland and was awarded the Iron Cross 2nd Class on 20 September 1939. The 1st Class was awarded on 11 May 1940, the day after the start of the campaign in the West. In July 1940, he led the highly success attack on convoy OA 178, and, for this, Dinort was awarded the Knight's Cross on 20 June 1940.

During operations over Greece and Crete, his crews believed the blast effect of their bombs used against infantry was greatly reduced due to the bombs penetrating the ground before exploding. Dinort came up with the idea of welding 8-cm rods (which became known as Dinort's Rods) with plates to the end of the bombs, allowing them to explode on impact. On 14 July 1941, he was awarded the Oak Leaves, and on 15 October, he took up a staff post. Dinort died on 27 May 1965 in Cologne, North Rhine-Westphalia.

161. *Major* Hans von SCHLEBRÜGGE

Von Schlebrügge was born on 1 May 1900 in Kassel. He fought in the First World War, being awarded the Iron Cross 1st and 2nd Class (1914). He was a company commander in Mountain *Jäger* Regiment 139 when he was awarded the Knight's Cross on 20 June 1940. Von Schlebrügge died on 26 April 1971 in Pullach, Bavaria.

162. *Major* Ludwig STAUTNER

Stautner was born on 4 May 1895 in Schrobenhausen. He fought in the First World War and was awarded the Iron Cross 1st and 2nd Class (1914). At the start of the Second World War, he was a battalion commander in 3rd *Jäger* Division, with which he saw action in Poland, France, and the Low Countries very briefly before being chosen to lead the attack on Narvik, Norway. His battalion landed at Bjervik, and although the town was taken with little opposition due to attacks by the Royal Navy, the German destroyer force was decimated leaving the troops with no support. So bad was it that any ships crews which made it to shore were pressed into front-line service as infantry.

The Germans came under intense attacks by well-trained Norwegian ski-troops. Attack after attack was fought off until the enemy gave up. For his part in the defence, Stautner was awarded the Knight's Cross on 20 June 1940. He died on 5 January 1983 in Garmisch-Partenkirchen, Bavaria.

163. *Hauptmann* Viktor SCHÖNBECK

Sechönbeck was born on 4 December 1910 in Pregarten. He was a company commander in Mountain *Jäger* Regiment 139 when was awarded the Knight's Cross on 20 June 1940. Sechönbeck died on 16 November 1983 and is buried in Petersfriedhof, Salzburg, Austria.

164. *Oberleutnant* Helmut CORTS

Corts was born on 22 February 1920 in Osnabrück. He was serving in Motorised Flak Regiment 64 when he was awarded the Knight's Cross on 20 June 1940. Corts died on 10 March 2000 and is buried in Hauptfriedhof, Koblenz, Rhineland-Palatinate.

165. Leutnant Hans ROHR

Rohr was born on 11 March 1912 in Rubland, Austria-Hungary. He was a platoon leader in *Jäger* Regiment 139 when he was awarded the Knight's Cross on 20 June 1940. Rohr died on 1 September 1998 in Paternion, Austria.

166. *Generaloberst* Wilhelm Ritter von LEEB

Ritter von Leeb was born on 5 September 1876 in Landsberg am Lech. He took part in the suppression of the Boxer Uprising in China. Von Leeb served as a staff officer throughout the First World War, being awarded the Iron Cross 1st and 2nd Class (1914). When Hitler came to power in 1933, von Leeb was a *Generalleutnant* and he helped rebuild the German Army, including founding the mountain troops. As a religious man, he was required to resign in 1938, but when the war started, he was reinstated as a *Generaloberst* commanding Army Group 'C', holding the Western Front during the Polish campaign. He was awarded the Iron Cross 1st and 2nd Class (1939). In June, his army group broke through the Maginot Line. For this, he was awarded the Knight's Cross on 24 June 1940 and promoted to *Generalfeldmarschall* in July.

In the Russian campaign, he commanded Army Group North, striking towards Leningrad. Stopping on the Führer's orders, he said: 'Hitler and Stalin seem to be allies'. Condemned to dig-in for the winter, their morale suffered and von Leeb asked to be relieved. He never commanded again. Captured by the Americans in 1945, he was tried as a war criminal and sentenced to five years. He was soon released and died from a heart attack on 29 April 1956 in Füssen. *Ritter* von Leeb is buried in Waldfriedhof, Munich.

167. *Generaloberst* Erwin von WITZLEBEN

Von Witzleben was born on 4 December 1881 in Breslau. He fought as a *Hauptmann* during the First World War, being awarded the Iron Cross 1st and 2nd Class (1914). After being severely wounded, he was sent to the General staff in 1918. Von Witzleben also fought in the *Freikorps* on the Polish frontier, and by 1931, he was an *Oberst*. With the coming of the Nazis, he achieved rapid promotion—*Generalmajor* in 1934, *Generalleutnant* in 1935, and full general the following year. He was, however, one of the earliest members of the military resistance to Hitler and was party to a number of plots to kill him. Promoted to *Generaloberst* in 1939, he was given command of 1st Army, which he took through the Maginot Line in June 1940. He was awarded the Iron Cross 1st and 2nd Class (1939) and the Knight's Cross on 24 June 1940. A promotion to *Generalfeldmarschall* followed in July.

After the fall of France, he was appointed supreme commander OB West, but in 1943, he had to retire due to ill-health. He kept in touch with the resistance, and when the bomb exploded on 20 July 1944, von Witzleben was in Berlin to take over the army. He was arrested and dishonourably expelled from the army, and he was sentenced to death by the notorious people's court. On 8 August 1944, he was hanged in Plötzensee Prison, Berlin, the highest-ranking officer to be executed as a result of the plot. He has no known grave.

168. General Friedrich DOLLMANN

Dollmann was born on 2 February 1882 in Würzburg. He fought in the First World War, being awarded the Iron Cross 1st and 2nd Class (1914). After the fall of Poland, he was awarded the Iron Cross 1st and 2nd Class (1939). Dollmann led the VII Army in France and was awarded the Knight's Cross on 24 May 1940.

He stayed in France and oversaw the defence of Brittany and Normandy. It was Dollmann that lowered the alert level due to the bad weather in the Channel in early June 1944. On 28 June 1944, after the fall of Cherbourg, Dollmann learnt he was to be court-martialled; it is unclear if he had a heart attack or killed himself following this news. He was awarded the Oak Leaves on 7 July 1944. He is buried in the German War Cemetery, Block 3, Row 13, Grave 1090, Champigny-Saint-André, Normandy, France.

169. General Alfred KELLER—'Iron Keller'

Keller was born in Bochum on 19 September 1882. On leaving school in 1897, he went into the army as a cadet; graduating in 1902, he was posted to Pioneer Battalion Nr. 7 at Thorn. Keller was commissioned a *Leutnant* in 1903. In the autumn of 1912, Keller applied for transfer to the German Army Air Service. On the outbreak of war in 1914, Keller was sent to the Western Front in command of *Kagohl* 27 and promoted to *Hauptmann*. He carried out a number of reconnaissance missions during the coming year, including a flight over Paris in October, causing a great deal of concern to Parisians who thought that the fighting was well away from them and offered no direct threat. This was to reveal the vulnerability of the city to its inhabitants; for this mission, Keller was awarded the Iron Cross 2nd Class. In 1915, Keller was given command of AFP 5 and saw extensive action in a reconnaissance role in the area of the Somme and Verdun. In September 1915, he was given command of *Kagohl* 40 until the autumn of 1916 when he was asked to command Night Flying Unit 1. Keller spent the next few months developing this unit, and then, on 1 April 1917, he was given command of *Bogohl* 1 and was awarded the Iron Cross 1st Class for his work in this field.

Bogohl 1 was the first official bombing *Jasta* to carry out night bombing, and Keller and his bomber crews carried out numerous missions, including one on Dunkirk in September 1917. Over 100,000 kg of bombs were dropped, causing a large number of casualties and considerable damage, which forced the British to move to the safety of Calais. For this, Keller was awarded the Knight's Cross with Swords of the Royal Hohenzollern House Order, and then, on 4 December 1917, he was awarded the *Pour le Mérite*.

Keller and his crews continued night bombing, and on the night of 30–31 January 1918, he led a surprise attack on Paris, causing great panic. Although the anti-aircraft guns put up a great deal of fire, all of the bombers returned safely. He continued to bomb the city with the result that vital artillery had to be moved from the front to defend the capital. At the war's end, Keller left the air service and became the head of the German *Luftreederei*, which was involved in airship transports.

In the early 1930s, Keller was asked by Göring to help build new the Luftwaffe. Keller joined the Luftwaffe in 1935 with the rank of *Oberst* and was given command of *Bogohl* 154. He was promoted to *Generalmajor* in April 1936, then to *Generalleutnant* on 1 February 1938, and given the post of commanding *General* of the East Prussian Luftwaffe. Keller held this post for one year, after which he was given command of the 4th Air Division HQ Brunswick. On 24 June 1940, he was awarded the Knight's Cross and promoted to *Generaloberst*. His next appointment was to commander-in-chief of *Luftflotte* 1 in Berlin and the Russian Front. At the end of the war, he was CO of the Luftwaffe Anti-Tank Service. Keller died on 11 February 1974 and is buried in Waldfriedhof, Feld 021, Grave 365–367, Wasgenensteig, Zehlendorf, Berlin.

170. General Heinrich-Gottfried von VIETINGHOFF (aka von SCHEELI)

Von Vietinghoff was born on 6 December 1887 in Mainz. He fought in the First World War and was awarded the Iron Cross 1st and 2nd Class (1914). Von Vietinghoff fought in Poland and was awarded the Iron Cross 1st and 2nd Class (1939). He was commander of XIII Army Corps when he was awarded the Knight's Cross on 24 June 1940.

Von Vietinghoff took part in the Balkans campaign and the invasion of Russia, where he was awarded the Oak Leaves on 16 April 1944. He also fought in some of the delaying battles in Italy. Von Vietinghoff surrendered his men to the British on 2 May 1945. He died on 23 February 1952 and is buried in Stadtfriedhof, Pfronten, Bavaria.

171. General Hubert WEISE

Weise was born on 29 December 1884 in Erfurt. He fought in the First World War and was awarded the Iron Cross 1st and 2nd Class (1914). Weise fought in Poland, from which he was awarded the Iron Cross 2nd Class (1939) in October 1939, and in France, from which he was awarded the Iron Cross 1st Class (1939) in May 1940. He was commander of I Falk Corps when he was awarded the Knight's Cross on 24 June 1940. Weise died on 14 February 1950 and is buried in St Rochus Friedhof, Abt A1, Row 1, Grave 5, Bad Kohlgrub, Bavaria.

172. Generalleutnant Wilhelm FAHRMBACHER

Fahrmbacher was born on 19 September 1888 in Zweibrücken. He fought in the First World War, being awarded the Iron Cross 1st and 2nd Class (1914). In France in May 1940, he was awarded the Iron Cross 2nd Class (1939), and he obtained the 1st Class on 11 June. This was followed by the Knight's Cross on 24 June 1940. Fahrmbacher was handed over to the French in 1945 and not released until 1950. He died on 27 April 1970 and is buried in Stadtfriedhof, Abt 111, Feld 3, Row 5, Grave 1, Garmisch-Partenkirchen, Bavaria.

173. Generalleutnant Robert Ritter von GREIM

Greim was born in Bayreuth on 22 June 1892. At the age of fourteen, he became a cadet, joining the regular army on 14 July 1911 at the age of nineteen. He was immediately put forward for officer training, and on 29 October 1912, he joined the Bavarian Field Artillery Regiment Nr. 8 and was commissioned a *Leutnant* on 25 October 1913. When the war broke out, his regiment was one of the first into action, he commanded a battery at the Battle of Lorraine at Nancy-Epinal, and at the assaults on Saint-Mihiel and Camp des Romains. For these actions, he was awarded the Iron Cross 2nd Class. On 15 March 1915, he was appointed the 1st Battalion's adjutant. At the end of April, Greim was awarded the Bavarian Military Merit Order 4th Class with Swords.

Like so many other young men, he began to look at the newly formed German Army Air Service and applied for a transfer. He started his training as an observer on 10 August 1915 and was posted to FFA 3b. Greim opened his tally by shooting down a Maurice Farman on 10 October. He was then sent to FA(A) 204 as an observer during the 1916 Battle of the Somme, but he applied for pilot training towards the end of the year. After graduating, he was sent to FA 46b as a reconnaissance pilot on 22 February 1917 and then to *Jastaschule* in March for single-seater training. On completing this, he was posted to *Jasta* 34b on 3 April 1917, and he now had his aircraft painted with his own markings of a red nose, two red fuselage bands, and a white/silvery tail. On 18 May 1917, he was awarded the Bavarian Military Merit Order 4th Class with Crown and Swords.

On 24 May, he shot down a Spad over Mamey, but this was unconfirmed. The next day, he shot down a Caudron R.4 over Ramaucourt and was awarded the Iron Cross 1st Class. By the end of 1917, he had brought down seven enemy aircraft. On 29 April 1918, with his tally at nine, he was awarded Knight's Cross with Swords of the Royal Hohenzollern House Order. On 21 March, he was given command of *Jagdgruppe* Nr. 10 and later *Jagdgruppe* Nr. 9. April, May, and June only saw him bring down four enemy aircraft, but in August, he shot down six, including two on the 8th. On 8 October 1918, he was awarded the *Pour le Mérite*, and by the end of the month, he had brought his score to twenty-eight, and this was followed by the Bavarian Max Joseph Medal, allowing him to use '*Ritter* von' thus making him a knight. He was also promoted to *Oberleutnant*. After the war, he was serving with the Bavarian Air Service and later became an adviser to the Chinese Nationalist Air Force.

In the early 1930s, he became director of the Bavarian Sport Flyers' Association. Then, in 1934, he joined the newly formed Luftwaffe with the rank of *Major*, taking command of the Richthofen *Geschwader*.

In 1938, he was promoted to *General*, and during the Second World War, he commanded V *Fliegerkorps*. He was awarded the Knight's Cross on 24 June 1940. The Oak Leaves followed on 2 April 1943 and the Swords on 7 August 1944. By 1944, he was commanding the *Luftflottes* in Russia with the rank of *Generaloberst*. When he was captured by the Americans in 1945, he was head of the Luftwaffe, a post given to him by Hitler who also promoted him to *Generalfeldmarschall*. He committed suicide on 24 May 1945, his last words being: 'I'm head of the Luftwaffe with no Luftwaffe'. He is buried in the Kommunal Friedhof, Military Section, Salzburg, Austria.

174. Generalleutnant Rudolf KOCH-ERPACH

Koch-Erpach was born on 9 April 1886 in Munich. He fought in the First World War and was awarded the Iron Cross 1st and 2nd Class (1914). Koch-Erpach fought in Poland in 1939 and was captured. Released after the surrender, he commanded 8th Infantry Division in France, for which he was awarded the Knight's Cross on 24 June 1940. He spent most of the remainder of the war in admin post until 1945 when he commanded the LVI Panzer Corps on the Eastern Front.

Surrounded, he was assisted by Alfons Rebane, an Estonian officer who was famous for breaking out. Rebane was awarded the Oak Leaves for this. Koch-Erpach died on 27 November 1971 and is buried in Beiertheim Friedhof, Karlsruhe, Baden-Württemberg.

175. Generalmajor Otto DESSLOCH

Dessloch was born on 11 June 1889 in Bamberg. He fought in the First World War and was awarded the Iron Cross 1st and 2nd Class (1914). Dessloch was awarded the Iron Cross 1st and 2nd Class (1939) in May 1940 and the Knight's Cross on 24 June 1940 as a Luftwaffe commander.

He commanded in Russia and was awarded the Oak Leaves on 10 May 1944. After the liberation of Paris, it was aircraft under his command that bombed the city. Dessloch died on 13 May 1977 and is buried in Waldfriedhof, Feld Mauer, Grave 165, Aschauffenburg, Bavaria.

176. *Oberleutnant* Hans LINGNER

Lingner was born on 17 January 1909 in Berlin. He was commander of Infantry Regiment 65 when he was awarded the Knight's Cross on 24 June 1940. Lingner died of wounds on 28 August 1941 and is believed to be buried in the German War Cemetery (as unknown), Sebastopol, Ukraine.

177. *Oberleutnant* Erich OECKEL

Oeckel was born on 8 June 1916 in Stettin. He was a company commander in Rifle Regiment 4 when he was awarded the Knight's Cross on 24 June 1940. Oeckel was killed in action on 13 July 1943 and is buried in the German War Cemetery (as unknown), Kharkov, Ukraine.

178. *Oberleutnant* Wilhelm WALTHER

Walther was born on 27 January 1910 in Dresden. He was commander of Construction Training Battalion 800 when he was awarded the Knight's Cross on 24 June 1940. Walther died on 25 November 2010 in Leimen, Baden-Württemberg.

179. Leutnant Alois PROCHAZKA

Prochazka was born on 9 May 1915 in Vienna. He was a company commander in Infantry Regiment 38 when he was awarded the Knight's Cross on 24 June 1940. Prochazka died on 8 November 1987 and is buried in Zentralfriedhof, Vienna.

180. Leutnant Wolfgang SEMMER

Semmer was born on 24 February 1917 in Munich. He was a company commander in Infantry Regiment 85 when he was awarded the Knight's Cross on 24 June 1940. Semmer died on 2 December 1947 in Belgrade as a POW and has no known grave.

181. General Hermann GEYER

Geyer was born on 7 July 1882 in Stuttgart. He fought in the First World War and was awarded the Iron Cross 1st and 2nd Class (1914). Geyer took part in the campaign in the West and was awarded the Knight's Cross on 25 June 1940. He was also involved in the invasion of Russia, where he stayed until retiring in 1943. Geyer took no further part in the war. He killed himself on 10 April 1946 near Wildsee.

182. Oberstleutnant Adolf RAEGENER

Raegener was born on 17 February 1895 in Klein-Leinungen. He fought in the First World War and was awarded the Iron Cross 1st and 2nd Class (1914). Raegener took part in the Polish campaign, being awarded the Iron Cross 2nd Class (1939). He was commander of Infantry Regiment 309 when he was awarded Iron Cross 1st Class (1939) in May 1940, and he was awarded the Knight's Cross on 25 June 1940 for his part in the campaign in the West.

Raegener also fought in Russia and was awarded the Oak Leaves on 17 April 1945. He died on 17 August 1983 and is buried in Hauptfriedhof, Feld 30 I, Grave 44–45, Braunschweig, Lower Saxony.

183. Oberstleutnant Eberhard RODT

Rodt was born on 4 December 1895 in Munich. He fought in the First World War and was awarded the Iron Cross 1st and 2nd Class (1914). Rodt was commander of Reconnaissance Battalion 25 when he awarded the Iron Cross 1st and 2nd Class (1939) in May 1940 and the Knight's Cross on 25 June 1940.

He also fought in Russia and Italy and was awarded the Oak Leaves on 28 April 1945. Rodt died on 14 December 1979 and is buried in Waldfriedhof, Munich.

184. *Oberleutnant* Gerhard VOIGT

Voigt was born on 19 September 1910 in Kulmsee (present-day Chełm⊠a). He was a company commander in Pioneer Battalion 18 when he was awarded the Knight's Cross on 25 June 1940. Voigt died on 9 June 1969 in Runding, Bavaria.

185. Feldwebel Heinz REINEFARTH

Reinefarth was born in Gnesen, West Prussia, on 26 December 1903. He joined the SS before the war, but on mobilisation, he was called up into the army. Reinefarth fought in Poland and was awarded the Iron Cross 2nd Class; the 1st Class came in May 1940 for action in the West. He was awarded the

Knight's Cross on 25 June 1940. After France, Reinefarth was demobilised and joined the police, serving until 1944 when he joined the *Waffen*-SS.

During the Warsaw Uprising, he commanded a *Kampfgruppe*, but Reinefarth was not a good commander at this level and men under his command acted with considerable barbarity. Despite this, he was awarded the Oak Leaves on 30 September 1944. He was captured by the British at the end of the war. Despite demands from Poland for him to be extradited for the murder of civilians during the Warsaw Uprising, he was exonerated at his trial. Reinefarth died on 7 May 1979 in Westerland, on the Island of Sylt, Schleswig-Holstein.

186. General Eugen Ritter von SCHOBERT

Ritter von Schobert was born on 13 March 1883 in Würzburg. He fought in the First World War and was awarded the Iron Cross 1st and 2nd Class (1914). Von Schobert fought in Poland as commander of VII Army Corps and, after the fall of France, was awarded the Knight's Cross on 29 June 1940.

He took part in the invasion of Russia, but he was killed when his light aircraft crashed on 12 September 1941. Von Schobert is buried near the monument for fallen soldiers of the Crimean War, Nikolajev, Ukraine.

187. General Viktor von SCHWEDLER

Von Schwedler was born on 18 January 1885 in Sankt Goarshausen. He fought in the First World War, being awarded the Iron Cross 1st and 2nd Class (1914). Von Schwedler was commander of IV Army Corps when he was awarded the Knight's Cross on 29 June 1940.

He took part in the invasion of Russia but was placed on the reserve list in October 1942. In March 1943, he was appointed commander of the 4th Military District in Dresden, a post he held until January 1945. However, he was still responsible for measures after the bombing of Dresden in February. Von Schwedler died on 30 October 1954 and is believed to be buried in Hauptfriedhof, Friedhofstrasse 8, Freilburg im Breisgau, Baden-Württemberg.

188. General Maximillian Freiherr von und zu WEICHS an der GLON

Freiherr von und zu Weichs an der Glon was born on 27 September 1954 in Dessau. He fought in the First World War and was awarded the Iron Cross

1st and 2nd Class (1914). In Poland, he commanded Army Corps 'Weichs', and in France, the 2nd Army, for which he was awarded the Knight's Cross on 29 June 1940. In Russia, still commanding the 2nd Army, he took part in the fighting at Kiev, Smolensk, Vyazma, and Bryansk.

In 1942, he led Army Group 'B' to the Stalingrad area and warned Hitler about the risk of being stretched to thin. After the Russian counterattack cut off the 6th Army, he suggested retreating, for which he was relieved of his command in early 1943. Recalled in August, he was sent to the Balkans and fought against the partisans, and in late 1944, he oversaw the retreat from Greece and Yugoslavia. Awarded the Oak Leaves on 5 February 1945, he was finally retired in March 1945 but taken prisoner by the Americans for war crimes in the Balkans. The charges were dropped due to ill health, and he died on 27 September 1954. He is buried in the village cemetery, Gut Rossberg, Baden-Württemberg.

189. Generalleutnant Franz BÖHME

Böhme was born on 15 April 1885 in Zeltweg, Austria-Hungary. He fought in the First World War and was awarded the Iron Cross 1st and 2nd Class (1914). Böhme took part in the Polish campaign and was awarded the Iron Cross 1st and 2nd Class (1939). He also fought in France and was awarded the Knight's Cross on 29 June 1940.

Between September and December 1941, he was commanding general of Serbia, during which time he had 100 Serbs shot for every German soldier killed and fifty Serbs shot for every German soldier wounded. Böhme ended the war in Norway where he was captured by the British. Sent for trial for war crimes in Serbia, he killed himself by jumping from the fourth floor of his prison cell. He is buried in St Leonhard Friedhof, Graz, Austria.

190. Generalleutnant Friedrich-Karl CRANZ

Cranz was born on 14 November 1886 in Culm. He fought in the First World War and was awarded the Iron Cross 1st and 2nd Class (1914). Cranz fought in Poland and France, being awarded the Iron Cross 1st and 2nd Class (1939). He was commander of Infantry Regiment 18 when he was awarded the Knight's Cross on 29 June 1940.

Cranz was killed in a training accident by friendly artillery fire at Neuhammer on 24 March 1941 and was buried in the Invaliden Friedhof, Feld D, Plot 3, Grave 17, Scharnhorstrasse, Berlin.

191. Generalleutnant Karl WEISENBERGER

Weisenberger was born on 29 September 1890 in Würzburg. He fought in the First World War and was awarded the Iron Cross 1st and 2nd Class (1914). Weisenberger was awarded the Knight's Cross as commander of the 71st Infantry Division on 29 June 1940, after the fall of France. He died on 28 March 1952 in Kempten, Bavaria.

192. Oberst Otto SCHMIDT-HARTUNG

Schmidt-Hertung was born on 9 February 1892 in Weinheim. He fought in the First World War and was awarded the Iron Cross 1st and 2nd Class (1914). Schmidt-Hertung was commander of Infantry Regiment 35 when he was awarded the Knight's Cross on 29 June 1940. He died on 19 February 1976 and is buried in German War Cemetery, Heidelberg, Baden-Württemberg.

193. *Hauptmann* Horst von PETERSDORFF

Von Petersdorff was born on 30 December 1892 in Posen. He was commander of III Battalion, Infantry Regiment 189, when he was awarded the Knight's Cross on 29 June 1940. Von Petersdorff died on 12 July 1962 in Prien am Chiemsee, Bavaria.

194. *Oberleutnant* Ernst-Georg BUCHTERKIRCH

Buchterkirch was born on 10 September 1914 in Stolp. He fought in the Spanish Civil War. Buchterkirch was awarded the Iron Cross 2nd Class in September 1939 and the 1st Class in May 1940. He was a platoon commander in Panzer Regiment 6 when he was awarded the Knight's Cross on 29 June 1940.

Buchterkirch also fought in Russia and was awarded the Oak Leaves on 31 December 1941. He ended the war as an *Oberstleutnant* on the General Staff. Buchterkirch died on 17 July 1969 in Krummendeich, Lower Saxony.

195. SS-Obergruppenführer Josef DIETRICH—'Sepp'

Dietrich was born on 28 May 1892 in Hawangen. He served during the First World War, becoming an NCO in a Panzer unit, and was awarded the Iron Cross 1st and 2nd Class (1914). Dietrich also fought in the *Freikorps* after the war. One of Hitler's earliest followers and a founder member of the SS, by 1933, he was a *Generalmajor*. He took part in the arrest and execution of SA leaders in 1934. In Poland (where he was awarded Iron Cross 1st and 2nd Class (1939)) and in the campaign in the West, he led the Motorised Regiment of the LAH, under Guderian. Dietrich was usually in the thick of the fighting and was nearly killed when his staff car was shot up. Awarded the Knight's Cross on 4 July 1940 and given command of the now divisional strength and renamed 1st SS Panzer Divison LAH, he took part in the invasion of Greece. Dietrich was the first member of the *Waffen*-SS to be awarded the Knight's Cross.

His division took part in the invasion of the Russia in July 1941 and fought with great success, gaining the respect of the army who thought them not 'proper soldiers'. Dietrich was awarded the Oak Leaves on 31 December 1941 and the Swords on 14 March 1943 for action at Kharkov and Kursk. He was moved to the West in 1944 to command the 2nd SS Panzer Corps under von Rundstedt. When the invasion came, he was in command of the armoured counterattacks in the area of Caen, but Allied air power prevented any success. It was around this time that Dietrich started to become disillusioned and openly critical of Hitler. After the 20 July bomb plot, he was given command of the much-weakened 5th Panzer Army and awarded the Diamonds on 6 August 1944. After the loss of most their equipment in the Falaise Pocket, the army made its long retreat into Germany.

Dietrich's next command was the 6th Panzer Army in the Ardennes Offensive, which he did not believe would work. After the failure, he was sent with the 6th Panzer Army to Hungary, and in the closing stages of the war, Hitler ordered the SS divisions to remove their unit arm bands for not holding on longer. Dietrich was furious and was said to have packed his decorations in a chamber pot and sent them to Hitler. After the war, he was imprisoned for life for war crimes, but he was released in 1955 only to be tried again by the West German government for his part in the executions of the SA. He received eighteen months. Another commander who was denied a pension, but thousands of his soldiers contributed funds to help him survive. Dietrich died from a heart attack on 21 April 1966 and is buried in Neuer Friedhof, Abt 75, Ludwigsburg, Baden-Württemberg.

196. Generalmajor Stefan FRÖHLICH

Fröhlich was born on 7 October 1889 in Orşovo, Austria-Hungary. He fought in the First World War, being awarded the Iron Cross 2nd Class (1914). In 1939, he was a *Kommodore* in the Luftwaffe and took part in the Polish and French campaigns, including some combat missions. He was awarded the Iron Cross 1st and 2nd Class (1939). Promoted to *Generalmajor* on 1 July 1940, he was awarded the Knight's Cross on 4 July 1940.

Sent to Africa in February 1941 to help the Africa Corps, he built up the Luftwaffe presence there from almost nothing. Back in Germany on 15 March 1942 to oversee the formation of the 2nd Air Division late in the war, he was named commander of *Luftflotte* 10. Fröhlich died on 2 October 1978 and is buried in Zentralfriedhof, Graz, Austria.

197. Generalmajor Karl KRIEBEL

Kriebel was born on 26 February 1888 in Metz. He fought in the First World War and was awarded the Iron Cross 1st and 2nd Class (1914). Kriebel was commander of 56th Infantry Division when he was awarded the Knight's Cross on 4 July 1940. He died on 28 November 1961 in Aufkirchen, Bavaria, but there are also references to him dying in Sparenberg, Baden-Württemberg.

198. Generalmajor Friedrich KÜHN—'Fritz'

Kühn was born on 7 August 1889 in Eutin. He fought in the First World War, being awarded the Iron Cross 1st and 2nd Class (1914). Kühn was commander of 3rd Panzer Brigade when he was awarded the Knight's Cross on 4 July 1940. He was appointed General for Army Mechanisation at OKH and, in April 1943, chief of the Wehrmacht Motor Transport and Mechanisation. Kühn was killed in an air raid in Berlin on 15 February 1944 and has no known grave.

199. Generalmajor Wolff von STUTTERHEIM

Von Stutterheim was born on 17 January 1893 in Königsberg. He fought in the First World War and was awarded the Iron Cross 1st and 2nd Class (1914), as well as the *Pour le Mérite*. Von Stutterheim was a *Kommodore* in Bomber Wing 77 when he was severely wounded in combat over France on 15 June 1940.

He was awarded the Knight's Cross on 4 July and died on 3 December 1940. Von Stutterheim is buried in the Invaliden Friedhof, Feld F, Plot 7, Grave 15 (next to Mölders and Udet), Scharnhorstrasse, Berlin.

200. General Ernst UDET—'The Flying Clown'

Udet was born on 26 April 1896 in Frankfurt am Main. Udet had a flair for anything mechanical and owned a motorcycle. Udet tried to join the army first at the age of seventeen but was rejected several times before being accepted on 21 August 1914, as a motorcycle messenger for the 26th Württemberg Reserve Division. For the next few months, he delivered messages up and down the lines. Then, one night, he swerved to miss a shell hole and crashed; after ten days in hospital, he was sent to find his division but could not. While in Liege, he met a pilot, *Leutnant* von Waxheim, who convinced him to join the German Army Air Service.

Udet made several applications but all were refused, and he was ordered back home. He trained as a pilot at his own expense while putting forward more requests to fly. In early 1915, he was ordered to Darmstadt for pilot training, after completion of which, he was sent to FA(A) 206 with the rank of *Gefreiter*. *Leutnant* Bruno Justinus was appointed as his observer, and after three weeks—in which time they never even saw an Allied aircraft—they spotted a French monoplane attacking a railway station. As they approached, it was obvious the Frenchman was having difficulties. Udet flew in behind him and noticed the monoplane had a machine gun mounted behind the propeller. The French pilot, encouraged by Udet, made a forced landing on the German side of the lines, and before he could set fire to his machine, it was captured by German soldiers. The pilot was Roland Garros and the capture of his aircraft with its machine gun and crude interruptor gear was to alter the course of the war in the air. For this, Udet was awarded the Iron Cross 2nd Class.

On 18 March 1916, he was posted to FA 68 (which later became *Kek* Habsheim and, in September, *Jasta* 15), on the same day that Udet shot down his first enemy aircraft, a French Farman F40 over Milhausen. It is said that he attacked twenty-two enemy aircraft single-handedly. He would only score two more by the end of the year. At the beginning of January 1917, Udet was awarded the Iron Cross 1st Class and commissioned a *Leutnant* on 22 January. After his sixth victory, he requested transfer to *Jasta* 37 and was posted there on 19 June. On 7 November, Udet was appointed commander of *Jasta* 37 after the death of its commander and his friend, Heinrich Gontermann. He was also awarded the Knight's Cross with Swords of the Royal Hohenzollern House Order on 13 November. He continued to score steadily, and by the end of 1917, he had sixteen confirmed victories.

With his tally at twenty, Udet was made acting commander of *Jasta* 11 on 23 March 1918, a post he held until 8 April. On the 9th, he was awarded the *Pour le Mérite* and given command of *Jasta* 4. Most of Udet's aircraft had his fiancée's initials, 'LO', painted on the fuselage. His Fokker DVII had a red fuselage, with the top surfaces of the wing 'candy striped' red and white. Written on the top of his rear tail surface was '*Du noch nicht*!'—'Not you yet'. With his score at forty, he was in a dogfight with a French Breguet two-seater on 29 July and was forced to jump from his aircraft; he landed by parachute in a shell hole. In August 1918, Udet shot down twenty enemy aircraft, including three on the 1st and the 8th and two on the 9th, 10th, 21st, and 22nd. Udet was awarded the Lübeck Hanseatic Cross in August and the Hamburg Hanseatic Cross in September. Then, on 26 September, after shooting down his sixty-first and sixty-second, Udet was badly wounded in the thigh, putting an end to his combat days. However, he had become the second highest-scoring German pilot of the war and the highest-surviving ace of the war.

After the war, Udet became something of an adventurer, flying all over the world. He was also involved in stunt flying for films and a test pilot. At the start of the Second World War, he was persuaded to join the Luftwaffe and attained the rank of *Generaloberst*. He was awarded the Knight's Cross on 4 July 1940. He could not deal with the political in-fighting within the Luftwaffe, and on 17 November 1941, Udet killed himself. The German propaganda machine announced that he was killed while testing a new aircraft and he was given a state funeral. He is buried in the Invaliden Friedhof, Feld F, Plot 8, Grave 15 (next to Mölders and Stutterheim), Scharnhorstrasse, Berlin.

201. Oberst Alfred BÜLOWIUS

Bülowius was born on 14 January 1892 in Königsberg. He fought in the First World War, being awarded the Iron Cross 1st and 2nd Class (1914). Bülowius fought in Poland and France and was awarded the Iron Cross 1st and 2nd Class (1939). He was also awarded the Knight's Cross on 4 July 1940 as commander of Close Support Wing 1. Bülowius died on 9 August 1968 in Detmold, North Rhine-Westphalia.

202. Oberst Hans-Karl Freiherr von ESEBECK

Freiherr von Esebeck was born on 10 July 1892 in Potsdam. He fought in the First World War and was awarded the Iron Cross 1st and 2nd Class (1914). *Freiherr* von Esebeck was awarded the Iron Cross 2nd Class (1939) in September 1939 and the 1st Class (1939) in May 1940. He was commander of 6th Rifle Brigade when he was awarded the Knight's Cross on 4 July 1940. *Freiherr* von Esebeck commanded the 15th Panzer Division in Africa.

He was sympathetic to the plot to kill Hitler and was arrested on 21 July 1944; he spent the remainder of the war in concentration camps. *Freiherr* von Esebeck was released at the end of the war and spent the rest of his life in poverty. He died on 5 January 1955 and is buried in Hauptfriedhof, Iserlohn, North Rhine-Westphalia.

203. Oberst Hans-Karl von SCHEELE

Von Scheele was born on 23 May 1892 in Magdeburg. He fought in the First World War and was awarded the Iron Cross 1st and 2nd Class (1914). Von Scheele was awarded the Iron Cross 2nd Class (1939) in September 1939 and the 1st Class in May 1940. He was commander of Infantry Regiment 191 when he was awarded the Knight's Cross on 4 July 1940.

Von Scheele took part in the invasion of Russia and was awarded the Oak Leaves on 2 April 1943. He died on 8 October 1955 and is buried in Waldfriedhof, Abt Y1, Grave 178 (headstone removed), Bad Homburg, Hesse.

204. Oberst Alois STOECKL

Stoeckl was born on 22 August 1895 in Mühldorf. He fought in the First World War, being awarded the Iron Cross 1st and 2nd Class (1914). Stoeckl also took part in the Spanish Civil War and the Polish and French campaigns. Stoeckl was a *Kommodore* in Bomber Wing 55 when he was awarded the Knight's Cross on 4 July 1940.

He was killed in action over Beachy Head, England, on 14 August 1940 and is buried in the German War Cemetery, Block 2, Row 2, Grave 30–32–35, Camp Road, Cannock Chase, Staffordshire, England.

205. Oberstleutnant Heinrich EBERBACH

Eberbach was born on 24 November 1895 in Stuttgart. He fought in the First World War, being awarded the Iron Cross 1st and 2nd Class (1914); he also had his nose shot off. It was replaced by a rubber one. Eberbach fought in Poland and was awarded the Iron Cross 1st and 2nd Class (1939). He was commander of Panzer Regiment 35 when he was awarded the Knight's Cross on 4 July 1940.

Eberbach took part in the invasion of Russia and was awarded the Oak Leaves on 31 December 1941. Wounded in late 1942, he became inspector of armoured troops on the Home Front. He later fought in Normandy and was captured by the British at Amiens in September 1944. Eberbach died on 13 July 1992 in Stadtfriedhof, Notzingen, Baden-Württemberg.

206. *Major* Bruno CHROBEK

Chrobek was born on 9 October 1895 in Pless. He fought in the First World War and was awarded the Iron Cross 2nd Class (1914). Chrobek fought in

Poland and France and was commander of I Battalion, Infantry Regiment 54, when he was awarded the Knight's Cross on 4 July 1940.

He took part in the invasion of Russia and was killed in action on 8 December 1942. Chrobek is buried in the German War Cemetery (as unknown), Rossoschka, Volgograd, Russia.

207. *Oberleutnant* Ludwig KLOTZ

Klotz was born on 27 September 1895 in Augsburg. He was a company commander in Infantry Regiment 423 when he was awarded the Knight's Cross on 4 July 1940. Klotz was killed in action in Lopanez, Russia, on 14 February 1944 and has no known grave.

208. Leutnant Hans-Günther STOTTEN

Stotten was born in Berlin on 7 October 1916. He fought in Poland and was awarded the Iron Cross 1st and 2nd Class. In France, he led his panzer company through some fortifications and all the way to the coast. For this, he was awarded the Knight's Cross on 4 July 1940.

He served in the Balkans and in Russia, where, in October 1941, he was wounded outside of Moscow. Stotten did not return to combat until September 1942 when he was sent to Africa. Promoted to battalion commander, Stotten fought in all the tank battles from El Alamein to Tunisia. Stotten stormed the Kasserine Pass and destroyed the enemy anti-tank guns there, clearing the way for the panzers. For this, he was awarded the Oak Leaves on 10 May 1943. Wounded again, he left Africa, and on his recovery, he saw action in Russia, He was captured on 4 April 1945 and the next day was shot dead at Wolfsgraben, Austria, while trying to escape; he has no known grave.

209. Feldwebel Albert BRACHAT

Brachat was born on 27 March 1915 in Hilzingen. He fought in Poland and France, and he was awarded the Iron Cross 1st and 2nd Class in June 1940 and the Knight's Cross on 4 July 1940 as commander of I Battalion, Infantry Regiment 14. Brachat was killed in action near Karachev, Russia, on 14 August 1943 and has no known grave.

210. Feldwebel Joseph LANG

Lang was born on 20 February 1914 in Stetten. He was a section leader in Pioneer Battalion 15 when he was awarded the Knight's Cross on 4 July 1940. Lang died of wounds at Kelkolowo, Russia, on 27 July 1943 and has no known grave.

211. Unteroffizier Herbert NELKE

Nelke was born on 20 March 1915 in Barnitz. He was a gun commander in Motorised Flak Regiment 23 when he was awarded the Knight's Cross on 4 July 1940. Nelke was killed in an accident on 30 January 1941 and is buried at Carei, Romania; his remains are awaiting transfer to a German war cemetery.

212. General Friedrich FROMM

Fromm was born on 8 October 1888 in Berlin. He fought in the First World War, being awarded the Iron Cross 1st and 2nd Class (1914). Fromm was commander of the armament of the army and the replacement army when he was awarded the Knight's Cross on 6 July 1940.

Fromm was aware of the plot to kill Hitler and agreed to take part if he was given a position in the new government. When an attempt failed, he withdraw from the plotters and had no more to do with it. After the 20 July bomb plot failed to kill Hitler, Fromm tried to arrest them but was overpowered and put in a cell. When the mutiny failed, Fromm was released and, against Hitler's orders, had the conspirators executed immediately. This did not save him and he was arrested, but as no direct link could be made between him and the plot, he was charged with cowardice before the enemy and executed at Brandenburg-Görden Prison on 19 March 1945. His last words were 'I die because it was ordered. I had always wanted only the best for Germany'. Fromm has no known grave.

213. Generalmajor Joachim COELER

Coeler was born on 1 June 1891 in Posen. He fought in the navy during the First World War, being awarded the Iron Cross 1st and 2nd Class (1914). Coeler was commander of 9th Flieger Division when he was awarded the Knight's Cross on 12 July 1940. He died on 14 May 1955 and is buried in Stadtfriedhof, Garmisch-Partenkirchen, Bavaria.

214. Generalleutnant Theodor ENDRES

Endres was born on 25 September 1876 in Ansbach. He fought in the First World War and was awarded the Iron Cross 1st and 2nd Class (1914). Endres also fought in France and was awarded the Iron Cross 2nd (1939) in June 1939 and the 1st Class (1939) in September 1940. He was commander of 212th Infantry Division when he was awarded Knight's Cross on 13 July 1940. Endres died on 19 January 1956 and is buried in Waldfriedhof, Feld 12, Row 1, Grave 1–2, Traunstein, Bavaria.

215. Generalleutnant Ferdinand SCHAAL

Schaal was born on 7 February 1889 in Freiburg. He fought in the First World War, being awarded the Iron Cross 1st and 2nd Class (1914). Schaal commanded the 10th Panzer Division in Poland, for which he was awarded the Iron Cross 2nd Class (1939), and France, for which he was awarded the Iron Cross 1st Class (1939). He was awarded the Knight's Cross on 13 July 1940.

Schaal went on to command the same unit in Russia until he was appointed commander of Bohemia and Moravia in August 1943. Involved in the 20 July bomb plot he was arrested, but unlike most of the other plotters, he was not executed. Schaal died on 9 October 1962 and is buried in Hauptfriedhof, Baden Baden, Baden-Württemberg.

216. Oberst Eugen-Felix SCHWALBE

Schwalbe was born on 25 March 1892 in Kleinpriessligk. He fought in the First World War and was awarded the Iron Cross 1st and 2nd Class (1914). Schwalbe fought in Poland and France as commander of Infantry Regiment 461; it was in this role that he was awarded the Knight's Cross on 13 July 1940. Schwalbe went on to fight in Russia, Normandy, and the Netherlands. He died on 12 June 1974 and is believed to be buried in Sennefriedhof, Bielefeld, North Rhine-Westphalia.

217. *Major* Leopold BÖHMER

Böhmer was born on 3 January 1882 in Cologne. He was commander of III Battalion, Infantry Regiment 270, when he was awarded the Knight's Cross on 13 July 1940. Böhmer died on 15 May 1949 in Grossrückerswalde, Saxony.

218. Rittmeister Horst NIEMACK

Niemack was born on 10 March 1909 in Hanover. He fought in France and was awarded the Iron Cross 1st and 2nd Class. Niemack was commander of Reconnaissance Battalion 5 when he was awarded the Knight's Cross on 13 July 1940. In Russia, he was awarded the Oak Leaves on 10 August 1941 and the Swords on 4 June 1944. Niemack was severely wounded on 20 August 1944 when he was pulled from his burning armoured car and flown to Berlin. The surgeon managed to save his left arm. Niemack died on 7 April 1992 and is buried in Gross Hehlen Friedhof, Celle, Lower Saxony.

219. *Hauptmann* Hans Freiherr von WOLFF

Freiherr von Wolff was born on 19 March 1903 in Riga, Latvia. He fought in Poland, for which he obtained the Iron Cross 2nd Class (1939), and France, for which he was rewarded the Iron Cross 1st Class (1939). Von Wolff was commander of I Battalion, Rifle Regiment 8, when he was awarded the Knight's Cross on 13 July 1940.

He also fought in the Balkans campaign and in Russia, where he was awarded the Oak Leaves on 16 January 1942. Von Wolff died of wounds at Brest, Russia, on 28 June 1944 and has no known grave.

220. *Oberleutnant* Wilhelm CIRENER

Cirener was born on 19 March 1913 in Dinslaken. He was a company commander in Pioneer Battalion 33 when he was awarded the Knight's Cross on 13 July 1940. Cirener was killed in action on 1 May 1941 and is buried in the German War Cemetery, Tobruk, Libya.

221. *Oberleutnant* Gerd Freiherr von KETELHODT

Freiherr von Ketelhodt was born on 17 March 1915 in Rudolstadt. He was a company commander in Infantry Regiment 472 when he was awarded the Knight's Cross on 13 July 1940. Von Ketelhodt died on 4 August 1976 and is believed to be buried in Erbach Friedhof, Homburg, Saarland.

222. Leutnant Herbert NAUE

Naue was born on 14 December 1906 in Berlin. He was a company commander in Infantry Regiment 178 when he was awarded the Knight's Cross on 13 July 1940. Naue was killed in action on 17 June 1942 and is buried in the German War Cemetery (as unknown), Sebastopol, Ukraine.

223. Oberfeldwebel Fritz GEBAUER

Gebauer was born on 5 February 1910 in Friedrichsfeld. He was a platoon leader in Frontier Pioneer Battalion 74 when he was awarded the Knight's Cross on 13 July 1940. Gebauer was posted missing near Orša, Russia, on 1 June 1944.

224. General Fritz-Erich von MANSTEIN

Born von Lewinski in Berlin on 24 November 1887, von Manstein was brought up by an aunt who adopted him. He was severely wounded during the First Would World, being awarded the Iron Cross 1st and 2nd Class (1914). When the Second World War started, he was chief-of staff to von Rundstedt's army group and, as such, took part in the Polish campaign. He came up with the idea of attacking France through the Ardennes, but the High Command did not think it would work. When dining with Hitler, he told him of the plan and Hitler promptly adopted it. He took part in the French campaign with his corps and was awarded the Knight's Cross on 19 July 1940.

In the invasion of the Soviet Union in July 1941, he commanded a Panzer corps, and in five days, he penetrated 150 miles. In 1942, he was appointed to command the 11th Army and told to capture the Crimea. He took Sebastopol and was promoted to *Generalfeldmarschall* in July 1942. In November, he commanded Army Group Don, responsible for defending a 600-mile front with an average of sixty divisions. His immediate problem was Stalingrad, where he was unable to relieve the 6th Army. He repeatedly urged Hitler to shorten the line to conserve manpower. Von Manstein was awarded the Oak Leaves on 14 March 1943 and the Swords on 30 March 1944. His HQ was back on the Polish border by March 1944. He was sacked at the end of the month and took no further part in the war. Marshal Malinovski said of him: 'We regarded the hated Erich von Manstein as our most dangerous opponent. His technical mastery of every situation was incomparable'.

Unjustly tried by the British for complicity to murders carried out behind the lines, his defence was paid for by British officers who disagreed with his being tried. He was sentenced to eighteen years, but was released in 1953. He died from a stroke on 9 July 1973 and was buried with full military honours in Dorfmark Friedhof, Bad Fallingbostel, Lower Saxony. His son-in-law was Knight's Cross holder Edel-Heinrich Zachariae-Lingenthal.

225. General Georg STUMME

Stumme was born on 29 July 1886 in Halberstadt. He fought in the First World War and was awarded the Iron Cross 1st and 2nd Class (1914). Stumme took part in the Polish and French campaigns. He was commander of XXXX Army Corps when he was awarded the Knight's Cross on 19 July 1940. Stumme also saw action in the Balkans.

He took part in the invasion of Russia, but in 1942, he was court-martialled when some plans were captured by the enemy. Sentenced to five years, he was instead released and sent to Africa. On 24 October 1942, he drove to the front near El Alamein when his car came under enemy fire. Stumme jumped out of the car and held on while his driver got them out of range. His body was found the next day; with no visible wounds, it is believed he had a heart attack. He is buried in the German War Cemetery, Tobruk, Libya.

226. General Albert WODRIG

Wodrig was born on 16 July 1883 in Berlin. He fought in the First World War and was awarded the Iron Cross 1st and 2nd Class (1914). Wodrig saw action in Poland and France as commander of XXVI and was awarded the Knight's Cross on 19 July 1940. He also saw action in Russia. Wodrig died on 31 October 1972 and is believed to be buried in Bad Oeynhausen Friedhof, North Rhine-Westphalia.

227. Generalleutnant Hans von SALMUTH

Von Salmuth was born on 29 November 1888 in Metz. He fought in the First World War and was awarded the Iron Cross 1st and 2nd Class (1914). Von Salmuth was chief-of-staff for Army Group 'B' during the Polish and French campaigns and was awarded the Knight's Cross on 19 July 1940. He fought in Russia until August 1943 when he was given command of XV Army in the Pas-de-Calais area.

After the Allied break-out from Normandy in August 1944, Von Salmuth was relieved of his command and did not take any further part in the war.

After the war, he was charged with war crimes relating to the mistreatment of POWs, enemy belligerents, and civilians in occupied counties. Von Salmuth was sentenced to twenty years but was released in 1953. He died on 1 January 1962 and is buried in the Nordfriedhof, Abt 12, Grave 001–003, Wiesbaden, Hesse.

228. Generalleutnant Georg von SODENSTERN

Von Sodenstern was born on 15 November 1889 in Kassel. He fought in the First World War and was awarded the Iron Cross 1st and 2nd Class (1914). Von Sodenstern also took part in the French campaign and was awarded the Knight's Cross on 19 July 1940. He died on 20 July 1955 in Frankfurt am Main.

229. Generalmajor Erich STRAUBE

Straube was born on 11 December 1887 in Elsterwerda. He fought in the First World War, being awarded the Iron Cross 1st and 2nd Class (1914). Straube also fought in France and was awarded the Iron Cross 1st and 2nd Class (1939). He was commander of 268th Infantry Division when he was awarded the Knight's Cross on 19 July 1940.

Straube fought in Russa and Normandy, where he was awarded the Oak Leaves on 30 September 1944. He died on 31 March 1971 and is believed to be buried in Osterode Friedhof, Lower Saxony.

230. Oberst Hans Reichsführer von BOINEBURG-LENGSFELD

Reichsführer von Boineburg-Lengsfeld was born on 9 June 1889 in Eisenach. He fought in the First World War and was awarded the Iron Cross 1st and 2nd Class (1914). Von Boineburg-Lengsfeld fought in Poland, being awarded the Iron Cross 1st and 2nd Class (1939). He was commander of the 4th Rifle Brigade when he was awarded the Knight's Cross on 19 July 1940. He died on 20 November 1980 and is buried in the grounds of the family estate, Felsberg-Altenburg, Hesse.

231. Oberst Fritz-Hubert GRÄSER

Gräser was born on 3 November 1888 in Frankfurt an der Oder. He fought in the First World War and was awarded the Iron Cross 1st and 2nd Class (1914). Gräser was awarded the Iron Cross 2nd Class (1939) in September and the Iron Cross 1st Class (1939) in October 1939. He took part in the French campaign and was awarded the Knight's Cross on 19 July 1940.

Gräser also fought in Italy and Russia, and he was awarded the Oak Leaves on 26 June 1944. The Swords were awarded on 8 May 1945 (this award was made in accordance with the Dönitz-Decree). He died on 4 October 1960 and is buried in Stadtfriedhof, Plot EU 24, Grave 5, Göttingen, Lower Saxony.

232. Fregattenkapitän Fritz BERGER

Berger was born on 15 April 1900 in Allenstein, East Prussia. He was awarded the Iron Cross 1st and 2nd Class (1939) in 1939. Berger fought at the Battle of Narvik as commander of Destroyer Flotilla 1 and was awarded the Knight's Cross on 19 July 1940. He died on 27 June 1973 and is believed to be buried in Johannesfriedhof, Bielefeld, North Rhine-Westphalia.

233. Oberstleutnant Eugen GARSKI

Garski was born on 8 June 1897 in Thorn. He fought in the First World War and was awarded the Iron Cross 1st and 2nd Class (1914). Garski took part in the campaign in the West and was awarded the Knight's Cross on 19 July 1940 as commander of III Battalion, Infantry Regiment 'GD'.

He also fought in the Balkans. Garski was killed in action on 30 September 1942 and is buried at Alenino-Melechowo, Russia. His remains are awaiting transfer to a German war cemetery.

234. Oberstleutnant Oskar RADWAN

Radwan was born on 3 July 1894 in Guttentag (present-day Dobrodzień). He was commander of II Battalion, Infantry Regiment 93, when he was awarded the Knight's Cross on 19 July 1940. Radwan was killed in action at the Mius River, Russia, on 18 June1942 and has no known grave.

235. *Major* Herbert BÖHME

Böhme was born on 21 April 1898 in Rattwitz. He was commander of III Battalion, Infantry Regiment 28, when he was awarded the Knight's Cross on 19 July 1940. Böhme was killed in action near Vitebsk, Belarus, on 27 December 1943 and has no known grave.

236. *Major* Josef GOLLÉ

Gollé was born on 27 October 1895 in Lödersdorf. He was commander of I Battalion, Infantry Regiment 339, when he was awarded the Knight's Cross on 19 July 1943. Gollé died on 16 July 1971 in Brannenburg, Bavaria.

237. *Major* Franz-Josef WELZEL

Welzel was born on 27 January 1895 in Altwilmsdorf. He was commander of I Battalion, Infantry Regiment 461, when he was awarded the Knight's Cross on 19 July 1940. Welzel died on 15 August 1978 in Bad Salzuflen, North Rhine-Westphalia.

238. *Hauptmann* Leo DROSSEL

Drossel was born on 2 February 1903 in Berlin. He fought in Poland and France as commander of III Battalion, Infantry Regiment 102. Drossel was awarded the Knight's Cross on 19 July 1940. He also fought in Russia as commander of III Battalion, Infantry Regiment 261. He died on 16 July 1983 and is buried in Planegg Friedhof, Munich.

239. *Oberleutnant* Heinrich BORGMANN

Borgmann was born on 15 August 1912 in Angermünde. He fought in Poland and was awarded the Iron Cross 1st and 2nd Class. Borgmann was a company commander in Infantry Regiment 46 when he was awarded the Knight's Cross on 19 July 1940 for his part in the French campaign. In Russia, he was awarded the Oak Leaves on 11 February 1942 and posted to Hitler's HQ staff in October 1943.

Borgmann was seriously injured in the 20 July bomb plot; he was standing very close to the bomb when it exploded. After recovering, he was posted to the Eastern Front and died of wounds on 5 April 1945. Borgmann is buried in Waldfriedhof, Hüttenweg, Dahlem, Berlin.

240. Leutnant Michael PÖSSINGER

Pössinger was born on 18 January 1919 in Ettal. He fought in Poland, for which he was awarded the Iron Cross 2nd Class, and France, where he manned his anti-tank gun single handed and knocked-out seven French tanks and damaged four more. Later, he almost single-handedly captured a bridge over the Char River. For these actions, he was awarded the Iron Cross 1st Class and the Knight's Cross on 19 July 1940. While in France, Pössinger met and became friends with Adolf Galland.

Next, he fought in the Balkans and then Russia, where he spent a great deal of time behind enemy lines during the winter of 1941–42. In 1942, his ski unit went to the Caucasus Mountains; badly wounded, he was sent to hospital but returned to his men in time for the retreat. In April 1943, his division was moved to the Balkans for rest. After landing in Corfu in September to disarm 4,000 Italians, Pössinger was finally promoted to *Hauptmann*. Next he fought against Tito's partisans before returning to the Russian Front in the summer of 1944. In East Prussia, Pössinger's anti-tank guns knocked-out forty-two tanks, for which he was awarded the Oak Leaves on 28 February 1945. He was also awarded the Close Combat Clasp in Gold, the Wound Badge in Gold, and five Tank Destruction Badges. He surrendered to US forces in March 1945. Pössinger took part in the 1956 Olympics. He died on 23 May 2003 in Garmisch-Partenkirchen, Bavaria.

241. Feldwebel Franz BERGER

Berger was born on 6 August 1916 in Vienna. He fought in Poland, for which he obtained the Iron Cross 2nd Class, and France, for which he was awarded the Iron Cross 1st Class. Berger was a section leader in Infantry Regiment 130 when he was awarded the Knight's Cross on 19 July 1940. He was killed in action on 29 November 1942 and is believed to be buried in the German War Cemetery (as unknown), Rossoschka, Volgograd, Russia.

242. Oberstleutnant Carl-Alfred (or Carl-August) SCHUMACHER

Schumacher was born on 19 February 1896 in Rheine. He fought in the artillery and the navy during the First World War. Schumacher commanded Fighter Wing 1 when he shot down his only two aerial victories on 18 and 27 December 1939, both British bombers. He was awarded the Knight's Cross on 21 July 1940 for his outstanding leadership. Schumacher was the first pilot to be awarded the Knight's Cross.

He was relieved of his command for a short time for accidently shooting down a Finnish Air Force aircraft in November 1941. Schumacher died on 22 May 1967 in Bad Godesberg, and at his own request, his ashes were scattered in the North Sea.

243. *Major* Walter HAGEN

Hagen was born on 16 March 1897 in Kiel. He fought in the First World War and was awarded the Iron Cross 1st and 2nd Class (1914). Hagen fought in Poland, for which he was awarded the Iron Cross 2nd Class (1939), and in France, for which he was rewarded the Iron Cross 1st Class (1939) on 9 June; he obtained the Knight's Cross on 21 July 1940 as a group commander in Dive Bomber Wing 1.

He also fought over England, the Balkans, the Mediterranean, and in Russia. Hagen was awarded the Oak Leaves on 17 February 1942. He died on 24 November 1963 and is buried in Parkfriedhof, Eichhofstrasse 56, Kiel, Schleswig-Holstein.

244. *Major* Clemens Graf von SCHÖNBORN-WIESENTHEID

Graf von Schönborn-Wiesentheid was born on 3 April 1905 in Munich. He was a group commander in Dive Bomber Wing 77 when he was awarded the Knight's Cross on 21 July 1940. He was kille din action on 30 August 1944 and is buried in the German War Cemetery, Sofia, Bulgaria.

245. *Hauptmann* Freidrich-Karl Freiherr von DALWIGK zu LICHTENFELS

Freiherr von Dalwigk zu Lichtenfels was born on 1 April 1907 in Torgau. He fought in Poland and France as a Stuka pilot. He was a group commander in Dive Bomber Wing 77 when he was killed in action over the English Channel on 9 July 1940; he has no known grave. Von Dalwigk zu Lichtenfels was awarded the Knight's Cross on 21 July 1940.

246. *Hauptmann* Walter ENNECCERUS

Enneccerus was born on 21 November 1911 in Trier. He served with the Condor Legion in the Spanish Civil War. Enneccerus fought in Poland, the campaign in the West, and the Battle of Britain as a pilot in Dive Bomber Wing 2. He was awarded the Knight's Cross on 21 July 1940.

Enneccerus went on to fly over Crete, Africa, and the Russian Front. He was removed from command for refusing to carry out what he considered to be a suicidal mission. Enneccerus died on 3 August 1971 and is believed to be buried in Waldfriedhof, Troisdorf North Rhine-Westphalia.

247. *Hauptmann* Hubertus HITSCHHOLD

Hitschhold was born on 7 July 1912 in Kurwin, South Africa. He fought in Poland, for which he obtained the Iron Cross 2nd Class, and France, for which he obtained the Iron Cross 1st Class. Hitschhold was awarded the Knight's Cross during the Battle of Britain on 21 July 1940 as a group commander in Dive Bomber Wing 2. He went on to fight in the Balkans, Crete, and Russia, where he was awarded the Oak Leaves on 31 December 1941. He died on 10 March 1966 and is buried in Söcking Friedhof, Bavaria.

248. *Hauptmann* Alois LINDMAYR

Lindmayr was born on 19 September 1901 in Laibach, Austria-Hungary. He led Bomber Wing 76 during the Polish and French campaign, for which he was awarded the Iron Cross 2nd Class on 20 September 1939 and the 1st Class on 23 May 1940. Lindmayr fought during the Battle of Britain and was awarded the Knight's Cross on 21 July 1940. From February 1944 until the end of the war, he was attached to training schools. Lindmayr died on 17 July 1965 in Enns, Austria.

249. *Hauptmann* Walter SIGEL

Sigel was born on 12 January 1906 in Ulm. He saw action over Poland, Belgium, France, and England. Sigel was awarded the Knight's Cross on 21 July 1940. He subsequently saw action in Crete and Africa. Sigel was awarded the Oak Leaves on 2 September 1942 in recognition of his unit's actions in Africa.

Later he fought on the ground with a battle-group made up of aircrew against partisans and US forces in Italy. In April 1944, he was sent to Norway as commander of the Luftwaffe there. Sigel was killed when his light aircraft struck telephone wires. He is buried in the Byaasen/Trondheim-Havstein Military Cemetery, Row 6, Grave 5, Norway.

250. *Hauptmann* Egon THIEM

Thiem was born on 5 October 1911 in Posen. He was a squadron leader in Close Support Wing 2 when he was awarded the Knight's Cross on 21 July 1940. Thiem died on 16 October 1959 and is believed to be buried in Sennefriedhof, Bielefeld, North Rhine-Westphalia.

251. *Oberleutnant* Karl GÖTZE

Götze was born on 20 February 1913 in Ludwigslust. He was a company commander in Motorised Flak Regiment 37 when he was awarded the Knight's Cross on 21 July 1940. Götze died on 10 August 1987 in Lüdenscheid, North Rhine-Westphalia.

252. *Oberleutnant* Horst Freiherr GROTE

Grote was born on 12 May 1912 in Gleiwitz. He was a squadron leader in Close Support Wing 2 when he was awarded the Knight's Cross on 21 July 1940. Grote died on 5 June 2008 in Hanover.

253. *Oberleutnant* Wolfdietrich PEITSMEYER

Peitsmeyer was born on 16 April 1914 in Stargard. He was a squadron leader in Close Support Wing 2 when he was awarded the Knight's Cross on 21 July 1940. Peitsmeyer was killed in action over the Mediterranean Sea on 10 December 1942 and has no known grave.

254. Oberstleutnant Johannes HINTZ

Hintz was born on 1 October 1898 in Metz. He fought in the First World War and was awarded the Iron Cross 1st and 2nd Class (1914). Hintz was commander of Motorised Flak Regiment 101 when he was awarded the Iron Cross 1st and 2nd Class (1939) in May 1940 and the Knight's Cross on 29 July 1940. He was injured in a car crash in Paris and died on 21 May 1944.

255. Oberstleutnant Walter von HIPPEL

Von Hippel was born on 27 May 1897 in Friedrichsthal. He fought in the First World War and was awarded the Iron Cross 1st and 2nd Class (1914). Von Hippel was commander of Motorised Flak Regiment 102 when he was awarded the Knight's Cross on 29 July 1940. He died on 29 November 1972 and is buried in Buchholz Friedhof, Lower Saxony.

256. Oberstleutnant Walter LOEBEL

Loebel was born on 23 June 1902 in Berlin. He was a *Kommodore* in Bomber Wing 30 when he was awarded the Knight's Cross on 29 July 1940. Loebel was killed in action over Smolensk on 6 September 1941 and has no known grave.

257. *Major* Adolf GALLAND—'Dolfo'

Galland was born on 19 March 1912 in Westerholt. He fought with the Condor Legion in Spain. Galland took part in the Polish campaign, but it was on 12 May 1940 that he scored his first air victory shooting down three Hurricanes. By the end of the campaign, he had shot down seven enemy aircraft and been awarded the Iron Cross 1st Class. He became one of the top scoring pilots of the Battle of Britain, having shot down seventeen enemy aircraft by 29 July 1940, the day he was awarded the Knight's Cross. After Galland shot down his fortieth enemy aircraft, bringing his score equal to Mölders, he was awarded the Oak Leaves on 24 September 1940.

Galland became the first man to be awarded the Swords on 21 June 1941, having shot down his seventieth enemy aircraft. After the death of Mölders. Galland became inspector of fighters and was only answerable to Göring. On 28 January 1942, with his tally at ninety-four (all earned on the Western Front), Galland was awarded the Diamonds

As the war dragged on through 1942–43, Galland visited the squadrons. Communicating his concerns to OKL, he found himself in conflict with Göring. At a conference in early 1943, Göring rated that his fighter pilots were cowards who obtained their medals by deception. Galland, enraged by this, ripped his Knight's Cross with Oak Leaves, Swords and Diamonds from his neck and threw it on the table. He refused to wear them for six months. By the end of 1943, he was also inspector of night fighters, a post that was forced on him.

During 1944, the Allied bombing campaign over Germany built up into a massive assault. Galland, now a *Generalleutnant*, planned a single concentrated operation to hit the US bombers with every fighter he could in the hope of inflicting such losses that they would be forces to rethink their tactics. OKL overruled him and used the fighters for a wasteful attack against Allied airfields in Europe in support of the failed Ardennes Offensive. Relieved of his command and under threat of arrest, Galland contemplated suicide before Hitler allowed him to return to combat flying.

He flew Me 262 jet fighters and shot down his last four aircraft using these jets, bringing his total to 104 enemy aircraft shot down. Galland was wounded during one fight but managed to land safely. He was taken prisoner by US forces on 5 May 1945. Galland is author of *The First and The Last*. He died in Bonn on 9 February 1996 and is buried in St Laurentius Churchyard (actually the Oberwinter Friedhof nearby), Ma Bergquell, Remagen-Oberwinter, Rhineland-Palatinate. I was lucky enough to meet him at an air show in the 1980s and I got his autograph. Galland's three brothers also served in the Luftwaffe: Wilhelm-Ferdinand shot down fifty-five enemy aircraft and was also awarded the Knight's Cross; Paul shot down seventeen enemy aircraft before being killed in action; and Fritz was a reconnaissance pilot who survived the war.

258. *Oberleutnant* Walter KRAUSS

Krauss was born on 11 March 1917 in Erlangen. He was a pilot in Dive Bomber Wing 2 when he was awarded the Knight's Cross on 29 July 1940. The Oak Leaves followed on 3 January 1944. Krauss was killed in action on 17 July 1943 and is buried at Orel, Russia; his remains are awaiting transfer to a German war cemetery.

259. Oberst Gustav von VAERST

Von Vaerst was born on 19 April 1894 in Meiningen. He fought in the First World War and was awarded the Iron Cross 1st and 2nd Class (1914). Von Vaerst was commander of the 2nd Rifle Brigade when he was awarded the Knight's Cross on 30 July 1940. He died on 10 October 1975 in Stockheim, Wiesbaden.

260. Feldwebel Karl HUBER

Huber was born on 3 December 1914 in Immendingen. He was a platoon leader in Motorised Reconnaissance Battalion 20 when he was awarded the Knight's Cross on 30 July 1940. Huber died on 24 February 1993 in Immendingen, Baden-Württemberg.

261. Kapitänleutnant Wilhelm ROLLMANN

Rollmann was born on 5 August 1907 in Wilhelmshaven. When the war started, Rollmann was already at sea with *U-34*. On 7 September 1939, he sank the 5,809-ton *Puccastan*, and the next day, he torpedoed the 5,548-ton British tanker *Kennebec*. He has success in October and November. On 20

January 1940, the 7,907-ton tanker *Caroni River* sank after hitting a mine laid by *U-34*, and on 28 January, *U-34* sank the *Eleni Stathatos*. During July 1940, he sank twelve ships, including the British destroyer *Whirlwind*, the Estonian steamer *Vapper*, the 9,337-ton *Accra* and the 10,364-ton British tanker *Thiara*. He was awarded the Knight's Cross on 31 July 1940.

Rollmann commissioned *U-848* on 20 February 1943 and sank the 4,573-ton *Baron Semple* on 2 November, but then, on 6 November 1943, he was attacked by US aircraft and sunk. Rollmann did not survive. He sank twenty-two ships (a total of 100,838 tons).

262. Leutnant Albert von SCHWERIN

Von Schwerin was born on 11 September 1904 in Janow. He was a pilot in Bomber Wing 26 when he was awarded the Knight's Cross on 31 July 1940. Von Schwerin was killed in action on 19 November 1940 and is buried in the German War Cemetery, Camp Road, Cannock Chase, Block 9, Row 5, Grave 30, Staffordshire, England.

263. Oberfeldwebel Gerhard RENZ

Renz was born on 22 July 1910 in Halle. He was a pilot in Bomber Wing 26 when he was awarded the Knight's Cross on 31 July 1940. Renz died on 16 February 1946 in Lubeck, Schleswig-Holstein.

264. Korvettenkapitän Rudolf PETERSEN

Petersen was born on 15 June 1905 in Atzerballig. When the war started, he was commander of S-Boat Flotilla 2 at Heligoland. By the spring of 1940, his flotilla was operating out of Borkum. On 28 May 1940, Petersen was awarded the Iron Cross 1st Class; the next day, he sank the destroyer HMS *Wakeful*. The following day, the French destroyers *Siroco* and *Cyclone* were also sunk. After the campaign in the West, his boats were engaged in attacking convoys in the Channel. In June, the 3,000-ton steamer *Roseburn* was sent to the bottom. During July and August, the boats were laid over 130 mines. For his flotilla's efforts, Petersen was awarded the Knight's Cross on 4 August 1940.

On 1 October 1941, Petersen was posted to the Admiralty Staff as commander of torpedo boats. He returned to S-boats when he was appointed commander of S-boats on 20 April 1942. It is interesting to note when the new badge awarded to S-boat crews was redesigned, Petersen was consulted.

He was awarded the Oak Leaves on 13 June 1944 for the success of units under his command. Petersen was one of only a handful of men to be awarded the S-boat War Badge with Diamonds, presented to him personally by Raeder. Petersen died on 2 January 1983 and is buried in Addelby Neuer Friedhof, Gravesite 71 A3, Flensburg, Schleswig-Holstein.

265. Korvettenkapitän Max-Eckart WOLFF

Wolff was born on 19 December 1902 in Wernigerode. He was awarded the Iron Cross 2nd Class in November 1939. On 10 April 1940, as commander of the destroyer Z2 *Georg Thiele*, he sank destroyers HMS *Hardy* and *Hunter*, and on 13 April, Wolff damaged HMS *Eskimo*. He was awarded the Iron Cross 1st Class in May 1940 and the Knight's Cross on 4 August 1940. Wolff died on 9 November 1988 and is buried in Osterholz Friedhof, Bremen.

266. *Kapitänleutnant* Otto KRETSCHMER—'Silent Otto'

Kretschmer was born in Heidau on 1 May 1912. He commanded *U-35* during the Spanish Civil War but did not sink any ships. At the beginning of the war, Kretschmer was commanding *U-23* in the North Sea. He laid mines and sunk eight ships, including the 10,517-ton *Denmark* on 12 January 1940. He commissioned *U-99* on 18 April 1940 and sunk eleven ships on his first patrol, including the 13,212-ton *Auckland Star*. He attacked convoy HX72, sinking three ships, one of which was the 9,154-ton tanker *Invershannon*. He was known for only using one torpedo per ship and is credited with the quote 'one torpedo ... one ship'. He was awarded the Knight's Cross on 4 August 1940. On one patrol in September 1940, he picked up a lone survivor from a small raft and transferred him to a lifeboat. Kretschmer was awarded the Oak Leaves on 4 November 1940. In two days, he sank eight ships from convoy SC7. In November, he sank the 18,724-ton *Riesen Laurentic* and the 11,314-ton *Patroclus*, and on 1 December, he sank the 16,402-ton *Forfar*.

On 3 March 1941, he sank the 20,638-ton factory whaling ship *Terje Viken*. He also sank seven ships from convoys ON293 and HX112. Then, on 17 March 1941, he was attacked by the destroyers *Walker* and *Vanoc*; unable to dive, the boat was scuttled and her crew taken prisoner. He was awarded the Swords on 26 December 1941. In 1943, the Germans tried to rescue him in a daring plan coded named Operation *Kiebitz*, but it failed. 'Silent Otto', as he was known, sunk fifty-six ships (a total of 313,611 tons), more than any other U-boat commander. He died in a boating accident on the Danube on 5 August 1998 and his ashes were scattered at sea.

267. General Otto HARTMANN

Hartmann was born on 11 September 1884 in Munich. He fought in the First World War and was awarded the Iron Cross 1st and 2nd Class (1914). Hartmann was commander of XXX Army Corps when he was awarded the Knight's Cross on 5 August 1940. He died on 10 July 1952 and is buried in Bergfriedhof, Miesbach, Bavaria.

268. Generalleutnant Arnold Freiherr von BIEGELEBEN

Freiherr von Biegeleben was born on 16 April 1883 in Darmstadt. He fought in the First World War and was awarded the Iron Cross 1st and 2nd Class (1914). Von Biegeleben was awarded the Iron Cross 1st and 2nd Class (1939) in October 1939. He was commander of the 6th Infantry Division when he was awarded the Knight's Cross on 5 August 1940. *Freiherr* von Biegeleben died from a heart attack on 11 October 1940 and is buried in the German War Cemetery, Block 47, Grave 232, La Cambe, Normandy, France.

269. Generalleutnant Franz KARL

Karl was born on 1 January 1888 in Glonn. He fought in the First World War and was awarded the Iron Cross 1st and 2nd Class (1914). Glonn was commander of the 263rd Infantry Division when he was awarded the Knight's Cross on 5 August 1940. He died on 18 March 1964 in Munich.

270. Generalleutnant Georg LINDEMANN

Lindemann was born on 8 March 1884 in Osterburg. He fought in the First World War and was awarded the Iron Cross 1st and 2nd Class (1914). Lindemann was awarded the Iron Cross 1st and 2nd Class (1939) after the fall of Poland. He commanded the 36th Infantry Division during the French campaign and was awarded the Knight's Cross on 5 August 1940.

Lindemann took part in the invasion of Russia as commander of 'L' Army Corps, striking towards Leningrad. On 21 August 1942, he was awarded the Oak Leaves but was relieved of his command in July 1944 and placed on the reserve list. Lindemann ended the war as commander of Denmark. He died on 25 September 1963 and is buried in Ahldorf Friedhof, Abt 2, Grave 13–14, Freudenstadt, Baden-Württemberg. His cousin, Ernst Lindemann, was also awarded the Knight's Cross.

271. Generalleutnant Friedrich MATERNA

Materna was born on 21 June 1885 in Hof, Austria-Hungary. He fought in the Austro-Hungarian Army during the First World War. Materna was commander of Infantry Division 45 when he was awarded the Knight's Cross on 5 August 1940. He went on to command XX Army Corps and Military District XVII before being retired in 1944. Materna died on 11 November 1946 and is buried in Zentralfriedhof, Vienna.

272. Oberst Günther ANGERN

Angern was born on 5 March 1893 in Kolberg. He fought in the First World War and was awarded the Iron Cross 1st and 2nd Class (1914). Angern fought in Poland, being awarded the Iron Cross 1st and 2nd Class (1939).

In France, he commanded the 11th Rifle Brigade and was awarded the Knight's Cross on 5 August 1940. Angern fought in Russia and committed suicide at Stalingrad on 2 February 1943; he has no known grave.

273. Oberst Gustav FEHN

Fehn was born on 21 February 1892 in Nuremberg. He fought in the First World War and was awarded the Iron Cross 1st and 2nd Class (1914). Fehn was awarded the Iron Cross 1st and 2nd Class (1939) after the fall of Poland. He was commander of Rifle Regiment 33 when he was awarded the Knight's Cross on 5 August 1940.

Fehn was the last commander of the Africa Corps, with whom he was wounded. In January 1943, he sent a final message to the High Command: 'Ammunition Exhausted. Equipment destroyed. In accordance with orders received, the Africa Corps has fought to the last man'. After recovery, he commanded LXXXVI Panzer Corps from July to August 1943, and XXI Army Corps from October 1943 until July 1944. He ended the war in the Balkans fighting partisans. Fehn was shot without trial on 5 June 1945 by partisans and has no known grave.

274. Oberst Walter NEUMANN-SILKOW

Neumann-Silkow was born on 10 April 1894 in Gross-Silkow. He fought in the First World War and was awarded the Iron Cross 1st and 2nd Class (1914). Neumann-Silkow was commander of the 8th Rifle Brigade when he was awarded the Knight's Cross on 5 August 1940. He died of wounds on 9 December 1941 and is buried in the German War Cemetery, Tobruk, Libya.

275. Oberst Hermann RECKNAGEL

Recknagel was born on 18 July 1892 in Strauehmühle. He fought in the First World War and was awarded the Iron Cross 1st and 2nd Class (1914). He was awarded the Iron Cross 1st and 2nd Class (1939) after the fall of Poland, and he received the Knight's Cross on 5 August 1940.

Recknagel fought in Russia, and as commander of the 111th Infantry Division, he was awarded the Oak Leaves on 6 November 1943. Given command of XXXXII Army Corps, he was awarded the Swords on 23 October 1944. Recknagel was killed by partisans on 23 January 1945 and is believed to be buried in the Laurahütte German War Cemetery (as unknown), Siemianowice Śląskie, near Bytom, Poland.

276. Oberstleutnant Hans-Ulrich BACK

Back was born on 26 August 1896 in Saarbrücken. He fought in the First World War and was awarded the Iron Cross 1st and 2nd Class (1914). Back took part in the Polish and French campaigns, being awarded the Iron Cross 1st and 2nd Class (1939). The Knight's Cross followed on 5 August 1940 for his command of Rifle Regiment 2. He died on 14 February 1976 in Hagen, North Rhine-Westphalia.

277. Oberstleutnant Julius von BERNUTH

Von Bernuth was born on 12 August 1897 in Metz. He fought in the First World War and was awarded the Iron Cross 1st and 2nd Class (1914). Von Bernuth was chief of General Staff of XV Army Corps when he was awarded the Knight's Cross on 5 August 1940. He died on 12 July 1942 when his aircraft exploded near Ssoehkranaja, Russia, and has no known grave.

278. Oberstleutnant Hans HECKER

Hecker was born on 26 February 1895 in Duisburg-Meiderich. He fought in the First World War and was awarded the Iron Cross 1st and 2nd Class (1914). Hecker fought in Poland and France as commander of Motorised Pioneer Battalion 29 when he was awarded the Knight's Cross on 5 August

1940. He also saw action in Russia, Africa, and Italy. Hecker died on 1 May 1979 in Hannoversch, Münden, Lower Saxony.

279. Oberstleutnant Karl LÖWRICK

Löwrick was born on 8 November 1894 in Podlechen. He fought in the First World War and was awarded the Iron Cross 1st and 2nd Class (1914). Löwrick was commander of III Battalion, Infantry Regiment 272, when he was awarded the Knight's Cross on 5 August 1940. The Oak Leaves followed on 17 May 1943. He died in an accident near Pillau on 28 March 1945 and has no known grave.

280. Oberstleutnant Karl-August POCHAT

Pochat was born on 28 October 1897 in Königsberg. He was commander of Reconnaissance Battalion 29 when he was awarded the Knight's Cross on 5 August 1940. Pochat was killed in action on 30 June 1942 and is buried in the German War Cemetery, Kharkov, Ukraine.

281. Oberstleutnant Josef RINTELEN

Rintelen was born on 7 March 1897 in Esch. He fought in the First World War and was awarded the Iron Cross 1st and 2nd Class (1914). Rintelen was commander of Infantry Regiment 478 when he was awarded the Knight's Cross on 5 August 1940. He died on 14 July 1981 and is buried in Ohlsdorf Friedhof, AA22, 156-157, 162, Fuhlsbüttler Strasse, Hamburg.

282. Oberstleutnant Walter RÖDLICH

Rödlich was born on 19 May 1896 in Eilenburg. He was commander of II Battalion, Panzer Regiment 4, when he was awarded the Knight's Cross on 5 August 1940. Rödlich died accidentally at Golovisce, Russia, on 23 July 1942 and has no known grave.

283. Oberstleutnant Franz SCHEIDIES

Scheidies was born on 22 February 1890 in Gross Pelken. He fought in the First World War. Scheidies was awarded the Iron Cross 1st and 2nd Class in

1939 and the Knight's Cross on 5 August 1940 as commander of Fortress Infantry Regiment 'C'.

He took part in the invasion of Russia and was awarded the Oak Leaves on 31 December 1941 while commanding Infantry Regiment 22. Scheidies was shot dead by a Russian sniper near Gluschitza on 7 April 1942 and has no known grave.

284. Oberstleutnant Hans TRAUT

Traut was born on 25 January 1895 in Saargemünd. He fought in the First World War and was awarded the Iron Cross 1st and 2nd Class (1914). Traut fought in Poland and was awarded the Iron Cross 1st and 2nd Class (1939). He was commander of I Battalion, Infantry Regiment 90, when he was awarded the Knight's Cross on 5 August 1940.

Traut took part in the invasion of Russia and was awarded the Oak Leaves on 23 January 1942. He was recommended for the Swords in December 1943, but it was turned down. Traut was captured by the Russians in 1944 and sentenced to twenty-five years' hard labour. He was released in 1955. Traut died on 9 December 1974 and is believed to be buried in Waldfriedhof, Darmstadt, Hesse.

285. *Major* Lothar BERGER

Berger was born on 31 December 1900 in Halberstadt. He fought in the First World War and was awarded the Iron Cross 1st and 2nd Class (1914). Berger took part in the Polish campaign and was awarded the Iron Cross 1st and 2nd Class (1939). In France, he was commander of III Battalion, Infantry Regiment 84, when he was awarded the Knight's Cross on 5 August 1940.

Berger fought in Italy and Russia, where he was awarded the Oak Leaves on 28 March 1945. He was captured by the Russians but handed over to the British who released him in 1946. Berger died on 5 November 1971 and is buried in the Evangelical Lutheran Friedhof, Bad Schwartau, Schleswig-Holstein.

286. *Major* Franz-Xaver RAUCHEISEN

Raucheisen was born on 17 October 1889 in Baar. He was commander of I Battalion, Infantry Regiment 131, when he was awarded the Knight's Cross on 5 August 1940. Raucheisen was killed accidently on 11 January 1941 and is buried in the German War Cemetery, Block 5, Row 24, Grave 860, Berneuil, near Saintes, Aquitaine, France.

287. *Major* Hans SCHÜLER

Schüler was born on 1 August 1885 in Thorn. He was commander of Infantry Regiment 633 when he was awarded the Knight's Cross on 5 August 1940. Schüler was killed in action on 10 December 1944 and has no known grave.

288. *Major* Adolf SEITZ

Seitz was born on 24 August 1891 in Munich. He was commander of II Battalion, Mountain Jäger Regiment 99, when he was awarded the Knight's Cross on 5 August 1940. Seitz died on 10 November 1945 in Heidelberg, Baden-Württemberg, as a prisoner of the Americans.

289. *Hauptmann* Alexander von ARENTSCHILDT

Von Arentschildt was born on 27 April 1911 in Berlin. He fought in Poland, for which he was awarded the Iron Cross 1st and 2nd Class. For action in France, he was awarded the Knight's Cross on 5 August 1940 as a company commander in Panzer Battalion 67. Von Arentschildt died on 22 June 1999 in Alfeld, Bavaria.

290. *Oberleutnant* Wilhelm RENNER

Renner was born on 17 April 1915 in Stuttgart. He was a company commander in Rifle Regiment 2 when he was awarded the Knight's Cross on 5 August 1940. Renner died on 3 June 1982 and is buried in Hergensweiler Friedhof, Bavaria.

291. *Oberleutnant* Walter SCHEUNEMANN

Scheunemann was born on 26 March 1909 in Bankau. He fought in Poland and France, where he was awarded the Knight's Cross on 5 August 1940 as a company commander in Infantry Regiment 272.

Scheunemann also fought in Russia, where he was awarded the Oak Leaves on 6 March 1943 as *hauptmann* and commander of I Battalion, Infantry Regiment 272. He died on 29 December 1949 and is buried in Stadtfriedhof, Göttingen, Lower Saxony.

292. Leutnant Karl-Heinz NOAK

Noak was born on 30 July 1916 in Berlin. He fought in Poland, being awarded the Iron Cross 2nd Class. Noak also fought in France and was awarded the Iron Cross 1st Class in June 1940 and the Knight's Cross on 5 August 1940.

He took part in the invasion of Russia, for which he was awarded the Oak Leaves on 16 January 1941. Noak fought in Normandy and the Ruhr Pocket. He died on 14 November 1978 and is believed to be buried in Hauptfriedhof, Koblenz, Rhineland-Palatinate.

293. *Kapitänleutnant* Fritz-Julius LEMP

Lemp was born on 19 December 1913 in Tsingtao, China. When war was declared on 3 September 1939, Lemp was at sea commanding *U-30* and received Dönitz's signal 'Begin Hostilities against England immediately'. That night, he sighted a troop transport running without lights and torpedoed it. It was the liner *Athenia* with 1,428 passengers on board, of which 128 died in the sinking. For this act, Lemp was disciplined on his return to base.

During December, he sank four ships and torpedoed a steamer and the British battleship *Barham*. He had more success during a June–July 1940 patrol and was awarded the Knight's Cross on 14 August 1940. On 21 November 1940, Lemp commissioned *U-110* and sailed on his first patrol on 9 March 1941, sinking two ships and torpedoing two more. His second patrol began on 15 April 1941, and when he made contact with convoy OB318 in the Atlantic, he torpedoed two ships on 9 May 1941. The same day, his boat was attacked by the destroyers HMS *Bulldog* and *Broadway*. *U-110* was damaged and abandoned, but when the British sent a boarding party, Lemp swam back to scuttle it. It is believed that he was killed by a burst of machine-gun fire. However, the British have always maintained that he drowned. The U-boat was captured.

294. *Kapitänleutnant* Heinrich LIEBE

Liebe was born on 29 January 1908 in Gotha. He was commander of *U-2* from 1936 to 1937 and an instructor at Kiel. On 24 October 1938, he commissioned *U-38* and was at sea on 3 September 1939, sinking two large British ships. One of his largest successes was the 14,172-ton British *Highland Patriot*. He was awarded the Knight's Cross on 14 August 1940 while at sea. Liebe sank ships from convoys SC7 and HX79. In May and June 1941, he sank eight ships (a total tonnage of 47,279) off the coast of Freetown.

On 10 June 1941, he was awarded the Oak Leaves. Liebe became an official in the OKM in August 1944, where he stayed until the end of the war. He sank a total of thirty-two ships (168,506 tons). Liebe died on 27 July 1997 in Eisenach, Thuringia.

295. *Oberleutnant* zur See Kurt FIMMEN

Fimmen was born on 4 May 1911 in Wittenberg. He was commander of torpedo boat *S-26* in S-Boat Flotilla 1 when he was awarded the Iron Cross 2nd Class in May and the 1st Class in June, followed by the Knight's Cross on 14 August 1940. Fimmen died on 6 May 2001 and is buried in Neuer Friedhof, Nordhorn, Lower Saxony.

296. *Oberleutnant* zur See Götz Freiherr von MIRBACH

Freiherr von Mirbach was born on 12 September 1915 in Berlin. He took part in the Spanish Civil War. Von Mirbach was commander of *S-21* in S-Boat Flotilla 9 when he was awarded the Iron Cross 1st and 2nd Class in April and May 1940, as well as the Knight's Cross on 14 August 1940.

He was commander of S-Boat Flotilla 9 when he was awarded the Oak Leaves on 14 June 1944. Von Mirbach was part of the 1952 German Olympic sailing team. He died on 6 August 1968 and is buried in Ohlsdorf Friedhof, Fuhlsbüttler Strasse, Hamburg.

297. Generalleutnant Freidrich-Wilhelm von CHAPPUIS

Von Chappuis was born on 13 September 1886 in Schubin. He fought in the First World War, being awarded the Iron Cross 1st and 2nd Class (1914). Von Chappuis took part in the Polish campaign and was awarded the Iron Cross 1st and 2nd Class (1939). He commanded the 15th Infantry Division in the French campaign and was awarded the Knight's Cross on 15 August 1940.

Von Chappuis also fought in Russia, but he killed himself on 27 August 1942 and is buried in Charlottenburg Friedhof, Trakehnerallee, Berlin.

298. Generalleutnant Eccard Freiherr von GABLENZ

Freiherr von Gablenz was born on 26 January 1891 in Königsberg. He fought in the First World War and was awarded the Iron Cross 1st and 2nd Class (1914).

Von Gablenz took part in the Polish and French campaigns and was awarded the Knight's Cross on 15 August 1940 as commander of the 7th Infantry Divison.

He fought in Russia and was flown out of the Stalingrad pocket in December 1942. Von Gablenz went on to fight in Italy where he was captured by the British. He died on 17 December 1978 and is buried in Waldfriedhof, Rheinbach, North Rhine-Westphalia.

299. Generalleutnant Mauritz (von?) WIKTORIN

Wiktorin was born on 23 August 1883 in Hainburg, Austria-Hungary. He fought in the First World War and was awarded the Iron Cross 2nd Class (1914). He took part in the Polish and French campaigns. Wiktorin was awarded the Knight's Cross on 15 August 1940 as commander of the 20th Infantry Division. He fought in Russia and was discharged from the Wehrmacht in November 1944 due to age. Wiktorin died on 16 August 1956 in Nuremberg.

300. Generalmajor Willibald Freiherr von LANGERMANN und ERLENCAMP

Freiherr von Langermann und Erlencamp was born on 29 March 1890 in Karlsruhe. He fought in the First World War and was awarded the Iron Cross 1st and 2nd Class (1914). Von Langermann und Erlencamp took part in the French campaign as commander of the 29th Infantry Division and was awarded the Iron Cross 1st and 2nd Class (1939) in May and June 1940, and the Knight's Cross on 15 August 1940.

He took part in the invasion of Russia, where he was awarded the Oak Leaves on 17 February 1942. Von Langermann und Erlencamp was killed in action near Storoshewoje, Russia, on 3 October 1942 and has no known grave.

301. Generalmajor Friedrich-Wilhelm von ROTHKIRCH und PANTHEN

Von Rothkirch und Panthen was born on 16 February 1884 in Darmstadt. He fought in the First World War and was awarded the Iron Cross 1st and 2nd Class (1914). Von Rothkirch und Panthen took part in the Polish and French campaigns and was awarded the Knight's Cross on 15 August 1940 as commander of the 13th Infantry Division. He retired from active duty in November 1943 and died on 24 December 1953; he is buried in Hauptfriedhof, Am Stadion 1, Trier, Rhineland-Palatinate.

302. Generalmajor Walther von SEYDLITZ-KURZBACH

Von Seydlitz-Kurzbach was born on 22 August 1888 in Eppendorf. He fought in the First World War and was awarded the Iron Cross 1st and 2nd Class (1914). Von Seydlitz-Kurzbach was commander of the 12th Infantry Division when he was awarded the Iron Cross 1st and 2nd Class in May 1940 and the Knight's Cross on 15 August 1940.

He took part in the invasion of Russia and was awarded the Oak Leaves on 31 December 1941. Trapped in Stalingrad, he fled under German fire to the Russians lines. He was used by them to help others to follow him, but after the war, the Russians tried him for war crimes and sentenced him to twenty-five years. Von Seydlitz-Kurzbach was released in 1955. He died on 28 April 1976 and is buried in Riensberg Friedhof, Feld R, Grave 175, Bremen.

303. Generalmajor Rudolf SINTZENICH

Sintzenich was born on 13 July 1889 in Munich. He fought in the First World War and was awarded the Iron Cross 1st and 2nd Class (1914). Sintzenich took part in the Polish and French campaigns and was awarded the Knight's Cross on 15 August 1940 as commander of the 33rd Infantry Division. He also fought in the Balkans and Russia. Sintzenich died on 24 December 1948 and is buried in Waldfriedhof, Munich.

304. SS-Oberführer Georg KEPPLER

Keppler was born on 7 May 1894 in Mainz. He fought in the First World War and was awarded the Iron Cross 1st and 2nd Class (1914). Keppler commanded SS-*Regiment Der Führer* during the campaign in the West, for which he was awarded the Knight's Cross on 15 August 1940.

He saw action during the early stages of the invasion of Russia but was taken ill with a brain tumour in late 1941. This kept him away from the front until April 1942 when he returned as commander of the 2nd SS-Panzer Division. But in February 1943, under advice from his doctor, he assumed a number of admin roles. Keppler once again returned to active duty and saw action in the later stages of the Normandy fighting before being sent to Russia. He surrendered to US forces on 22 May 1945. Keppler died on 16 June 1966 and is buried in Ohlsdorf Friedhof, Fuhlsbüttler Strasse, Hamburg.

305. SS-Oberführer Felix STEINER

Steiner was born on 23 May 1896 in Ebenrode. He fought in the First World War, being awarded the Iron Cross 1st and 2nd Class (1914). He took part in the attack on Poland, for which he is best known for capturing the fort at Modlin with over 1,200 men. For this, he was awarded the Iron Cross 1st and 2nd Class (1939). In the campaign in the West, his men broke through the Weygand Line and penetrated deep into enemy territory; for this, he was awarded the Knight's Cross on 15 August 1940.

In Russia, he commanded the SS-Viking Division and was awarded the Oak Leaves on 23 December 1942 and the Swords on 10 August 1944. Steiner's men were often referred to as the European-SS, being largely from the Netherlands, Denmark, and Sweden. In 1945, he was ordered by Hitler to break the encirclement of Berlin, but knowing the futility of such an order, he refused to sacrifice his men. Steiner died on 12 May 1966 and is buried in Perlacher Forst Friedhof, Plot 201, Row A, Grave 16, Munich.

306. Oberst Rudolf von BÜNAU

Von Bünau was born on 19 August 1890 in Stuttgart. He fought in the First World War and was awarded the Iron Cross 1st and 2nd Class (1914). Von Bünau took part in the Polish campaign, being awarded the Iron Cross 1st and 2nd Class (1939), and the French campaign, for which he was awarded the Knight's Cross on 15 August 1940.

He also fought in Russia and Austria where he was awarded the Oak Leaves on 5 March 1945. Von Bünau died on 14 January 1962 and is buried in Waldfriedhof, Aht 7H, Grave 5061, Stuttgart, Baden-Württemberg. His two sons, Rudolf and Günther, were both killed in action; Rudolf was also awarded the Knight's Cross.

307. Oberst Kurt-Jürgen Freiherr von LÜTZOW

Freiherr von Lützow was born on 7 August 1892 in Marienwerder. He fought in the First World War and was awarded the Iron Cross 1st and 2nd Class (1914). Von Lützow took part in the Polish campaign and was awarded the Iron Cross 1st and 2nd Class (1939). He also fought in France and was awarded the Knight's Cross on 15 August 1940 as commander of Infantry Regiment 89.

Von Lützow also fought in Russia, where he was awarded the Oak Leaves on 21 October 1941. He died on 20 July 1961 and is buried in Stadtfriedhof (headstone removed), Seelhorst, Hanover.

308. Oberst Walter WESSEL

Wessel was born on 21 April 1892 in Lautenthal. He fought in the First World War and was awarded the Iron Cross 1st and 2nd Class (1914). Wessel also took part in the Polish and French campaigns and was awarded the Knight's Cross on 15 August 1940 as commander of Motorised Infantry Regiment 15.

Wessel was awarded the Oak Leaves while in Russia on 17 February 1942. He later severed in Italy, where he was killed in a car crash near Morano on 20 July 1943. Wessel is buried in Hauptfriedhof (military section) Block 57, Grave 210, Tannenkeckerweg 6, Kassel, Hesse. He was responsible for the massacre at Ciepielów, Poland.

309. Oberstleutnant Karl EIBL

Eibl was born on 23 July 1891 in Steg Oberdonau, Austria-Hungary. He fought in the First World War in the Austro-Hungarian army. In the Polish campaign, Eibl was awarded the Iron Cross 1st and 2nd Class (1939). He fought in France and the Low Countries, and for the defeat of an enemy brigade and taking important territory near Chuignolles, he was awarded the Knight's Cross on 15 August 1940.

Eibl fought in Russia, and for his successful command, he was awarded the Oak Leaves on 31 December 1941. He was awarded the Swords on 19 December 1942 during heavy fighting north of Stalingrad. Now in command of XXIV Panzer Corps, Eibl was badly wounded in the legs on 21 January 1943 when his HQ vehicle was mistaken for Russians by an Italian unit. He underwent emergency amputation but died a few hours later; Eibl is buried at Nagornoje, Ukraine, and his remains are awaiting transfer to a German war cemetery.

310. Oberstleutnant Henning SCHÖNFELD

Schönfeld was born on 19 May 1894 in Stettin. He fought in the First World War, being awarded the Iron Cross 1st and 2nd Class (1914). Schönfeld took part in the Polish campaign and was awarded the Iron Cross 1st and 2nd Class (1939). In France, he was commander of Reconnaissance Battalion 20 when he was awarded the Knight's Cross on 15 August 1940.

Schönfeld fought in Italy, but he was retired from the army in 1944. He was captured by the British but released in 1947. Schönfeld died on 7 March 1958 and is buried in Stadtfriedhof, Partenkirchen, Bavaria.

311. Oberstleutnant Paul VELKE

Velke was born on 19 November 1890 in Velpke. He was commander of Pioneer Battalion 45 when he was awarded the Knight's Cross on 15 August 1940. Velke was killed in action on 28 July 1942 and is buried in the German War Cemetery (as unknown), Rossoschka, Volgograd, Russia.

312. Oberstleutnant Thomas-Emil von WICKEDE

Von Wickede was born on 23 April 1893 in Verden an der Aller. He fought in the First World War and was awarded the Iron Cross 1st and 2nd Class (1914). Von Wickede fought in Poland and France as commander of Infantry Regiment 4 and was awarded the Knight's Cross on 15 August 1940.

He also fought in Russia, but he was killed with Karl Eglseer, Eduard Dietl, and Franz Rossi when his aircraft crashed on 23 June 1944 near Hartberg, Austria; Wickede has no known grave.

313. Major Hans KRATZENBERG

Kratzenberg was born on 9 October 1890 in Wenzlow. He was commander of III Battalion, Rifle Regiment 3, when he was awarded the Knight's Cross on 15 August 1940. Kratzenberg died on 24 January 1976 and is buried in German War Cemetery, Bad Oldesloe, Schleswig-Holstein.

314. *Major* Gerhard WENDENBURG

Wendenburg was born on 23 October 1890 in Stuttgart. He was commander of Panzer Battalion 67 when he was awarded the Knight's Cross on 15 August 1940. Wendenburg died on 9 March 1952 and is buried in Alter Friedhof, Bonn.

315. *Major* Hermann-Eberhard WILDERMUTH

Wildermuth was born on 23 October 1890 in Stuttgart. He fought in the First World War and was awarded the Iron Cross 1st and 2nd Class (1914). Wildermuth was commander of II Battalion, Infantry Regiment 272, when he was awarded the Knight's Cross on 15 August 1940 for the French campaign.

He also took part in the fighting in the Balkans, Russia, and Italy. In August 1944, he was appointed commander of Fortress Le Havre, but this fell into British hands in September. After the war, he went into politics, and his greatest success was the First Housing Act in which more than 4 million homes were built in seven years. Wildermuth died on 9 March 1952 and is buried in Stadtfriedhof, Gmelinstrasse 20, Tübingen, Baden-Württemberg.

316. *Hauptmann* Theodor FRIEDMANN

Friedmann was born on 20 September 1903 in Fürth. He was commander of I Battalion, Artillery Regiment 156, when he was awarded the Knight's Cross on 15 August 1940. Friedmann died of wounds near Semenovka, Russia, on 10 January 1942 and has no known grave.

317. *Hauptmann* Heinrich SCHWARTING

Schwarting was born on 8 September 1888 in Lintel. He was a company commander in Infantry Regiment 154 when he was awarded the Knight's Cross on 15 August 1940. Schwarting was killed in action on 26 August 1941 and is buried in the German War Cemetery, Narva, Estonia.

318. *Oberleutnant* Hans MÖLLER

Möller was born in Berlin on 30 June 1912. He was *aide-de-camp* in the 15th Infantry Division when he was awarded the Knight's Cross on 15 August 1940. Möller died on 18 December 1999 in Langen, Hesse.

319. Leutnant Edwin-Oskar-Heinrich DIETZ

Dietz was born on 4 July 1914 in Dortmund. He was a platoon leader in Rifle Regiment 11 when he was awarded the Knight's Cross on 15 August 1940. Dietz died of wounds on 16 July 1941 and is buried at Bila Tserkva, Ukraine; he is waiting transfer to a German war cemetery.

320. Leutnant Fritz STEGER

Steger was born on 10 January 1915 in Pechbrunn. He was a platoon leader in Motorised Infantry Regiment 20 when he was awarded the Knight's Cross on 15 August 1940. Steger died on 20 March 2003 and is believed to be buried in Waldfriedhof, Munich.

321. *Major* Ludwig SCHULZ

Schulz was born on 4 August 1896 in Lissa. He fought in the First World War and was awarded the Iron Cross 1st and 2nd Class (1914). Schulz was a group commander in Bomber Wing 76 when he was awarded the Iron Cross 1st and 2nd Class (1939) in May 1940 and the Knight's Cross on 16 August 1940.

He was commander of a *Kampfgruppe* in Fortress Breslau when awarded the Oak Leaves on 19 February 1945. Schulz died on 10 December 1966 and is buried in Hauptfriedhof, Zeppelinstrasse, Mülheim, North Rhine-Westphalia.

322. Feldwebel Otto EICHLOFF

Eichloff was born on 19 April 1916 in Willenberg. He was a pilot in Bomber Wing 30 when he was awarded the Knight's Cross on 16 August 1940. Eichloff died on 3 June 1987 in Erding, Bavaria.

323. *Hauptmann* Anton KEIL

Keil was born on 21 October 1910 in Plattling. He was a group commander in Dive Bomber Wing 1 when he was awarded the Knight's Cross on 19 August 1940. Keil was killed in action on 29 August 1941 and is buried in the German War Cemetery, Block 2, Row 3, Grave 116, Kiev, Ukraine.

324. *Hauptmann* Walter RUBENSDÖRFFER

Rubensdörffer was born on 1 August 1910 in Basel. He was a group commander in Erprobungsgruppe 210 when was killed in action on 15 August 1940 and is buried in the German War Cemetery, Block 9, Row 4, Grave 20, Camp Road, Cannock Chase, Staffordshire, England. Rubensdörffer was awarded the Knight's Cross on 20 August 1940.

325. *Hauptmann* Walter OESAU—'Gulle'

Oesau was born on 28 June 1913 in Farnewinkel. He started his military career in the army before transferring to the Luftwaffe in the early 1930s. Oesau fought in the Spanish Civil War, shooting down eight enemy aircraft. In the campaign in the West, he added another five aircraft shot down and was awarded the Iron Cross 1st and 2nd Class. By August 1940, his tally was at twenty, which brought him the awarding of the Knight's Cross on 20 August 1940. By 5 February 1941, Oesau had brought down forty enemy aircraft, for which he was awarded the Oak Leaves the following day.

Moved to the East at the start of that campaign, he soon added to his score, and on 15 July 1941, he was awarded the Swords for shooting down eighty enemy aircraft. On 26 October 1941, with his tally at 100, he was ordered to give up combat flying and posted to the staff. Recalled to combat due to the lack of experienced pilots, he became an expert in shooting down four-engined bombers—shooting down fourteen. Then, on 11 May 1944, with his tally at 127, he was shot down and killed by a P-38 Lightning over St Vith, Belgium. Oesau is buried in Stadtfriedhof, family plot, Feld A, Row 4, Grave 208, Meldorf, Schleswig-Holstein.

326. *Hauptmann* Horst TIETZEN—'Jakob'

Tietzen was born on 19 July 1912 in Arnswalde. He fought in the Spanish Civil War, shooting down seven enemy aircraft. He shot down a French bomber on 20 April 1940 for his first victory of the Second World War. By 25 July 1940, he had increased that to seventeen aircraft shot down, and on 15 August, he shot down three British Hurricanes. Then, on 18 August 1940, with twenty-seven victories to his credit, Tietzen was shot down over the Thames Estuary. His body later washed ashore at Calais. He is buried in the German War Cemetery, Block 17, Row 1, Grave 10, Bourdon, Picardy, France. Tietzen was awarded the Knight's Cross on 20 August 1940.

327. Generalmajor Theodor OSTERKAMP—'Uncle Theo'

Osterkamp was born in Düren on 15 April 1892. He was studying forestry when the war started, and he volunteered for the Naval Flying Corps in August 1914, requesting to be trained as a pilot. However, the need for observers was greater at that time. On completion of his training, he was posted to the Marine Flying Detachment, with whom, for the next two years, he flew reconnaissance missions along the Belgian coast. Osterkamp's success was rewarded with the Iron Cross 2nd Class and a commission to *Leutnant zur See* in June 1916.

The routine of these missions soon started to get to him, and in February 1917, he applied for and was accepted in March for pilot training. On graduating on 14 April, Osterkamp was posted to MFJ I; the same week, he shot down his first enemy aircraft—a Sopwith Camel—while on patrol over Oostkerke. By the end of July, his tally was five, and on 29 August, he was awarded the Iron Cross 1st Class and the Knight's Cross of the Royal Hohenzollern House Order. His sixth victory came on 24 September when he shot down a Spad from *Escadrille* 31. Then, on 15 October 1917, he was given command of MFJ I and promoted to *Oberleutnant zur See*.

While on a solo familiarisation flight in a new Fokker EV monoplane, he was jumped by three Spads; Osterkamp had to bale out of his aircraft, landing behind his own lines. At the beginning of 1918, he spent some time reorganising his unit to make it more efficient, and the results soon started to show. By the end of July, his personal tally had risen to nineteen, and by the end of August, this was at twenty-three. On 2 September 1918, he was awarded the *Pour le Mérite*. His total stood at thirty-two by the war's end. After the Armistice, he, along with Peter Jacobs and Gotthard Sachsenberg, fought the communists in the Baltic.

Osterkamp took part in the FAI International Tourist Plane Contest Challenge in 1930 (finishing eleventh), 1932 (twelfth), and 1934 (fifth). In 1935, he joined the Luftwaffe and was given command of *Jagdfliegerschule* Nr. I in 1939. During the invasion of France, Osterkamp was almost immediately in action, shooting down four enemy aircraft in May and two more during the Battle of Britain (so perhaps his final score should be thirty-eight). For this, he was awarded the Knight's Cross on 22 August 1940. He was appointed commander of fighters in north France and later Sicily, with the rank of *Generalleutnant*. He was very critical of the High Command and the way they were directing the air war, and because of this, he was retired in 1944. It was probably the respect that Luftwaffe pilots and ground crew held for him that prevented a worse fate. He died on 2 January 1975 and is buried in Hauptfriedhof, Baden Baden, Baden-Württemberg.

328. Oberst Max IBEL

Ibel was born on 2 January 1896 in Munich. He fought in the First World War, being awarded the Iron Cross 1st and 2nd Class (1914). Ibel was commander of Fighter Wing 27 during the French campaign and the Battle of Britain, for which he was awarded the Knight's Cross on 22 August 1940. He died on 19 March 1981 and is buried in the Waldfriedhof, Old Section, Feld 96, Row W, Grave 40, Munich.

329. Oberstleutnant Harry von BÜLOW-BOTHKAMP

Von Bülow-Bothkamp was born on 19 November 1897 in Bothkamp. He fought in the First World War in the infantry and as a pilot, shooting down six enemy aircraft, including the British ace Capt. Cecil Clark. Von Bülow-Bothkamp was also awarded the Iron Cross 1st and 2nd Class (1914). He fought in France in 1940, shooting down twelve enemy aircraft—not bad for a man of forty-three years! Von Bülow-Bothkamp also saw action during the Battle of Britain and was awarded the Knight's Cross on 22 August 1940.

He was given command of a night-fighter training unit in September 1940 and commanded it until October 1943. Von Bülow-Bothkamp died on 27 February 1976 and is buried with his two brothers (both killed in the First World War) in the grounds of family ancestral castle at Kirchbarkau, Schleswig-Holstein.

330. *Major* Dietrich Freiherr von MASSENBACH

Freiherr von Massenbach was born on 12 February 1902 in Wreschen. He was a group commander in Bomber Wing 4 when he was awarded the Knight's Cross on 27 August 1940. Von Massenbach died on 22 July 1973 in Seeheim-Jugenheim, Hesse.

331. *Oberleutnant* Helmut WICK

Wick was born on 5 August 1915 in Mannheim. He missed the Polish campaign but shot down twelve aircraft over France in 1939–40 and was awarded the Iron Cross 1st and 2nd Class. His tally rose during the Battle of Britain, and with twenty enemy aircraft to his credit, he was awarded the Knight's Cross on 27 August 1940.

By 5 October 1940, he had doubled his score to forty, and the next day, he was awarded the Oak Leaves. On 28 November 1940, he shot down two aircraft over England, bringing his total to fifty-six, more than Galland (fifty-two) and Mölders (fifty-four). On the return journey to France, he was attacked by Fg Off. John Dundas and badly shot up; Wick baled out just as his Me 109 blew up. He landed in the Channel but was never seen again.

332. Korvettenkapitän Hans-Rudolf RÖSING

Rösing was born on 28 September 1905 in Wilhelmshaven. At the outbreak of war, he was commander of the 5th U-Boat Flotilla in Kiel. Rösing took over command of *U-48* when her captain was taken ill and sailed on his first war patrol on 26 May 1940. He sank seven ships between 6 and 20 June, and another was damaged. His second patrol began on 7 August, during which he sank five ships, including the Swedish *Hedrun*. Two more were torpedoed. He returned to Lorient on 28 August 1940 and was awarded the Knight's Cross the next day.

Dönitz then sent him to the staff of the commander of Italian submarines, Admiral Perona, in an effort to achieve better co-operation. From 1942 until the end of the war, he was commander of U-Boats West. He died on 16 December 2004 and is buried in Parkfriedhof, Eichhofstrasse 56, Kiel, Schleswig-Holstein.

333. *Kapitänleutnant* Fritz FRAUENHEIM

Frauenheim was born in Berlin on 9 March 1912. He transferred to the U-boat service in April 1939 and served in the Spanish Civil War. Under his command, *U-21* went into action at the very start of the war. He laid mines in the Firth of Forth—HMS *Belfast* struck one of these and was badly damaged—and he also sank five ships. On 11 March 1940, he commissioned *U-101*, and on his first patrol, he sank seven ships, including the British 13,212-ton *Wellington Star*. He was awarded the Knight's Cross on 29 August 1940. On his next patrol on 1 September, he sank the *Efploia* in the Atlantic. On his fourth patrol, he sank four ships from convoy SC 7.

In September 1941, Frauenheim took command of the 23rd U-Boat Flotilla in Salamis. From May 1942 until July 1943, he led the 29th U-Boat Flotilla in La Spezia/Toulon. His last command was as chief-of-staff of the admiral in charge of special assault units. He died on 28 September 1969 in Hamburg.

334. *Hauptmann* Hans-Karl MAYER

Mayer was born on 9 March 1911 in Roufach. He fought in Spain with the Condor Legion, shooting down eight aircraft. Mayer shot down his first enemy aircraft of the war on 5 November 1939, a French Potez. He shot down eight more during the campaign in the West, including five on 14 May 1940.

During the Battle of Britain, Meyer shot down two Hurricanes on 12 August, and by 25 August, his score was at fifteen, including two aces. He was awarded the Knight's Cross on 3 September 1940. Then, on 17 October, with his score at thirty-nine, Mayer was shot down over the English Channel and is buried in the German War Cemetery (New Cemetery), Block O, Grave 405, Aerodrome Road, Hawkinge, near Folkestone, Kent, England.

335. Unteroffizier Gerhard HEIN

Hein was born on 9 July 1916 in Klein Paniow. He fought in France and was awarded the Iron Cross 1st and 2nd Class in June and the Knight's Cross on 3 September 1940. Hein also fought in Russia and was awarded the Oak Leaves on 6 September 1942 as *Leutnant* and a company commander in Infantry Regiment 209. In December 1944, he took part in the Ardennes Offensive. Hein died on 6 June 2008 in Harrislee, Schleswig-Holstein.

336. General Walter HEITZ

Heitz was born on 8 December 1878 in Berlin. He fought in the First World War and was awarded the Iron Cross 1st and 2nd Class (1914). Heitz fought in Poland, for which he was awarded the Iron Cross 2nd Class (1939), and France, for which he was awarded the Iron Cross 1st Class (1939) in May and the Knight's Cross on 4 September 1940.

Heitz commanded the VIII Army Corps in Russia and was awarded the Oak Leaves on 21 December 1942, but he was taken prisoner at Stalingrad. He died from cancer on 9 February 1944 and is buried in the German War Cemetery, Section 1, Grave 77, Krasnogorsk, Russia.

337. General Joachim von KORTZFLEISCH

Von Kortzfleisch was born on 3 January 1890 in Braunschweig. He fought in the First World War and was awarded the Iron Cross 1st amd 2nd Class (1914). Von Kortzfleisch was commander of XI Army Corps when he was awarded the Knight's Cross on 4 September 1940.

For most of the remainder of the war, Von Kortzfleisch was commander of the Defence Group III (Berlin). He was killed in actionon 20 April 1945 and is buried in the German War Cemetery, Feld A, Grave 294, Schulstrasse, Breuna, Hesse.

338. Oberst Gustav SCHMIDT

Schmidt was born on 24 April 1894 in Karsdorf. He fought in the First World War, being awarded the Iron Cross 1st and 2nd Class (1914). Schmidt fought in Poland, for which he was awarded the Iron Cross 1st and 2nd Class, and Belgium and France, for which he was awarded the Knight's Cross on 4 September 1940.

He took part in the invasion of Russia, seeing action at Minsk, Moscow, and Kursk. Schmidt was awarded the Oak Leaves on 6 March 1943, but he committed suicide on 7 August 1943 near Berezovka to avoid being captured by the Russians. He is believed to be buried in the German War Cemetery (as unknown), Kharkov, Ukraine.

339. Oberstleutnant Bruno GERLOCH

Gerloch was born on 11 November 1890 in Teschen, Austria-Hungary. He fought in the First World War. Gerloch took part in the Polish and French campaigns and was awarded the Knight's Cross on 4 September 1940 as commander of Artillery Regiment 90. He went on to fight in Russia and Normandy. Gerloch died on 7 September 1954 and is buried in Zentralfriedhof, Vienna.

340. Oberstleutnant Wolf HAGEMANN

Hagemann was born on 20 July 1898 in Glashütte. He fought in the First World War and was awarded the Iron Cross 1st and 2nd Class (1914). Hagemann fought in Poland, for which he was awarded the Iron Cross 2nd Class, and Norway, for which he was awarded the Iron Cross 1st Class and the Knight's Cross on 4 September 1940. He took part in the invasion of Russia and was awarded the Oak Leaves on 4 June 1944. Hagemann died on 12 September 1983 and is believed to be buried in St Nikolaus Friedhof, Murnau, Bavaria.

341. Oberstleutnant Erich Freiherr von SECKENDORFF

Freiherr von Seckendorff was born on 21 September 1897 in Görz, Austria-Hungary. He fought in the First World War, being awarded the Iron Cross 1st and 2nd Class (1914). Von Seckendorff fought in Poland and France, where he was awarded the Knight's Cross on 4 September 1940.

He took part in the invasion of Russia, seeing action at Moscow and Leningrad. Von Seckendorff was killed in action near Lagarde, France, on 23 September 1944. He is buried in the village cemetery, Obernzenn, Bavaria.

342. Oberstleutnant Richard von WERDER

Von Werder was born on 22 May 1897 in Uchte. He was commander of II Battalion, Infantry Regiment 102, when he was awarded the Knight's Cross on 4 September 1940. Von Werder died on 28 February 1984 in Berlin.

343. *Major* Arthur HAUSSELS

Haussels was born on 4 February 1895 in Glauchau. He was commander of II Battalion, Mountain Jäger Regiment 139, when he was awarded the Knight's Cross on 4 September 1940. Haussels died of wounds on 13 February 1943 and is buried in the German War Cemetery, Block 16, Grave 1037, Cassino, Italy.

344. *Major* Ernst-Wilhelm HOFFMANN

Hoffmann was born on 27 September 1904 in Nuremberg. He fought in Poland and France and was awarded the Knight's Cross on 4 September 1940. Hoffmann also fought in Russia; he was awarded the Oak Leaves on 9 June 1944 as commander of *Panzergrenadier* Regiment 12. He died on 27 August 1994 and is buried in Gräfelfing Friedhof, Bavaria.

345. *Major* Albrecht LANZ

Lanz was born on 7 September 1891 in Entringen. He was commander of I Battalion, Infantry Regiment 396, when he was awarded the Knight's Cross on 4 September 1940. Lanz died form wounds on 27 January 1942 and is buried at Orša, Belarus; his remains are awaiting transfer to a German war cemetery.

346. *Major* Johannes MEDER

Meder was born on 28 May 1902 in Babilon. He was commander of III Battalion, Infantry Regiment 19, when he was awarded the Knight's Cross on 4 September 1940. Meder died of wounds near Dimitrovsk, Russia, on 7 April 1943 and has no known grave.

347. SS-Sturmbannführer Fritz WITT

Witt was born on 27 May 1908 in Hohenlimburg. He was one of the original 120 members of the *Leibstandarte*-SS Adolf Hitler when it was formed. Witt took part in the Polish campaign and was awarded the Iron Cross 2nd Class on 19 September 1939 followed by the 1st Class six days later. Now a battalion commander, he fought in the Netherlands and France in 1940 with considerable *élan*. For this, he was awarded the Knight's Cross on 4 September 1940.

Witt was awarded the Oak Leaves on 1 March 1943 for action in Russia. When the *Hitlerjugend* division was formed in 1943, Witt was give command of the unit. The division was thrown into the battle for Normandy in June 1944, and on 16 June, Witt and his staff were playing cards during a lull in the fighting when a barrage of heavy calibre shells fired from a battleship crashed into the German positions. Witt and a number of his staff were killed instantly. On hearing the news of his death, Sepp Dietrich reportedly said: 'That's one of the best gone. Witt was too good a soldier to survive for so long'. He is buried in the German War Cemetery, Block 8, Row 12, Grave 1027, Champigny-St André, Normandy, France.

348. *Major* Hermann ZIMMERMANN

Zimmermann was born on 18 November 1897 in Magdeburg. He was commander of II Battalion, Rifle Regiment 3, when he was awarded the Knight's Cross on 4 September 1940. Zimmermann died on 11 January 1978 and is buried in St Katharina Friedhof, Lensahn, Schleswig-Holstein.

349. *Hauptmann* Erich LÖWE

Löwe was born on 24 September 1906 in Mühlhausen. He took part in the Polish campaign and was awarded the Iron Cross 1st and 2nd Class. Löwe also took part in the campaign in the West and was awarded the Knight's Cross on 4 September 1940. Given command of Heavy Panzer Battalion 65, he was killed in action at Losovka, Russia, on 24 December 1943 and has no known grave. Löwe was awarded the Oak Leaves on 8 February 1944.

350. *Oberleutnant* Helmut BECK-BROICHSITTER

Beck-Broichsitter was born on 30 August 1914 in Kiel. He fought in France and was awarded the Knight's Cross on 4 September 1940 as a company commander in Infantry Regiment 'GD'. Beck-Broichsitter also took part in the invasion of Yugoslavia and Russia. He died on 25 September 2000 in Heist, Schleswig-Holstein.

351. *Oberleutnant* Hans-Günther BETHKE

Bethke was born on 20 May 1913 in Königsberg. He fought in Poland, for which he obtained the Iron Cross 2nd Class in September 1939, and France, for which he was awarded the Iron Cross 1st Class in June 1940, as well as the Knight's Cross on 4 September 1940. Bethke took part in the invasion of Russia and died of wounds on 14 September 1942. He is buried in the German War Cemetery, Block 10 (as unknown), Sologubowka, Russia.

352. *Oberleutnant* Gustav HIPPLER

Hippler was born on 25 July 1903 in Gronau. He was a company commander in Motorised Infantry Regiment 74 when he was awarded the Knight's Cross on 4 September 1940. Hippler died of wounds on 22 August 1942 and is buried at Bryansk, Russia; his remains are awaiting transfer to a German war cemetery.

353. SS-Obersturmführer Fritz VOGT

Vogt was born in Munich on 17 March 1918. He fought in Poland, being awarded the Iron Cross 2nd Class, and in France and the Low Countries. His unit was tasked with capturing a bridge over the River Kleve in the Netherlands. Vogt led the attack, which knocked-out eight bunkers and captured 200 men. Soon afterwards, he spotted a French column; Vogt went into action, managing to take the French by surprise and capture 650 prisoners with his thirty-man unit. Then, on 7 June 1940, he came upon another French column, which he quickly overcame, adding 250 more prisoners to his tally. The Iron Cross 1st Class was immediately awarded, but as news of his exploits became know, it was clear that something more was called for. Vogt was awarded the Knight's Cross on 4 September 1940.

Vogt took part in the invasion of Russia but contracted typhus and was sent home. He returned to the Eastern Front, fighting at Leningrad. At the end of 1944, he was involved in the fighting to relieve Budapest, during which his unit knocked-out fifty-three of 200 enemy tanks destroyed; Vogt personally knocked-out three tanks. For this, he was awarded the Oak Leaves on 16 March 1945. On 3 April 1945, Vogt's car was attacked by aircraft at Fürstenfeld and he was mortally wounded. Karl Ullrich took off his own Oak Leaves and put hung them around Voght's neck to ensure his dying comrade received the honour he deserved. He is buried in the German War Cemetery, Feld 52A, Row 18, Grave 180, Graz/Steiermark, Austria.

354. Oberfeldwebel Hans HINDELANG

Hinelang was born on 16 April 1912 in Trossingen. He was a platoon leader in Motorised Infantry Regiment 'GD' when he was awarded the Knight's

Cross on 4 September 1940. Hinelang died on 1 June 2004 in Trossingen, Baden-Württemberg.

355. SS-Hauptscharführer Ludwig KEPPLINGER

Kepplinger was born on 31 December 1911 in Linz, Austria-Hungary. During the campaign in the West, his section attacked the Dutch fort at Westervoort, which commanded the bridge over the Issel River. They found the bridge blown on their arrival, but with just two men, Kepplinger crossed over the wreckage and attacked the enemy position with grenades; over ninety Dutch soldiers surrendered to him. Another thirty were captured later the same day. Then, acting alone, he attacked more bunkers with grenades, quickly neutralising enemy fire. For this, he was awarded the Iron Cross 1st and 2nd Class and, on 4 September 1940, the Knight's Cross. He was the first NCO in the *Waffen*-SS to be awarded it.

Later, he commanded a tank battalion, and on 6 August 1944, in Villiers-Charlemagne, Normandy, he was in charge of a group of stragglers when the truck they were in was ambushed; Kepplinger, who was in the front, was killed instantly. He is buried in the German War Cemetery, Crypt 68, Grave Chamber 168, Mont-de-Huisnes, Normandy, France.

356. Oberfeldwebel Johann PONGRATZ

Pongratz was born on 19 January 1913 in Furth im Wald. He was a platoon leader in Infantry Regiment 74 when he was awarded the Knight's Cross on 4 September 1940. Pongratz died on 1 August 1997 in Munich.

357. Feldwebel Karl JÜRGENS

Jürgens was born on 4 July 1911 in Kamin. He was a platoon leader in Infantry Regiment 73 when he was awarded the Knight's Cross on 4 September 1940. Jürgens was killed in action on 16 October 1941 and is buried at Ilyinskoye/Maloyaroslavets, Russia; his remains are awaiting transfer to a German war cemetery.

358. Oberstleutnant Otto HÖHNE

Höhne was born on 30 April 1895 in Woinowitz, Poland. He fought in the First World War and shot down six enemy aircraft, including Canadian ace

Alan Duncan Bell-Irving. Höhne was awarded the Iron Cross 1st and 2nd Class (1914).

He took part in the Polish campaign and the campaign in the West, for which he was awarded the Knight's Cross on 5 September 1940. Höhne was badly wounded in a crash on 15 August 1941, and after recovering, he served as commander of a flight combat school. He died on 29 November 1969 and is buried in the village cemetery, Jachenau, Bavaria.

359. Oberstleutnant Johann (or Hans) SCHALK

Schalk was born on 19 September 1903 in Krems, Austria-Hungary. He shot down five enemy aircraft in the campaign in the West and six during the Battle of Britain using the Bf 110. Three of these victories were shot down by his rear gunner, *Unteroffizier* Scheuplein. Schalk was awarded the Knight's Cross as a group commander in Heavy Fighter Wing 26 on 5 September 1940. He was the first heavy fighter pilot to be awarded it. He died on 9 November 1987 and is buried in Zentralfriedhof, Graz, Austria.

360. *Oberleutnant* Engelbert ENDRASS

Endrass was born on 2 March 1911 in Bamberg. He was watch officer on board *U-47* under Günther Prien when he sank the *Royal Oak* in Scapa Flow. On his first patrol as commander of *U-46*, he sank a number of ships, including the 20,277-ton British armed merchantman *Carinthia*. Endrass attacked convoys OB 205d, SC 7, and HX 79, sinking eight ships. He was awarded the Knight's Cross on 5 September 1941. In March 1941, *U-46* was in the waters south of Greenland when Watch Officer Helmut Pöttgen was washed overboard, a search of the area proved fruitless.

During his next patrol on 6 June, the U-boat was rammed by a 10,000-ton tanker. The chief engineer managed to stop the boat plunging into the depths, and the damaged U-boat sank three more ships on its way home. Endrass was awarded the Oak Leaves on 10 June 1941.

His next patrol was with a new boat, *U-567*, which was successful. On 18 December 1941, he sailed on his second patrol with *U-567*, joining other boats attacking convoy HG 76 on 21 December. He sank a steamer and was then attacked by the sloop *Deptford* and the corvette *Samphire*. *U-567* was lost with all hands. Endrass sank a total of 142,105 tons.

361. *Oberleutnant* Heinrich PAEPCKE

Paepcke was born on 11 December 1910 in Wattenscheid. He took part in the invasion of Norway and the Battle of Britain, for which he was awarded the Knight's Cross on 5 September 1940 as a squadron leader in Bomber Wing 30. Paepcke also saw action in Russia. He was killed in action over Malta on 17 October 1942 and has no known grave. Paepcke was awarded the Oak Leaves on 19 December 1942.

362. Oberfeldwebel Werner MACHOLD

Machold was born on 29 July 1913 in Unterneubrunn. He was a pilot in Fighter Wing 2; he fought in France and the Battle of Britain. Machold shot down thirty-two enemy aircraft and was awarded the Knight's Cross on 5 September 1940. On 9 June 1940, he was shot down over Portland, England, and taken prisoner. He died on 2 April 1968 and is believed to be buried in Waldfriedhof, Landsberg am Lech, Bavaria.

363. Oberstleutnant Joachim-Friedrich HUTH

Huth was born on 31 July 1896 in Neuhof. He fought in the First World War in the infantry and later as a pilot and was awarded the Iron Cross 1st and 2nd Class (1914). Huth was also badly wounded and lost part of his lower right leg. He commanded Heavy Fighter Wing 26 during the French campaign and during the Battle of Britain, for which he was awarded the Knight's Cross on 11 September 1940. Huth died on 27 March 1962 and is buried in Gatow Friedhof (next to the church), Alt Gatow, Berlin.

364. *Hauptmann* Gerhard SCHÖPFEL

Schöpfel was born on 19 December 1912 in Erfurt. He fought in the skies over France and during the Battle of Britain, shooting down twenty enemy aircraft, including four on 18 August 1940, two of which were aces. Schöpfel was awarded the Knight's Cross on 11 September 1940.

He stayed on the Western Front during the invasion of Russia and increased his score to forty-five by January 1943, when he took up an admin post; he later returned to combat in the defence of the Reich in May 1944. Although he only spent a very short time on the Eastern Front and had not shot anything down, he was imprisoned by the Russians and released in 1949. He died on 15 May 2003 in Bergisch Gladbach, North Rhine-Westphalia.

365. *Oberleutnant* Herbert IHLEFELD—'Ihle'

Ihlefeld was born on 1 June 1914 in Pinnow. He fought in the Spanish Civil War, shooting down seven aircraft. Ihlefeld also fought in the Polish campaign, for which he was awarded the Iron Cross 2nd Class, and in the West, for which he was awarded the Iron Cross 1st Class. During the Battle of Britain, he was awarded the Knight's Cross for shooting down his twenty-first aircraft on 13 September 1940.

When Ihlefeld shot down his fortieth enemy aircraft, he was awarded the Oak Leaves on 27 June 1941. After shooting down his 100th, he was awarded the Swords on 24 April 1942. By the end of the war, he had shot down 132 enemy aircraft, including fifteen four-engined bombers, and he had been shot down himself eight times. Ihlefeld died on 8 August 1995 and is believed to be buried in Knigge Friedhof, Wennigsen, Lower Saxony.

366. Oberstleutnant Walter GRABMANN

Grabmann was born on 20 September 1905 in Reichenhall. He took part in the Spanish Civil War and shot down five aircraft. He fought in Poland and was wounded on the very first day of the war. Grabmann also fought in France and was shot down in his Bf 110. Captured by the French, he was freed by an advancing panzer column.

The Battle of Britain followed, and for his part, he was awarded the Knight's Cross on 14 September 1940. He spent the remainder of the war in command of heavy fighter units in the West. Grabmann died on 11 July 1992 in Munich.

367. *Hauptmann* Rolf PINGEL

Pingel was born on 1 October 1913 in Kiel. He took part in the Spanish Civil War, shooting down six enemy aircraft. Pingel shot down his first enemy aircraft of the war on 10 September 1939 over Saarlautern. During the Battle of Britain, his tally increased and he was awarded the Knight's Cross on 14 September 1940. Then, on 28 September, his fighter was badly shot up over Maidstone, and he was forced to ditch in the Channel. Pingel was picked up by the German Air Sea Rescue.

With his score at twenty-eight, plus six for Spain, he was shot down on 10 July 1941 by a Short Stirling bomber that he was pursuing, crash landing near St Margaret's Bay. Pingel was taken prisoner by the Home Guard. He died on 4 April 2000 and is buried in Odenhausen Friedhof, Lollar, Hesse.

368. *Oberleutnant* Joachim MÜNCHEBERG— 'The Hunter of Malta'

Müncheberg was born on 31 December 1918 in Friedrichshof. He shot down nine enemy aircraft in the western campaign and fought in the Battle of Britain. Müncheberg was awarded the Knight's Cross on 14 September 1940 after his twentieth victory. Sent to Italy in early 1941, he raised his total to forty-three and was awarded the Oak Leaves on 7 May 1941. Most of his victories at this time were scored over Malta. After a brief stop in Africa, he was back on the Channel Coast, where he shot down another thirty-five aircraft before transferring to Russia in August 1942. The Swords were awarded to him on 9 September 1942 after his 103rd victory.

Müncheberg returned to Africa and raised his score to 135 enemy aircraft. Then, on 23 March 1943, he shot down US Captain Sweetland. Sweetland's Spitfire struck Müncheberg's wing, tearing it off. Both aircraft crashed to the ground. Müncheberg was killed and is buried in the German War Cemetery, Ossario 6B, Panel 19, Bordj-Cedria, Tunisia.

369. *Oberleutnant* Hermann-Friedrich JOPPIEN (also spelt JOPPLEN)—'Jupp'

Joppien was born on 19 July 1912 in Bochum. He was awarded the Iron Cross 2nd Class in December 1939 for shooting down enemy aircraft over France. During the 1940 French campaign, Joppien shot down another four more and was awarded the Iron Cross 1st Class. He fought in the Battle of Britain where he shot down twenty-six enemy fighters, most of which were Spitfires. Joppien was awarded the Knight's Cross on 16 September 1940.

He shot down his fortieth aircraft on 21 April 1941 and was awarded the Oak Leaves two days later. Joppien took part in the invasion of Russia and his score increased rapidly until 5 July 1941, when, with his tally at fifty-eight, he was shot down by returning fire from a bomber; he spent several weeks in hospital. On 25 August 1941, with his total at seventy, Joppien was shot down near Yelnya, Russia, and died; he has no known grave.

370. *Major* Heinz CRAMER

Cramer was born on 24 May 1911 in Strasbourg. He was a pilot in Close Support Wing 1, with which he saw action in Poland, Norway, and France, as well as taking part in the Battle of Britain. Hoffman was awarded the Knight's Cross on 18 September 1940, the same month he was shot down over England; he was a POW for the rest of the war. He died on 5 September 2003 in Hamburg.

371. *Major* Günther LÜTZOW

Lützow was born on 4 September 1912 in Kiel. He fought in the Spanish Civil War with the Condor Legion, shooting down five enemy aircraft. Lützow was sent to train new pilots after returning from Spain. He then fought in the Battle of Britain and was awarded the Iron Cross 1st and 2nd Class in May and June and the Knight's Cross on 18 September 1940 for shooting down his fifteenth enemy aircraft. By the time his unit was moved to the east for the invasion of Russia, he had raised his total to forty.

In Russia, he was awarded the Oak Leaves on 20 July 1941 and his tally rapidly increased until 11 October 1941, when, with ninety-two enemy aircraft destroyed, Lützow was awarded the Swords. He was withdrawn from combat and sent into a number of admin roles. Then, in January 1945, during a conference with Göring, he had a frank exchange of views with the *Reichsmarschall*, criticising Göring's failure to support his pilots, his offensive remarks that they were cowards, the conduct of the war, and the sacking of Adolf Galland. Göring threaten to have Lützow court-martialled but instead sent him to Italy, as far away as he could get him from Berlin. In the dying days of the war, Lützow managed to return to combat using the Me 262 jet fighter, shooting down two more enemy aircraft before being reported missing on 24 April 1945 near Donauwörth, Bavaria. Lützow is credit with 110 victories.

372. *Major* Wolfgang SCHELLMANN

Schellmann was born on 2 March 1911 in Kassel. He fought in the Spanish Civil War and shot down twelve enemy aircraft. Schellmann took part in the Polish campaign and in France, where he shot down his first enemy aircraft of the war. Five more would follow before the fall of France. His first victory during the Battle of Britain was on 18 July 1940. Schellmann was awarded the Knight's Cross on 18 September 1940 with his tally at twenty-three.

Moved to the Balkans, he shot down only one enemy aircraft. On 22 June 1941, the opening day of the invasion of Russia, Schellmann shot down an enemy aircraft over Grodno, bringing his total to twenty-five, but he was then rammed; Schellmann managed to bale out but was never seen again. It is thought that he was captured by the Russians and shot.

373. *Oberleutnant* Johannes BRANDENBURG

Brandenburg was born on 28 July 1910 in Innien. He fought in Poland, France, and the Battle of Britain, for which he was awarded the Knight's Cross on 18 September 1940 as a squadron commander in Dive Bomber Wing 2. Brandenburg was killed in action on 28 February 1942 and is buried in the German War Cemetery, Block 16 (as unknown), Korpowo, Russia.

374. *Kapitänleutnant* Günter KUHNKE

Kuhnke was born in Elbing on 7 September 1912. At the start of the war, he was commander of *U-28*, he sank his first ship—the British 4,955-ton *Vancouver City*—on 14 September 1939, followed by two steamers in November. In January 1940, the British steamer *Protesilaus* sank after hitting a mine laid by *U-28*. He sank two ships in both March and June. On 27 August, he torpedoed a ship from convoy SC1 and finished it off with gunfire. The next day, he sank two ships from convoy SC2.

After sighting convoy OA210 on 11 September, he fired three torpedoes, sinking one ship and damaging another. He was awarded the Knight's Cross on 19 September 1940. Kuhnke torpedoed the *Marina* on 26 October 1940, but she was finished off by *U-31*. He commissioned *U-125* on 3 March 1941. His last command was the 33rd U-Boat Flotilla. He died on 11 October 1990 and is buried in Neuer Friedhof, Plaggestrasse 26, Lower Saxony.

375. *Kapitänleutnant* Joachim SCHEPKE

Schepke was born in Flensburg on 8 March 1912. When the war started, he was in command of *U-3*. His first patrols were mine-laying off the English coast. The merchant ship *Vendia* was the first to be sunk by his torpedoes on 30 September 1939. In January 1940, he took command of *U-19* and led the boat on several patrols with only a few small ships sunk. Things only got better when he commissioned *U-100* on 30 May; he attacked convoy HX72, sinking six ships, including the 10,525-ton British tanker *Frederick S. Fales* and the 10,364-ton tanker *Torinia*. He was awarded the Knight's Cross on 24 September 1940.

In the 'Night of the Long Knives' against convoy SC7, Schepke sunk three ships and torpedoed three more. His best success was on 23 November 1940 when he sank seven ships in thirteen hours from convoy SC11. The Oak Leaves were awarded to him on 1 December 1940. Schepke sank three ships, including the 10,116-ton *Napier Star* in December. On 17 March 1941, he was forced to the surface following a long pursuit and was rammed by the destroyer *Vanoc*, sinking the U-boat; only five of her crew survived, Schepke was not one of them. He was known as 'Her Majesty's best looking officer'. Schepke sank thirty-seven ships (a total of 145,842 tons).

376. *Hauptmann* Wolfgang LIPPERT

Lippert was born on 14 September 1914 in Fraureuth. As part of the Condor Legion in Spain, he shot down five enemy aircraft. Lippert shot down eight more enemy aircraft over France starting on 30 September 1939. During the Battle of Britain, seven fell to his guns, including British ace Archie McKeller. Lippert was awarded the Knight's Cross on 24 September 1940, with his tally at eighteen victories.

Next, he took part in the invasion of Russia, shooting down another four before being moved to North Africa. Here shot down five more, and then, on 23 November, he was shot down over Allied lines; when Lippert baled out, he hit his tailplane. He had both his legs removed but gangrene set in and he died on 3 December 1941. He is buried in the German War Cemetery, Block 29, Row D, Grave 22, Fayid, Egypt.

377. *Oberleutnant* Hans HAHN—'Assi'

Hahn was born on 14 April 1914 in Gotha. He fought over France, and for his first victory, he shot down two Hurricanes on 14 May 1940, followed by another three aircraft before the fall of France. During the Battle of Britain, Hahn was awarded the Iron Cross 2nd Class in May and the 1st Class in June 1940. With his tally at twenty, he was awarded the Knight's Cross on 24 September 1940. Staying in the West, Hahn was awarded the Oak Leaves on 14 August 1941, having shot down forty-one enemy aircraft.

With his score at sixty-six, Hahn was moved to the Eastern Front in November 1942 and in three mouths he had shot down forty-two Russian aircraft, his 100th coming on 27 January 1943. On 21 February 1943, Hahn shot down his 118th enemy aircraft but was himself shot down and captured near Staraya. He was not released until 1950. Hahn's memoirs are called *I Tell the Truth*, in which he details his life in the Luftwaffe and as a POW. He died on 18 December 1982 and is believed to be buried in Waldfriedhof, Munich.

378. Oberstleutnant Theodor ROWEHL

Rowehl was born on 9 February 1894 in Barstede. He fought in the First World War as a navy pilot. Rowehl was commander of the Reconnaissance Group of

OBdl when he was awarded the Knight's Cross on 27 September 1940. He resigned from the Luftwaffe in 1943 to care for his children when his wife was killed in an air raid. Rowehl died on 6 June 1978 and is buried in Zentralfriedhof, Münster.

379. Generalleutnant Erich-Heinrich CLÖSSNER

Clössner was born on 17 September 1888 in Giessen. He fought in the First World War and was awarded the Iron Cross 1st and 2nd Class (1914). Clössner was commander of 25 Infantry Division when he was awarded the Knight's Cross on 29 September 1940. He died on 28 March 1976 and is buried in Stadtfriedhof, Feld A, Grave 140–141, Braunfels, Hesse.

380. Oberst Georg von BISMARCK

Von Bismarck was born on 25 February 1891 in Neumühl. He saw action in the First World War, being awarded the Iron Cross 1st and 2nd Class (1914). Von Bismarck fought in the Polish campaign and was awarded the Iron Cross 1st and 2nd Class (1939). In France, he distinguished himself by leading his regiment's breakthrough to the coast. For this, he was awarded the Knight's Cross on 29 September 1940.

In the Russian campaign, he commanded the 20th Rifle Brigade until December 1941. In January 1942, he was assigned to the staff of Panzer Army Africa. Rommel placed him in command of the 21st Panzer Division, with which von Bismarck led a charge though Cyrenaica all the way to the approaches to El Alamein. Promoted to *Generalleutnant* on 1 August 1942, he was killed in an air attack on 31 August 1942 and is buried in the German War Cemetery, Tobruk, Libya.

381. Oberstleutnant Joachim von STOLZMANN

Von Stolzmann was born on 6 February 1898 in Berlin. He was commander of III Battalion, Infantry Regiment 17, when he was awarded the Knight's Cross on 29 September 1940. Von Stolzmann died on 29 May 1971 in Kiel, Schleswig-Holstein.

382. *Major* Gustav HERTZ

Hertz was born on 13 April 1886 in Kleptow. He was commander of I Battalion, Artillery Regiment 258, when he was awarded the Knight's Cross on 29 September 1940. Hertz died on 25 February 1967 in Verden an der Aller, Lower Saxony.

383. *Major* Günther KRATSCH

Kratsch was born on 13 September 1896 in Kassel. He was commander of I Battalion, Motorised Artillery Regiment 65, when he was awarded the Knight's Cross on 29 September 1940. Kratsch died on 30 December 1984 and is believed to be buried in Hauptfriedhof, Tannenkeckerweg 6, Kassel, Hesse.

384. *Major* Ernst SEIFERT

Seifert was born on 30 May 1898 in Margonin. He was commander of II Battalion, Heavy Artillery Regiment 48, when he was awarded the Knight's Cross on 29 September 1940. Seifert died on 27 July 1991 and is believed to be buried in Stadtfriedhof, Celle, Lower Saxony.

385. *Hauptmann* Adalbert SCHULZ—'Panzer Schulz'

Schulz was born on 20 December 1903 in Berlin. He first saw action as a panzer commander in the campaign in the West. Schulz distinguished himself, capturing a fiercely defended position in the forest of Saumont. He then held it against numerous counterattacks. For this, he was awarded the Iron Cross 1st and 2nd Class, as well as the Knight's Cross on 29 September 1940.

In Russia during 1941, he again distinguished himself at the Minsk Pocket, the Dnieper, Smolensk, and on the approach to Moscow. For this, he was awarded the Oak Leaves on 21 December 1941. He fought through the winter and his unit was moved to France for rest and refit in May 1942. He was sent back to Russia to fight in the winter battles of 1942–43, where one of his panzers knocked-out 100 enemy tanks and artillery guns. Schulz commanded a panzer regiment at Kursk, for which he was awarded the Swords on 6 August 1943. In fierce fighting around Kiev and Zhitomir, his regiment attacked the flanks of the Russians, destroying over 150 enemy tanks and stopping their advance. For this, he was awarded the diamonds on 14 December 1943.

On 28 January 1944, while in command of the 7th Panzer Division, Schulz was conducting a battlefield conference when he was wounded by a nearby shall burst. He was rushed to the aid station but died before he could be treated. Schulz is buried at Starokostiantyniv, Ukraine; his remains are awaiting transfer to a German war cemetery.

386. *Oberleutnant* Hans DAUMILLER

Daumiller was born on 24 August 1910 in Kempten. He was a company commander in Mountain Jäger Regiment 98 when he was awarded the Knight's Cross on 29 September 1940. Daumiller was accidently shot on 12 January 1942 and is buried at Roslawl, Russia; his remains are awaiting transfer to a German war cemetery.

387. Leutnant Rudolf NEUBRANDT

Neubrandt was born on 23 September 1919 in Eschweiler. He was a platoon leader in Panzer Reconnaissance Battalion 37 when he was awarded the Knight's Cross on 29 September 1940. Neubrandt was killed in action at Wiasma, Russia, on 11 October 1941 and has no known grave.

388. Oberst Hubert LANZ

Lanz was born on 22 May 1896 in Entringen. He fought in the First World War and was awarded the Iron Cross 1st and 2nd Class (1914). Lanz was on the staff of XVIII Army Corp in the French campaign and was awarded the Knight's Cross on 1 October 1940. In April 1941, he was involved in the fighting in Yugoslavia with the II Army. Lanz took part in the invasion of Russia as commander of 1st *Jäger* Division. During the drive to the Caucasus Mountains, Lanz sent some men to raise the German flag on Mount Elbrus. Widely publicised by Goebbels, Hitler was furious and relieved him of his command on 17 December 1942; however, he was still awarded the Oak Leaves six days later.

After the fall of Stalingrad, Lanz was given a new command and tasked to hold the around Kharkov, although outnumbered four to one. When Kharkov fell, he was again relieved of his command. Lanz was part of a plan to arrest Hitler, but this failed. On 9 September Lanz assumed a command in Greece, where men under his command carried out executions of civilians—something Lanz did not order or initially agree with this. However, after the death of *Generalleutnant* Salminger in a guerrilla ambush, Lanz ordered 'ruthless retaliatory action' in a large area around the place of the ambush. Over 200 civilians were executed. When Italy surrendered to the Allies, Lanz was ordered to overcome all Italian forces in the Ionian Islands. After initial resistance, the Italians surrendered, but over 5,000 Italians were shot on Lanz's orders. He ended the war in Austria and was captured by US forces and tried for war crimes. Sentenced to twelve years, he was released in 1951. Lanz died on 12 May 1982 and is believed to be buried in Waldfriedhof, Munich.

389. Oberstleutnant Benno KOSCH

Kosch was born on 12 March 1900 in Rovereto. He was a group commander in Fighter Wing 1 when he was awarded the Knight's Cross on 1 October 1940. Kosch died on 16 June 1975 in Vienna.

390. *Major* Wolfgang FALCK

Falck was born on 19 August 1910 in Berlin. He flew over Poland in a Bf 110 heavy fighter, shooting down three enemy aircraft. After Poland, his unit was sent to Jever to protect the naval bases at Wilhelmshaven. On 18 December 1939, he shot down two Wellington bombers but was forced down himself by return fire. On 9 April 1940, during the invasion of Denmark, Falck shot down his seventh enemy aircraft.

He was appointed the first commander of Night Fighter Wing 1 in June 1940 and was awarded the Knight's Cross on 1 October 1940. In July 1943, he was given overall responsibility for air defence of the Reich. Falck was captured by US forces in May 1945. He died on 13 March 2007 in St Ulrich, Austria.

391. *Hauptmann* Erich GROTH

Groth was born on 4 January 1907 in Wesermünde. He was a group commander in Heavy Fighter Wing 76 when he was awarded the Knight's Cross on 1 October 1940. Groth was killed in action at Stavanger, Norway, on 11 August 1941 and has no known grave.

392. *Hauptmann* Martin LUTZ

Lutz was born on 10 March 1913 in Mannheim. He was a squadron leader in Heavy Fighter Wing 1 when he was killed in action over Bristol on 27 September 1940 and is buried in the German War Cemetery, Block 8, Row 2, Grave 32, Camp Road, Cannock Chase, Staffordshire, England. Lutz was awarded the Knight's Cross on 1 October 1940.

393. *Oberleutnant* Hans-Joachim JABS

Jabs was born on 14 November 1917 in Lubeck. He flew a Bf 110 heavy fighter over France and during the Battle of Britain, shooting down eight enemy aircraft. Jabs was awarded the Iron Cross 1st and 2nd Class in May 1940 and the Knight's Cross on 1 October 1940. By the end of the year, he had shot down sixteen aircraft.

Moved to night fighting in 1941, Jabs raised his tally to forty-five aircraft shot down by January 1944. On 29 April 1944, he shot down two Spitfires before being forced down himself. Jabs was awarded the Oak Leaves on 24 March 1944 and ended the war with fifty aerial victories. He died on 26 October 2003 and is buried in Oberrahmede Friedhof, Lüdenscheid, North Rhine-Westphalia.

394. *Oberleutnant* Wilhelm-Richard RÖSSIGER

Rössiger was born on 12 December 1913 in Eidelstedt. He was a squadron leader in Test Wing 210 when he was killed in action over England on 27 September 1940. He has no known grave. Rössiger was awarded the Knight's Cross on 1 October 1940.

395. *Oberleutnant* Fritz SCHÜRMEYER

Schürmeyer was born on 15 May 1913 in Quedlinburg. He was a squadron leader in Reconnaissance Group des OB der Luftwaffe when he was awarded the Knight's Cross on 1 October 1940. Schürmeyer died on 8 October 1982 and is buried in Südfriedhof, Göttingen, Lower Saxony.

396. Leutnant Gustav SPRICK 'Micky'

Sprick was born on 29 November 1917 in Biemsen. He shot down his first enemy aircraft on 10 May 1940, the first day of the campaign in the West. By the end of this campaign, he had raised his tally to ten, but had also been shot down himself.

Sprick shot down another eleven enemy aircraft during the Battle of Britain and was awarded the Knight's Cross on 1 October 1940. He stayed in France, and by 28 June 1941, he had shot down thirty-one enemy aircraft. On this same day, he was killed in action. He is buried in the German War Cemetery, Block 32, Row 8, Grave 305, Bourdon, Picardy, France.

397. Oberfeldwebel Wilhelm-Friedrich ILLG

Illg was born on 9 September 1911 in Stuttgart. He was a pilot in Bomber Wing 76 when he was awarded the Knight's Cross on 1 October 1940. Illg died on 7 July 1968 and is buried in the German War Cemetery, Grave 31, Schorndorf, Baden-Württemberg.

398. Oberst Wolfgang von CHAMIER-GLISCZINKI

Von Chamier-Glisczinki was born on 16 April 1894. He fought in the First World War and was awarded the Iron Cross 1st and 2nd Class (1914). Von Chamier-Glisczinki was a *Kommodore* in Bomber Wing 3 when he was awarded the Knight's Cross on 6 October 1940. He was killed when his aircraft crashed on 22 August 1943 and is buried in the German War Cemetery (as unknown), Zagreb-Mirogoi, Croatia.

399. Korvettenkapitän Gerhard von KAMPTZ

Von Kamptz was born on 27 December 1902 in Koppaschütz. He was awarded the Iron Cross 1st and 2nd Class in May 1940. Von Kamptz was commander of R-Boat Flotilla 2 when he was awarded the Knight's Cross on 6 October 1940. He was awarded the Oak Leaves on 14 April 1943. He was captured by the Russians in May 1945 and not released until 1954. Von Kamptz died on 16 May 1998 and is buried in Nordfriedhof, Feld B, Grave 47, Kiel, Schleswig-Holstein.

400. Korvettenkapitän Kurt THOMA

Thoma was born on 4 August 1901 in Staufen. He took part in the Spanish Civil War, and he was awarded the Iron Cross 2nd Class in 1939 and the 1st Class in May 1940. Thoma was commander of M-Boat Flotilla 2 when he was awarded the Knight's Cross on 6 October 1940. He died on 11 April 1971 in Oldenburg, Lower Saxony.

401. Kapitän zur See Kurt BÖHMER

Böhmer was born on 31 December 1892 in Magdeburg. He fought in the First World War and was awarded the Iron Cross 2nd Class (1914). Böhmer also took part in the Spanish Civil War. He was awarded the Iron Cross 1st and 2n+d Class (1939) in April 1940. Böhmer was chief-of-staff to the commander of the security of the North Sea when he was awarded the Knight's Cross on 6 October 1940. He was killed in actions by partisans on 1 October 1944.

Böhmer is buried at Ventspils, Latvia; his remains are awaiting transfer to a German war cemetery.

402. *Hauptmann* Wilhelm MAKROCKI

Makrocki was born on 23 August 1905 in Schroda. He was a group commander in Heavy Fighter Wing 26 when he was awarded the Knight's Cross on 6 October 1940. Makrocki was posted missing over Crete on 21 May 1941.

403. *Oberleutnant* Werner STREIB

Streib was born on 13 June 1911 in Pforzheim. His first and only daylight victory came on 10 May 1940 when he downed a Bristol Blenheim while flying a Bf 110 heavy fighter. His next victory came on 20 July 1940 when he shot down a RAF Whitley bomber. With eight victories, he was awarded the Knight's Cross on 6 October 1940. With his score at forty-two enemy aircraft shot down, Streib was awarded the Oak Leaves on 26 February 1943.

On the night of 11–12 June 1943, Streib shot down five Lancaster bombers in thirty minutes using a new prototype of the He 219. On 11 March 1944, he was awarded the Swords, with his final score at sixty-six enemy aircraft shot down. On 23 March, Streib was made inspector of night fighters—a post he held until the end of the war. He died on 15 June 1986 and is buried in Ostfriedhof, Plot 41, Row 1, Grave 5, Munich.

404. Oberst Friedrich HOSSBACH

Hossbach was born on 21 November 1894 in Unna. He fought in the First World War and was awarded the Iron Cross 1st and 2nd Class (1914). Hossbach was commander of Infantry Regiment 82 when he was awarded the Knight's Cross on 7 October 1940. The Oak Leaves were awarded on 11 September 1943 while he was commander of LVI Panzer Corps. Hossbach was recommended for the Swords, but they were never awarded.

He was responsible for planning and executing an operation to set up 'typhus camps' in the path of the Russian Army to cause an epidemic. It is estimated that over 10,000 civilians died as a result. Hossbach died on 10 September 1980 and is buried in Stadtfriedhof, Feld WD4, Grave 60, Göttingen, Lower Saxony.

405. *Oberleutnant* zur See Hans JENISCH

Jenisch was born in Gerdauen on 19 October 1913. He took over command of *U-32* before the outbreak of war and scored his first success in March 1940. In early June, he sank one steamer and two sailing ships, followed by the Polish *Labud* on 19 June and the 9,026-ton Norwegian *Egli Knudsen* on 22 June.

He attacked convoy HX66, sinking three steamers before being forced away by depth charges. On 1 September 1940, he attacked a group of warships, torpedoing the 8,000-ton cruiser *Fiji*. On his next patrol, he sighted the 42,348-ton *Empress of Britain* under tow after being bombed. Two torpedoes sent her to the bottom. This was the largest merchant ship sunk during the war. He was awarded the Knight's Cross on 7 October 1940. Then, on 30 October 1940, *U-32* was attacked by the British ships *Harvester* and *Highlander*; Jenisch and some of his crew were taken prisoner after the sinking of his boat. His sank a total of 115,207 tons. He died on 29 April 1982 and is believed to be buried in Urnenfriedhof, Kronshagen, Schleswig-Holstein.

406. Oberstleutnant Friedrich VOLLBRACHT

Vollbracht was born on 8 February 1897 in Hamburg. He was commander of Heavy Fighter Wing 2 when he was awarded the Knight's Cross on 13 October 1940. Vollbracht died on 24 August 1968 and is buried in Hauptfriedhof, Baden Baden, Baden-Württemberg.

407. *Major* Erich BLOEDORN

Bloedorn was born on 6 July 1902 in Mühlhausen. He was a group commander in Bomber Wing 4 when he was awarded the Knight's Cross on 13 October 1940. Having fought in North Africa, he was assigned to Albert Kesselring's Staff in 1943. Bloedorn died on 30 November 1975 and is buried in Stadtfriedhof, Ansbach, Bavaria.

408. *Oberleutnant* Hans-Joachim HERRMANN—'Hajo'

Herrmann was born on 1 August 1913 in Kiel. He fought in Spain with the Condor Legion as a bomber pilot. Herrmann fought in Poland, for which he was awarded the Iron Cross 2nd Class, and France, for which he was awarded the Iron Cross 1st Class; he also fought in the Battle of Britain. He was awarded the Knight's Cross on 13 October 1940. In February 1941, his unit was moved to Sicily, where he carried out attacks on Malta and Greece. During one raid on Piraeus harbour, he dropped a bomb on the ammunition ship SS *Clan Fraser*; the resulting explosion sank eleven ships and made the port unusable for months. In early 1942, Herrmann was stationed in Norway, attacking the Arctic convoys, including PQ-17.

In July 1942, having sunk 70,000 tons of shipping, he was appointed to the Luftwaffe operational staff. Heavily involved in the defence of the Reich, Herrmann flew fifty night missions and shot down nine RAF bombers. He was awarded the Oak Leaves on 2 August 1943 and the Swords on 23 January 1944. Herrmann was a supporter of using young untrained pilots to ram enemy bombers; during one attack of 138 aircraft, only fifty returned. Captured by the Russians in May 1945, he was not released until 1955. Herrmann died on 5 November 2010 and his ashes were scattered in the Baltic Sea at Kiel, Schleswig-Holstein.

409. *Major* Friedrich KLESS

Kless was born on 7 October 1906 in Bayreuth. He was a group commander in Bomber Wing 55 when he was awarded the Knight's Cross on 14 October 1940. Kless died on 6 April 1994 and is believed to be buried in Stadtfriedhof, Krailling, Bavaria.

410. *Oberleutnant* Dietrich PELTZ

Peltz was born on 9 June 1914 in Gera. He was a Stuka pilot who fought in Poland, for which he was awarded the Iron Cross 2nd Class, and France, for which he obtained the Iron Cross 1st Class. During the Battle of Britain, he switched to flying the Ju 88 medium bomber. Peltz was awarded the Knight's Cross on 14 October 1940.

On the Russian Front, he was instrumental in developing accurate bombing techniques, thus allowing better success with fewer bombers. For this, he was awarded the Oak Leaves on 31 December 1941. He later flew missions from Sardinia, where he was awarded the Swords on 23 July 1943. This was followed by more attacks on England, during which his crews suffered heavy losses. Peltz became an advocate of using poorly trained pilots to ram Allied four-engined bombers. He died on 10 August 2001 in Munich. His brother-in-law, Hans-Karl Stepp, was also awarded the Knight's Cross.

411. Generalleutnant Hermann Ritter von SPECK

Ritter von Speck was born on 8 August 1888 in Munich. He fought in the First World War and was awarded the Iron Cross 1st and 2nd Class (1914). Von Speck fought in France as commander of XXVIII Army Corps. He was killed in action at Pont sur Yonne on 15 June 1940 and has no known grave. Von Speck was awarded the Knight's Cross on 17 October 1940. It is said that he sought death in battle as he could not break his oath to the army.

412. Kapitän zur See Friedrich BONTE

Bonte was born on 19 October 1896 in Potsdam. In April 1940, he commanded *Kampfgruppe* Narvik during the invasion of Norway and was an important part of its success. At 4.30 a.m. on 10 April 1940, Bonte's force came under torpedo attack by three British destroyers. His ship, the *Z-21 Wilhelm Heidkamp*, was struck by the first torpedo; Bonte was killed in the attack and he went down with his ship. He was awarded the Knight's Cross on 17 October 1940 for his part in command of the *Kampfgruppe*.

413. *Oberleutnant* Josef PRILLER—'Pips'

Priller was born on 27 July 1915 in Ingolstadt. He shot down six enemy aircraft during the French campaign, and by the end of August 1950, he had claimed fifteen aerial victories. Priller was awarded the Knight's Cross on 19 October 1940 after shooting down his twentieth opponent. Between 16 June and 11 July 1941, Priller shot down nineteen RAF aircraft. He was awarded the Oak Leaves on 20 July 1941, with his tally at forty-one.

Still in the West, he was now shooting down bombers as well as fighters. By the end of 1942, his tally stood at eighty-one aerial victories. On 5 June 1944, Priller and his wingman got drunk, and the next morning, they attacked the beaches with a hangover. It is said that Priller was the only German fighter pilot to get through to strafe the Normandy beaches on D-Day. Not only was he was accompanied by his wingman Heinz Wodarczyk, several others also made attacks on the beaches that day. He shot down his 100th opponent for which he was awarded the Swords on 2 July 1944. He ended the war with 110 enemy aircraft to his credit (sixty-eight of which were Spitfires—the most shot down by anyone—eleven Hurricanes, five US fighters, five medium bombers, and eleven US four-engined bombers). Priller died from a heart attack on 20 May 1961 and is buried in Westfriedhof, Feld 28, Central G31, Augsburg, Bavaria.

414. *Major* Joachim HAHN

Hahn was born on 17 March 1903 in Hirschberg. He was commander of *Kampfgruppe* 606 when he was awarded the Knight's Cross on 21 October 1940. Hahn was killed in action on 3 June 1942 and is buried in the German War Cemetery, Block 17, Row 22, Grave 1217, Champigny-St André, Normandy, France.

415. *Kapitänleutnant* Victor OEHRN

Oehrn was born in Kedabeck, Russia, on 21 October 1907. He took command of *U-14* in 1936 and later served on the staff. He only ever carried out two war patrols, both as commander of *U-37*. The first was in the waters off Cape Finisterre, and although his torpedoes were not working properly, by the time he returned to base, he had sunk eleven ships (a total of 45,111 tons) and damaged one (a total of 9,494 tons). On his second patrol, he sank the British anti-submarine ship *Penzance* on 8 August 1940. This was followed by eleven merchant ships (totalling 63,639 tons). Thus, in two patrols, he had sunk twenty-three ships, a total of 108,750 tons of shipping. He was awarded the Knight's Cross on 21 October 1940.

Afterwards, he served as commander of U-Boats in the Mediterranean. He was wounded and captured while on a special mission in July 1942, but he was released in a prisoner exchange in April 1944. Returning to Germany, he spent the rest of the war in staff positions. He died on 26 December 1997 and is believed to be buried in Alter Friedhof, Bonn.

416. *Major* Edgar PETERSEN

Petersen was born on 26 April 1904 in Strasbourg. He was a group commander in Bomber Wing 40 when he was awarded the Knight's Cross on 21 October 1940. Petersen died on 10 June 1986 and is believed to be buried in Friedhof, Machtlfing, Andechs, Bavaria.

417. *Hauptmann* Heinz BRETNÜTZ—'Pietzsch'

Bretnütz was born on 24 January 1914 in Mannheim. He fought in the Spanish Civil War and shot down two enemy aircraft. Bretnütz's first victory of the Second World War was on 25 September 1939—a French Curtiss P-36 Hawk shot down over Bienwald. During the Battle of Britain, he was one of the most successful pilots. For his twentieth aerial victory (plus twelve barrage balloons), he was awarded the Knight's Cross on 21 October 1940.

Bretnütz shot down his thirtieth opponent on 3 May 1941, the last on the Western Front. On 22 June 1941, the first day of the invasion of Russia, he shot down a twin-engined bomber but was himself wounded in the left knee and forced down behind enemy lines. Found and hid by Russian farmers, Bretnütz was handed over to the advancing Germans four days later. He was rushed to hospital and had his leg removed, but he died on 27 June 1941 and is buried in the German War Cemetery, Insterburg, Russia.

418. *Hauptmann* Dietrich HRABAK—'Dieter'

Hrabak was born on 19 December 1914 in Gross-Deuben. During the Polish campaign, he was shot down (for the first of eleven times) on his first mission. Hrabak shot down his first enemy aircraft on 13 May 1940—a French Potez 63—and would add five more before the end of the campaign. He shot down another ten enemy aircraft during the Battle of Britain and was awarded the Knight's Cross on 21 October 1940.

He fought in the Balkans before taking part in the invasion of Russia. In August 1943, he shot down his 100th opponent and was awarded the Oak Leaves on 25 November 1943. Hrabak ended the war with 125 aerial victories to his credit. One of his favourite sayings was 'if you return from a mission with a victory, but without your wingman, you have lost your battle'. He died on 15 September 1995 and is buried in Waldfriedhof, Feld 4, Grave 202–202A, Fürstenfeldbrück, Bavaria.

419. Kapitän zur See Friedrich RUGE

Ruge was born on 24 December 1894 in Leipzig. He fought in the First World War and was awarded the Iron Cross 1st and 2nd Class (1914). Ruge took part in operations during the Polish campaign and was awarded the Iron Cross 1st and 2nd Class (1939). He was awarded the Knight's Cross on 21 October 1940.

Until 1943, he was stationed in France, then he was sent to Italy to become Rommel's naval advisor. In August 1944, Ruge became director of ship construction. In the film *The Longest Day*, he plays himself. Ruge died on 3 July 1985 and is buried in Stadtfriedhof, Gmelinstrasse 20, Tübingen, Baden-Württemberg.

420. *Hauptmann* Walter STORP

Storp was born on 2 February 1910 in Schnecken. He took part in the Spanish Civil War as a pilot onboard the heavy cruiser *Admiral Scheer*. Storp was awarded the Iron Cross 1st and 2nd Class after the Polish campaign. He took part in the Battle of Britain and carried out a low-level bombing attack over the Midlands on 27 September 1940. He was a group commander in Bomber Wing 76 when he was awarded the Knight's Cross on 21 October 1940.

Storp was involved in the invasion of Russia and was awarded the Oak Leaves on 14 July 1941. He was transferred to a staff appointment in October 1941. Storp ended the war in Norway. He died on 9 August 1981 and is buried Feldstrasse Friedhof, Section 11, Goslar, Lower Saxony.

421. *Oberleutnant* Gerd SUHREN

Suhren was born on 16 May 1914 in Tafaigata, Samoa. He served as leading engineer on *U-37* under three of its captains. As such, he played a major role in the success of the U-boat and on several occasions prevented *U-37* from sinking after heavy depth-charge attacks. He was awarded the Knight's Cross on 21 October 1940, the first leading engineer to be awarded it. He then served on the staff of U-boat HQ, and his last posting was as leading engineer on *U-2511*. Gerd died on 6 May 1991 and is believed to be buried in Alter Friedhof, Bonn. His brother, Reinhard, was also awarded the Knight's Cross while serving in the U-boat arm.

422. *Oberleutnant* Hans PHILIPP

Philipp was born on 17 March 1917 in Meissen. He fought in Poland, France, and during the Battle of Britain, where, on 20 October 1940, he brought down his twelfth enemy aircraft. He was awarded the Knight's Cross two days later. After a brief time in the Balkans, Philipp saw action in Russia where he was awarded the Oak Leaves on 24 August 1941.

Philipp was awarded the Swords on 12 March 1942, with his score at eighty-two aerial victories. In April 1943, with his tally at 200, he was transferred to home defence, where command responsibility kept him on the ground more often than not. On 8 October 1943, however, he took off to intercept 150 bombers and 250 fighters heading for the shipyards in northern Germany. Philipp was heard claiming his first bomber 'kill', but he was then shot down and killed himself. His final score was 206 enemy aircraft shot down. Philipp is buried in Trinitis Friedhof, Meissen, Lower Saxony.

423. *Kapitänleutnant* Heinrich BLEICHRODT—'Ajax'

Bleichrodt was born on 21 October 1909 in Berga, Kyffhäusser. He joined the navy in 1933, spending some time on the heavy cruiser *Admiral Hipper*. His first patrol was on *U-48* as its third commander, sinking eight ships, including the 11,081-ton *City of Benares*. During his second patrol, he sunk seven more ships, one of which—the *Port Gisborn*—was in excess of 10,000 tons. He was awarded the Knight's Cross on 24 October 1940, but he refused to wear it until his second in command Reinhard Suhren was also awarded it as he had overseen all surface shooting. On 28 June 1941, Bleichrodt left port on his first patrol with *U-109*, but he scored no hits. On his next patrol, he sank five ships.

He enjoyed great success off Bermuda and the East Coast of the USA, with the *Harpagon* exploding after being struck by one of his torpedoes. Bleichrodt's fifth patrol started on 18 July 1942 and he soon sank a Norwegian tanker as well as the 11,449-ton *Tuscan Star*. On his return to port, he sank the steamer *Peterton*. He was awarded the Oak Leaves on 23 September 1942. His last post was as commander of the 22nd U-Boat Flotilla with the rank of *Korvettenkapitän*. He sank twenty-eight ships (a total of 162,171 tons). He was charged with war crimes by the Allies after the war. When seen wearing the Knight's Cross by a British admiral, Bleichrodt was ordered to remove it because of the swastika. He merely turned it around, showing the date of 1813. When seen by the admiral again, Bleichrodt just reminded him that it was the Prussians at Waterloo who saved the day for Wellington, surely the British could not object to that. He died in Munich on 9 January 1977.

424. *Oberleutnant* zur See Wolfgang LÜTH

Lüth was born on 15 October 1913 in Riga, Latvia. He served on *U-38* under Liebe as a trainee commander. In December 1939, Lüth took command of *U-9* and sank the French submarine *Doris*. He was awarded the Knight's Cross on 24 October 1940. As commander of *U-138* and *U-43*, he achieved great success against large steamers and tankers, including the 13,801-ton *New Sevilla*. The Oak Leaves were awarded to him on 13 November 1942. He sank eleven ships in three patrols, spending 192 days at sea on *U-43*. He was awarded the Swords on 15 April 1943. On 9 May, Lüth commissioned *U-181*, and he was awarded the diamonds on 9 August 1943 before taking *U-181* out on 12 September 1943 for 129 days at sea; during his time at sea on *U-181*, he sank twelve ships.

His last patrol was for 205 days, between Cape Town and Madagascar. Ten ships were destroyed, including the 10,528-ton *Clan McArthur*. Dönitz ordered him to be sent to the Naval Academy in Flensburg-Murwik as commander. He was accidentally shot and killed by a sentry on 14 May

1945 after he failed to answer a challenge. Lüth was given a state funeral, the only U-boat commander to be so honoured. He is buried in Addelby Neuer Friedhof, Flensburg, Schleswig-Holstein. During his career, Lüth sank forty-seven ships (a total of 221,981 tons—the second highest tonnage of the war).

425. *Hauptmann* Otto BERTRAM—'Otsch'

Bertram was born on 30 April 1916 in Wilhelmshaven. He fought in Spain with the Condor Legion, shooting down nine enemy aircraft. His first claim of the Second World War was on 20 April 1940 when he shot down French ace Antoine Casenobe, but this was unconfirmed. Bertram shot down four enemy aircraft before the end of the French campaign but was also shot down himself. During the Battle of Britain, he shot down seven British fighters between 2 and 6 September 1940. His last two victories came on 9 October, when he shot down two Bristol Blenheim fighter bombers over Le Havre. Bertram was awarded the Knight's Cross on 28 October 1940 and banned from flying as his two brothers had been killed in action. As the last surviving brother, he was excused further combat. He spent the remainder of the war in staff and training posts. Bertram died on 8 February 1987 and is believed to be buried in Hauptfriedhof, Freiburg im Breisgau, Baden-Württemberg.

426. Korvettenkapitän Hellmuth von RUCKTESCHELL

Von Ruckteschell was born on 23 March 1890 in Hamburg. He fought in the First World War and was awarded the Iron Cross 1st and 2nd Class (1914). He was commander of the armed merchant raider *Widder* (HSK 3), which he took to sea on 6 May 1940 and returned on 31 October 1940. During this raid, he sank or captured ten enemy ships. For this, he was awarded the Knight's Cross on 31 October 1940.

On his second voyage, he commanded the armed raider *Michel* (HSK9) and the voyage lasted from 9 March 1942 to 1 March 1943. During this raid, he sank or captured fifteen enemy ships; he was awarded the Oak Leaves on 23 December 1942. For his two voyages, he is credited with 152,727 tons of shipping destroyed or captured. After the war, he was tried for war crimes, namely that, on several occasions, he continued to fire on ships that had surrendered. He was sentenced to ten years. However, there were serious concerns about the trial as only one junior naval officer sat as judge, the rest being army officers who would have only a limited knowledge of naval warfare. Von Ruckteschell died in Hamburg prison on 24 September 1948, shortly after being told he would be released due to bad health. He has no known grave.

427. Oberst Karl ANGERSTEIN

Angerstein was born on 4 December 1890 in Mühlhausen. He fought in the First World War and was awarded the Iron Cross 1st and 2nd Class (1914). Angerstein was a *Kommodore* in Bomber Wing 1 when he was awarded the Knight's Cross on 2 November 1940. He died on 20 September 1985 in Feldkirchen, Bavaria.

428. *Hauptmann* Rudolf KALDRACK

Kaldrack was born on 25 June 1913 in Stargard. He took part in the Spanish Civil War, shooting down three enemy aircraft. He fought at the Battle of Heligoland Bight, France, and the Battle of Britain. Kaldrack was awarded the Knight's Cross on 2 November 1940 as a group commander in Heavy Fighter Wing 76.

Kaldrack was killed in action on 3 February 1942 and is buried at Bassary/Welikije Luki, Russia; his remains are awaiting transfer to a German war cemetery. Kaldrack had twenty-four victories to his credit and was awarded the Oak Leaves on 9 February 1942.

429. *Hauptmann* Wilhelm KNAPP

Knapp was born on 25 August 1912 in Lubeck. He was a squadron leader in Reconnaissance Group 123 when he was awarded the Knight's Cross on 2 November 1940. Knapp was killed in action over Obernau on 10 June 1944 and has no known grave.

430. *Hauptmann* Heinz NACKE

Nacke was born on 22 December 1909 in Ullendorf. He took part in the Spanish Civil War. Nacke fought over France and during the Battle of Britain flying a Bf 110 heavy fighter. He was a squadron commander in Heavy Fighter Wing 76 when he was awarded the Knight's Cross on 2 November 1940. He later took part in the Defence of the Reich and ended the war with fourteen victories to his credit. Nacke died on 16 September 1984 and is believed to be buried in Hoppenlau Friedhof, Stuttgart, Baden-Württemberg.

431. Korvettenkapitän Hans ERDMENGER

Erdmenger was born on 29 October 1903 in Gersthofen. He was commander of the destroyer *Z-21* when he was awarded the Knight's Cross on 3 November 1940. Erdmenger was killed in action in the Bay of Biscay on 27 December 1943 when his ship, the *Z-27*, was sunk by HMS *Glasgow* and HMS *Enterprise*. He went down with his ship.

432. *Oberleutnant* zur See Reinhard SUHREN—'Teddy'

Suhren was born on 16 April 1916 in Langenschwalbach, Czechoslovakia. He served as watch officer on *U-48* under Heinrich Bleichrodt and participated in his early success; he was awarded the Knight's Cross on 3 November 1940 after Bleichrodt's insisted. On 3 April 1941, Suhren commissioned *U-564* and scored his first big success against convoy HX133, sinking two ship, both of which were over 8,000 tons, and damaging another larger ship. Next he attacked convoy OG76, sinking two ships and torpedoing a third. On 23 August 1941, he sank the corvette *Zinnia*.

On his next patrol, he sank two large ships from convoy HG75. Suhren was awarded the Oak Leaves on 31 December 1941. In Febraruy 1942, he sank the 11,410-ton Canadian tanker *Victolite*. On his next patrol, he sank three ships and torpedoed two more. Teddy, as his crew called him, attacked convoy OS34 and sank two ships of 5,000 tons. He ended his patrol by sinking the 8,176-ton tanker *Vardaas* on 30 August 1942. His award of the Swords came on 1 September 1942. He ended the war in command of U-Boats Norway and the Arctic. Suhren died on 25 August 1984 in Halstenbek, near Hamburg. His ashes were scattered at sea, close to where *U-564* was sunk. His brother, Gerd, was also awarded the Knight's Cross while serving in the U-boat arm.

433. *Oberleutnant* Arnold LIGNITZ

Lignitz was born on 25 March 1913 in Insterburg, Russia. He flew over France, England, and Yugoslavia. Lignitz was awarded the Knight's Cross on 5 November 1940 as a group commander in Fighter Wing 54. He took part in the invasion of Russia, and with his score of victories at twenty-five, he was posted missing over Leningrad on 30 September 1941.

434. Leutnant Heinz EBELING

Ebeling born on 2 January 1918 in Karlsruhe. A fighter pilot, he shot down five enemy aircraft by the end of the French campaign. During the initial stages of the Battle of Britain, Ebeling shot down ten aircraft in August, including three on the 12th and two on the 15th. On 31 August 1940, he was shot up and ditched his fighter in the Channel, being picked up by a German seaplane. He was back in combat the same day.

After shooting down three more in September, his unit was converted to heavy fighters, mostly likely the Bf 110. On 5 November 1940, Ebeling collided with his wingman, Walter Braun, over Dungeness, spending the rest of the war as a POW. He was awarded the Knight's Cross the same day. Ebeling died on 30 November 1987 in Obsteig, Austria.

435. Stabsobersteuermann Heinrich PETERSEN

Petersen was born in Hamburg on 3 November 1902. He served on *U-23* and *U-99* under Kretschmer as watch officer. Whenever he took a fix on the ship's position, it was accurate to the last degree, which was an advantage in closing quickly with a convoy. He was awarded the Knight's Cross on 5 November 1940. On 17 March 1941, *U-99* was attacked by the destroyers *Walker* and *Vanoc*; unable to dive, the boat was scuttled. It was Petersen who signalled the destroyers to pick up survivors. He died on 6 June 1963 and is buried in Parkfriedhof, Eichhofstrasse 56, Kiel, Schleswig-Holstein.

436. Leutnant Siegfried SCHNELL—'Wumm'

Schnell was born on 23 January 1916 in Zielenzig. He shot down his first enemy aircraft on 14 May 1940. During the Battle of Britain, he raised his score to twenty by November and was awarded the Knight's Cross on 9 November 1940. As the war moved east, Schnell stayed in the West. He shot down nine Spitfires in two days—on 8 and 9 July 1941—bringing his tally to forty-four aerial victories. He was awarded the Oak Leaves on 9 July 1941.

Schnell scored his fifty-second victory during the 'Channel Dash' on 12 February 1942, and during the Dieppe Raid on 19 August 1942, he shot down five Spitfires to bring his tally to seventy-one. Moved to the defence of the Reich, he shot down three B-17 four-engined bombers on 11 January 1944 to reach ninety victories. In total, he would bring down twelve four-engined bombers before being sent to the Eastern Front. On 25 February 1944, with his total at ninety-three, he was shot down and killed over Narva, Estonia, and has no known grave.

437. *Hauptmann* Walter ADOLPH

Adolph was born on 11 June 1913 in Fântânele, Romania. He fought in the Spanish Civil War, shooting down one enemy aircraft. Adolph fought in Poland but did not score any victories. His first victory in the Second World War came on 1 October 1939 when he shot down a Bristol Blenheim. During the French campaign, he would bring down another five aircraft, including three Blenheims in five minutes on 12 May 1940.

During the Battle of Britain, he raised his tally to fifteen and was awarded the Knight's Cross on 13 November 1940. With his score at twenty-five, Adolph was shot down and killed on 18 September 1941. He is buried in the German War Cemetery, Block 38, Grave 459, Kattenbos N746, Lommel, Belgium.

438. *Hauptmann* Karl-Heinz KRAHL

Krahl was born on 25 September 1914 in Breslau. He fought with the Condor Legion in Spain. Krahl took part in the Battle for France and the Battle of Britain; he also helped with the defence of the Reich.

He was a group commander in Fighter Wing 2 when he was awarded the Knight's Cross on 13 November 1940. Krahl was killed in action when he was shot down by anti-aircraft fire over Malta on 14 April 1942. He is buried in the German War Cemetery, Block 1, Grave 60, Cagliari, Sardinia, Italy. Krahl has been credited with between fourteen and twenty-four aerial victories.

439. Oberst Günter SCHWARTZKOPFF

Schwartzkopff was born on 4 August 1898 in Forbach. He fought in the First World War and was awarded the Iron Cross 1st and 2nd Class (1914). Schwartzkopff took part in the Polish campaign. On 14 May 1940, just four days into the French campaign, he was killed in action; he is buried in the German War Cemetery, Block 4, Grave 3970, Noyers-Pont-Maugis, Champagne-Ardenne, France. Schwartzkopff was awarded the Knight's Cross on 24 November 1940.

440. *Hauptmann* Joachim HELBIG

Helbig was born on 10 September 1915 in Börln. He started the Polish campaign but was injured in a motorcycle accident within a few days and missed most of it. Helbig was involved in anti-shipping raids for the next few months, for which he was awarded the Iron Cross 2nd Class. He saw action in the invasion of Norway and, on one occasion, had to bring his badly damaged bomber home. During the campaign in the West, he was awarded the Iron Cross 1st Class. On one occasion, he sank a British warship and afterwards despatched three Spitfires, throwing his twin-engined bomber around like a fighter. Despite damage to his aircraft and his own wounds, which one of his crew bandaged as he flew the plane, Helbig managed to return to his base at Düsseldorf.

On 13 August 1940, his squadron was at the rear of a large formation attacking the British airfield at Worthy Down when they were jumped by eighty fighters. The German formation was torn apart, and Helbig's was the only aircraft from his squadron to get away; with his port engine shot up and his gunner and radio operator wounded, he headed back to the channel. As he reached the coast, a British fighter appeared and Helbig waited for the *coup de grâce*. The British pilot did not open fire but instead escorted the bomber across the Channel. With the French coast in sight, he saluted, waggled his wings, and turned for home.

Helbig was awarded the Knight's Cross on 24 November 1940 and transferred to the Mediterranean area, to take part in attacks on Malta. He was awarded the Oak Leaves on 16 January 1942 and the Swords on 28 September 1942. The British called his squadron 'The Helbig Flyers'. He destroyed much shipping, and the British even resorted to a commando raid on his airfield to put him out of action. Many of his aircraft were destroyed on the ground, but Helbig was back in action soon afterwards, bringing his total of enemy shipping sunk to over 200,000 tons—like Baumbach, his was more than some of the U-boat aces. Helbig was transferred to non-combat duties but saw action over Anzio and Normandy before the end of the war. He died in a car accident in Malente, Spain, on 5 October 1985.

441. *Hauptmann* Robert KOWALEWSKI

Kowalewski was born on 15 March in Berlin. He was a pilot in X *Fliegerkorps* when he was awarded the Knight's Cross on 24 November 1940. Kowalewski died on 5 July 1996 and is believed to be buried in Waldfriedhof, Herdecke, North Rhine-Westphalia.

442. *Hauptmann* Hermann KÜHL

Kühl was born on 6 March 1909 in Bliesdorf. He was a squadron leader in Bomber Wing 4 when he was awarded the Knight's Cross on 24 November 1940. Kühl was killed in action on 22 July 1942 and is buried in the German War Cemetery, Block 10, Row 52, Grave 6222, Kharkov, Ukraine.

443. *Oberleutnant* Sigmund-Ulrich Freiherr von GRAVENREUTH

Freiherr von Gravenreuth was born on 21 October 1909 in Munich. He fought in Poland, France, the Battle of Britain, and the Battle of the Atlantic. Von Gravenreuth was a pilot in Bomber Wing 30 when he was awarded the Knight's Cross on 24 November 1940. He was killed when his bomber crashed near Breslau on 16 October 1944; he has no known grave. Von Gravenreuth was awarded the Oak Leaves on 9 January 1945.

444. *Oberleutnant* Otto HINTZE

Hintze was born on 9 October 1914 in Munich. He was a squadron leader in Ergänzungs Wing 210 when he was awarded the Knight's Cross on 24 November 1940. Hintze died on 9 May 1999 in Munich.

445. *Oberleutnant* Gerhard RICHTER

Richter was born on 21 November 1913 in Niederogebra. He fought in Spain with the Condor Legion. Richter took part in the Polish campaign and was awarded the Iron Cross 2nd Class. In France, he was awarded the 1st Class. He fought in the Battle of Britain as well as the Balkans campaign. Richter was awarded the Knight's Cross on 24 November 1940. He later fought in the Mediterranean area. Richter died on 10 March 1995 and is buried in Neckargemünd Friedhof, Baden-Württemberg.

446. *Major* Wilhelm SCHMALZ

Schmalz was born on 1 March 1901 in Reussen. He fought in Poland and was awarded the Iron Cross 1st and 2nd Class. Schmalz took part in the Balkans campaign and was awarded the Knight's Cross on 28 November 1940. In Russia, he was awarded the Oak Leaves on 23 December 1943. Schmalz was captured by US forces in Italy in May 1945 and accused of war crimes, but the charges were dropped. He died on 14 March 1983 and is buried in Stadtfriedhof, Feld C, Grave 1, Weilmunster, Hesse.

447. *Hauptmann* Franz Graf von BELLEGARDE

Graf von Bellegarde was born on 28 July 1912 in Bruck an der Mur, Austria-Hungary. He fought in Poland and France. Von Bellegarde was a company commander in Reconnaissance Battalion 4 when he was awarded the Knight's Cross on 28 November 1940. He died of wounds on 19 December 1941 and is believed to be buried in the German War Cemetery (as unknown), Kursk-Besedino, Russia.

448. *Hauptmann* Martin EDER

Eder was born on 22 December 1902 in Bruck. He was a company commander in Infantry Regiment 481 when he was awarded the Knight's Cross on 28 November 1940. Eder died on 6 April 1983 in Regensburg, Bavaria.

449. *Hauptmann* Wilhelm SÖTH

Söth was born on 15 February 1903 in Wilster. He was commander of II Battalion, Artillery Regiment 56, when he was awarded the Knight's Cross on 28 November 1940. Söth died on 6 July 1978 and is buried in the village cemetery, Hollern, near Stade, Lower Saxony.

450. *Oberleutnant* Ernst PHILIPP

Philipp was born on 13 October 1912 in Senitz. He fought in Poland and was awarded the Iron Cross 1st and 2nd Class. Philipp also fought in France as a company commander in Panzer Regiment 1, and he was awarded the Knight's Cross on 28 November 1940. He spent most of the remainder of the war on the Eastern Front and was awarded the Oak Leaves on 30 September 1944. Philipp died on 16 March 2005 and is believed to be buried in Warendorf Friedhof, North Rhine-Westphalia.

451. Leutnant Hans BECKER

Becker was born on 30 May 1914 in Golzwarden. He was awarded the Iron Cross 1st and 2nd Class on 3 June 1940 and the Knight's Cross on 28 November 1940 as a company commander in Infantry Regiment 116. Becker died on 15 January 2004 and is buried in Hauptfriedhof, Oberursel, Hesse.

452. Leutnant Anton MOSANDL

Mosandl was born on 5 May 1912 in Aschbuch. He was a platoon leader in Mountain *Jäger* Regiment 99 when he was awarded the Knight's Cross on 28 November 1940. Mosandl died of wounds on 2 December 1942 at Guicu, Russia, and has no known grave.

453. Feldwebel Bernhard KLUTH

Kluth was born on 17 January 1914 in Arnoldsweiler. He was a platoon leader in Rifle Regiment 4 when he was awarded the Knight's Cross on 28 November 1940. Kluth died on 1 December 1993 in Kierpe, North Rhine-Westphalia.

454. Unteroffizier Karl BRÜGGEMANN

Brüggemann was born on 1 December 1915 in Stettin. He was a section leader in Infantry Regiment 5 when he was awarded the Knight's Cross on 28 November 1940. Brüggemann died on 19 June 1987 in Düsseldorf.

455. Unteroffizier Willy MODER

Moder was born on 17 November 1916 in Berlin. He was a section leader in Rifle Regiment 3 when he was awarded the Knight's Cross on 28 November 1940. Moder was killed in action near Dinnyés, Hungary, on 14 March 1945 and has no known grave.

456. Konteradmiral Hans STOHWASSER

Stohwasser was born on 4 May 1884 in Dresden. He fought in the First World War and was awarded the Iron Cross 1st and 2nd Class (1914). Stohwasser was awarded the Iron Cross 2nd Class (1939) in November 1939 and the 1st Class in April 1940. He was commander of the security of the Baltic Sea when he was awarded the Knight's Cross on 30 November 1940. Stohwasser died on 30 May 1967 in Neumunster, Schleswig-Holstein.

457. *Major* Bernd von DOERING

Von Doering was born on 16 January 1903 in Smachowo. He was commander of II Battalion, Rifle Regiment 79, when he was awarded the Knight's Cross on 30 November 1940. Von Doering fought in France, Yugoslavia, Greece, and Russia. He was killed in action on 7 July 1944 and is buried in the German War Cemetery, Block 8, Grave 1065, Costermano, Italy.

458. *Major* Klaus Freiherr von HARDENBERG

Hardenberg was born on 25 August 1898 in Oberwiederstedt. He was serving in Motorised Infantry Regiment 25 when he was awarded the Knight's Cross on 30 November 1940. Hardenberg was killed in an accident on 3 November 1942 and is buried in the German War Cemetery, Crypt 2, El Alamein, Egypt.

459. *Hauptmann* Wilhelm DÜRBECK

Dürbeck was born on 25 January 1912 in Nuremberg. He was squadron leader in Close Support Wing 1 when he was awarded the Knight's Cross on 3 December 1940. Dürbeck was posted missing over Malta on 19 January 1941.

460. Kapitän zur See Bernhard ROGGE

Rogge was born on 4 November 1899 in Schleswig. He fought in the First World War and was awarded the Iron Cross 1st and 2nd Class (1914). Rogge was commander of the armed raider *Atlantis* (HSK2) when he was awarded the Knight's Cross on 7 December 1940 and the Oak Leaves on 31 December 1941.

Praised by many of the ships' crews he sank, Rogge was the one of only a few surface raider captains not to be arrested for war crimes. He and his ship are depicted in the 1960 film *Under Ten Flags*. Rogge died on 29 June 1982 and is buried in Stadtfriedhof, Reinbek, Schleswig-Holstein.

461. Korvettenkapitän Viktor SCHÜTZE

Schütze was born on 16 February 1906 in Flensburg. He took his first patrol as commander of *U-25* in October 1939 and sank the 5,874-ton French ship *Baoulé*. From 12 January to 13 February 1940, he sank six ships (a total of

27,000 tons). He fired on several ships during the Norwegian campaign, but none of his torpedoes exploded. He commissioned *U-103* on 5 July 1940 and took her out in October, torpedoing a tanker on the 6th. On the 9th, he fired four torpedoes at a convoy, sinking three ships and damaging another. In November, he sank two ships from convoy OB244. He sank another five ships on this patrol.

He was awarded the Knight's Cross on 11 December 1940. On his next patrol, he sank three ships on 17 December from convoy HX107, including the 10,455-ton tanker *Edwy R. Brown*. A patrol in April–May 1941 resulted in a record thirteen ships sunk (a total of 65,172 tons). He was awarded the Oak Leaves on 14 July 1941. In total, he sank thirty-five ships (a total of 180,053 tons of shipping). He died in Frankfurt am Main on 23 September 1950.

462. *Hauptmann* Waldemar PLEWIG

Plewig was born on 6 January 1911 in Ostrowo. He was a group commander in Dive Bomber Wing 77 when he was awarded the Knight's Cross on 14 December 1940. Plewig died on 10 September 1983 in Mooregge, Schleswig-Holstein.

463. *Hauptmann* Joachim SCHLICHTING

Schlichting was born on 1 February 1914 in Kassel. He fought in the Spanish Civil War, shooting down five enemy aircraft. He fought in Poland and France, shooting down three more aircraft. Schlichting was shot down over Shoeburyness, England, on 6 September 1940 and spent the reminder of the war as a POW.

He was awarded the Knight's Cross on 14 December 1940 in recognition of his outstanding commitment as fighter escort to the bombers, at the expense of personal success in the air. Schlichting died on 7 July 1982 and is buried in Hornli Friedhof, Basel, Switzerland.

464. *Oberleutnant* Karl BARTH

Barth was born on 29 December 1914 in Lengenfeld. He was a pilot in Coastal Fighter Wing 506 when he was awarded the Knight's Cross on 14 December 1940. Barth was posted missing over the Mediterranean Sea on 9 November 1942.

465. *Oberleutnant* Franz Xaver Freiherr von WERRA—'The One that Got Away'

Werra was born on 13 July 1914 in Leuk, Switzerland. He fought as a fighter pilot in Poland but shot down his first enemy aircraft over France, where he was awarded the Iron Cross 2nd Class. Von Werra was shot down on 5 September 1940 during the Battle of Britain and captured. He made three attempts to escape, in the last of these, he simply walked on to a RAF airfield claiming to be a shot-down Dutch pilot looking to get back to his base. He was actually at the controls of a Hurricane when recaptured. Sent to Canada with other POWs, von Werra jumped from a moving train and walked across the frozen St Laurence River into the USA, which was still neutral at that time.

Von Werra arrived back in Berlin to a hero's welcome on 18 April 1941. Although awarded the Knight's Cross on 14 December 1940, von Werra was presented with it personally by Hitler. Von Werra wrote a book called *My Escape from England*, but it was never published. He fought in Russia and shot down a total of twenty-one enemy aircraft. Rotated back to the Netherlands, he was killed on 25 October 1941 when his engine failed and his fighter crashed into the sea. His body was never recovered. Von Werra's story was made into the film *The One That Got Away* in 1957 staring Hardy Krüger.

466. *Kapitänleutnant* Wolfgang KADEN

Kaden was born on 5 December 1899 in Leipzig. He was commander of *U-Jäger 116* when he was awarded the Knight's Cross on 18 December 1940. Kaden is credited with sinking at least three submarines, including HMS *H49* on 18 October 1940 and the Russian *K-23* on 12 May 1942. He was killed in action off the coast of Hammerfest on 9 July 1942 when his ship, *U-Jäger 1110*, hit a mine—although some say he was torpedoed by a Russian submarine.

467. *Oberleutnant* Alfred BOPP

Bopp was born on 4 June 1915 in Offenburg. He was a company commander in Infantry Regiment 216 when he was awarded the Knight's Cross on 21 December 1940. Bopp died on 18 August 1983 and is buried in Beiertheim Friedhof, Karlsruhe, Baden-Württemberg.

468. *Oberleutnant* Kurt BUDÄUS

Budäus was born on 6 March in Leipzig. He was a platoon leader in Infantry Regiment 307 when he was awarded the Knight's Cross on 21 December 1940. Budäus died on 16 April 1963 and is buried in Waldfriedhof, Velbert, North Rhine-Westphalia.

469. *Oberleutnant* Alfons KÖNIG

König was born on 29 December 1898 in Munich. He fought in the First World War and was awarded the Iron Cross 1st and 2nd Class (1914). König was a company commander in Infantry Regiment 199 when he was awarded the Iron Cross 1st and 2nd Class (1939) in June and the Knight's Cross on 21 December 1940. He was awarded the Oak Leaves on 21 February 1943 and the Swords on 9 June 1944. König was killed in action on 12 July 1944 and is buried at Orša, Belarus; his remains are awaiting transfer to a German war cemetery.

470. Leutnant Hermann DANZER

Danzer was born on 25 June 1916 in Vienna. He was a platoon leader in Panzer Pioneer Battalion 57 when he was killed in action on 20 June 1940. Danzer was awarded the Knight's Cross on 21 December 1940. He is buried in the German War Cemetery, Block 33, Row 10, Grave 697, Andilly, near Toul, Lorraine, France.

471. Leutnant Wilhelm SPINDLER

Spindler was born on 5 July 1914 in Stuttgart. He fought in Poland, for which he was awarded the Iron Cross 2nd Class, and France, for which he was awarded the Iron Cross 1st Class. Spindler was awarded the Knight's Cross on 21 December 1940 as a platoon leader in Mountain *Jäger* Regiment 98.

He took part in the invasion of Yugoslavia in April 1941 and of Russia in June 1941, where he spent the reminder of the war. Spindler was awarded the Oak Leaves on 31 January 1945. He died on 20 August 1997 and is buried in Hoppenlau Friedhof, Stuttgart, Baden-Württemberg.

472. Kapitän zur See Otto KÄHLER

Kähler was born on 3 March 1894 in Hamburg. He fought in the navy during the First World War and was awarded the Iron Cross 2nd Class (1914). Kähler was captain of the merchant raider *Thor*, with which he sank or captured twelve enemy ships (a total of 96,000 tons of shipping). For this, he was awarded the Knight's Cross on 22 December 1940. The Oak Leaves followed on 15 September 1944 when he was commander of Fortress Brest. Kähler died on 2 November 1967 and is buried in Parkfriedhof, Eichhofstrasse 56, Kiel, Schleswig-Holstein.

473. Kapitän zur See Ernst-Felix KRÜDER

Krüder was born on 6 December 1897 in Hamburg. He fought in the navy during the First World War and was awarded the Iron Cross 1st and 2nd Class (1914). Krüder was captain of the auxiliary cruiser *Pinguin* (HSK5) when he was awarded the Iron Cross 2nd Class (1939) in August 1940, the 1st Class (1939) on 11 October, and the Knight's Cross on 22 October 1940.

He was killed in action on 8 May 1941 when his ship was sunk in the Indian Ocean by HMS *Cornwall* with all hands, including 200 prisoners. Krüder was awarded the Oak Leaves on 15 November 1941.

474. *Hauptmann* Günther Freiherr von MALTZAHN

Freiherr von Maltzahn was born in Wodarg on 20 October 1910. He took part in the Spanish Civil War as a fighter pilot. Von Maltzahn also fought in Poland, France, and the Battle of Britain, being awarded the Knight's Cross on 30 September 1940 with just twelve enemy aircraft to his credit. The award was given for his outstanding leadership rather than his aerial victories. In 1941, he took part in the invasion of Russia where his score rapidly increased, reaching forty-three, for which he was awarded the Oak Leaves on 24 July 1941.

Moved to the Mediterranean area in November 1941, von Maltzahn took part in raids on Malta, the Western Desert, and Tunisia during 1942 and the spring of 1943. In the autumn of 1943, with sixty-eight aerial victories, he was grounded with malaria. Von Maltzahn spent the reminder of the war in staff posts. He survived the war, but his health declined steadily due to the malaria and he died on 24 June 1953. He is believed to be buried in Nordfriedhof, Düsseldorf.

475. *Oberleutnant* Bernhard JOPE

Jope was born on 10 May 1914 in Leipzig. He was a Fw 200 'Condor' pilot (Germany's only four-engined bomber) when, on 26 October 1940, he bombed the *Empress of Britain*, badly damaging her. She was later sunk by *U-32*. Jope was awarded the Knight's Cross on 30 December 1940.

On 9 September 1943, he led an attack on the Italian fleet *en route* to surrender to the British at Malta. Using 'Fritz X' radio-controlled bombs, the battleship *Roma* was hit twice and sunk. The *Roma*'s sister ship, *Italia*, was also hit but made it to Malta. Later, Jope scored hits with the 'Fritz X' on the battleship HMS *Warspite*, the cruiser HMS *Uganda*, and the cruiser USS *Savannah*. He was awarded the Oak Leaves on 24 March 1944. Jope died on 31 July 1995 and is buried in Stadtfriedhof, Feld 111, Grave 171, Königstein im Taumus, Hesse.

3

1941

476. Oberstleutnant Ernst BORMANN

Bormann was born on 5 November 1897 in Kirchbrak. He fought in the First World War, shooting down seventeen enemy aircraft, and he was awarded the Iron Cross 1st and 2nd Class (1914). Bormann was awarded the Iron Cross 1st and 2nd Class (1939) after the fall of Poland. He was a *Kommodore* in Bomber Wing 76 when he was awarded the Knight's Cross on 5 January 1941.

Bormann was awarded the Oak Leaves on 3 September 1942 and was captured by the Russians in May 1945; he was not released until 1955. Bormann died on 1 August 1960 and is buried in Nordfriedhof, Düsseldorf.

477. Major Anton HOLZINGER

Holzinger was born on 30 December 1901 in Pola, Austria-Hungary. He was commander of I Battalion, Jäger Regiment 138, when he was awarded the Knight's Cross on 11 January 1941. Holzinger died on 6 April 1989 and is buried in St Barbara Friedhof, Graz, Austria.

478. Korvettenkapitän Hans-Gerrit von STOCKHAUSEN

Stockhausen was born in Kassel on 11 August 1907. Before commissioning *U-65* in February 1940, he was serving at the U-Boat HQ. On 21 June 1940, he destroyed the 28,124-ton *Champlain*, which had run aground. A Dutch steamer followed, as did the 5,802-ton *Clan Ogilvy*, which was torpedoed. On 1 July, he torpedoed the 8,156-ton *Amstelland*.

U-65 put to sea again in September, sinking three ships in twenty-four hours, including the 7,614-ton Norwegian tanker *Havbör*. On 18 November, von Stockhausen torpedoed the tanker *Congonian*. His fourth patrol began in December 1940, sinking four ships, of which three were large tankers. Von Stockhausen was awarded the Knight's Cross on 14 January 1941. On his return, he handed the boat over and took up staff work again. Von Stockhausen was killed in a car crash in Berlin on 15 January 1943.

479. Konteradmiral Oskar KUMMETZ

Kummetz was born on 21 July 1891 in Illowo. He fought in the First World War and was awarded the Iron Cross 1st and 2nd Class (1914). Kummetz was captain of the *Blücher* and was awarded the Knight's Cross on 18 January 1941 for his part in the Battle of Drøbak Sound. He also fought in the naval action at the Barents Sea. Kummetz died on 17 December 1980 and is buried in Haardt Friedhof, Neustadt an der Weinstrasse, Rhineland-Palatinate.

480. Kapitän zur See Hellmuth HEYE

Heye was born on 9 August 1895 in Beckingen. He fought in the First World War and was awarded the Iron Cross 1st and 2nd Class (1914). Heye was captain of the heavy cruiser *Admiral Hipper* when, on 8 April 1940, he encountered HMS *Glowworm* and sank her, but not before the *Glowworm* rammed him. Heye sent word of the *Glowworm*'s brave action to the British Admiralty via the Red Cross, and the *Glowworm*'s captain Gerard Roope was awarded the Victoria Cross.

He was awarded the Knight's Cross on 18 January 1941. Heye died on 10 November 1970 and is buried in Nordfriedhof, Feld 38 (by the wall), Wiesbaden, Hesse.

481. Kapitän zur See August THIELE

Thiele was born on 26 August 1893 in Charlottenburg. He fought in the First World War and was awarded the Iron Cross 1st and 2nd Class (1914). Thiele was commander of the heavy cruiser *Lützow* and was awarded the Knight's Cross for his command of the ship and his leadership of *Kampfgruppe* V on 18 January 1941. He was awarded the Oak Leaves on 8 April 1945. Thiele died on 31 March 1981 in Mölln, Schleswig-Holstein.

482. *Oberleutnant* Georg Freiherr von BOESELAGER

Freiherr von Boeselager was born on 25 August 1015 in Kassel. He fought in Poland, for which he was awarded the Iron Cross 2nd Class in October 1939, and France, for which he was awarded the Iron Cross 1st Class in June 1940. Von Boeselager was awarded the Knight's Cross on 18 January 1941. He took part in the invasion of Russia and was awarded the Oak Leaves on 31 December 1941.

Von Boeselager became involved in the plot to kill Hitler along with his brother, Philipp. After the 20 July bomb plot failed to kill Hitler, von Boeselager returned to the front, well aware that his life was in danger. It seems he wanted a hero's death to save his family from persecution. He was killed in action between 26 and 29 August 1944 and is buried at Łomża, Poland; von Boeselager's remains are awaiting transfer to a German war cemetery. He was awarded the Swords on 28 November 1944. His brother, Philipp, was also awarded the Knight's Cross.

483. Leutnant Georg MICHAEL

Michael was born on 10 February 1917 in Hamburg. He fought in Poland and France, being awarded the Iron Cross 2nd Class on 25 May 1940 and the 1st Class on 27 June 1940. At the end of June, he captured 500 men and held open a village in France with just two men. For this, he was awarded the Knight's Cross on 19 January 1941.

Michael took part in the invasion of Russia and fought at the crossing of the Dnieper and at Smolensk in 1941. In 1942, he was part of the drive towards Stalingrad, where he showed much determination in numerous actions. He was awarded the Oak Leaves on 25 January 1943. His unit was sent to France for rest and refit during March and April 1943. He served briefly in Italy before returning to Russia in time for another horrific winter. Michael died of wounds on 19 January 1944 and is believed to be buried in the German War Cemetery (as unknown), Kirovograd, Ukraine.

484. Unteroffizier Willi HILSS

Hilss was born on 8 January 1916 in Frankfurt am Main. He was a gun commander in Panzer *Jäger* Battalion 46 when he was awarded the Knight's Cross on 19 January 1941. Hilss died on 13 April 1995 in Assenheim, Rhineland-Palatinate.

485. Oberst Johannes STREICH

Streich was born on 16 April 1891 in Augustenburg. He fought in the First World War and was awarded the Iron Cross 1st and 2nd Class. During the 1940 French campaign, his regiment cracked the blocking position near La Bassée barring the way to the coast, taking 20,000 prisoners. For this, he was recommended for the Knight's Cross, but he was not awarded it until 31 January 1941, after a second recommendation had been submitted.

He fought in Africa but was dismissed by Rommel for 'caring for his troops'. He then fought in Russia before becoming inspector of fast troops. Streich ended the war in Berlin. He died 20 August 1977 and is believed to be buried in Ohlsdorf Friedhof, Fuhlsbüttler Strasse, Hamburg.

486. *Major* Hans CHRISTERN

Christern was born on 24 January 1900 in Lauenburg. He fought in the First World War and was awarded the Iron Cross 1st and 2nd Class (1914). Christern was commander of II Battalion, Panzer Regiment 31, when he was awarded the Knight's Cross on 31 January 1941. He died on 17 June 1966 in Georgenhof, Bavaria.

487. *Hauptmann* Edmund DASER

Daser was born on 1 October 1908 in Augsburg. He was a squadron leader in Bomber Wing 40 when he was awarded the Knight's Cross on 21 February 1941. Daser died on 6 October 1974 and is buried in Cimitero di Locarno, Switzerland.

488. Kapitän zur See Theodor KRANCKE

Krancke was born on 30 March 1893 in Magdeburg. He fought in the First World War and was awarded the Iron Cross 1st and 2nd Class (1914). Krancke was captain of the pocket battleship *Admiral Sheer*. On 15 November 1940, he encountered convoy HX-84 and was engaged by the armed merchant cruiser *Jervis Bay*, which he sank. Captain Edward Fegen of the *Jervis Bay* was awarded the Victoria Cross for this action.

Krancke also sank thirteen merchant ships and captured three more during this raid (a total of 115,195 tons). For this, he was awarded the Knight's Cross on 21 February 1941. Krancke was awarded the Oak Leaves on 18 October 1944. He died on 18 June 1973 and is buried in the village cemetery, Wentorf, near Hamburg.

489. *Oberleutnant* zur See Werner TÖNIGES

Töniges was born on 7 January 1910 in Oberhausen. He took part in the Spanish Civil War onboard the pocket battleship *Admiral Graf Spee*. Töniges transferred to fast attack boats and was awarded the Iron Cross 1st and 2nd Class in 1940. During this time, he commanded *S-24*, *S-26*, and *S-102* and sank eighteen ships (a total of 86,200 tons).

Töniges was awarded the Knight's Cross on 25 February 1941. The Oak Leaves followed on 13 November 1942. In September 1942, he was sent to train new sailors. Töniges died on 25 January 1995 in Essen, North Rhine-Westphalia.

490. *Kapitänleutnant* Heinrich LEHMANN-WILLENBROCK

Lehmann-Willenbrock was born on 11 December 1911 in Bremen. He commissioned *U-96* on 14 September 1940, and on 5 December, he sailed for his first patrol, during which he sank five ships. On his next patrol, he sank the British steamer *Oropesa* on 16 January 1941 and the *Almeda Star* on the 17th, both 14,000-ton ships. He was awarded the Knight's Cross on 26 February 1941 and the Oak Leaves on 31 December.

His third patrol began on 30 January 1942, and by the time he returned to St Nazaire on 28 February, he had sunk another seven ships, including a tanker. His next three patrols were not so successful. In February and March 1942, he sank five ships off the US coast. After these patrols, he took leave and was appointed commander of the 9th U-Boat Flotilla in Brest on his return. When Brest was surrounded in 1944, he was able to escape to Bergen, where he became commander of the 11th U-Boat Flotilla, a position he held until the end of the war. Lehmann-Willenbrock sank twenty-five ships (a total of 183,253 tons). He died on 18 April 1986 and is believed to be buried in Osterholz Friedhof, Bremen. The film *Das Boot* was based on *U-96*.

491. *Kapitänleutnant* Karl-Heinz MOEHLE

Moehle was born on 31 July 1910 in Norden. He took over the *U-20* in October 1937 and he went on a mine-laying operation. On 22 November 1939, the steamer *Ionian* struck one of his mines and sunk. The *Willowpool* also struck a mine, while the *Magnus* was torpedoed and sunk.

On 30 May 1940, Moehle commissioned *U-123*, and in October, he sank the *Beatus* and the *Boekolo*. He also finished off the *Snefjeld* and the

Shakatika, which had been torpedoed by *U-10* and *U-100*. His last success on this patrol was the *Clintonia*. In attacks on convoy OB244, he sank six ships in thirty-six hours (a total of 27,895 tons). *U-123* returned to sea in January 1941 and sank four more ships, including the Dutch ship *Grootekerk*. He was awarded the Knight's Cross on 26 February 1941. His last patrol with *U-123* only saw one ship sunk, the 6,991-ton Swedish *Venezuela*. On his return, Moehle handed the boat over to Hardegen. He then took command of the 5th U-Boat Flotilla and submarine base at Kiel. After the war, Moehle was tried for passing on the 'Laconia Order' and sentenced to five years' imprisonment. He died on 17 November 1996 and is believed to be buried in Evangel Friedhof, Ahrensburg, Schleswig-Holstein.

492. Kapitän zur See Wilhelm MEISEL

Meisel was born on 4 November 1893 in Zwickau. He fought in the First World War and was awarded the Iron Cross 1st and 2nd Class (1914). Meisel commanded a destroyer flotilla during the Polish campaign and was awarded the Iron Cross 2nd Class (1939). In 1940, he was given command of the heavy cruiser *Admiral Hipper* and awarded the Iron Cross 1st Class (1939).

Meisel was awarded the Knight's Cross on 26 February 1941 and made chief-of-staff of Naval Group West in 1943, and later the same year, he was made chief of naval staff. He died on 7 September 1974 and is believed to be buried in Hauptfriedhof, Zeppelinstrasse, Mülheim, North Rhine-Westphalia.

493. *Oberleutnant* Hans-Ekkehard BOB

Bob was born on 24 January 1917 in Freilburg im Breisgau. He shot down his first enemy aircraft on 10 May 1940 over Tongeren, Belgium. Bob took part in the Battle of Britain, during which he raised his aerial victories' tally to nineteen. During the Balkans campaign, he shot down two more and was awarded the Knight's Cross on 7 March 1941.

In Russia, he added thirty-seven enemy aircraft to his tally. He was also forced down four times behind enemy lines, but he always managed to get back. Bob was on the home front in April 1943 and brought down a B-17 bomber by ramming it—his fifty-seventh victory. He was involved with the Me 262 jet at the end of the war. Bob died on 12 August 2013 and is buried in Staufen Friedhof, Staufen im Breisgau, Baden-Württemberg.

494. *Oberleutnant* Heinrich HANBAUER

Hanbauer was born on 14 January 1917 in Wiener Neustadt, Austria-Hungary. He was a company commander in Rifle Regiment 86 when he was awarded the Knight's Cross on 7 March 1941. Hanbauer was killed in action at Beredino, Russia, on 3 July 1941 and has no known grave.

495. *Oberleutnant* Helmut MEIER

Meier was born on 30 January 1915 in Dresden. He was a company commander in Infantry Regiment 79 when he was killed in action on 17 June 1940. He is buried in the German War Cemetery, Block 14, Row 3, Grave 201, Andilly, near Toul, Lorraine, France. Meier was awarded the Knight's Cross on 7 March 1941.

496. Leutnant Karl HÖFLINGER

Höflinger was a born on 13 July 1917 in Kirchheim unter Teck. He was a pilot in Bomber Wing 77 when he was awarded the Knight's Cross on 7 March 1941. Höflinger was killed in action over England on 18 April 1941 and has no known grave.

497. Feldwebel Karl OFFSCHANY

Offschany was born on 23 November 1912 in Radzein, Austria-Hungary. He was a platoon leader in Infantry Regiment 191 when he was awarded the Knight's Cross on 7 March 1941. Offschany was killed in action on 4 October 1944 and is buried in the German War Cemetery, Block 15, Grave 867, Costermano, Italy.

498. Unteroffizier Walter PAPE

Pape was born on 20 December 1914 in Balagansk. He was a section leader in Infantry Regiment 211 when he was awarded the Knight's Cross on 7 March 1941. Pape died on 27 June 1989 in Magdeburg, Saxony.

499. Gefreiter Hubert BRINKFORTH

Brinkforth was born on 15 April 1916 in Marl. He fought in Poland and France, where his 37-mm anti-tank gun knocked-out nine British tanks in twenty minutes. It seems he was nominated for the Knight's Cross for this action, but he was not awarded it until 7 March 1941. Brinkforth was killed in action at Pogostje on 5 June 1942 and is buried in the German War Cemetery, Block 4, Row 12, Grave 1184, Sologubowka, Russia.

500. *Kapitänleutnant* Bernd KLUG

Klug was born on 12 December 1914 in Wuppertal. He took part in the Spanish Civil War. Klug was awarded the Iron Cross 1st and 2nd Class in 1940. He was commander of *S-28* from S-Boat Flotilla 1 when he was awarded the Knight's Cross on 12 March 1941. The Oak Leaves followed on 1 January 1944.

Klug's best action came on 28 February 1944 when he led the attack on Convoy T-4 consisting of LSTs, which were carrying out large-scale rehearsals for D-Day in the English Channel. *LST-507* and *LST-531* were sunk, and *LST-289* was badly damaged. Over 700 American servicemen were killed. This near disaster for the Allies was kept a secret for many years. The Germans had no idea how close they came to seriously upsetting the D-Day operation. Klug died on 15 June 1975 and is believed to be buried in Parkfriedhof, Eichhofstrasse 56, Kiel, Schleswig-Holstein.

501. Kapitän zur See Hans BÜTOW

Bütow was born on 28 December 1894 in Volpersdorf, Silesia. He fought in the First World War and was awarded the Iron Cross 1st and 2nd Class (1914). He was awarded the Iron Cross (1939) in 1940. Bütow was commander of Torpedo Boats when he was awarded the Knight's Cross on 12 March 1941. He died on 9 May 1974 in Hamburg.

502. *Hauptmann* Josef-Franz ECKINGER

Eckinger was born on 17 February 1904 in Steyr, Austria-Hungary. He was awarded the Iron Cross 1st and 2nd Class in 1940. Eckinger was commander of II Battalion, Rifle Regiment 1, when he was awarded the Knight's Cross on 17 March 1941. He was killed in action on 17 October 1941 and is buried at Tver, Russia; Eckinger's remains are awaiting transfer to a German war cemetery. He was awarded the Oak Leaves on 31 December 1941.

503. *Oberleutnant* Herbert GÖBEL

Göbel was born on 23 August 1913 in Dortmund. He was a company commander in Infantry Regiment 461 when he was awarded the Knight's Cross on 19 March 1941. Göbel died of wounds at Rusanowo, Russia, on 10 October 1941 and has no known grave.

504. *Oberleutnant* Joachim GENZOW

Genzow was born in Berlin on 13 December 1915. He was a squadron leader in Bomber Wing 2 when he was awarded the Knight's Cross on 23 March 1941. Genzow died on 7 March 1989 in Berlin.

505. Leutnant Heinz GESCHWILL

Geschwill was born on 25 April 1920 in Brühl. He was a pilot in Fighter Wing 3 when he was awarded the Knight's Cross on 23 March 1941. Geschwill died on 6 May 2009 and is buried in Beiertheim Friedhof, Karlsruhe, Baden-Württemberg.

506. *Oberleutnant* Hans BUCHHOLZ

Buchholz was born on 27 August 1908 in Altlandsberg. He was a pilot in Bomber Wing 40 when he was awarded the Knight's Cross on 24 March 1941. Buchholz was killed in action over the Atlantic on 19 May 1941; his body was not recovered.

507. *Hauptmann* Fritz FLIEGEL

Fliegel was born on born on 30 November 1907 in Berlin. He was a group commander in Bomber Wing 40 when he was awarded the Knight's Cross on 25 March 1941. Fliegel was killed in action when he was shot down over the Atlantic on 18 July 1941; his body was not recovered.

508. *Kapitänleutnant* Jürgen OESTEN

Oesten was born in Berlin on 24 October 1913. He transferred to the U-boat arm in 1937 and commissioned *U-61* on 12 August 1939. His first two patrols were to lay mines. The steamer *Gryfevale* was damaged by one and the *Ferryhill* sank by another. *U-61* sank its first ship with torpedoes on 22 January 1940, followed by four more shortly thereafter. On 29 September, he commissioned *U-106*; a spread of its torpedoes sank the 10,578-ton ship *Zealandic* on 16 January 1941 and the *Sesostris* on the 29th. Off Freetown, he sank the 7,506-ton *Memmon* on 11 March and damaged the battleship *Malaya* on 20 March. He was awarded the Knight's Cross on 26 March 1941.

On 2 September 1943, Oesten commissioned *U-861* and undertook his first patrol in the Indian Ocean in July 1944, sinking two ships *en route*. On 20 August 1944, he sank the *Berwickshire*, the *Ioannis Fafalios*, and torpedoed the 8,138-ton tanker *Daronia*. The submarine was taken to England on 29 May 1945 and sunk as part of Operation Deadlight. He sank nineteen ships altogether (a total of 101,744 tons). Oesten died on 5 August 2010 in Hamburg.

509. *Kapitänleutnant* Georg-Wilhelm SCHULZ

Schulz was born on 10 March 1906 in Cologne. He commissioned *U-64* on 16 December 1939 and sailed for Narvik on 11 April 1940. The boat was depth-charged and then sunk by bombs from HMS *Furious* on 13 April. Schulz and forty of his crew were rescued with help from the alpine infantry. On 11 June 1940, he commissioned *U-124*. On his fourth patrol, he sank eleven ships and torpedoed another two. He was awarded the Knight's Cross on 4 April 1941.

Schulz took command of the 6th U-Boat Flotilla, and on 4 October 1943, he transferred to the staff of the commander of training U-boats. His last command was the 25th U-Boat Flotilla. He died on 5 July 1986 in Hamburg.

510. Oberstleutnant Gustav PONATH

Ponath was born on 27 February 1898 in Hansfelde. He fought in Poland and France. Sent to Africa in February 1941, his unit fought as part of a battlegroup. Derna was taken on 8 April and, two days later, Ponath marched into the southern sector of Tobruk. He led several assaults on the fortress. Ponath was awarded the Knight's Cross on 13 April 1941. He died of wounds on 25 April 1941 and is buried in the German War Cemetery, Tobruk, Libya.

511. Oberstleutnant Irnfried Freiherr von WECHMAR

Freiherr von Wechmar was born in Berlin on 12 February 1899. He fought in the First World War, being awarded the Iron Cross 1st and 2nd Class (1914). Von Wechmar fought in France and Poland and was awarded the Iron Cross 1st and 2nd Class (1939). In Africa, he commanded the 3rd Reconnaissance Battalion; he captured En Nofilia, Agedabia, El Agheila, Solluch, and Benghazi. For this, he was awarded the Knight's Cross on 13 April 1941 personally by Rommel.

Constantly in contact with the enemy, in attack or defence, the battalion covered the withdrawal into the Agedabia position. Von Wechmar gave up his battalion and was made head of Army Propaganda Troops. In 1943–44, he fought on the Russian Front, but he surrendered in Denmark. Von Wechmar died on 27 November 1959 and is believed to be buried in Alter Friedhof, Bonn.

512. *Major* Otto HEYMER

Heymer was born on 29 September 1903 in Heepen. He was known as the man with the vision of a falcon and was indispensable to Rommel. He provided Rommel with information to plan his lightning raids by finding gaps in the enemy lines and reporting them to him. He was personally recommended for the Knight's Cross by Rommel and was awarded it on 13 April 1941.

He was forced to leave Africa due to illness and then served in several Luftwaffe staff positions. Heymer was killed on 25 February 1943 while on an inspection flight and is buried in the German War Cemetery, Smolensk-Nishnjaja Dubrowinka, Russia.

513. General Gustav von WIETERSHEIM

Von Wietersheim was born on 11 February 1884 in Breslau. He fought in the First World War and was awarded the Iron Cross 1st and 2nd Class (1914). He commanded the XIV Motorised Corps in Poland, France, Yugoslavia, and Russia, and he was awarded the Knight's Cross on 20 April 1941. He was later dismissed from command by Paulus for suggesting withdrawal at Stalingrad. He held no further commands, although he enlisted in the *Volkssturm* in 1945 at sixty-one years old. Von Wietersheim died on 25 April 1974 in Essen, North Rhine-Westphalia.

514. Generalleutnant Alfred Ritter von HUBICKI

Ritter von Hubicki was born on 5 February 1887 in Friedrichsdorf, Austria-Hungary. He fought in the Austrian Army during the First World War and was awarded the Iron Cross 2nd Class (1914). Von Hubicki commanded the 9th Panzer Division in Poland, the Netherlands, France, and the Balkans. He was awarded the Knight's Cross on 20 April 1941.

Promoted in October 1942, he commanded a special unit at the OKW and was then appointed as head of the German Military Mission to Slovakia. Von Hubicki was retired in March 1945. He died on 14 July 1971 and is buried in Zentralfriedhof, Vienna.

515. Generalmajor Ferdinand SCHÖRNER—'Bloody Ferdinand'

Schörner was born on 12 June 1892 in Munich. He fought in the First World War as a *Leutnant* and was awarded the Iron Cross 1st and 2nd Class (1914). On 5 December 1917, he was awarded the *Pour le Mérite*. He also fought in the *Freikorps*, but in the 1920s, he qualified for the General Staff. Promoted to *Oberstleutnant* in 1937, he commanded *Jäger* Regiment 98 in Poland and in the West. He was awarded the Iron Cross 1st and 2nd Class (1939). He led *Jäger* Regiment 6 in Greece, breaching the famous Metaxas Line; for this, he was awarded the Knight's Cross on 20 April 1941. He was always 'up front' and driving his men on. 'Sweat saves Blood' was one of his sayings.

Throughout the bitter fighting in Russia, he rose steadily in rank, always being sent to the trouble spots. It is said that during a Russian counteroffensive, he took part in hand-to-hand fighting. He was awarded the Oak Leaves on 17 February 1944, the Swords on 28 August 1944, and the Diamonds on 1 January 1945. Appointed to command the central group of armies on the Eastern Front in early 1945, *Generaloberst* Schörner managed to stabilise the front and fight a series of delaying actions.

In April 1945, he was the last man to be promoted to *Generalfeldmarschall*. Sentenced to twenty-five years' imprisonment by the Russians, he was released in 1955, but then had to face charges from a West German court for the execution of several deserters for which he served two years. Denied a pension from the German Government, he was paid the equivalent from a voluntary collection of veterans of *Jäger* Regiment 6. He died from a heart attack on 2 July 1973 and is buried Stadtfriedhof, Mittenwald, Bavaria. Marshal Koniev said of him: 'If it had not been for Schörner, the Red Army would have marched right through Bavaria'.

516. *Major* Walter GORN

Gorn was born on 24 September 1898 in Bieganin. He fought in the First World War and was awarded the Iron Cross 2nd Class (1914). He was a company commander in Rifle Regiment 10 when he was awarded the Knight's Cross on 20 April 1941. The Oak Leaves followed on 17 August 1942 and the Swords on 8 June 1943. Gorn ended the war as a *Generalmajor*. He died on 10 July 1968 and is buried in Rosenheim Friedhof, Bavaria.

517. SS-Obersturmführer Gerhard PLEISS—'Gerd'

Pleiss was born on 20 April 1915 in Remscheid. He awarded the Iron Cross 1st and 2nd Class for his part in the French campaign. Pleiss fought in the Balkans, during which he captured a key position, over 100 British prisoners, and twenty machine guns. For this, he was awarded the Knight's Cross on 20 April 1941.

He took part in the invasion of Russia, but during the fighting for Rostov, he stood on a mine and lost both legs; he died on the way to hospital. Pleiss was buried on the railway embankment at Taganrog, Russia.

518. *Oberleutnant* Erwin FISCHER

Fisher was born on 14 August 1912 in Dresden. He was a pilot in Reconnaissance Group 121 when he was awarded the Knight's Cross on 21 April 1941. The Oak Leaves followed on 8 February 1943. He flew over Poland, Denmark, Norway, France, Britain, Malta, and Russia. Fisher died on 10 December 1996 in Hamburg.

519. *Oberleutnant* Erich ZÜRN

Zürn was born on 23 July 1906 in Stuttgart. He was the leading engineer on *U-48* under Schulte, Rösing, and Bleichrodt. Zürn distinguished himself on a number of occasions, keeping a clear head. As Schultze put it, he was the 'soul' of the boat. He had already recommended him for the Knight's Cross and made another recommendation after he saved the boat from sinking a second time. Bleichrodt described him as 'always slate', meaning he could be depended upon. Zürn was awarded the Knight's Cross on 23 April 1941.

Later, as the 5th U-Boat Flotilla's engineer, he introduced a number of improvements that helped the flotilla's efficiency. He died on 9 August 1965 in Grossholzleute, Baden-Württemberg.

520. *Oberleutnant* zur See Klaus FELDT

Feldt was born on 14 April 1912 in Kiel. He awarded the Iron Cross 1st and 2nd Class after the Polish campaign. Feldt was commander of *S-30* in S-Boat Flotilla 2 when he was awarded the Knight's Cross on 25 April 1941. The Oak Leaves followed on 1 January 1944. Feldt died on 7 September 2010 in Wiesbaden, Hesse.

521. Leutnant Erich RUDORFFER—'The Fighter of Libau'

Rudorffer was born on 1 November 1917 in Zwochau. He shot down nine enemy aircraft by the end of the Battle for France. During the Battle of Britain, Rudorffer was said to have been pursued down Croydon High Street at below rooftop level by a Hurricane. He was awarded the Iron Cross 1st and 2nd Class in May and June 1940. Rudorffer was awarded the Knight's Cross on 1 May 1941, with nineteen victories to his credit. Rudorffer shot down twenty-six enemy aircraft over Tunisia and was recommended for the Oak Leaves when he shot down eight US aircraft on 9 February and another seven in just twenty minutes on 15 February 1943, but the award was not forthcoming.

Twice in Russia he shot down eleven aircraft in one day. Rudorffer was awarded the Oak Leaves on 11 April 1944 and the Swords on 26 January 1945. From February to April 1945, he flew the Me 262 jet, shooting down twelve enemy aircraft, including ten four-engined bombers. Rudorffer was shot down himself no less than sixteen times. By the end of the war, he had shot down 222 enemy aircraft; many of these were multiple victories, his best ever being thirteen victories in just seventeen minutes. He died on 8 April 2016 in Bad Schwartau, Schleswig-Holstein.

522. *Oberleutnant* zur See Georg CHRISTIANSEN

Christiansen was born on 21 October 1914 in Flensburg. He was awarded the Iron Cross 1st and 2nd Class in 1940. Christiansen was commander of torpedo boat *S-101* when he was awarded the Knight's Cross on 8 May 1941. He was awarded the Oak Leaves on 13 November 1943 as commander of S-Boat Flotilla 1. Christiansen died on 14 June 1997 in Kruså, Denmark.

523. Generalmajor Günther KORTEN

Korten was born on 26 July 1898 in Cologne. He fought in the First World War and was awarded the Iron Cross 1st and 2nd Class (1914). Korten was chief of the General Staff of *Luftflotte* 4 during the Battle for France and the Battle of Britain. For the Balkans campaign, he was moved to *Luftflotte* 4 and awarded the Knight's Cross on 13 May 1941.

Korten fought in Russia as commander of *Luftflotte* 4 until he was appointed chief-of-staff of the Luftwaffe in August 1943. He was mortally wounded in the 20 July bomb plot and died two days later. Korten was buried at the Tannenberg Memorial. As the Russians neared, his remains were exhumed and reburied in Bergstrasse Friedhof, Munich.

524. Generalmajor Wilhelm von APELL

Von Apell was born on 16 January 1892 in Bückeburg. He fought in the First World War and was awarded the Iron Cross 1st and 2nd Class (1914). Von Apell took part in the Polish campaign and was awarded the Iron Cross 1st and 2nd Class (1939).

He also took part in the campaigns in the West and the Balkans. Von Apell was commander of Rifle Brigade 9 when he was awarded the Knight's Cross on 14 May 1941. He fought in Russia. Von Apell died on 7 March 1969 and is buried in the village cemetery, Varnholt, near Baden Baden, Baden-Württemberg.

525. Generalmajor Ludwig CRÜWELL

Crüwell was born on 20 March 1892 in Dortmund. He fought in the First World War, being awarded the Iron Cross 1st and 2nd Class (1914). He was promoted to *Generalmajor* in December 1939 and awarded the Iron Cross 1st and 2nd Class in 1940 (1939). Crüwell was severing on the Army General Staff, and in August 1940, he became commander of 11th Panzer Division. Crüwell led his division in Yugoslavia and Greece, taking Belgrade and Saloniki. For this, he was awarded the Knight's Cross on 14 May 1941.

During Operation Barbarossa, his division captured Berdichev, smashed two bunker lines, and reached the area south of Zhitomir. For the battle at the Teterov River, Crüwell was awarded the Oak Leaves on 1 September 1941. He continued to distinguish himself in the battles of encirclement at Uman and Kiev. Crüwell commanded the Africa Corps in 1941, inflicting a severe defeat on the enemy at Sidi Rezegh. Shot down while on a reconnaissance flight, he was captured by the British. Crüwell died on 25 September 1958 and is buried in Ostfriedhof, Feld 9, Grave 10A–10B, Am Ostpark 3, Dortmund, North Rhine-Westphalia.

526. Generalmajor Heinrich KIRCHHEIM

Kirchheim was born on 6 April 1882 in Gross-Salze. He fought in the First World War, being awarded the Iron Cross 1st and 2nd Class (1914), as well as the *Pour le Mérite*. He was commander of the 169th Infantry Division during campaign in the West, for which he was awarded the Iron Cross 1st and 2nd Class (1939).

In March 1941, Rommel made Kirchheim leader of the Special HQ Libya, but he was often called upon to commanded units at the front. In April, he seized Barce and Derna, and although wounded, he took part in the battles for Tobruk. For this, he was awarded the Knight's Cross on 14 May 1941. At the end of May, he was appointed to the OKH in Berlin. Kirchheim was retired at the end of 1944 due to illness. He died on 14 December 1973 and is buried in Oberrahmede Friedhof, Lüdenscheid, North Rhine-Westphalia.

527. Oberst Helmuth BEUKEMANN

Beukemann was born on 9 May 1894 in Hamburg. He fought in the First World War and was awarded the Iron Cross 1st and 2nd Class (1914). Beukemann fought in Poland, for which he was awarded the Iron Cross 1st and 2nd Class (1939). He was commander of Infantry Regiment 382 in the Balkans when he was awarded the Knight's Cross on 14 May 1941. Beukemann died on 13 July 1981 and is buried in Bergstadt Friedhof, Hamburg.

528. *Major* Karl ENS

Ens was born on 21 March 1896 in Schön-Münzach. He was commander of II Battalion, Motorised Infantry Regiment 125, when he was awarded the Knight's Cross on 14 May 1941. Ens was posted missing near Görlitz on 15 April 1945.

529. *Major* Günther HOFFMANN-SCHÖNBORN

Hoffmann-Schönborn was born on 1 May 1905 in Posen. He was awarded the Iron Cross 1st and 2nd Class in 1940. Hoffmann-Schönborn was commander of Assault-Gun Battalion 191 when he was awarded the Knight's Cross on 14 May 1941 for breaching the Metaxas Line, and he was awarded the Oak Leaves on 31 December 1941 for penetrating 75 miles and securing the Dnjepr Bridge. He died on 4 April 1970 in Bad Kreuznach, Rhineland-Palatinate.

530. *Major* Heinrich KODRÉ

Kodré was born on 8 August 1899 in Vienna. He was commander of II Battalion, Infantry Regiment 123, when he was awarded the Knight's Cross on 14 May 1941. Kodré died on 22 May 1977 and is believed to be buried in St Barbara Friedhof, Linz, Austria.

531. *Kapitänleutnant* Herbert KUPPISCH

Kuppisch was born on 10 December 1909 in Hamburg. He commissioned *U-58* on 4 February 1939, and on 31 December, he torpedoed a British destroyer. He sank his first ship on 1 January 1940 followed by another two days later. Further success was limited, but he did sink the 8,401-ton British steamer *Astronomer*.

On 10 August 1940, Kuppisch commissioned *U-94* and scored his first success in December against convoy HX90; this was followed by another five ships on the same patrol. He was awarded the Knight's Cross on 14 May 1941. While attacking convoy OB318, he fired at four steamers, sinking the 10,263-ton British *Ixion* and the 5,658-ton Norwegian *Eastern Star*. In May, he also picked of three ships from convoy HX126, including the Norwegian tanker *John P. Pedersen*. Now in command of *U-847* in the Sargasso Sea, he was attacked by aircraft from the US carrier *Card* on 27 August 1943; the U-boat was sent to the bottom, and there were no survivors.

532. *Major* Theodor Graf SCHIMMELMANN von LINDENBURG

Graf Schimmelmann von Lindenburg was born on 3 March 1896 in Ahrensburg. He was commander of II Battalion, Panzer Regiment 15, when he was awarded the Knight's Cross on 14 May 1941. Graf Schimmelmann von Lindenburg died on 19 November 1970 in Ahrensburg, Schleswig-Holstein.

533. SS-Hauptsturmführer Fritz KLINGENBERG

Klingenberg was born on 17 December 1912 in Röversahgen. He fought in France, being awarded the Iron Cross 1st and 2nd Class. During the Balkans campaign, Klingenberg, with just eleven other men, entered Belgrade and persuaded the mayor to surrender. For this, he was awarded the Knight's Cross on 14 May 1941.

He spent more of the remainder of the war training foreign volunteers for the *Waffen*-SS. In January 1945, he was given command of the 17th

SS-*Panzergrenadier* Division. Klingenberg was killed in action on 25 March 1945 and is buried in the German War Cemetery, Block 35, Row 132, Grave 730, Andilly, near Toul, Lorraine, France.

534. *Oberleutnant* Johann RAST

Rast was born on 21 April 1914 in Traisen. He was a company commander in Mountain Pioneer Battalion 85 when he was awarded the Knight's Cross on 14 May 1941. Rast was killed in action on 31 August 1944 and is buried in the Laurahütte German War Cemetery, Block 4, Row 53, Grave 1257, Siemianowice Śląskie, near Bytom, Poland.

535. *Oberleutnant* Fritz SCHIRRMACHER

Schirrmacher was born on 25 March 1915 in Neuhöfchen. He was a company commander in Panzer Pioneer Battalion 13 when he was awarded the Knight's Cross on 14 May 1941. Schirrmacher was posted missing near Eisenbrod during April 1945.

536. Leutnant Rolf SCHNEEGE

Schneege was born on 2 October 1918 in Königsberg. He was a platoon leader in Motorised Infantry Regiment 129 when he was killed in action on 15 June 1940; he is buried in the German War Cemetery, Block 21, Row 13, Grave 390, Niederbronn-les-Bains, France. Schneege was awarded the Knight's Cross on 14 May 1941.

537. Oberfeldwebel Walter MEYER

Meyer was born on 2 February 1912 in Freiburg. He was a section leader in Infantry Regiment 125 when he was awarded the Knight's Cross on 14 May 1941. Meyer died on 2 July 1992 in Freiburg im Breisgau, Baden-Württemberg.

538. Oberfeldwebel Peter VEESER

Veeser was born on 25 July 1915 in Nusplingen. He was a section leader in Infantry Regiment 125 when he was awarded the Knight's Cross on 14 May 1941. Veeser died on 10 April 1989 in Nusplingen, Baden-Württemberg.

539. *Major* Ernst BOLBRINKER

Bolbrinker was born on 23 October 1898 in Graz, Austria-Hungary. He fought in the First World War and was awarded the Iron Cross 1st and 2nd Class (1914). Awarded the Iron Cross 2nd Class for the Polish campaign, he also fought in France. By April 1940, he was a *Major* in Panzer Regiment 1. Bolbrinker was reassigned to Panzer Regiment 5 and sent to Africa on 11 March 1941, and he was awarded the Iron Cross 1st Class in April 1941.

His tanks were soon in action, knocking-out two British tanks and capturing Marsa el Brega. At Mechili, he stormed into the fort behind an enemy column; three out of four of his tanks were put out of action, but they still managed to destroy the British anti-tank guns. With the fall of Mechili, 2,000 prisoners, including two generals, were taken. For this, he was awarded the Knight's Cross on 15 May 1941. Recalled to Germany, he spent the rest of the war in staff posts. Bolbrinker died on 2 July 1962 in Bielefeld, North Rhine-Westphalia.

540. *Kapitänleutnant* Herbert WOHLFARHT

Wohlfarht was born on 5 June 1915 in Kanagawa, Japan. He commanded *U-14* when the war started, and he carried out several mine-laying missions. On 15 June 1940, Wohlfarht commissioned *U-137* and sunk three ships on his first patrol. He had more success in October and November before commissioning *U-556* on 6 February 1941.

While on his next patrol, he attacked convoy OB314, sinking several ships and torpedoing the 13,000-ton tanker *San Felix*, but she was towed to port. It was while on this patrol that Wohlfarht was awarded the Knight's Cross on 15 May 1941. With no torpedoes left, he headed for home; *en route*, he sighted the ships pursuing the *Bismarck* and reported their position in an attempt to help her. *U-556* returned to sea, and on 27 June 1941, while engaging convoy HX133, she was depth-charged and forced to the surface; she was sunk by the corvettes *Celandine*, *Gladiolus*, and *Nasturtium*—five were killed and the rest taken prisoner. Wohlfarht died on 13 August 1982 in Villingen, Baden-Württemberg.

541. *Oberleutnant* Winrich BEHR—'Teddy'

Behr was born on 22 January 1918 in Berlin. He fought in Poland and France with Armoured Reconnaissance Battalion 3. In February 1941, the battalion was moved to North Africa, where it was immediately sent into action. Behr and his motorcycle troops were sent toward El Agheila and Behr accounted for the first enemy armoured car knock-out by the Germans in Africa.

On 24 March 1941, Behr drove into El Agheila, breaking all resistance. He then drove around Marsa el Brega and headed for Benghazi. Behr captured six guns, stormed enemy nests, and captured Fort Benina. Behr's motorcycle troops spearheaded the subsequent advance, capturing two enemy tanks and Bardia. Already awarded the Iron Cross 1st and 2nd Class, he was awarded the Knight's Cross on 15 May 1941. Falling ill, he was sent home in December 1941 and, following promotion to *Hauptmann*, spent the remainder of the war on the staff. Behr died on 25 April 2011 and is buried in Hubbelrath Friedhof, Düsseldorf.

542. *Hauptmann* Klaus NÖSKE

Nöske was born on 26 November 1911 in Potsdam. He fought in Poland, France, and the Battle of Britain. Nöske was a squadron leader in Bomber Wing 4 when he was awarded the Knight's Cross on 15 May 1941 for combat in Russia. He died on 15 May 1978 and is believed to be buried in Stadtfriedhof, Göttingen, Lower Saxony.

543. *Oberleutnant* Gerhard CZERNIK

Czernik was born on 12 January 1913 in Breslau. He fought in the Condor Legion in Spain. Czernik also saw action in Poland, France, the Battle of Britain, and the Balkans. He was a squadron leader in Bomber Wing 2 when he was awarded the Knight's Cross on 16 May 1941. Czernik was killed in action near Sloterdijk on 20 October 1941 and is buried in the German War Cemetery, Block CW, Row 6, Grave 143, Timmermansweg, Ysselsteyn, the Netherlands.

544. Generalmajor Hans von GREIFFENBERG

Von Greiffenberg was born on 12 October 1893 in Radensfelde. He fought in the First World War and was awarded the Iron Cross 1st and 2nd Class (1914). Von Greiffenberg was chief of the General Staff of XII Army when he was awarded the Knight's Cross on 18 May 1941. He died on 30 June 1951 and is believed to be buried in Stadtfriedhof, Königstein im Taumus, Hesse.

545. Oberst Kurt ZEITZLER

Zeitzler was born on 9 June 1895 in Gossmar. He fought in the First World War and was awarded the Iron Cross 1st and 2nd Class (1914). Zeitzler was chief-of-staff to Siegmund List during the Polish campaign. In March 1940, he became chief-of-staff to von Kleist. In this post, he served in France and brilliantly organised and managed the panzers through the Ardennes. After the Balkans, he was awarded the Knight's Cross on 18 May 1941.

His greatest success was in Russia, where he managed to supply his panzer army on the long marches deep into enemy territory. In January 1942, he was posted as chief-of-staff to von Rundstedt and played an important role in responding to the British raid on Dieppe in August 1942. On 24 September 1942, Zeitzler was made chief of the General Staff serving directly under Hitler. It was not long before the two would argue over the conduct of the war, and in July 1944, Zeitzler reported he could no longer serve due to ill health. Zeitzler died on 25 September 1963 in Hohenaschau, Bavaria.

546. SS-Sturmbannführer Kurt MEYER—'Panzer Meyer'

Meyer was born on 23 December 1910 in Jerxheim. He fought in Poland, for which he was awarded the Iron Cross 2nd Class, and France, for which he was awarded the Iron Cross 1st Class. Mayer also fought in Greece where he personally led his men in the capture of the Klissura Pass, for which he was awarded the Knight's Cross on 18 May 1941. He took part in the invasion of Russia and was awarded the Oak Leaves on 23 February 1943 for his part in the battle for Kharkov.

Meyer was given command of a regiment in the 12th SS-Panzer Division and commanded it in Normandy. Later, he would command the division. For his actions in Normandy, he was awarded the Swords on 27 August 1944.

Eleven days later, he was captured by Belgian partisans and handed to the British. Meyer was tried for crimes committed by men under his command and sentenced to death. Following a wave of protests, his sentence was commuted to life; he was released in 1954. Kurt 'Panzer' Meyer died from a heart attack on 23 December 1961 and is buried in Stadtfriedhof, Block 16, Grave 16, Kuhlestrasse, Hagen, North Rhine-Westphalia. His funeral was attended by thousands of his comrades.

547. *Major* Hermann STIEFVATER

Stiefvater was born on 11 June 1903 in Freilburg im Breisgau. He was commander of Panzer *Jäger* Battalion 173 when he was awarded the Knight's Cross on 18 May 1941. Stiefvater died on 16 April 1977 and is believed to be believed to be buried in Isola di San Michele, Venice, Italy.

548. *Hauptmann* Wilhelm Prinz von SCHÖNBURG-WALDENBURG

Prinz von Schönburg-Waldenburg was born on 3 April 1913 in Guteborn-Schwarz-Bach. He was a company commander in Panzer Regiment 31 when he was awarded the Knight's Cross 18 May 1941. Von Schönburg-Waldenburg was killed in action near Villers-Bocage on 11 June 1944 and is buried in Dorffriedhof, Parfouru-sur-Odon, France.

549. *Kapitänleutnant* Georg SCHEWE

Schewe was born on 24 November 1909 in Ueckermünde. At the start of the war, he was at sea on *U-60* laying mines, and on 17 December 1939, the British ship *City of Kobe* was sunk by one of them. On 10 September 1940, he commissioned *U-105*, and on his first patrol in January 1941, he sank two ships. In March, he sank seven ships, mostly from convoy SL68. On 6 May, he sank three ships, and then, on the 16th, one of his torpedoes stopped the merchant ship *Rodney*, which was finished off with gunfire. The last ship sunk on this patrol was the 4,719-ton *Scottish Monarch*. He was awarded the Knight's Cross on 23 May 1941.

He sank another ship on 11 September, before attacking convoy SC42, sinking a small steamer. Forced to submerge and withdraw due to serious damage, he returned to base. Schewe handed his boat over to *Kapitänleutnant* Nissen and became an official in the OKM. He died on 16 September 1989 in Hamburg.

550. Konteradmiral Eberhard WOLFRAM

Wolfram was born on 24 July 1882 in Gerbstedt. He fought in the First World War and was awarded the Iron Cross 1st and 2nd Class (1914). Wolfram was commander-in-chief of the security for the North Sea when he was awarded the Knight's Cross on 25 May 1941. He died on 6 January 1947 in Hamburg.

551. Korvettenkapitän Adalbert SCHNEIDER

Schneider was born on 31 December 1913 in Halle. He was first gunnery officer on the battleship *Bismarck* when, on 24 May 1941, after firing only five salvos, she hit HMS *Hood*, which exploded, sinking her and killing all but three of her crew. For this, Schneider was awarded the Knight's Cross on 27 May 1941, but he was never to wear it as the *Bismarck* was sunk the same day by HMS *Rodney* and HMS *King Gorge V*. He went down with his ship.

552. *Kapitänleutnant* Claus KORTH

Korth was born in Berlin on 7 October 1911. He joined the *Reichsmarine* in April 1932. When the war stared, he was on patrol from the very first days; commanding *U-37*, he sank two ships on 19 November 1939. Another followed in December and two more in January 1940. Then, on 14 February, he sank the 10,191-ton British tanker *Gretafield*. In March, he sank two more ships.

He commissioned *U-93* on 30 July 1940, and on his first patrol, he sank the 9,331-ton *Huruni*; two more ships went to the bottom on 17 October. In January 1941, he attacked convoy SC19; firing all of his torpedoes, he sank three ships, including the 10,468-ton tanker *W. B. Walker*. Another ship was sunk in February. On a patrol in May, he attacked convoy HX126, firing two torpedoes at the 6,235-ton Dutch tanker *Elusa*, which sank. He was awarded the Knight's Cross on 29 May 1941. Korth's last command was as officer in charge of the TVA-North. He died on 25 January 1988 and is believed to be buried in Parkfriedhof, Eichhofstrasse 56, Kiel, Schleswig-Holstein.

553. Oberstleutnant Gustav-Georg KNABE

Knabe was born on 8 July 1897 in Wichmannsdorf. He fought in the First World War and was awarded the Iron Cross 1st and 2nd Class. Knabe commanded a battalion in the 1940 western campaign. In Africa, his battalion captured Sollum and Capuzzo. On 1 June 1941, he was awarded the Knight's Cross. Knabe was forced to leave Africa due to illness, after which he held staff posts. His wartime career came to an end when he was injured in a car crash. Knabe died on 13 December 1972 and is buried in Hauptfriedhof, Bad Dürkheim, Rhineland-Palatinate.

554. *Oberleutnant* Fritz HEIDENREICH

Heidenreich was born on 29 June 1916 in Bielefeld. He was an observer in Reconnaissance Group 120 when he was awarded the Knight's Cross on 3 June 1941. He was killed in action on 30 May 1944 off the coast of Norway and has no known grave.

555. *Oberleutnant* Siegfried GRABERT

Grabert was born on 11 January 1916 in Schorndorf. He fought in Poland and France and was awarded the Iron Cross 1st and 2nd Class in 1940. Grabert also fought in the Balkans campaign and in Russia. He was awarded the Knight's Cross on 10 June 1941. Grabert was killed in action on 25 July 1942 near Batajsk, Russia, and has no known grave. He was awarded the Oak Leaves on 6 November 1943.

556. Leutnant Otto TOLL

Toll was born on 5 September 1917 in Schönborn. He was a platoon leader in Pioneer Battalion 200 when he was awarded the Knight's Cross on 10 June 1941. At some point, he was transferred to the *Waffen*-SS. Toll was killed in action on 10 June 1944 and is buried in the German War Cemetery (as unknown), La Cambe, Normandy, France.

557. Generalmajor Julius RINGEL—'Papa'

Ringel was born on 16 November 1889 in Völkermarkt, Austria-Hungary. He fought in the Austrian Army during the First World War. Ringel took part in the French campaign and commanded the 3rd Mountain Division in the Balkans and Crete. For his outstanding leadership, he was awarded the Knight's Cross on 13 June 1941.

In November 1941, his division played a major part in defeating the Volkhov Front; for this, he was awarded the Oak Leaves on 25 October 1943. Ringel later fought in Italy, but he ended the war in Croatia. Ringel died on 10 February 1967 in Bayerisch Gmain, Bavaria.

558. Oberst Maximilian von HERFF

Von Herff was born in Hannover on 17 April 1893. He fought in the First World War, being awarded the Iron Cross 1st and 2nd Class (1914). At the start of the Second World War, he was adjutant with XVII Army Corps. In Africa, he commanded the 115th Rifle Regiment, and he and his battle group stormed east and captured a number of enemy positions. Von Herff's forces were also involved in the Battle of Halfaya Pass and in defeating British attacks; on his own initiative, von Herff stormed up the pass to Capuzzo and Sollum, capturing both places. Rommel personally recommended him for the Knight's Cross, which was awarded on 13 June 1941.

Summoned to Berlin, von Herff was transferred to the *Waffen*-SS and served in the Main Personnel Office of the SS. He was in Warsaw during the uprising in 1943. Taken prisoner by the British, von Herff died from a stroke on 6 September 1945 and is buried in the German War Cemetery, Block 3, Row 7, Grave 223, Camp Road, Cannock Chase, Staffordshire, England.

559. Oberstleutnant Karl DECKER

Decker was born on 30 November 1897 in Borntin. He fought in the First World War, being awarded the Iron Cross 1st and 2nd Class (1914). Decker fought in Poland and was awarded the Iron Cross 1st and 2nd Class (1939). He also took part in the French and Balkans campaigns and was awarded the Knight's Cross for his personal bravery on 13 June 1941.

Decker was awarded the Oak Leaves in Russia on 4 May 1944. He committed suicide on 21 April 1945 in the Ruhr Pocket and has no known grave. Decker was awarded the Swords on 26 April 1945 (date assigned by the AKCR).

560. *Major* Albin ESCH

Esch was born on 22 June 1901 in Dieburg. He was commander of III Battalion, Mountain *Jäger* Regiment 85, when he was awarded the Knight's Cross on 13 June 1941. Esch died on 3 March 1959 and is buried in Alter Friedhof, Schorndorf, Baden-Württemberg.

561. *Hauptmann* Albert GAUM

Gaum was born on 15 October 1914 in Kempten. He was commander of II Battalion, Mountain *Jäger* Regiment 100, when he was awarded the Knight's Cross on 13 June 1941. Gaum died on 19 July 1977 in Korsika, Hesse.

562. *Hauptmann* Heinrich NIETSCHE

Nietsche was born on 5 March 1907 in Marburg. He was commander of III Battalion, Infantry Regiment 105, when he was awarded the Knight's Cross on 13 June 1941. Nietsche killed himself near Litoměřice on 9 May 1945 and has no known grave.

563. *Hauptmann* Franz PFEIFFER

Pfeiffer was born on 23 October 1907 in Munich. He fought in Poland, for which he was awarded the Iron Cross 2nd Class, and France, being awarded the Iron Cross 1st Class. Pfeiffer also fought in Yugoslavia, Crete, and Russia. He was a company commander in Mountain *Jäger* Regiment 100 when he was awarded the Knight's Cross on 13 June 1941. Pfeiffer died on 20 November 1994 and is believed to be buried in Waldfriedhof, Munich.

564. *Hauptmann* Heribert RAITHEL

Raithel was born on 14 June 1910 in Ingolstadt. He was commander of II Battalion, Mountain Artillery Regiment 95, when he was awarded the Knight's Cross on 13 June 1941. Raithel died on 14 July 1976 in Erding, Bavaria.

565. *Oberleutnant* Karl-Peter JACOB

Jacob was born on 30 December 1909 in Kaiserslautern. He was a company commander in Mountain *Jäger* Regiment 143 when he was awarded the Knight's Cross on 13 June 1941. Jacob died on 22 February 1992 in Berg, Bavaria.

566. *Oberleutnant* Karl MICKLEY

Mickley was born on 1 October 1901 in Förderstedt. He was a company commander in Rifle Regiment 304 when he was awarded the Knight's Cross on 13 June 1941. Mickley died on 25 January 1987 and is buried in Wathlingen Friedhof, Lower Saxony.

567. *Oberleutnant* Egon ORINSCHNIG

Orinschnig was born on 30 December 1913 in Pola. He was a company commander in Infantry Regiment 266 when he was awarded the Knight's Cross on 13 June 1941. Orinschnig was killed in action on 11 September 1942 and is buried in the German War Cemetery (as unknown), Rzhev, Russia.

568. Leutnant Hans DROSTE

Droste was born on 29 March 1915 in Wuppertal. He was a shock troop leader in Infantry Regiment 124 when he was awarded the Knight's Cross on 13 June 1944. Droste died on 13 July 1976 and is buried in Burgtor Friedhof, Lubeck, Schleswig-Holstein.

569. Oberjäger Johann SANDNER

Sandner was born on 15 October 1921 in Osterhofen. He was a section leader in *Jäger* Regiment 100 when he was awarded the Knight's Cross on 13 June 1941. Sandner died on 26 December 1983 and is believed to be buried in Marzoll Friedhof, Bad Reichenhall, Bavaria.

570. Gefreiter Helmuth VALTINER

Valtiner was born on 7 October 1919 in Lana. He was a section leader in Mountain *Jäger* Regiment 143 when he was awarded the Knight's Cross on 13 June 1941. Valtiner died on 4 March 1987 in Lana, Italy.

571. Generalmajor Eugen MEINDL

Meindl was born on 16 July 1892 in Donaueschingen. He fought in the artillery during the First World War, being awarded the Iron Cross 1st and 2nd Class (1914). In November 1939, he was made commander of *Jäger* Artillery Regiment 112 with the rank of *Oberstleutnant*. His first jump was at Narvik, although he was not officially transferred to the Luftwaffe until November 1940; by then, he had been awarded the Iron Cross 1st and 2nd Class (1939). In Crete, as *Generalmajor*, he was seriously wounded in the chest near the Platanias Bridge. Meindl was awarded the Knight's Cross on 14 June 1941.

On 26 February 1942, he became commander of Luftwaffe Division Meindl in Russia, and on 26 September, he took over XII *Fliegerkorps*, later I Luftwaffe Field Corps. He commanded II Parachute Corps in Normandy and was awarded the Oak Leaves on 31 August 1944. He also commanded his unit at Cleve, the Reichswald, Goch, and in the Wesel bridgehead. Meindl was awarded the Swords on 8 May 1945 (this award was made in accordance with the Dönitz-Decree). He died on 24 January 1951 and is buried in Stadtfriedhof, Donaueschingen, Baden-Württemberg.

572. Oberst Richard HEIDRICH

Heidrich was born on 27 July 1896 in Lewalde. He served in the First World War, being awarded the Iron Cross 1st and 2nd Class (1914). Heidrich formed a parachute battalion in 1938, which became part of *Fallschirmjäger* Regiment 1. He left the Luftwaffe for a short time, but was persuaded by Student to return and lead *Fallschirmjäger* Regiment 3 during the invasion of

Above left: Fedor von Bock.

Above right: Wilhelm Keitel.

Right: Wilhelm List.

Above left: Johannes Blaskowitz.

Above right: Albert Kesselring.

Left: Günther von Kluge.

Above left: Walter von Reichenau.

Above right: Günther Prien.

Right: Heinz Guderian.

Above left: Franz Halder

Above right: Erich Hoepner.

Left: Freidrich Olbricht.

Above left: August Schmidt.

Above right: Walter Koch.

Right: Joachim Meissner.

Above left: Helmut Arpke.

Above right: Ewald von Kleist.

Left: Herbert Schmidt.

Above: Ernst Busch.

Right: Hans von Schlebrügge.

Friedrich Dollmann.

Alois Stoeckl.

Above left: Alois Lindmayr.

Above right: Adolf 'Dolfo' Galland.

Right: Albert von Schwerin.

Above: Arnold von Biegeleben.

Below left: Heinrich Liebe.

Below right: Kurt Fimmen.

Above: Walter Rubensdörffer.

Below left: Helmut Wick.

Below right: Hans-Rudolf Rösing.

Above left: Fritz Witt.

Above right: The grave of Fritz Witt.

Ludwig Kepplinger.

Above left: Joachim Schepke.

Above right: Georg von Bismarck.

Right: Martin Lutz.

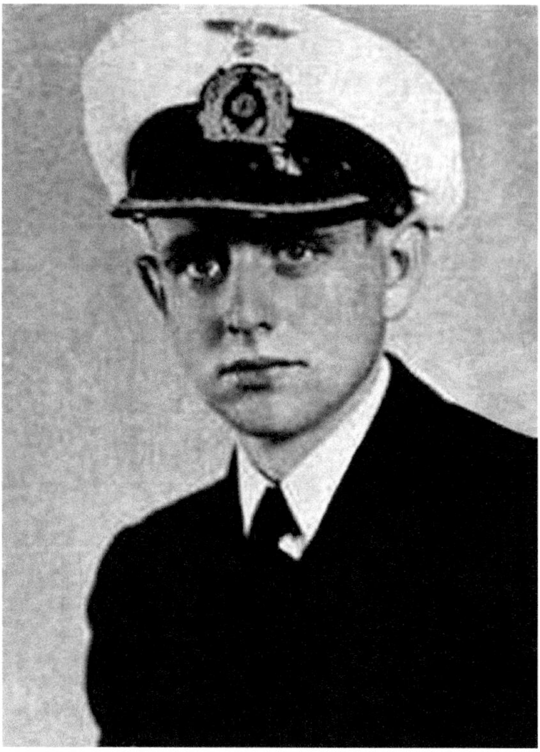

Above left: Gerd Suhren.

Above right: Walter Adolph.

Left: Hermann Kühl.

Above left: Franz Xaver von Werra—'The One that Got Away'.

Above right: Hans-Gerrit von Stockhausen.

Right: Erich Rudorffer.

Above left: Gerhard Czernik.

Above right: Maximilian von Herff.

Left: Richard Heidrich.

Above left: Walter Gericke.

Above right: Erich Topp.

Right: Erich Marcks.

Ludwig Streil.

Above: Walter Model—'Hitler's Fireman'.

Below left: Friedrich August von der Heydte.

Below right: Karl-Heinz Becker.

Hans Hahn.

Paul Gildner

Otto Lasch.

Walter K. Nehring.

Jost Metzler.

Hugo Dahmer.

KONRAD EYDT
UFFZ.
30.7.1899 † 28.6.44
FRANZ BEYER
MAJOR
22.4.18 † 11.2.44
L
11-263

Franz Beyer.

Above: Reinhold Eckardt.

Below: Herbert Huppertz.

Kurt Ubben.

Above: Josef Wurmheller.

Left: Hermann Hogeback..

Konrad-Oskar Heinrichs.

Walter Bradel.

Heinrich Wittkopf.

Above: Willi Welsch.

Left: Kurt von der Chevallerie.

Above left: Rolf Mützelburg.

Above right: Wilhelm Falley.

Alfred Gause.

Fritz Bayerlein.

Crete in 1941. Heidrich was awarded the Iron Cross 1st and 2nd Class (1939) on 25 May 1941 and the Knight's Cross on 14 June 1941. He commanded the 1st Parachute Division on the Eastern Front in 1942.

From 12 July 1943, his division was redeployed to Sicily and fought around the Primosole Bridge. His division fought in Italy in the Anzio/Nettuno area and during the three battles for Cassino. He was awarded the Oak Leaves on 5 February 1944 and the Swords on 25 March 1944. He oversaw the withdrawal up the entire length of Italy and was captured by the Americans on 2 May 1945 and handed over to the British. He died in hospital on 23 December 1947 and is buried in Bergedorf Friedhof, Hamburg.

573. *Major* Ludwig HEILMANN

Heilmann was born on 9 August 1903 in Würzburg. He was awarded the Iron Cross 1st Class for the invasion of France in 1940 while serving with Infantry Regiment 91. He joined the airborne forces and dropped into Crete in May 1941 while commanding III Battalion, *Fallschirmjäger* Regiment 1. He was awarded the Knight's Cross on 14 June 1941. In the late autumn, his battalion was sent to Russia where they fought as infantry at the Vyborgskaya bridgehead. Heilmann was given command of *Fallschirmjäger* Regiment 3 in November 1943 and parachuted into Sicily to reinforce the Hermann Göring Panzer Division. On the Italian mainland, his regiment fought near Ortona, which he held until 28 December.

His regiment also fought at Cassino and the Monastery Mountain. He was awarded the Oak Leaves on 2 March 1944 and the Swords on 15 May 1944. Heilmann commanded the 5th Parachute Division in the Ardennes offensive. He was captured just at the end of the war. He died on 26 October 1959 in Kempten, Bavaria.

574. *Hauptmann* Walter GERICKE

Gericke was born on 23 December 1907 in Bilderlahe. He joined *Fallschirmjäger* Regiment 1 in April 1938 and took part in the invasion of Denmark in April 1940, capturing the Storstromm Bridge. He was awarded the Iron Cross 2nd Class on 10 April 1940. During the invasion of the Netherlands, his men captured the Dordrecht Bridge, for which he was awarded the Iron Cross 1st Class on 12 May 1940.

In Crete, he commanded the Glider Assault Regiment's IV Battalion. He pinned down the enemy on the coastal road east of Maleme and, on his own initiative, launched an attack in the direction of Chania, capturing the citadel.

For this, he was awarded the Knight's Cross on 14 June 1941. Gericke's most daring jump was into the Italian HQ on Monte Rotondo after the Italians left the Axis alliance. Next, he fought in the Anzio/Nettuno area and was awarded the Oak Leaves on 17 September 1944 for his successful blocking operations. He died on 19 October 1991 and is buried in Alsfeld Friedhof, Hesse.

575. *Hauptmann* Kuno HOFFMANN

Hoffmann was born on 24 May 1907 in Posen. He was a group commander in Close Support Wing 1 when he was awarded the Knight's Cross on 14 June 1941. Hoffmann was killed in action in Berlin on 25 January 1944 and has no known grave.

576. *Hauptmann* Ralph von RETTBERG

Von Rettberg was born on 1 March 1911 in Bad Homburg. He was a group commander in Heavy Fighter Wing 26 when he was awarded the Knight's Cross on 14 June 1941. Von Rettberg died on 25 February 2004 and is believed to be buried in Waldfriedhof, Munich.

577. *Hauptmann* Gerhart SCHIRMER

Schirmer was born in Chemnitz on 9 January 1913. He transferred to the Airborne Arm in May 1939, and on 15 September, he became commander of the 6th Company, *Fallschirmjäger* Regiment 2. Schirmer took part in the airborne attack on the Corinth Canal in Greece, taking command of the II Battalion when its commander was injured on landing. He occupied the airfield and pursued the enemy across the Peloponnese, capturing seventy-two British Officers and 1,200 other ranks, along with 9,000 Greek troops, including the CO of the army of the Peloponnese. He was awarded the Iron Cross 1st and 2nd Class on 28 May 1940.

In Crete, he landed at Heraklion as commander of the strategic reserve and captured Hill 296. For this, he was awarded the Knight's Cross on 14 June 1941. In Tunisia, he commanded III Battalion, *Fallschirmjäger* Regiment 5, in the defensive fighting and later took command of the regiment when Koch was put out of action. On 1 January 1944, Schirmer became commander of *Fallschirmjäger* Regiment 16 on the Eastern Front, with which he fought during the retreat into positions guarding East Prussia and in the Memel bridgehead. He was awarded the Oak Leaves on 18 November 1944. On 8 May 1945,

Schirmer was taken prisoner by the Red Army. It was almost eleven years before he was released. He died on 5 September 2004 in Lauf-Aubach, Bavaria.

578. *Hauptmann* Wilhelm SPIES

Spies was born on 26 August 1913 in Rimpar. He was a Bf 110 pilot in the Polish campaign, for which he was awarded the Iron Cross 2nd Class, and the French campaign, for which he was awarded the Iron Cross 1st Class. Spies also took part in the Battle of Britain and the Balkans campaign. He was a squadron leader in Heavy Fighter Wing 26 when he was awarded the Knight's Cross on 14 June 1941.

With twenty victories to his credit, Spies was shot down and killed on 27 January 1942 near Suchinitschi, Russia. He has no known grave. Spies was awarded the Oak Leaves on 5 April 1942.

579. *Oberleutnant* Sophus BAAGOE

Baagoe was born on 4 March 1915 in Flensburg. He fought in France as a Bf 110 pilot, shooting down his first four enemy aircraft and being awarded the Iron Cross 1st and 2nd Class. Baagoe also fought in the Battle of Britain, during which he shot down another nine enemy aircraft—very good for a twin-engined heavy fighter.

His last victory was over Crete on 20 April 1941 when he shot down British ace Pat Marmaduke (whom he claimed with Theodor Rossiwall). Baagoe was shot down on 14 May 1941 and is buried in the German War Cemetery, Block 1, Grave 480, Hill 107, Maleme, Crete. He was awarded the Knight's Cross on 14 May 1941.

580. *Oberleutnant* Johannes DIENHOLD

Dienhold was born on 23 February 1901 in Dresden. He was a company commander in Motorised Flak Regiment 23 when he was awarded the Knight's Cross on 14 June 1941. Dienhold died on 4 November 1990 and is buried in Hauptfriedhof, Am Stadion 1, Trier, Rhineland-Palatinate.

581. *Oberleutnant* Heinz FORGATSCH

Forgatsch was born on 8 March 1915 in Bunzlau. He was a pilot in *Kampfgruppe* 806 when he was awarded the Knight's Cross on 14 June 1941.

Forgatsch was killed in action at Rechlin on 23 September 1941 and has no known grave.

582. *Oberleutnant* Alfred GENZ

Genz was born in Berlin on 8 March 1916. He took part in the invasion of Poland with *Fallschirmjäger* Regiment 1. He fought in Crete and was awarded the Knight's Cross on 14 June 1941. He saw action in Tunisia with *Fallschirmjäger* Regiment 5 and was later appointed to Student's staff.

On 1 December 1943, he took command of *Fallschirmjäger* Assault Regiment 12, and on 1 January 1945, he was charged with forming a replacement parachute battalion. In April 1945, he took command of *Fallschirmjäger* Regiment 29. At the war's end, he was captured by the Soviets. Genz died on 23 April 2000 and is buried in Westfriedhof, 235U, Grave 127, Munich.

583. *Oberleutnant* Gerhard HOMUTH

Homuth was born in Kiel on 20 September 1914. In 1940, he fought over France and Britain, shooting down fifteen enemy aircraft. He was transferred to Africa in March 1941, where there was some friction between Homuth and Marseille. He was awarded the Knight's Cross on 14 June 1941 after shooting down his twenty-second enemy aircraft.

In February 1943, he was assigned to the air *attaché* in Sofia, but returned to flying in June. Homuth was shot down on 3 August 1943 over Orel, Russia, and has no know grave.

584. *Oberleutnant* Rudolf TOSCHKA

Toschka was born on 26 September 1911 in Berlin. He was a platoon leader in *Fallschirmjäger* Regiment 1 and took part in the attack on 'Fortress Holland', landing by glider. He held the rank of *Oberfeldwebel*. Toschka was awarded the Iron Cross 1st and 2nd Class, and on 20 May 1940, he was promoted to *Leutnant* for bravery in the face of the enemy. He landed on Crete by glider near enemy flak positions south of Chania. He destroyed the enemy there and put the flak battery out of action but was badly wounded. He was awarded the Knight's Cross on 14 June 1941 for 'opening the way to Chania'.

Toschka was promoted to *Hauptmann* on 14 October 1942, and after recovering from his wounds, he took command of I Battalion, Parachute Assault Regiment, which he led in Russia. Toschka was killed in action on 20

February 1944 in the Anzio-Nettuno bridgehead and is buried in the German War Cemetery, Block L, Grave 13, Pomezia, Italy.

585. Leutnant Rudolf BRAUN

Braun was born on 30 August 1913 in Brannenburg. In 1938, he was part of the notorious exercise at the Neuhammer Training Grounds; at least thirteen men were killed when their aircraft crashed in the Sagan Heath during think fog. As a Stuka pilot, he took part in the Polish campaign, the French campaign, and the Battle of Britain. Braun also saw action over the Balkans and Crete, where he flew in support of the parachute troops and against British shipping in the Mediterranean Sea. He was awarded the Knight's Cross on 14 June 1941.

In November 1941, he was sent to Africa where he was shot down over Tobruk, his gunner being killed. Back in the Balkans, he flow anti-partisan missions until he took command of a Dive Bomber Wing, a post he held until January 1945. He ended his career on the Eastern Front flying the Fokker Wolf Fw 190. Braun died on 4 April 1990 and is buried in Protestantischer Friedhof, Augsburg, Bavaria.

586. Leutnant Wilhelm FULDA

Fulda was born on 21 May 1909 in Antwerp. He first saw action after landing his glider on the Belgian Fort Eben-Emael in 1940 and was awarded the Iron Cross 2nd Class on 12 May and the 1st Class on 13 May 1940. Next, as a *Leutnant*, Fulda commanded a glider platoon at the Corinth Canal in Greece. His most daring landing was on Crete, for which he was awarded the Knight's Cross 14 June 1941.

Fulda flew over Russia as part of a special transport group, and on 1 November 1943, he joined JG 301 as part of the German air defence. On 25 November 1944, he became commander of JG 400, which was equipped with rocket-powered Me 163s. Fulda died on 8 August 1977 and is buried in Wandsbek Friedhof, Hamburg.

587. Leutnant Hans TEUSEN

Teusen was born on 26 July 1917 in Salz. He joined *Fallschirmjäger* Regiment 2 in November 1939 and was promoted to *Leutnant* in December. Teusen first action was at the Corinth Canal, landing in gliders; his platoon eliminated a flak battery, but was unable to prevent the bridge from being blown. Later, over 1,200 officers and men surrendered to his platoon; for this he was awarded the Knight's Cross on 14 June 1941.

He became adjutant of the II Battalion in October 1941 and took command of a company in March 1943. In September, he was promoted to *Hauptmann* and saw action at the Mius River, Russia. Teusen also fought in the hellish Battle at Volkhov. After a brief period in Italy, the regiment was sent back to Russia in November 1943, where he was severely wounded, near Zhitomir. Teusen ended the war as operations officer of the 1st Parachute Army. He died on 11 February 2001 in Bad Neuenahr, Rhineland-Palatinate.

588. Leutnant Armin THIEDE

Thiede was born on 30 December 1917 in Gross Lipke. He took part in the French campaign, the Battle of Britain, the Balkans, Crete, and the invasion of Russia. Thiede was a pilot in Dive Bomber Wing 2 when he was awarded the Knight's Cross on 14 June 1941. Thiede was killed when his transport aircraft crashed on 9 July 1943. He is buried in the German War Cemetery, Block 6, Row 5, Grave 128, Zagreb-Mirogoi, Croatia.

589. *Oberleutnant* zur See Erich TOPP

Topp was born in Hannover on 2 July 1914. He served as watch officer on *U-46* before taking command of *U-57* in June 1940. On his second patrol, he sunk a number of ships, including the 10,939-ton steamer *Cumberland*. While returning from this patrol, he was rammed by the Norwegian freighter *Rona*, which sank with six of her crew. On 4 December 1940, Topp commissioned *U-552*, and on his first patrol, he sank the 12,062-ton tanker *Cadillac*. On his next patrol, he sank the 10,160-ton *Beacon Grange*, followed by the 10,948-ton *Norfolk* in June. Topp was awarded the Knight's Cross on 20 June 1941.

Then, on 31 October 1941, he sank the US destroyer *Reuben James*, which was illegally hunting for U-boats. His next three patrols were off the US coast, attacking westbound convoys; this resulted in sixteen ships sunk and two torpedoed. He was awarded the Oak Leaves on 11 April 1941 and the Swords on 17 August 1941. In 1942, he controversially sank the US *David H. Atwater*. Topp took command of the Tactical U-Boat Flotilla in Gotenhafen, but his last command was *U-2513*, which he scuttled on 8 May 1945. He sank thirty-five ships during his career (a total of 192,611 tons). His autobiography is called *The Odyssey of a U-Boat Commander: The Recollections of Erich Topp*. He died on 26 December 2005 and his ashes were scattered at sea.

590. Oberst August KRAKAU

Krakau was born on 12 September 1894 in Pirmasens. He fought in the First World War and was awarded the Iron Cross 1st and 2nd Class (1914). Krakau fought in Poland and France, for which he was awarded the Iron Cross 1st and 2nd Class (1939) in June 1940.

He was commander of Mountain *Jäger* Regiment 85 when he was awarded the Knight's Cross on 21 June 1941. Krakau died on 7 January 1975 and is believed to be buried in Katherinefriedhof, Amberg, Bavaria.

591. Oberst Willibald UTZ

Utz was born on 20 January 1983 in Furth im Wald. He fought in the First World War and was awarded the Iron Cross 1st and 2nd Class (1914). Utz was the commander of *Jäger* Regiment 100 when he was awarded the Knight's Cross on 21 June 1941. He died on 20 April 1954 and is buried in Bergfriedhof, Bad Reichenhall, Bavaria.

592. Oberstleutnant August WITTMANN

Wittmann was born on 20 July 1895 in Munich. He was commander of Mountain Regiment 95 when he was awarded the Knight's Cross on 21 June 1941. Wittmann died on 29 March 1977 in Glonn, Bavaria.

593. *Hauptmann* Heinrich BRÜCKER

Brücker was born on 5 May 1913 in Kiel. He fought in the Spanish Civil War. Brücker also took part in the Polish campaign, the French campaign, the Battle of Britain, Crete, and the invasion of Russia. He was a group commander in Dive Bomber Wing 2 when he was awarded the Knight Cross on 22 June 1941. Brücker died on 14 June 1984 in Eckernförde, Schleswig-Holstein.

594. *Hauptmann* Günther SCHWÄRZEL

Schwärzel was born on 13 February 1912 in Altona. He was a squadron leader in Dive Bomber Wing 2 when he was awarded the Knight's Cross on 22 June 1941. He died of wounds on 26 September 1942 near Kursk, Russia, and has no known grave.

595. *Oberleutnant* Erich HEINRICHS

Heinrichs was born on 5 November 1912 in Naugard. He was a pilot in Bomber Wing 54 when he was killed in action over the Atlantic, west of Ireland, on 28 May 1941. Heinrichs was awarded the Knight's Cross on 22 June 1941.

596. *Oberleutnant* Lothar LAU

Lau was born on 30 January 1913 in Königsberg. He was a squadron leader in Dive Bomber Wing 2 when he was awarded the Knight's Cross on 22 June 1941. Lau died on 4 September 1981 in Würzburg, Bavaria.

597. *Oberleutnant* Helmut NAUMANN

Naumann was born on 12 August 1912 in Magdeburg. He was a squadron leader in Dive Bomber Wing 3 when he was awarded the Knight's Cross on 22 June 1941. Naumann died on 21 June 1997 and is believed to be buried in German War Cemetery, Heidelberg, Baden-Württemberg.

598. *Oberleutnant* Frank NEUBERT

Neubert was born on 28 September 1915 in Bad Herrenalb. He took part in the Polish campaign and was probably the first victor in air combat when he shot down Captain Medwecki in the early hours of 1 September 1939. Neubert fought in France, the Battle of Britain, Yugoslavia, Cretem and Russia. He was squadron leader in Dive Bomber Wing 2 when he was awarded the Knight's Cross on 22 June 1941. Neubert died on 13 December 2003 in Gütersloh, North Rhine-Westphalia.

599. *Oberleutnant* Dietrich PEKRUN

Pekrun was born on 15 July 1917 in Dresden. He was a pilot and adjutant in Dive Bomber Wing 2 when he was awarded the Knight's Cross on 22 June 1941. Pekrun died on 18 July 2005 and is believed to be buried in Waldfriedhof, Aachen, North Rhine-Westphalia.

600. *Oberleutnant* Gustav RÖDEL

Rödel was born on 24 October 1915 in Merseburg. He served in the Condor Legion in Spain. Rödel fought in the Battle for France and the Battle of Britain, shooting down ten enemy aircraft on the Channel Front. Sent to Africa, he soon increased his score to twenty and was awarded the Knight's Cross on 22 June 1941.

His score increased steadily until 20 June 1943, when he was awarded the Oak Leaves with seventy-eight victories to his credit. He went on to shot down another twenty aircraft, including twelve four-engined bombers. Rödel died on 6 February 1995 and is buried in Rüngsdorf Friedhof, Abt II, Grave 708, Bad Godesberg, North Rhine-Westphalia.

601. *Oberleutnant* Götzpeter VOLLMER

Vollmer was born on 9 November 1915 in Berlin. He was a squadron leader in Dive Bomber Wing 2 when he was awarded the Knight's Cross on 22 June 1941. Vollmer was killed in an accident near Königsberg on 19 December 1944 and has no known grave.

602. *Kapitänleutnant* Günther HESSLER

Hessler was born in Beerfeld on 14 June 1909. He served initially on the battleship *Schlesien* and then on torpedo boats. After transferring to the U-boat service, Hessler's first command was *U-107*, which was commissioned on 8 October 1940. During his first patrol, he sank four ships. On his next patrol, he sank fourteen ships (a total of 86,699 tons), the most successful patrol by a German U-boat of the entire war.

On his third patrol, he sank four ships in a lengthy pursuit. He was awarded the Knight's Cross on 24 June 1941. Promoted to *Fregattenkapitän*, he was appointed to the staff of the commander of U-Boats. His destroyed a total tonnage of 118,822. After the war, he attended the Nuremberg trials as a witness to speak on behalf of the U-boat service and his father-in-law, Dönitz. He is the author of *The U-Boat War in the Atlantic*. Hessler died on 4 April 1968 and is buried in Hauptfriedhof, Bochum, North Rhine-Westphalia.

603. *Hauptmann* Hellmuth HALLAUER

Hallauer was born on 4 February 1904 in Saarbrücken. He was a company commander in Motorised Pioneer Battalion 59 when he died of wounds near

Kowno, Russia, on 24 June 1941; he has no known grave. Hallauer was awarded the Knight's Cross the same day.

604. Generalleutnant Erich MARCKS

Marcks was born on 6 June 1891 in Schöneberg. He fought in the First World War where he was awarded the Iron Cross 1st and 2nd Class (1914). Marcks commanded VIII Army Corps in Poland and was awarded the Iron Cross 1st and 2nd Class (1939). In the campaign in the West, he served as chief-of-staff in XVIII Army and altered the plan to stop the bombing of Bruges and Paris as he believe these were places of historical importance. Marcks requested a combat duty and commanded a light division in the Balkans campaign.

Badly wounded in Russia, he lost a leg. Marcks was awarded the Knight's Cross on 26 June 1941. After a year's recovery, he again asked to take part in combat duties, and he was sent to Italy. In Normandy, he commanded LXXXIV Army Corps and was killed on 12 June 1944 when, on a daily visit of units, he was mortally wounded by Allied aircraft. Marcks was awarded the Oak Leaves on 24 June 1944. He is buried (with his batman who was killed alongside him) in the German War Cemetery, Block 2, Row 38, Grave 1478, Marigny, Normandy, France.

605. Oberstleutnant Hans CRAMER

Cramer was born on 13 July 1896 in Minden. He fought in the First World War where he was awarded the Iron Cross 1st and 2nd Class (1914). He became the commander of the Armoured Reconnaissance Instruction Battalion in September 1939. Named CO of Panzer Regiment 8, he would led it with distinction in Africa. On 16 May 1941, Cramer stormed into Sidi Azeiz and, shortly afterwards, Capuzzo fell to him as well. Cramer also made a decisive contribution to the capture of the Halfaya Pass. For these exploits, he was awarded the Knight's Cross on 27 June 1941.

He was badly wounded at Sollum, but after his recovery, Cramer was made chief-of-staff to the general of Mobile Forces. On 1 October 1942, he was himself appointed to general of Mobile Forces and promoted to *Generalmajor*. He commanded 'Cramer Corps HQ' on the Don in Russia before being given command of the German Africa Corps on 1 March 1943. In May, he was promoted to *General der Panzertruppe*. But, on 16 May 1943, he was taken prisoner by the British. Cramer died on 28 October 1968 and is buried in Alter Friedhof, Porta Westfalica, North Rhine-Westphalia.

606. *Oberleutnant* Ott-Friedrich SENFT (or SENFFT) von PILSACH

Senft von Pilsach was born on 18 March 1913 in Halle. Sent to Africa in April 1941, he took part in the Battle of the Halfaya Pass with Panzer Regiment 5. At Sidi Suleiman, his company destroyed eleven enemy tanks and opened the way to Tobruk. For this, he was awarded the Knight's Cross on 27 June 1941.

Wounded near Sidi Rezegh, he was evacuated to hospital in Germany. On his recovery, he was sent to the panzer training department. At the war's end, Senft von Pilsach was serving in the staff of the armoured troops in Berlin. He died on 1 May 1979 in Darmstadt, Hesse.

607. General Richard RUOFF

Ruoff was born on 18 August 1883 in Messbach. He fought in the First World War and was awarded the Iron Cross 1st and 2nd Class (1914). Ruoff was commander of V Army Corps when he was awarded the Knight's Cross on 30 June 1941. He died on 30 March 1967 and is buried in Bergfriedhof, Abt 45, Grave 1, Galgenbergstrasse, Tübingen, Baden-Württemberg.

608. Generalmajor Gustav HÖHNE

Höhne was born on 17 February 1893 in Kruschwitz. He fought in the First World War and was awarded the Iron Cross 1st and 2nd Class (1914). Höhne fought in Poland and was awarded the Iron Cross 1st and 2nd Class (1939). He also fought in Belgium, France, and Russia.

Höhne was commander of 8 Infantry Division when he was awarded the Knight's Cross on 30 June 1941. He was awarded the Oak Leaves on 17 May 1943. Höhne died on 1 July 1951 and is buried in Hauptfriedhof, Oberursel, Hesse.

609. Oberstleutnant Helmuth THUMM

Thumm was born on 25 August 1895 in Ravensburg. He fought in the First World War and was awarded the Iron Cross 1st and 2nd Class (1914). Thumm was commander of Infantry Regiment 56 when he was awarded the Knight's Cross on 30 June 1941 and the Oak Leaves on 23 December 1942. He was relieved of his command for pulling teenage boys out of the front line against orders. Thumm died on 13 July 1977 and is buried in Alter Friedhof, Abt 2, Row 61, Grave 13, Welzheim, Baden-Württemberg.

610. *Hauptmann* Karl BAACKE

Baacke was born on 15 May 1907 in Aurich. He was awarded the Iron Cross 1st and 2nd Class in 1940. Baacke was a company commander in Frontier Infantry Regiment 124 when he was awarded the Knight's Cross on 30 June 1941. The Oak Leaves were awarded on 10 December 1943. Baacke was posted missing at Orinin, Ukraine, on 2 April 1944.

611. *Hauptmann* Kurt GIERGA

Gierga saw born on 3 March 1909 in Pritzwalk. He took part in the campaign in the West with Panzer Regiment 5. Moved to Africa with his regiment, he was engaged in heavy fighting at Tobruk and Sollum. His unit advanced into the area north of Sidi Omar and continued the attack west of Sidi Azeiz towards Sidi Suleiman. In the Battle of Halfaya Pass, Gierga and his company punched through the enemy front, demolishing the British anti-tank line. For this, he was awarded the Knight's Cross on 30 June 1941.

Gierga fought on in Africa until wounded in July 1943 and was sent home. He fought in Russia and was wounded again. His last service position was with the office of replacement for armoured forces. Gierga died on 25 June 1961 and is believed to be buried in Alter Friedhof, Geesthacht, Schleswig-Holstein.

612. *Oberleutnant* Theodor SCHWABACH

Schwabach was born on 11 January 1912 in Ludwigshafen. He was became CO of a flak battery on in September 1940 with which he went to Africa. At Sollum, he fought with a total disregard for his own life—his battery was often ahead of the panzers. By 17 June 1941, his four 88-mm guns had knocked-out thirty-four tanks, and on one occasion, he captured a 150-mm howitzer battery.

Schwabach's battery was ordered to hold a strong point near Sollum, with no ammunition or food resupply; he held out for two months. For this action, he was awarded the Knight's Cross on 30 June 1941. Schwabach was cut off at the Halfaya Pass and, on 17 June 1942, had to surrender. He died on 13 June 1981 in Emden, Lower Saxony.

613. *Oberleutnant* Ludwig STREIL

Streil was born on 21 January 1893 in Zusamzell. He was commander of Infantry Regiment 61 when he was killed in action on 17 May 1940. He is buried in the German War Cemetery, Block 49, Grave 264, Kattenbos N746, Lommel, Belgium. Streil was awarded the Knight's Cross on 30 June 1941.

614. Leutnant Eberhard ZAHN

Zahn was born on 2 January 1910 in Wuppertal. He fought in France with an anti-tank gun unit and was awarded the Iron Cross 1st and 2nd Class. Zahn was sent to Africa with his unit from the very start, and he fought there until the end of the campaign. During the Battle for Capuzzo, Zahn was captured by the British, but he managed to escape and make his way back to the German lines. He was awarded the Knight's Cross on 30 June 1941.

Zahn distinguished himself in Tunisia and was awarded the Oak Leaves on 6 March 1943. After Africa, he spent some time on the staff before commanding a heavy anti-gun battalion, equipped with tank destroyers. He fought with his unit on the Eastern Front until the end of the war. In January 1945, he was awarded the Gold Wound Badge. Zahn was held by the Russians but managed to escape. He died on 7 February 2010 in St Wolfgang am See, Austria.

615. Hauptfeldwebel Wilhelm WENDT

Wendt was born on 11 October 1911 in Friedrichshof. He was the Spiess of the 5th Panzer Regiment's 5th Company. Sent to Africa in March 1941, Wendt made a frontal attack on El Agheila and was present at the capture of Marsa el Brega. For his part in the capture of Mechili, he was awarded the Iron Cross 1st Class.

On 16 June 1941, at Sidi Omar, part of the Battle for Sollum, Wendt led a platoon of tanks; he destroyed four or five enemy tanks, and his was the first tank to break through enemy lines. For this, he was awarded the Knight's Cross on 30 June 1941. Later, he served in Russia before being transferred to an admin job. Wendt died on 19 February 1984 and is believed to be buried in Zentralfriedhof, Münster.

616. Unteroffizier Reinhard MELZER

Melzer was born on 26 November 1914 in Bauerwitz. He fought in France with a flak battalion and was sent to Africa with the unit in early 1941. During the advance, Melzer repeatedly displayed his initiative by attacking enemy tanks whenever he sighted them. Only opening fire at close range, in this manner, he knocked-out thirteen tanks.

His greatest success came in the tank battle at Sollum. Again, he intervened at a critical time and helped to master a number of difficult situations. For this, he was awarded the Knight's Cross on 30 June 1941. On 17 January 1942, during the retreat from the Sidi Rezegh area to El Agheila and Agedabia, Melzer, with his gun out of action, was captured by the British. He died on 19 November 1994 and is buried in Unna Friedhof, North Rhine-Westphalia.

617. *Hauptmann* Josef FÖZÖ—'Joschko'

Fözö was born on 7 November 1912 in Vienna. He fought in the Spanish Civil War with the Condor Legion, claiming three enemy aircraft shot down. Fözö's first victory of the war was a balloon on 16 April 1940 during the French campaign. After thirteen victories during the Battle of Britain, he was made a group commander in Fighter Wing 51.

By the time of the invasion of Russia, Fözö had fifteen victories to his credit. He was awarded the Knight's Cross on 2 July 1941, with his tally at twenty-two. He was baldy injured in a take-off accident on 11 July 1941 and was hospitalised. In May 1942, he was injured again, this time in a landing accident at Tubelja. Fözö died on 4 March 1979 and is believed to be buried in Zentralfriedhof, Vienna.

618. Leutnant Heinrich (or Heinz) BÄR—'Pritzl' or 'Reeste'

Bär was born on 25 March 1913 in Sommerfeld. One of the great fighter pilots of the war, Bär shot down this first enemy aircraft on 25 September 1939. By the end of 1940, he had been awarded the Iron Cross 1st and 2nd Class. Bär was shot down into the English Channel; when asked by Göring what he was thinking about while in the water, he replied 'your speech about England no longer being an island'. He was awarded the Knight's Cross on 2 July 1941, after shooting down his twenty-seventh enemy aircraft. The Oak Leaves followed on 14 August 1941, for shooting down sixty aircraft. Ninety 'kills' brought him the Swords on 16 February 1942. He had been recommended for the Swords several times, but it was turned down by Göring.

Bär was never awarded the Diamonds as he was so outspoken, even to Göring. He did, however, receive the Golden Pilot's Badge with Diamonds from Göring. He fought on all fronts, including the defence of the Reich, shooting down twenty-one four-engined bombers, sixteen of them using the Me 262 jet fighter. His final tally was 220 enemy aircraft shot down and over 1,000 missions flown. He was also brought down himself several times. Bär died on 28 April 1957 when the light aircraft he was flying stalled and crashed to the ground, he is buried in Hauptfriedhof, Braunschweig, Lower Saxony.

619. Generalleutnant Johann SINNHUBER

Sinnhuber was born on 27 March 1887 in Wilkoschen. He fought in the First World War and was awarded the Iron Cross 1st and 2nd Class (1914). Sinnhuber was commander of the 28th Infantry Division when he was awarded the Knight's Cross on 5 July 1941. He died on 23 October 1979 in Augsburg, Bavaria.

620. Oberst Herbert RIECKHOFF

Rieckhoff was born on 25 December 1898 in Berlin. He fought in the First World War and was awarded the Iron Cross 1st and 2nd Class (1914). Rieckhoff was a *Kommodore* in Bomber Wing 2 when he was awarded the Knight's Cross on 5 July 1941. He died on 30 November 1948 and is buried in Eberhaldenfriedhof, Landenbergerstrasse, Esslingen am Necker, Baden-Württemberg.

621. *Major* Alexander von WINTERFELDT

Von Winterfeldt was born on 11 December 1898 in Berlin. He was a group commander in Fighter Wing 77 when he was awarded the Knight's Cross on 5 July 1941. Von Winterfeldt was killed in a flying accident near Vienna on 16 May 1942 and has no known grave.

622. *Major* Bernhard WOLDENGA

Woldenga was born on 4 December 1901 in Hamburg. He was commander of Fighter Wing 77 when he was awarded the Knight's Cross on 5 July 1941. Woldenga died on 19 January 1999 in Timmendorfer Strand, Schleswig-Holstein.

623. *Hauptmann* Gerhard KOLLEWE

Kollewe was born on 3 March 1912 in Deutsch-Kruschin. He took part in the Spanish Civil War with the Condor Legion. Kollewe took part in the sinking of the Polish destroyers ORP *Gryf* and ORP *Wicher* on the first day of the war. For this, he was awarded the Iron Cross 1st and 2nd Class.

He was involved in damaging the destroyers HMS *Ilex* and HMS *Isis* on 15 June 1941. Kollewe was awarded the Knight's Cross on 5 July 1941 and the

Swords on 12 August 1942. He was killed in action over Malta on 17 October 1942 and has no known grave.

624. *Oberleutnant* Willi DOUS

Dous was born on 16 June 1916 in Passenheim. He was a pilot in Bomber Wing 3 when he was awarded the Knight's Cross on 5 July 1941. Dous was posted missing near Jarcevo, Russia, on 2 September 1941.

625. *Oberleutnant* Heinrich EPPEN

Eppen was born in Winsen on 29 March 1915. In 1938, he was part of the notorious exercise at the Neuhammer Training Grounds; at least thirteen men were killed when their aircraft crashed in the Sagan Heath during thick fog. Eppen took part in the Polish and French campaigns. He distinguished himself in the Balkans and attacks on the fortifications of the Metaxas Line, for which he was awarded the Iron Cross 1st and 2nd Class. He dive-bombed and sank a destroyer off Crete. In total, Eppen was credited with sinking 50,000 tons of shipping. For this, he was awarded the Knight's Cross on 5 July 1941.

He was transferred to Africa in the autumn 1941, and he became one of the best-known Stuka pilots. He continued to support the Africa Corps until he was shot down by the South African Air Force over Tobruk on 4 June 1942; he is still listed as missing.

626. *Oberleutnant* Wolf-Dietrich (or Wolfdieter) HUY

Huy was born on 2 August 1917 in Freilburg im Breisgau. He was a fighter pilot and shot down his first enemy aircraft on 31 May 1940. Huy was soon moved to ground support missions over Greece and Crete and sunk 34,000 tons of shipping, including the 22,000-ton freighter *Hellas*. He also damaged the battleship HMS *Warspite*. Huy took part in the invasion of Russia and was awarded the Knight's Cross on 5 July 1941 for shooting down twenty-two aircraft. In early 1942, he was shot down twice, first by Russian ace Mikhail Avdeyev and then by German anti-aircraft fire. Huy was awarded the Oak Leaves on 17 March 1942. After recovery, his unit was posted to Africa where, with his total at forty, he was again shot down and taken prisoner. Huy died on 13 July 2003 and is buried in Evangelischer Friedhof, Gernsbach, Baden-Württemberg.

627. *Oberleutnant* Erich JÄGER

Jäger was born on 17 September 1916 in Simmern. He was a platoon leader in Motorised Flak Regiment 19 when he was awarded the Knight's Cross on 5 July 1941. Jäger died on 21 March 1981 and is buried in Hauptfriedhof, Würzburg, Bavaria.

628. *Oberleutnant* Hermann MUGLER

Mugler was born on 26 April 1914 in Munich. He was a company commander in *Jäger* Regiment 54 when he was awarded the Knight's Cross on 5 July 1941. Mugler died of wounds on 4 March 1943 and is buried at Sablino, Ukraine; his remains are awaiting transfer to a German war cemetery.

629. Leutnant Gerhard BRENNER

Brenner was born on 29 August 1918 in Ludwigsburg. He was a pilot in Bomber Wing 1 when he was awarded the Knight's Cross on 5 July 1941. Brenner sank HMS *Fiji* and HMS *Jackal*, as well as eleven merchant ships (a total of 61,000 tons). He was killed in action on 14 June 1942 south of Gavdos in the Aegean Sea; he has no known grave.

630. Leutnant Heinrich HUNGER

Hunger was born on 28 October 1918 in Weimer. He was a pilot in Bomber Wing 2 when he was awarded the Knight's Cross on 5 July 1941. Hunger was killed in action on 14 August 1941 and is buried at Novgorod, Russia; his remains are awaiting transfer to a German war cemetery.

631. Leutnant Hans SAUER

Sauer was born on 22 May 1912 in Wiesbaden. He was a pilot in Close Support Wing 1 when he was awarded the Knight's Cross on 5 July 1941. Sauer was killed in action in the Mediterranean area during August 1941; he has no known grave.

632. Oberfeldwebel Josef WENIGMANN

Wenigmann was born on 7 October 1914 in Beuel. He was a pilot in Dive Bomber Wing 3 when he was awarded the Knight's Cross on 5 July 1941. Wenigmann was killed in action at El Alamein, North Africa, on 3 July 1942 and has no known grave.

633. General Leo Reichsfeiherr GEYR von SCHWEPPENBURG

Reichsfeiherr Geyr von Schweppenburg was born on 2 March 1886 in Potsdam. He fought in the First World War and was awarded the Iron Cross 1st and 2nd Class (1914). Geyr von Schweppenburg commanded panzer troops in Poland and France, being awarded the Iron Cross 1st and 2nd Class (1939). He took part in the invasion of Russia and was awarded the Knight's Cross on 9 July 1941.

In early 1943, he was moved to France to command the armoured troops that would fight against the Allies during the invasion. Wounded on 10 June 1944, Geyr von Schweppenburg was relieved of his command on 2 July 1944. He died on 27 January 1974 and is buried the village cemetery, Irschenhausen, Bavaria.

634. General Walther SCHROTH

Schroth was born on 3 June 1882 in Glumbowitz. He fought in the First World War and was awarded the Iron Cross 1st and 2nd Class (1914). Schroth was the commander of XII Army Corps when he was awarded the Knight's Cross on 9 July 1941. He was killed in a car crash on 6 October 1944 and is buried in Alter Südfriedhof, Grave 5, Wiesbaden, Hesse.

635. Generalleutnant Gerhard KAUFFMANN

Kauffmann was born on 29 June 1887 in Mariendorf. He fought in the First World War and was awarded the Iron Cross 1st and 2nd Class (1914). Kauffmann was commander of the 256th Infantry Division when he was awarded the Knight's Cross on 9 July 1941. He was retired from active service in September 1943 after arguing with Hitler. Kauffmann died on 16 June 1969 and is buried in the Invaliden Friedhof, Scharnhorstrasse, Berlin.

636. Generalleutnant Walter MODEL—'Hitler's Fireman'

Model was born in Genthin on 24 January 1891. He fought during the First World War and was wounded twice; awarded the Iron Cross 1st and 2nd Class (1914), he ended the war as a *Hauptmann*. In 1935, he took charge of a technical department concerned with new inventions, and he played a major role in the development of the assault gun. Promoted to *Generalmajor* in 1938, he became chief-of-staff to IV Army Corps, in which he served during the Polish campaign, being awarded the Iron Cross 1st and 2nd Class (1939). In the West, he was chief-of-staff to Busch's 16th Army, and by the end of 1940, he was commanding the 3rd Panzer Division with the rank of *Generalleutnant*. In 1941, his division stormed into Russia, and for this he was awarded the Knight's Cross on 9 July 1941. In October, he was promoted to *General* and given command of XXXI Panzer Corps; two days later, he was in command of the 9th Army. Model helped stop the Russian winter offensive and was awarded the Oak Leaves on 17 February 1942 and was promoted to *Oberstgeneral*. Model led from the front and was frequently under fire. After Stalingrad, he protested that the men were not capable of another offensive. He was awarded the Swords on 2 April 1943 but was sacked in November.

He was recalled just two months later to sort out the situation facing Army Group North, for which he was promoted to *Generalfeldmarschall*, the youngest in the German Army. When von Manstein was sacked at the end of March 1944, Model took over Army Group North Ukraine and South and stopped another Soviet offensive. In June, he replaced Busch in command of Army Group Centre, but he still retained control over Army Group North Ukraine. Thus, he commanded more than 100 divisions. Time and again, he succeeded in closing gaps in the Eastern Front.

Awarded the Diamonds on 17 August 1944, Model moved to the West where he took over as supreme commander and commander of Army Group 'B' from von Kluge. Model struggled to stop the rot with the forces at his disposal, and in early September, von Rundstedt took over as supreme commander—though Modal kept Army Group 'B'. He organised the defence of the Netherlands when the Allies launched their airborne attack on 17 September 1944. Model did not believe in the Ardennes Offensive but was forced to carry it out. After its failure, his armies were driven across the Rhine and surrounded in the Rühr Pocket. Model killed himself on 21 April 1945 and was buried were he fell, but his son recovered his body and he was reburied in the German War Cemetery, Plot 1973, Grave 1974, Franziskusweg, Vossenack, North Rhine-Westphalia.

637. Generalmajor Josef KAMMHUBER

Kammhuber was born on 19 August 1896 in Burgkirchen. He fought in the First World War and was awarded the Iron Cross 1st and 2nd Class (1914). During the French campaign, he was shot down and captured, but he was released after the fall of France.

Put in charge of coordinating flak, searchlight, and radar units, Kammhuber came up with the system of radar, flak, and night fighters used throughout the remainder of the war. Kammhuber was awarded the Knight's Cross on 9 July 1941. In 1943, he was transferred to Norway after infighting with Milch over new night fighter designs. He died on 25 January 1986 and is buried in the Westfriedhof, Plot 451, Row 42, Grave 215, Munich.

638. Oberst Hans BERGEN

Bergen was born on 5 March 1890 in Munich. He fought in the First World War and was awarded the Iron Cross 1st and 2nd Class (1914). He took part in the Polish campaign and was awarded the Iron Cross 1st and 2nd Class (1939). Bergen was commander of Infantry Regiment 187 when he was awarded the Knight's Cross on 9 July 1941. He died on 17 February 1957 and is buried in Hauptfriedhof, Friedhofstrasse 1, Landshut, Bavaria.

639. Oberst Alfred STURM

Sturm was born on 23 August 1888 in Saarbrücken. He fought in the First World War as an infantryman before transferring to the air service. Sturm was awarded the Iron Cross 1st and 2nd Class (1914) before being shot down on 13 June 1917. At the age of fifty-two, in June 1940, he passed the parachute training course, and a month later, he was commanding *Fallschirmjäger* Regiment 2 with the rank of *Oberst*. His first combat jump was at the Corinth Canal, where his regiment prevented 10,000 British and Greek troops escaping to Crete, for which he was awarded the Iron Cross 2nd Class.

On the second day of the Crete operation, Sturm was captured by the British, but later freed. For his actions in Crete, he was awarded the Iron Cross 1st Class, which was followed by the Knight's Cross on 9 July 1941. Promoted to *Generalleutnant* on 1 August 1943 and after holding a number of posts, he was named head of the Wehrmacht Transport Service. Although released from the Wehrmacht on 21 January 1945, Sturm was arrested in April and held as a POW. He died on 8 March 1962 in Detmold, North Rhine-Westphalia.

640. *Major* Fritz BEIGEL

Beigel was born on 11 June 1900 in Ludwigsburg. He was commander of Panzer Pioneer Battalion 39 when he was awarded the Knight's Cross on 9 July 1941. Beigel died on 28 March 1985 and is believed to be buried in Hirschlanden Friedhof, Ditzingen, Baden-Württemberg.

641. *Major* Edgar STENTZLER

Stentzler was born in Dortmund on 27 March 1905. He was a cavalry officer before the war and won many competitions, including nine in the 1936 Olympic Games. He took part in the fighting in Poland and Norway, for which he was awarded the Iron Cross 1st and 2nd Class. On 20 June 1940, he joined the Parachute Replacement Battalion as a volunteer with the rank of *Hauptmann*. After training, he was made commander of II Battalion Parachute Assault Regiment and was promoted to *Major*.

Stentzler jumped into Crete east of Maleme, where he took part in the capture of Hill 107 and then assumed command of the regiment as *Generalmajor* Meindl had been wounded. For his action in Crete, he was awarded the Knight's Cross on 9 July 1941. He fought on the Russian Front in the winter of 1941 and was badly wounded on 3 October in an assault on the Petrushino bridgehead and died from his wounds on 20 October 1941 in Tilsit, Russia. He has no known grave.

642. *Major* Heinrich VOIGTSBERGER

Voigtsberger was born on 10 February 1903 in Untermhaus. He fought in France and was awarded the Iron Cross 2nd Class. In Africa, on 21 April 1941, he was awarded the Iron Cross 1st Class. His unit attacked the British positions from the flank and broke-through, then stormed towards Tobruk and held open the first breach in the defensive ring surrounding the fortress. For this, he was awarded the Knight's Cross on 9 July 1941.

Voigtsberger fell ill with dysentry and had to give up command of his battalion to leave Africa in July 1941. On his recovery, he was placed in command of the 60th Motorised Grenadier Regiment and sent to the Russian Front on 14 May 1942. Awarded the Oak Leaves on 9 December 1943 for his personal bravery, Voigtsberger fought until the end on the Russian Front, even defending the Reich capital. He died on 17 March 1959 and is buried in Stadtfriedhof, Starnberg, Bavaria.

643. *Hauptmann* Wilhelm BACH—'The Pastor in Purgatory'

Bach was born on 5 November 1892 in Oberwösheim. He fought in the First World War, being awarded the Iron Cross 1st and 2nd Class (1914). During this war, Bach was taken prisoner by the British. Between the wars, he became a pastor. As a reservist, Bach was called up and took part in the 1940 French campaign and was awarded the Iron Cross 1st and 2nd Class. Sent to Africa with the 104th Rifle Regiment, he took part in the Battle of Tobruk during April–May 1941. On 14 June, Bach ordered an offensive patrol and the next day captured the Halfaya Pass.

The British attacked this position three times as part of Operation Battleaxe, but Bach and his men could not be budged. For this action, he was awarded the Knight's Cross on 9 July 1941. He also became known as 'The Pastor in Purgatory of the Halfaya Pass'. In November 1941, Bach and his battalion were left alone in the pass. After using up their ammunition, Bach was forced to surrender and became a prisoner of the British for the second time. He died on 22 December 1942 and is buried in Woodland Cemetery, Arlington Boulevard, Kitchener, Ontario, Canada.

644. *Hauptmann* Walter FROMM

Fromm was born on 2 February 1910 in Dingelstädt. He fought in Spain with the Condor Legion. In Africa from 19 February 1941 with a flak regiment, he took part in the Battle of Sollum where his battalion knocked-out ninety-two enemy tanks in three days, including a number of Matilda tanks. For this action, he was awarded the Knight's Cross on 9 July 1941.

Badly wounded in late 1941, he was sent back to Germany, where, on his recovery, he trained replacement flak soldiers. At his own request, he was given command of the 69th Motorised Flak Battalion, which was responsible for anti-aircraft defence between Rhône in France and the Italian border. Fromm was captured on 27 August 1944 by the French and endured a series of humiliations, including several attempts to steal his Knight's Cross. He was not released until 1951. Fromm died on 27 April 1999 in Cologne, North Rhine-Westphalia.

645. *Hauptmann* Hans von HAHN

Von Hahn was born on 7 August 1914 in Frankfurt am Main. He was a group commander in Fighter Wing 3 when he was awarded the Knight's Cross on 9 July 1941; he shot down thirty-one enemy aircraft. Von Hahn died on 5 November 1957 in Frankfurt am Main.

646. *Hauptmann* Friedrich-August Freiherr von der HEYDTE

Von der Heydte was born on 30 March 1907 in Munich. He fought as an infantry officer during the Polish and French campaigns, being awarded the Iron Cross 1st and 2nd Class. He reported for parachute training in August 1940 and dropped into Crete as a *Hauptmann* in May 1941 with *Fallschirmjäger* Regiment 3. His men occupied Agya prison and, in the days that followed, tied down a numerically superior force near Peribolia and Pyrgos. On 25 May, he led his battalion in an attack over the Alikanpos–Chania road, and on 27 May, he took possession of the east side of the capital and pushed on to the harbour. He was awarded the Knight's Cross on 9 July 1941.

He fought Russia and North Africa, but while on a flight over Elda, his aircraft crashed, leaving him seriously injured. Von der Heydte became commander of *Fallschirmjäger* Regiment 6 in February 1944, and in Normandy, his regiment earned the nickname 'Lions of Carentan' from the US paratroops. In a daring raid at St Germain-sur-Seves, thirty-two of his men captured 265 Americans from the 90th Infantry Division. He was awarded the Oak Leaves on 30 September 1944. His men jumped into the Ardennes to hold open the bottlenecks for XI SS-Panzer Army but was not successful in this. He was wounded and captured on 24 December 1944. He died on 7 July 1994 and is believed to be buried in Hauptfriedhof, Friedhofstrasse 1, Landshut, Bavaria.

647. *Hauptmann* Lothar KELLER

Keller was born on 7 April 1914 in Dresden. He fought in the Spanish Civil War with the Condor Legion, shooting down three enemy aircraft. Keller shot down another nineteen aircraft during the Second World War. Then, on 26 June 1941, he was killed in a collision. He is buried at Sokol, Ukraine; his remains are awaiting transfer to a German war cemetery. Keller was awarded the Knight's Cross on 9 July 1941.

648. *Hauptmann* Ferdinand SCHNEIDER-KOSTALSKI

Schneider-Kostalski was born on 20 July 1908 in Judenburg. He was commander of III Battalion, Panzer Regiment 6, when he was awarded the Knight's Cross on 9 July 1941. Schneider-Kostalski was killed in action on 7 August 1944 and is buried in the German War Cemetery, Block 4, Row 5, Grave 450, Champigny-St André, Normandy, France.

649. *Oberleutnant* Josef BARMETLER

Barmetler was born in Kempten on 11 March 1904. In September 1940, he became commander of *Fallschirmjäger* Assault Regiment 7. He fought at Hill 107 on Crete, helping to take out some anti-aircraft guns. He also provided effective support to the mountain infantry on 25 May 1941. He was severely wounded during his action and, as a result, was only fit for home duties. Barmetler was awarded the Knight's Cross on 9 July 1941.

He was promoted to *Hauptmann* on 25 July 1941 and to *Major* on 1 June 1944. Barmetler was hospitalised in Kempten at the end of 1944 due to his wounds and died on 20 February 1945.

650. *Oberleutnant* Karl-Heinz BECKER

Becker was born on 2 January 1914 in Schwedt an der Oder. On 1 January 1939, he joined *Fallschirmjäger* Regiment 1, becoming commander of the 11th Company on 1 April 1940. He took part in the operation to capture Rotterdam airport, for which he was awarded the Iron Cross 1st Class. Becker took part in the capture of Heraklion during the invasion of Crete in 1941. He was awarded the Knight's Cross on 9 July 1941.

During the winter of 1941, he took part in the fighting around Neva, Russia. On 28 December 1942, he was involved in the last attempt to relieve the garrison of the Velikiye Luki fortress. Becker was wounded on 16 January 1943 on the Russian Front and returned home. In Normandy, he fought at Saint-Lô and saw action at Arnhem and in the Ardennes Offensive before leading his men back through the Westwall. The award of the Oak Leaves came on 12 March 1945. He died on 3 October 2002 in Bargum, Schleswig-Holstein.

651. *Oberleutnant* Reinhard EGGER

Egger was born on 11 December 1905 in Klagenfurt, Austria-Hungary. He joined *Fallschirmjäger* Regiment 1 on 2 October 1940 as a company commander. Egger led his company in the invasion of Crete fighting for eight days to capture Heraklion, for which he was awarded the Knight's Cross on 9 July 1941.

He fought in Russia, and he was promoted to *Major* in 1942 with *Fallschirmjäger* Regiment 4 and fought in Sicily. Commanding I Battalion, he took part in the third battle for Cassino and assumed command of the regiment when *Oberst* Walther was wounded. Egger played a key role in the fighting withdrawal up the Italian mainland, being awarded the Oak Leaves on 24 June 1944. He was captured when his position was overrun on 31 July 1944. Egger died on 10 June 1987 in Seeboden, Austria.

652. *Oberleutnant* Andreas HAGL

Hagl was born in Farchant on 21 April 1911. He took part in the Polish campaign, for which he was awarded the Iron Cross 2nd Class. In the battle for 'Fortress Holland', he was awarded the Iron Cross 1st Class. Promoted to *Leutnant* on 1 November 1940 with *Fallschirmjäger* Regiment 3, he was an *Oberleutnant* by the time he dropped into Crete in 1941. His platoon was dropped in the wrong place and had to fight its way through elements of the 10th New Zealand Division and Greek forces to join up with his battalion. He took over the defensive sector on the Cladiso.

On 26 May, he assumed command of the 2nd Company, and although wounded in the right arm, he played a vital role in the battalion's success. For this, he was awarded the Knight's Cross on 9 July 1941. Hagl was severely wounded on the Russian Front and, after recovering, was assigned to the reserve; on 15 October 1942, he was assigned to the staff of *Fallschirmjäger* Regiment 3. He saw action in Italy and was wounded again. On recovery, he commanded the rearguard but was killed in action on 28 July 1944 at San Vito di Leguzzano. He has no known grave.

653. *Oberleutnant* Harry HERRMANN

Herrmann was born on 27 May 1909 in Berlin. He became adjutant of *Fallschirmjäger* Regiment 1 in January 1939 and took part in the attack on 'Fortress Holland', being awarded the Iron Cross 1st and 2nd Class. He dropped into Crete near Heraklion. During the attempted landing, he ended up hanging from his parachute and wounded in the head, which left him temporarily blinded, limiting his actions. He reached the airfield and provided his company with a shining example. Herrmann was awarded the Knight's Cross on 9 July 1941.

In 1942, he was appointed commander of the newly-formed Parachute Instruction Regiment, which he led in the Anzio/Nettuno area of Italy. In Russia, he fought to the end, commanding Parachute Anti-tank Battalion Herrmann. He was held by the Russians until 1955. Herrmann died on 12 March 1995 and is buried in Altenstadt Friedhof, Hesse.

654. *Oberleutnant* Johannes KÜMMEL—'The Lion of Capuzzo'

Kümmel was born on 21 July 1909 in Coswig. He fought in Poland and France, being awarded the Iron Cross 1st and 2nd Class with the 8th Panzer Regiment. Kümmel transferred to Africa with his regiment and arrived in time to see action in Operation Battleaxe in 1941. He attacked on his own initiative at Capuzzo when his CO was wounded. For this, Kümmel was awarded the Knight's Cross on 9 July 1941.

On 26 May 1942, the Africa Corps went on the offensive again, and on 15 June, Kümmel's unit reached the coast first; that evening, his panzers overran Fort Pilastrino and Tobruk fell. He was awarded the Oak Leaves on 11 October 1942. After Africa, he fought in Anzio-Nettuno area of Italy. On 26 February 1944, at Cisterna, his car was involved in an accident; Kümmel was killed in the collision. He is buried in the German War Cemetery, Block C, Grave 4, Pomezia, Italy.

655. *Oberleutnant* Karl-Wolfgang REDLICH

Redlich was born on 13 December 1914 in Hamburg. He fought in Spain with the Condor Legion, shooting down his first enemy aircraft there. He fought over France and during the Battle of Britain. In Africa, his score continued to rise and Redlich was awarded the Knight's Cross on 9 July 1941, with twenty-one victories to his credit. In September, his squadron was sent back to Germany to re-equip; Redlich, who had shot down forty-one enemy aircraft, was transferred to the staff.

In May 1944, Redlich retuned to combat flying and shot down two four-engined bombers on his first sortie. However, he was shot down and killed over St Pölten on 29 May 1944 and has no known grave.

656. *Oberleutnant* Arnold von ROON

Von Roon was born on 19 July 1914 in Berlin. He served in the Condor Legion and was awarded the Spanish Cross in Gold with Swords in 1939. In April 1940, he became commander of a company in *Fallschirmjäger* Regiment 2, with the rank of *Oberleutnant*. Von Roon saw action in the Netherlands, where most of his company landed in the wrong place; the company managed to fight its way to the regiment. He was awarded the Iron Cross 1st and 2nd Class for his part in Dutch campaign.

He saw action at the Corinth Canal in Greece and in Crete as company CO. Von Roon landed 7 km from his objective, Rethymnon airfield. Nevertheless, he fought his way through a vineyard hill and through to the airfield, finally capturing Hill 156 on 27 May 1941. For this, he was awarded the Knight's Cross on 9 July 1941. He spent the rest of the war in staff positions. Roon died on 24 October 1990 in Miesbach, Bavaria.

657. *Oberleutnant* Horst TREBES

Trebes was born on 22 October 1916 in Cologne. He saw action in Poland and the Netherlands with *Fallschirmjäger* Regiment 1, being awarded the Iron Cross 1st and 2nd Class. He saw action in Crete with a battle group from 1st Parachute Assault Regiment, landing in gliders at the large bridge due west of Maleme. Trebes assumed command of the battle group when Braun and Schächter were put out of action. He fought his way through to IV Battalion. He also stormed through as far as the riverbed west of Platanias, playing a part in the capture of Hill 107. For this, he was awarded the Knight's Cross on 9 July 1941.

In Russia, he commanded a company in III Battalion, *Fallschirmjäger* Regiment 6. He was killed in action near Carentan, Normandy, on 29 July 1944 and is buried in the German War Cemetery (as unknown), La Cambe, Normandy, France.

658. Leutnant Hans HAHN

Hahn was born on 21 February 1919 in Rheydt. He was a pilot in Night Fighter Wing 2 when he was awarded the Knight's Cross on 9 July 1941. Hahn was killed in action on 11 October 1941 and is buried in the German War Cemetery, Block 3, Row 10, Grave 306, Camp Road, Cannock Chase, Staffordshire, England.

659. Oberfeldwebel Max BURGHARTSWIESER

Burghartswieser was born on 10 June 1914 in Wiesen. He was a section leader in *Jäger* Regiment 100 when he was awarded the Knight's Cross on 9 July 1941. Burghartswieser was killed in action on 22 August 1942 and is believed to be buried in the German War Cemetery (as unknown), Sologubowka, Russia.

660. Oberfeldwebel Hermann CONRAD

Conrad was born on 21 September 1913 in Heroldshof. He was a section leader in Infantry Regiment 330 when he was awarded the Knight's Cross on 9 July 1941. Conrad died of wounds on 6 October 1942 and is buried at Gagarin, Russia; his remains are awaiting transfer to a German war cemetery.

661. Oberfeldwebel Paul GILDNER

Gildner was born on 1 February 1914 in Nimptsch. As a heavy fighter pilot, he took part in the French campaign and the Battle of Britain. Transferred to night fighting in late 1940, he was awarded the Knight's Cross on 9 July 1941 for shooting down fourteen enemy aircraft.

With his tally at forty-eight—eight of which were four-engined bombers—he was killed when his Bf 110 crashed due to engine failure on 24 February 1943. Gildner was awarded the Oak Leaves two days later. He is buried in the German War Cemetery, Block M, Row 4, Grave 81 (next to Reinhold Knacke), Timmermansweg, Ysselsteyn, the Netherlands.

662. Feldwebel Gerhard REINICKE

Reinicke was born on 11 April 1914 in Berlin. He was a section leader in Panzer Regiment 6 when he was awarded the Knight's Cross on 9 July 1941. Reinicke died on 4 July 1997 in Viersen, North Rhine-Westphalia.

663. General Walter Graf von BROCKDORFF-AHLEFELDT

Graf von Brockdorff-Ahlefeldt was born on 13 July 1887 in Perleberg. He fought in the First World War, being awarded the Iron Cross 1st and 2nd Class (1914). Von Brockdorff-Ahlefeldt was commander of II Army Corps when he was awarded the Knight's Cross on 15 July 1941.

The Swords followed on 27 June 1942, but he was taken ill in November 1942 and sent home. He died on 9 May 1943 and is buried in Waldfriedhof, Wasgenensteig, Zehlendorf, Berlin. His son, Ernst-Albrecht, was also awarded the Knight's Cross.

664. Generalmajor Erich BRANDENBERGER

Brandenberger was born on 15 July 1892 in Augsburg. He fought in the First World War and was awarded the Iron Cross 1st and 2nd Class (1914). Brandenberger was commander of the 8th Panzer Division when he was awarded the Knight's Cross on 15 July 1941. The Oak Leaves followed on 12 November 1943. He died on 21 June 1955 and is buried in Alter Friedhof, Bonn.

665. Generalmajor Hans Freiherr von FUNCK

Freiherr von Funck was born on 23 December 1891 in Aachen. He fought in the First World War and was awarded the Iron Cross 1st and 2nd Class (1914). Von Funck served in the Spanish Civil War as leader of the German National Army. He commanded the 3rd Panzer Division in the 1940 French campaign and was awarded the Iron Cross 1st and 2nd Class (1939). In Russia, he commanded the 7th Panzer Division and was awarded the Knight's Cross on 15 July 1941 for actions at Vilnius and Białystok–Minsk and Wjasna.

For his part on the Don and Donets, von Funck was awarded the Oak Leaves on 22 August 1943. He was captured by the Russians in August 1945 and held until 1955. Von Funck died on 14 February 1979 and is buried in Auf der Loh Friedhof, Block 19, Grave 72D–72E, Viersen, North Rhine-Westphalia.

666. Generalmajor Walter KRÜGER

Krüger was born on 23 March 1892 in Zeitz. He fought in the First World War and was awarded the Iron Cross 1st and 2nd Class (1914). Krüger was awarded the Iron Cross 1st and 2nd Class (1939) in May 1940. He was commander of the 1st Rifle Brigade when he was awarded the Knight's Cross on 15 July 1941. The Oak Leaves followed on 24 January 1944. Krüger died on 11 July 1973 in Baden Baden, Baden-Württemberg.

667. Oberst Karl LOHMEYER

Lohmeyer was born on 25 December 1893 in Königsberg. He was commander of Infantry Regiment 505 when he was awarded the Knight's Cross on 15 July 1941. Lohmeyer was killed in action on 4 January 1942 and is buried in the German War Cemetery, Block 2, Row 82, Grave 8565, Sologubowka, Russia.

668. Oberst Richard KOLL

Koll was born on 7 April 1897 in Koblenz. He fought in the First World War and was awarded the Iron Cross 1st and 2nd Class (1914). Koll was commander of Panzer Regiment 11 when he was awarded the Knight's Cross on 15 July 1941. He died on 13 May 1963 and is buried in Waldfriedhof, Hüttenweg, Dahlem, Berlin.

669. Oberstleutnant Wilhelm CRISOLLI

Crisolli was born on 20 January 1895 in Berlin. He fought in the First World War and was awarded the Iron Cross 1st and 2nd Class (1914). Crisolli was awarded the Iron Cross 1st and 2nd Class (1939) after the fall of Poland in 1939. He was commander of Rifle Regiment 8 when he was awarded the Knight's Cross on 15 July 1941. Crisolli was killed in action by partisans on 5 September 1944 and is buried in the German War Cemetery, Block 22, Grave 22, Futa Pass, near Bologna, Italy.

670. Oberstleutnant Hartwig von LUDWIGER

Von Ludwiger was born on 29 June 1895 in Beuthen. He fought in the First World War and was awarded the Iron Cross 1st and 2nd Class (1914). Von Ludwiger was awarded the Iron Cross 1st and 2nd Class (1939) after the fall of Poland. He took part in the campaign in the West and the invasion of Russia, and he was awarded the Knight's Cross on 15 July 1941 as commander of Infantry Regiment 83. The Oak Leaves followed on 23 December 1942.

While in Yugoslavia during 1943, von Ludwiger had 500 civilians executed in reprisals for the murder by partisans of eight German soldiers and two Serbian mayors. He was also involved in reprisals in Greece and took part in the massacre of the Italian 'Acqui' Division in September 1943. After the war, he was tried for war crimes and executed at Belgrade during May 1947. He has no known grave.

671. *Major* Hermann-Heinrich BEHREND

Behrend was born on 25 August 1898 in Perleberg. He fought in the First World War and was awarded the Iron Cross 1st and 2nd Class (1914). Behrend was awarded the Iron Cross 1st and 2nd Class (1939) in 1940. He was commander of I Battalion, Infantry Regiment 489, when he was awarded the Knight's Cross on 15 July 1941. The Oak Leaves followed on 6 March 1944 and the Swords on 26 April 1945. He was also awarded the Wound Badge in Gold. Behrend died on 19 June 1987 in Soltau, Lower Saxony.

672. *Major* Wilhelm Ritter und Edler von PETER

Von Peter was born on 27 January 1899 in Friedberg. He was commander of I Battalion, Panzer Regiment 36, when he was awarded the Knight's Cross on 15 July 1941. Von Peter died of wounds following the assault on Mirgorod, Russia, on 26 September 1941 and has no known grave.

673. *Hauptmann* Hans STERN

Stern was born on 2 May 1907 in Kassel. He was a company commander in Panzer Regiment 11 when he was awarded the Knight's Cross on 15 July 1941. Stern died on 30 March 1972 and is buried in Horressen Friedhof, Rhineland-Palatinate.

674. *Oberleutnant* Harald KRIEG

Krieg was born on 7 February 1910 in Waldenburg. He was a company commander in Rifle Regiment 1 when he was awarded the Knight's Cross on 15 July 1941. Krieg died on 5 April 1973 and is buried in Hauptfriedhof, Koblenz, Rhineland-Palatinate.

675. *Hauptmann* Fritz GRASSAU

Grassau was born on 9 September 1905 in Rathenow. He was commander of II Battalion, Infantry Regiment 188, when he was awarded the Knight's Cross on 16 July 1941. Grassau was killed in action on 20 April 1945 and is buried in the Community Cemetery, Military Section, Wienrode, Saxony-Anhalt.

676. *Hauptmann* Helmut MAHLKE

Mahlke was born on 27 August 1913 in Berlin. A Stuka pilot, he flew in the French campaign and during the Battle of Britain, for which he was awarded both Iron Crosses. At the beginning of 1941, his unit was moved to the Mediterranean for attacks on Malta. For nine days, he attacked targets on Crete before returning to African to support Rommel. During the Battle for Tobruk, Mahlke flew through heavy flak to knock-out several defensive positions. For this, he was awarded the Knight's Cross on 16 July 1941.

Moved to the Russian Front, he was shot down three times, being wounded once. From April 1942 until the end of the war, Mahlke was a staff officer on the Russian front. Mahlke died on 26 December 1998 in Heikendorf, Schleswig-Holstein.

677. *Oberleutnant* Hermann STAIGER

Staiger was born on 6 April 1915 in Tennenbronn. He shot down his first enemy aircraft over Ghent on 31 May 1940. Staiger shot down seven British fighters during the Battle of Britain. On the first day of the invasion of Russia, he shot down three bombers, and on 30 June 1941, he shot down another four bombers; on 15 July 1941, he was himself seriously wounded by anti-aircraft fire. Staiger was awarded the Knight's Cross the next day, with twenty-five victories to his credit.

After recovery, he spent the next two years training pilots, only returning to combat at the end of May 1943. Over the next month, he shot down five US four-engined bombers, becoming one of the first 'bomber' aces. On 10 October 1943, he shot down his seventh B-17 but was wounded by return fire. In April 1944, Staiger shot down eight bombers, five of which were on the 24th. He ended the war with sixty-three victories, of which twenty-six were bombers. Staiger died on 22 June 1964 and is buried in Hauptfriedhof, Friedhofstrasse 8, Freilburg im Breisgau, Baden-Württemberg.

678. Generalleutnant Walter KEINER

Keiner was born on 30 December 1890 in Benshausen. He fought in the First World War and was awarded the Iron Cross 1st and 2nd Class (1914). Keiner was commander of the 62nd Infantry Division when he was awarded the Knight's Cross on 17 July 1941. He died on 23 January 1978 in Gelnhausen, Hesse.

679. Generalmajor Karl ALLMENDINGER

Allmendinger was born on 3 February 1891 in Abtsgemünd. He fought in the First World War and was awarded the Iron Cross 1st and 2nd Class (1914). He fought in Poland, for which he was awarded the Iron Cross 2nd Class (1939), and France, for which he was awarded the Iron Cross 1st Class (1939). Allmendinger was commander of the 5th Infantry Division when he was awarded the Knight's Cross on 17 July 1941. The Oak Leaves followed on 13 December 1942. He was retired from the army in 1944 and died on 2 October 1965. Allmendinger is buried in Schonenberg Friedhof, Ellwangen, Baden-Württemberg.

680. Oberst Albert BUCK

Buck was born on 23 January 1895 in Stuttgart. He fought in the First World War and was awarded the Iron Cross 1st and 2nd Class (1914). Buck was commander of Grenadier Regiment 305 when he was awarded the Knight's Cross on 17 July 1941. He was killed in action on 6 September 1942 near Novrossijsk, Russia, and has no known grave.

681. Oberst Otto LASCH

Lasch was born on 25 June 1893 in Pless. He fought in the First World War and was awarded the Iron Cross 1st and 2nd Class (1914). Lasch was awarded the Iron Cross 1st and 2nd Class (1939) after the fall of Poland. He was commander of Infantry Regiment 43 when he was awarded the Knight's Cross on 17 July 1941. The Oak Leaves followed on 10 September 1944.

From November 1944, Lasch was commandant of Königsberg in East Prussia. He surrendered the city on 9 April 1945. For this, Hitler condemned him and his family to death. However, his family were released at the end of the war. Lasch was taken prisoner and not released until 1953. Lasch wrote two books, the first about the fighting for Königsberg and the second about his time in a Russian prison camp. He died on 28 April 1971 and is buried in Zentralfriedhof, Abt XIV, Grave 682, Gotenstrasse, Bad Godesberg, North Rhine-Westphalia.

682. Oberstleutnant Heinz BAYER

Bayer was born on 8 August 1899 in Stollberg. He was commander of Motorcycle Battalion 22 when he was awarded the Knight's Cross on 17 July 1941. Bayer died on 12 August 1986 and is buried in Bad Krozingen Friedhof, Baden-Württemberg.

683. Oberstleutnant Max-Günther SCHRANK

Schrank was born on 19 November 1898 in Rieden. He fought in the First World War and was awarded the Iron Cross 1st and 2nd Class (1914). Schrank was commander of I Battalion, *Jäger* Regiment 100, when he was awarded the Knight's Cross on 17 July 1941. He died on 22 September 1960 in Grünwald, Bavaria.

684. *Major* Otto SCHURY

Schury was born on 22 October 1903 in Munich. He fought in Poland, for which he was awarded the Iron Cross 1st and 2nd Class, France, Yugoslavia, Crete, and Russia. Schury was commander of II Battalion, *Jäger* Regiment 100, when he was awarded the Knight's Cross on 17 July 1941. The Oak Leaves followed on 21 September 1944. He died on 11 December 1979 and is buried in Waldfriedhof, Plot 199, Row 1, Grave 6 (headstone removed), Munich.

685. *Hauptmann* Julius KIRN

Kirn was born on 26 June 1913 in Canstatt. He was a company commander in Panzer Regiment 18 when he was killed in action on 16 July 1941. He is buried in the German War Cemetery, Smolensk-Nishnjaja Dubrowinka, Russia. Kirn was awarded the Knight's Cross on 17 July 1941.

686. Leutnant Werner PFITZER

Pfitzer was born on 7 August 1913 in Schalkau. He was a shock troop leader in Rifle Regiment 113 when he was awarded the Knight's Cross on 19 July 1941. Pfitzer died on 21 November 1996 in Münhltal-Traisa, Hesse.

687. *Oberleutnant* Ludwig FRANZISKET

Franzisket was born on 26 June 1917 in Düsseldorf. He saw action in Poland and was stationed on the English Channel after the fall of France. In Africa, he was adjutant but also found the time to take part in combat flights, shooting down twenty-two enemy aircraft, including the South African ace Ken Driver. For this, he was awarded the Knight's Cross on 20 July 1941.

Later, he flew in the defence of the Reich, shooting down another twenty-one enemy aircraft, including four four-engined bombers. Franzisket died on 23 November 1988 in Münster.

688. Oberleutnant Karl-Heinz LEESMANN

Leesmann was born on 3 May 1915 in Osnabrück. He fought in France, the Battle of Britain, and Russia. Leesmann was a squadron leader in Fighter

Wing 52 when he was awarded the Knight's Cross on 23 July 1941. He was killed in action over Heligoland on 25 July 1943 and has no known grave.

689. *Oberleutnant* Erich THIEL

Thiel was born on 14 June 1912 in Heinrode. He was a squadron leader in Bomber Wing 27 when he was awarded the Knight's Cross on 23 July 1941. Thiel was killed in action on 22 April 1943 and has no known grave.

690. Leutnant Erich SCHMIDT—'Schmidtchen'

Schmidt was born on 17 November 1914 in Neuhaus. He shot down seventeen British aircraft during the Battle of Britain before being moved east for the invasion of Russia. With his total at thirty, Schmidt was awarded the Knight's Cross on 23 July 1941.

On 26 July, he shot down five bombers, and on the 29 July 1941, Schmidt brought down three aircraft to bring his total to forty-seven. He was shot down by flak behind enemy lines near Dubno, Russia, on 31 August 1941 and was posted missing the same day.

691. Stabsfeldwebel Rudolf NACKE

Nacke was born on 19 February 1914 in Dresden. He was a pilot in Bomber Wing 76 when he was awarded the Knight's Cross on 23 July 1941. Nacke died on 29 October 1988 and is buried in Südfriedhof, Hohr-Grenzhausen, Rhineland-Palatinate.

692. Generalmajor Walther K. NEHRING

Nehring was born on 15 August 1892 in Stettin. He fought in the First World War, being awarded the Iron Cross 1st and 2nd Class (1914). He was chief-of-staff of XIX Army Corps during the 1940 French campaign. In Russia, he commanded the 18th Panzer Division and was awarded the Knight's Cross on 24 July 1941. On 9 March 1942, he was named CO of the Africa Corps which, he led until wounded in August. Kesselring asked him to go Tunisia as CO of the V Panzer Army. Nehring carried out this 'footrace to Tunis' with a handful of men and emerged victorious. For this, he was recommended for the Oak Leaves, but they were not awarded until 8 February 1944.

While leading the XXIV Corps in the decisive battles in Russia, Nehring raised the art of commanding armoured forces to its highest level. Nehring was awarded the Swords on 22 January 1945 and was captured by US forces and released on 31 May 1948. He died on 20 April 1983 and is buried in Nordfriedhof, Düsseldorf.

693. Oberst Friedrich-August SCHACK

Schack was born on 27 March 1892 in Schmiedeberg (now Kowary). He fought in the First World War and was awarded the Iron Cross 1st and 2nd Class (1914). Schack fought in Poland, for which he was awarded the Iron Cross 2nd Class (1939), and France, for which he was awarded the Iron Cross 1st Class (1939). He was awarded the Knight's Cross on 24 July 1941 for the capture of Salla, Russia. For his defence of Caen, he was awarded the Oak Leaves on 21 September 1944.

But Schack was suffering from combat fatigue and was relieved of his command. Schack led the LXXXV Army Corps in the Ardennes Offensive and captured by US forces at the end of the war. He died on 24 July 1968 and is buried in Feldstrasse Friedhof, Feld 23, Grave 25–26, Goslar, Lower Saxony.

694. Oberstleutnant Willibald BOROWIETZ

Borowietz was born in Ratibor on 17 September 1893. He fought in the First World War and was awarded the Iron Cross 1st and 2nd Class (1914). In Poland, he commanded the 50th Anti-tank Battalion and was awarded the Iron Cross 2nd Class (1939). In Russia, he led the 10th Rifle Regiment, which spearheaded the division, being awarded the Iron Cross 1st Class (1939) there. His regiment destroyed ninety-two tanks, sixteen artillery pieces, and twelve anti-aircraft guns. For this, he was awarded the Knight's Cross on 24 July 1941.

After a brief period on the staff, he took command of the 15th Panzer Division in Africa. Borowietz fought in the final stages of the battles in Tunisia and was awarded the Oak Leaves on 10 May 1943. Three days later, he was forced to surrender. He died on 1 July 1945 in a car accident while a POW. He is buried at Fort Benning, Muscogee County, Georgia, USA.

695. Oberstleutnant Gerhard FRANZ

Franz was born on 26 February 1902 in Bobeck. He was chief-of-staff of the 29th Infantry Division when he was awarded the Knight's Cross on 24 July 1941. Franz died on 24 December 1975 and is buried in the village cemetery, Bad Wildungen, Hesse.

696. Oberstleutnant Erich FRONHÖFER

Fronhöfer was born on 27 December 1895 in Ragaischen. He fought in the First World War and was awarded the Iron Cross 1st and 2nd Class (1914). Fronhöfer was commander of Panzer Regiment 10 when he was awarded the Knight's Cross on 24 July 1941. He died on 12 January 1970 and is buried in Hauptfriedhof, Am Gottesacker 25, Dortmund, North Rhine-Westphalia.

697. Oberstleutnant Herbert SIMON

Simon was born on 27 March 1897 in Döse. He was commander of Rifle Regiment 112 when he was awarded the Knight's Cross on 24 July 1941. Simon died on 25 October 1971 and is believed to be buried in Südfriedhof, Lünen, Schleswig-Holstein.

698. *Major* Botho von la CHEVALLERIE

Von le Chevallerie was born on 1 August 1898 in Hanover. He fought in the First World War and was awarded the Iron Cross 1st and 2nd Class (1914). Von le Chevallerie was commander of I Battalion, Infantry Regiment 408, when he was awarded the Knight's Cross on 24 July 1941. He died of wounds on 16 November 1943 and is buried in the German War Cemetery, Block 13, Row 3, Grave 211, Kirovograd, Ukraine.

699. *Major* Hans REICHARDT

Reichardt was born on 18 April 1904 in Kirchberg. He was commander of III Battalion, Infantry Regiment 192, when he was awarded the Knight's Cross on 24 July 1941. Reichardt was killed in action at Steinau on 2 February 1945 and has no known grave. He was awarded the Oak Leaves on 5 March 1945.

700. *Hauptmann* Werner LUTZE

Lutze was born on 28 February 1902 in Preussisch. He was commander of II Battalion, Infantry Regiment 169, when he was awarded the Knight's Cross on 24 July 1941. Lutze died on 9 December 1981 and is buried in German War Cemetery, Bad Kissingen, Bavaria.

701. Oberfeldwebel Albert BLAICH

Blaich was born on 3 October 1913 in Unterreichenbach. He was a platoon leader in Panzer Regiment 6 when he was awarded the Knight's Cross on 24 July 1941. Blaich was killed in action at Dabas, Hungary, on 15 March 1945 and has no known grave.

702. Unteroffizier Oskar ALBRECHT

Albrecht was born on 24 September 1914 in Abtsbessingen. He was gun commander in Motorised Infantry Regiment 15 when he was awarded the Knight's Cross on 24 July 1941. Albrecht died on 13 November 1992 in Wallhausen, Baden-Württemberg.

703. Unteroffizier Otto BUKATSCHEK (later changed to WÜNSCHE)

Bukatschek was born on 14 January 1915 in Morgenthau. He was a section leader in Rifle Regiment 52 when he was awarded the Knight's Cross on 24 July 1941. Bukatschek died on 24 March 2003 and is buried in Renningen Friedhof, Baden-Württemberg.

704. General Joachim LEMELSEN

Lemelsen was born on 26 September 1888 in Berlin. He fought in the First World War and was awarded the Iron Cross 1st and 2nd Class (1914). Lemelsen commanded the 29th Infantry Division during the Polish campaign, which was involved in the massacre at Ciepielów on 8 September 1939. He was awarded the Iron Cross 1st and 2nd Class (1939) after the fall of Poland.

Lemelsen fought in France and Denmark, before commanding the XLVII Motorised Corps in the invasion of Russia. He was awarded the Knight's Cross on 27 July 1941. Lemelsen made a strongly worded protest about the shooting of unarmed prisoners during the early part of the campaign. He was awarded the Oak Leaves on 7 September 1943 and transferred to Italy. In May 1944, he was given command of First Army in France. After the Allied invasion of Normandy and the capture of Rome Lemelsen was sent back to Italy, where he stayed until the end of the war. He died on 30 March 1954 and is buried in Stadtfriedhof, Göttingen, Lower Saxony.

705. General Eberhard von MACKENSEN

Von Mackensen was born on 24 September 1889 in Bromberg. He fought in the First World War and was awarded the Iron Cross 1st and 2nd Class (1914). Von Mackensen took part in Poland and France as a chief-of-staff and was awarded the Iron Cross 1st and 2nd Class (1939) after the fall of Poland. He fought in Russia and was awarded the Knight's Cross on 27 July 1944 and the Oak Leaves on 26 May 1942.

Von Mackensen was sent to Italy in 1943, and following a partisan attack, he stated that the suggested reprisals were to 'excessive'. The matter was put to Keitel who ordered the execution of ten Italians for every German solder killed. Von Mackensen was retired from the army in the summer of 1944. He was arrested and tried for war crimes; von Mackensen was sentenced to death, but this was commuted to twenty-one years' imprisonment, but he was released in 1952. Von Mackensen died on 19 May 1969 and is believed to be buried in Einfeld Friedhof, Neumunster, Schleswig-Holstein.

706. General Hans von OBSTFELDER

Von Obstfelder was born on 6 September 1886 in Steinbach-Hallenberg. He fought in the First World War and was awarded the Iron Cross 1st and 2nd Class (1914). Von Obstfelder was awarded the Iron Cross 1st and 2nd Class (1939) in September 1939.

He was commander of XXIX Army Corps when he was awarded the Knight's Cross on 27 July 1941. The Oak Leaves followed on 7 June 1943 and the Swords on 5 November 1944. Von Obstfelder died on 20 December 1976 and is buried in Südfriedhof, Wiesbaden, Hesse.

707. Generalmajor Otto LANCELLE

Lancelle was born on 27 March 1885 in Xanten. He fought in the First World War and was awarded the Iron Cross 1st and 2nd Class (1914), as well as the *Pour le Mérite*. Lancelle was killed in action by a sniper near Krāslava, Latvia, on 3 July 1941 and is buried in Stadtfriedhof, Garmisch-Partenkirchen, Bavaria. He was awarded the Knight's Cross on 27 July 1941.

708. Generalmajor Hans ZORN

Zorn was born on 27 October 1891 in Munich. He fought in the First World War and was awarded the Iron Cross 1st and 2nd Class (1914). Zorn was commander of the 20th Infantry Division when he was awarded the Knight's Cross on 27 July 1941. He was killed in action at Kromy, Russia, on 2 August 1943 and has no known grave. Zorn was awarded the Oak Leaves on 3 September 1943.

709. *Major* Rudolf KÖHLER

Köhler was born on 9 July 1899 in Neu-Wallwitz. He was commander of I Battalion, Rifle Regiment 73, when he was awarded the Knight's Cross on 27 July 1941. Köhler was killed in action on 7 July 1943 near Belgorod, Russia, and has no known grave.

710. *Major* Johannes (aka Hannes) TRAUTLOFT—'The Father of Fighter Wing 54'

Trautloft was born on 3 March 1912 in Grossobringen. He took part in the Spanish Civil War and shot down five enemy aircraft. Trautloft took part in the Polish and French campaign and the Battle of Britain, bringing his tally to thirteen. He saw service in the Balkans and Russia. Trautloft was awarded the Knight's Cross on 27 July 1941, having shot down twenty enemy aircraft.

During 1942 and 1943, he raised his tally to fifty-eight, and on 6 July 1943, he was put in charge of all fighter units on the Eastern Front. In late 1944, Trautloft heard that Allied air crews were being held at Buchenwald Concentration Camp. He visited the camp and found over 160 Allied airmen imprisoned there. Within days, he had them moved to a POW camp. Trautloft died on 12 January 1995 and is buried in Waldfriedhof, Munich.

711. *Hauptmann* Curt EHLE

Ehle was born on 21 October 1899 in Salzwedel. He fought in the First World War and was awarded the Iron Cross 1st and 2nd Class (1914). In 1939, he joined Infantry Regiment 93, the same regiment that he served in during the First World War. Ehle fought in Poland and France, earning the Iron Cross 1st and 2nd Class (1939). Transferred to Africa in April 1941, he took part in the capture of Benghazi and stormed east along the Via Balbia to Capuzzo. His motorcycle battalion fought at Sollum and at the Halfaya Pass. Ehle was awarded the Knight's Cross on 27 July 1941, and in October, he took command of the battalion. He commanded this unit at Sidi Azeiz, Sidi Rezegh, and Bir el Gobi. Fighting with the rear guard, he covered the retreat from El Alamein to Agedabia.

In January 1942, his battalion advanced again now as part of the 104th *Panzergrenadier* Regiment. Ehle was badly wounded by enemy aircraft and evacuated to Germany. After recovering, he was sent back to Africa and became CO of the 104th *Panzergrenadier* Regiment. However, he was wounded again and sent home to recover. In September 1944, with the rank of *Oberstleutnant*, he took command of the 102nd *Panzergrenadier* Regiment in Russia. On 29 November 1944, he was awarded the Oak Leaves. Captured by the Soviets, it was many years before he was released. Ehle died on 16 August 1986 and is buried in Uelzen Friedhof, Lower Saxony.

712. *Hauptmann* Richard LEPPLA

Leppla was born on 9 June 1914 in Matzenbach. He shot down five enemy aircraft during the campaign in the West and a further eight during the Battle of Britain. Leppla fought in Russia and was awarded the Knight's Cross on 27 July 1941 after shooting down his twenty-seventh opponent. He shot down his fortieth on 10 October 1941 and his fiftieth on 9 February 1942.

With his total at sixty-eight in August 1942, Leppla collided with a Ju 52 transport aircraft on landing. He was severely injured, losing the sight in one eye. At the end of the war, he was interned by the Russians and not released until 1950. Leppla died on 4 August 1988 in Matzenbach, Rhineland-Palatinate.

713. *Oberleutnant* Hans KOLBOW

Kolbow was born on 8 January 1914 in Hamburg. He was a squadron leader in Fighter Wing 51 when he was killed in action on 16 July 1941. He is buried at Bychow, Belarus; Kolbow's remains are awaiting transfer to a German war cemetery. He was awarded the Knight's Cross on 27 July 1941. Kolbow is credited with shooting down twenty-seven enemy aircraft.

714. *Oberleutnant* Horst OHRLOFF

Ohrloff was born on 2 April 1917 in Eckersdorf. He was a company commander in Panzer Regiment 25 when he was awarded the Knight's Cross on 27 July 1941. Ohrloff died on 9 May 1997 in Buxtehude, Lower Saxony.

715. *Oberleutnant* Robert OLEJNIK

Olejnik was born on 9 March 1911 in Essen. He was awarded the Iron Cross 1st and 2nd Class in September 1940. Olejnik was a squadron leader in Fighter Wing 1 when he was awarded the Knight's Cross on 27 July 1941. He shot down forty-one enemy aircraft. Olejnik died on 29 October 1988 and is believed to be buried in Waldfriedhof, Munich.

716. *Oberleutnant* Wilhelm SPECHT

Specht was born on 2 February 1912 in Freilburg im Breisgau. He was a company commander in Infantry Regiment 62 when he was awarded the Knight's Cross on 27 July 1941. Specht died of wounds on 31 August 1944 and is buried in the German War Cemetery, Block 36, Row 7, Grave 273, Bourdon, Picardy, France.

717. Leutnant Theodor POPULO

Populo was born on 30 January 1916 in Herne. He was a company commander in Rifle Regiment 4 when he was awarded the Knight's Cross on 27 July 1941. Populo died on 18 May 2010 and is buried in Ostfriedhof, Herne, North Rhine-Westphalia.

718. Stabsfeldwebel Alfred SIMM

Simm was born on 12 July 1910 in Eppendorf. He was a platoon leader in Infantry Regiment 31 when he was awarded the Knight's Cross on 27 July 1941. The Oak Leaves followed on 14 April 1945. Simm died on 19 November 1973 in Eppendorf, Hamburg.

719. Feldwebel Otto ESKE

Eske was born on 12 June 1917 in Hagen. He was a platoon leader in Infantry Regiment 4 when he was awarded the Knight's Cross on 27 July 1941. Eske was killed in action on 8 November 1941 and is buried at Samoschenko, Russia; his remains are awaiting transfer to a German war cemetery.

720. Unteroffizier Otto BRAKAT

Brakat was born on 15 January 1916 in Labiau. He was awarded the Iron Cross 1st and 2nd Class in 1940. Brakat was section leader in Bicycle Battalion 1 when he was awarded the Knight's Cross on 27 July 1941. He died on 31 January 1978 and is buried in Hauptfriedhof, Moers, Rhineland-Palatinate.

721. Korvettenkapitän Gustav FORSTMANN

Forstmann was born on 10 June 1908 in Kiel. He was awarded the Iron Crass 2nd Class in November 1939 and the 1st Class in April 1940. Forstmann was commander of R-Boat Flotilla 1 when he was awarded the Knight's Cross on 28 July 1941. He died on 2 February 1985 in Wedel, Schleswig-Holstein.

722. *Kapitänleutnant* Jost METZLER

Metzler was born in Altshausen on 26 February 1909. He commissioned *U-69* on 21 November 1940 and fired his first torpedoes on 17 February 1941, sending the 8,456-ton *Siamese Prince* to the bottom. The next day, he sank the *Blanda*, which was followed by the *Temple Moat* on the 23rd. During his next patrol in March, he sank the *Coultran*. On 21 May 1941, *U-69* stopped the 4,000-ton *Robin Moore* as the ship was carrying contraband goods; it was sunk as per the prize order. Ten days later, he sank the *Sangara* in Accra Harbour. The *Robert Hughes* was sunk by mines laid by Metzler off the entrance to Lagos Harbour. *U-69* went on to sink three ships from convoy SL76. He was awarded the Knight's Cross on 28 July 1941.

In mid-August, Metzler was taken ill at sea with severe renal cholic and returned for hospital treatment. He was then appointed commander of a training flotilla, and in October 1943, he formed the 19th U-Boat Flotilla in Pillau, with which he transferred to Kiel in February 1945. In 1954, he published his memoir, *The Laughing Cow: The Story of U-69*. Metzler died on 29 September 1975 in Bavendorf-Ravensburg, Baden-Württemberg.

723. Generalmajor Walter DÜVERT

Düvert was born on 2 October 1893 in Görlitz. He fought in the First World War and was awarded the Iron Cross 1st and 2nd Class (1914). Düvert was awarded the Iron Cross 1st and 2nd Class (1939) in 1940. He was commander of the 13th Panzer Division when he was awarded the Knight's

Cross on 30 July 1941. Düvert retired from active duty in November 1944. He died on 4 February 1972 and is buried in Stoffeler Friedhof, Feld 17B, Düsseldorf.

724. Oberst Walter HOERNLEIN—'Papa'

Hoernlein was born on 2 January 1893 in Blüthen. He fought in the First World War and was awarded the Iron Cross 2nd Class (1914). Hoernlein was commander of Infantry Regiment 80 when he was awarded the Knight's Cross on 30 July 1941. The Oak Leaves followed on 15 March 1943. He died on 14 September 1961 in Cologne, North Rhine-Westphalia.

725. Oberstleutnant Maximilian Reichsführer von EDELSHEIM

Von Edelsheim was born on 6 July 1897 in Berlin. He fought in the First World War and was awarded the Iron Cross 1st and 2nd Class (1914). Von Edelsheim was awarded the Iron Cross 1st and 2nd Class (1939) after the fall of Poland. He was commander of Bicycle Battalion I when he was awarded the Knight's Cross on 30 July 1941. The Oak Leaves followed on 23 December 1942 and the Swords on 23 October 1944. Von Edelsheim died on 26 April 1994 and is buried in Konstanz Friedhof, Baden-Württemberg.

726. *Oberleutnant* Viktor BAUER

Bauer was born on 19 September 1915 in Löcknitz. He took part in the Battle for France and the Battle of Britain, shooting down three British aircraft. By November 1940, he had been awarded the Iron Cross 1st and 2nd Class. Bauer took part in the invasion of Russia, where his tally really started to mount up. In June 1941, he shot down fifteen enemy aircraft, including five bombers on the 26th. Bauer shot down seventeen aircraft in July, including another five bombers on 12th, but was himself shot down on the 23rd.

With his tally at thirty-five, he was awarded the Knight's Cross on 30 July 1941. On 26 July 1942, he was awarded the Oak Leaves for his 102nd victory. Bauer shot down his 106th and last aircraft on 9 August 1942, after which he was transferred to southern France. He died on 13 December 1969 and is believed to be buried in Waldfriedhof, Bad Homburg, Hesse.

727. *Oberleutnant* Arbogast Graf von KAGENECK—'Erbo'

Graf von Kageneck was born on 2 April 1918 in Bonn. In the West and over England, he shot down seventeen enemy aircraft while flying bomber escort and fighter sweeps. Moved to the Russian Front in 1941, he added forty-eight Russian aircraft to his total and was awarded the Knight's Cross on 30 July 1941.

Transferred to Africa, Graf von Kageneck was awarded the Oak Leaves on 26 October 1941. Then, on 24 December, he was badly shot up but managed to land at his own airfield. Following initial treatment, Graf von Kageneck was moved to Naples where he died of wounds on 12 January 1942; he has no known grave. His brother, Clemens-Heinrich, was also awarded the Knight's Cross with Oak Leaves.

728. Generalmajor Hans-Valentin HUBE—'The Human'

Hube was born on 29 October 1890 in Naumburg. He fought in the First World War, losing his left arm and being awarded the Iron Cross 1st and 2nd Class (1914). Hube took part in the Polish and French campaigns and was awarded the Iron Cross 1st and 2^{n+d} Class (1939). Between the wars, he wrote a two-volume work entitled *Der Infanterist*. He commanded a panzer division with distinction at Starya-Konstatynov, Russia, against a much larger force. For this, he was awarded the Knight's Cross on 1 August 1941.

For his actions during the winter battles of 1941–42, Hube was awarded the Oak Leaves on 16 January 1942. Appointed commander of XIV Panzer Corps in September 1942, he was awarded the Swords on 21 December 1942 for his corps actions during the thrust towards the Volga, north of Stalingrad. Hube was flown out of the pocket to receive his award but immediately flown back in. On Hitler's orders, he was flown out again on 18 January 1943. Hube pleaded with the Führer to allow the 6th Army to break out, but Hitler refused.

Posted to Sicily in July 1943, Hube commanded the army and flak troops on the island. He fought with great skill in Sicily and Italy, but he was unable to crush the Salerno landing. In October 1943, he was placed on the leadership reserve of the OKH, but in February 1944, he was sent to the Russian Front to command the 1st Panzer Army. Hube was responsible for the break-out from the Korsun Pocket in March–April 1944.

For his leadership in Sicily, Italy, and at Korsun, Hube was awarded the Diamonds on 20 April 1944. He was killed in a plane crash while returning to the front after the award ceremony. Hube is buried in the Invaliden Friedhof, Feld E, Plot 7, Grave 1, Scharnhorstrasse, Berlin.

729. *Hauptmann* Otto STAMS

Stams was born on 5 April 1903 in Grätz. He was a group commander in Bomber Wing 1 when he was awarded the Knight's Cross on 1 August 1941. Stams died on 16 May 1976 and is believed to be buried in Waldfriedhof, Munich.

730. *Oberleutnant* Erich LEIE

Leie was born on 10 September 1916 in Kiel. During the Battle for France and the Battle of Britain, he shot down eleven enemy aircraft. On 23 July 1941, Leie shot down six Spitfires and, with his tally at thirty-one, was awarded the Knight's Cross on 1 August 1941. On 19 August 1942, he shot down a Spitfire over Dieppe but was himself shot down.

In January 1943, he was transferred to the Russian Front and was shot down again in July. In November, he claimed his 100th enemy aircraft. Leie total score was 118, which included one four-engined bomber, thirty Spitfires, and thirty-two Sturmoviks. He was killed in action on 7 March 1945 when he collided with a Russian fighter, and has no known grave. Leie was recommended for the Oak Leaves, but they were not awarded.

731. *Oberleutnant* Karl-Gottfried NORDMANN

Nordmann was born on 22 November 1915 in Giessen. He was awarded the Iron Cross 1st and 2nd Class after the fall of Poland. By November 1940, he had shot down eight enemy aircraft. Nordmann took part in the invasion of Russia and, with his tally at thirty-one, was awarded the Knight's Cross on 1 August 1941. The Oak Leaves followed on 16 September 1941.

With his total at seventy-eight, Nordmann was involved in a mid-air collision with Rudolf Busch on 17 January 1943. Busch was killed and Nordmann was so badly injured that he did not fly again. He died on 22 July 1982 and is buried in Putnam Cemetery, Greenwich, Connecticut, USA.

732. *Oberleutnant* Rudolf PFLANZ—'Rudi'

Pflanz was born on 1 July 1914 in Ichenheim. He shot down his first enemy aircraft on 30 April 1940. During the Battle of Britain, Pflanz shot down eight more aircraft. With his tally at twenty, he was awarded the Knight's Cross on 1 August 1941. With his total at fifty-two (including forty-five Spitfires),

Pflanz was killed in action on 31 July 1942. He is buried in the German War Cemetery, Block 32, Row 7, Grave 276, Bourdon, Picardy, France.

733. *Oberleutnant* Karl-Heinz SCHNELL—'Bubi'

Schnell was born on 10 January 1915 in Essen. He was a fighter pilot and shot down nine enemy aircraft over France and during the Battle of Britain. Schnell soon started to rack up victories in Russia, and with his tally at thirty-one, he was awarded the Knight's Cross on 1 August 1941. Apart from a short visit to Italy, he would remain on the Eastern Front for the remainder of the war. His final tally was seventy-two victories. Schnell died on 13 March 2013.

734. Leutnant Egon MAYER—'Connie'

Mayer was born on 19 August 1917 in Konstanz. He was awarded the Iron Cross 2nd Class after the fall of Poland and the 1st Class in May 1940, but he did not shoot down his first enemy aircraft until 13 June 1940. Mayer was awarded the Knight's Cross on 1 August 1941 with his tally at twenty victories.

On 23 November 1942, he shot down his first two four-engined bombers, a B-17 and a B-24. Mayer was awarded the Oak Leaves on 16 April 1943 with sixty-three victories to his credit. With his tally at 102 (including twenty-six four-engined bombers), Mayer was shot down and killed on 2 March 1944; he was awarded the Swords the same day. Mayer was the first fighter ace to score 100 victories on the Western Front. He is buried in the German War Cemetery, Block 1, Row 8, Grave 67, St. Desiré-de-Lisieux, Normandy, France.

735. Oberwachtmeister Ernst ALEX

Alex was born on 1 March 1915 in Seifersdorf. He was platoon commander in Assault-Gun Battalion 243 when he was awarded the Knight's Cross on 1 August 1941. Alex died on 25 October 1965 and is buried in Hauptfriedhof, Tannenkeckerweg 6, Kassel, Hesse.

736. Oberfeldwebel Hugo DAHMER

Dahmer was born on 7 May 1918 in Koblenz. He was a pilot in Fighter Wing 5 when he was awarded the Knight's Cross on 1 August 1941. Dahmer is credited with shooting down between forty-five and fifty-seven enemy aircraft.

He died on 1 August 2006 and is buried in Waldfriedhof, Troisdorf, North Rhine-Westphalia.

737. Oberfeldwebel Kurt PRZYKLENK

Przyklenk was born on 2 January 1912 in Deumen. He was a section leader in Panzer Reconnaissance Battalion 40 when he was awarded the Knight's Cross on 1 August 1941. Przyklenk was killed in action on 10 January 1943 and is believed to be buried in the German War Cemetery (as unknown), Rossoschka, Volgograd, Russia.

738. General Christian HANSEN

Hansen was born 10 April 1885 in Schleswig. He fought in the First World War and was awarded the Iron Cross 1st and 2nd Class (1914). Hansen was commander of X Army Corps when he was awarded the Knight's Cross on 3 August 1941. He was retired due to ill health on 31 December 1944. Hansen died on 7 August 1972 and is buried in Stadtfriedhof, Abt 1, Feld 2, Row 10, Grave 7, Garmisch-Partenkirchen, Bavaria.

739. Korvettenkapitän Fritz BREITHAUPT

Breithaupt was born on 5 September 1892 in Bromberg. He fought in the First World War and was awarded the Iron Cross 1st and 2^{n+d} Class (1914). Breithaupt was awarded the Iron Cross 2nd Class (1939) after the fall of Poland and the 1st Class (1939) after the fall of France.

He was commander of M-Boat Flotilla 12 when he was awarded the Knight's Cross on 3 August 1941. The Oak Leaves followed on 10 February 1944. Breithaupt was killed in a flying accident on 24 December 1944 and is buried in the German War Cemetery, Block 8, Row 3, Grave 60, on the B-6600, Recogne-Bastogne, Belgium.

740. Korvettenkapitän Karl PALMGREEN

Palmgreen was born on 2 September 1891 in Stralsund. He fought in the First World War and was awarded the Iron Cross 1st and 2nd Class (1914). Palmgreen was commander of Mine Sweeper Pathfinder IX and I when he was awarded the Knight's Cross on 3 August 1941. The Oak Leaves followed on

11 July 1944. He died on 16 September 1970 and is buried in Stadtfriedhof, Göttingen, Lower Saxony.

741. *Oberleutnant* zur See Siegfried WUPPERMANN

Wuppermann was born on 15 December 1916 in Berlin. He was awarded the Iron Cross 1st and 2nd Class in 1940. Wuppermann was commander of torpedo boat *S-60* when he led an attack on 7 March 1941 in which two destroyers and three merchant ships were sank. For this, he was awarded the Knight's Cross on 3 August 1941. The Oak Leaves followed on 14 April 1943. He died on 15 April 2005 in Osnabrück, Lower Saxony.

742. General Ion ANTONESCU (Commander-in-Chief Romanian Army)—'The Red Dog'

Antonescu was born on 15 June 1882 in Piteşti, Romania. He took part in 1907 Peasants' Revolt and the 1913 Second Balkans War. Antonescu also fought in the First World War. In September 1940, he was made prime minister and *Conducător* of the State of Romania as King Michael II.

Romania joined Germany in the invasion of Russia, and Antonescu was awarded the Knight's Cross on 6 August and promoted to marshal of Romania by royal decree on 22 August 1941. Antonescu ordered a large-scale massacre of the Jewish population in reprisal for a bomb that killed a number of Romanian solders in Odessa. With the war turning against him, Antonescu was arrested on 23 August 1944 and sent to Moscow. After the war, he was sent back to Romania for war crimes trials; found guilty, he was shot by firing squad on 1 June 1946. Antonescu refused a blindfold and raised his hat in salute as the order to fire was given. He has no known grave.

743. Generalleutnant Walther FISCHER von WEIKERSTHAL

Fischer von Weikersthal was born on 15 September 1890 in Stuttgart. He fought in the First World War and was awarded the Iron Cross 1st and 2nd Class (1914). Fischer von Weikersthal was commander of the 35th Infantry Division when he was awarded the Knight's Cross on 6 August 1941. He died on 11 February 1953 and is buried in Alter Friedhof, Tettnang, Baden-Württemberg.

744. *Major* Fritz HOLZHÄUER

Holzhäuer was born on 8 July 1902 in Schwäbisch Gmünd. He was commander of III Battalion, Panzer Regiment 29, when he was awarded the Knight's Cross on 6 August 1944. Holzhäuer died on 14 December 1982 and is buried in Hauptfriedhof, Tannenkeckerweg 6, Kassel, Hesse.

745. *Hauptmann* Herbert KAMINSKI

Kaminski was born on 24 May 1909 in Ohmswalde. He fought in the Condor Legion during the Spanish Civil War. Kaminski shot down his first enemy aircraft over France and two more during the Battle of Britain before his Bf 110 was shot down into the English Channel. He also saw action over the Balkans and Crete before taking part in the invasion of Russia. Kaminski was awarded the Knight's Cross on 6 August 1941 with five victories to his credit.

He saw action over Malta where he shot down a Hurricane and later took part in the defence of the Reich, shooting down at lest one four-engined bomber. Kaminski died in a car crash on 18 July 1971 in Garmisch-Partenkirchen, Bavaria.

746. *Hauptmann* Theodor ROSSIWALL

Rossiwall was born on 13 October 1915 in Vienna. He fought in the Spanish Civil War and shot down two aircraft. Rossiwall went on to shot down a further seventeen enemy aircraft, including British ace Pat Marmaduke over Crete on 20 April 1941 (whom he claimed with Sophus Baagoe). He was awarded the Knight's Cross on 6 August 1941. Rossiwall died on 10 July 1979 and is buried in Zentralfriedhof, Vienna.

747. *Hauptmann* Wolf-Dietrich WILCKE—'Fürst'

Wilcke was born on 11 March 1913 at Schrimm. He served briefly with the Condor Legion in Spain. Wilcke shot down his first enemy aircraft, a French Potez 637, on 7 November 1939. In May 1940, he was shot down and taken prisoner by the French; he was released after the fall of France. By now awarded the Iron Cross 1st and 2nd Class, Wilcke was shot down into the Channel on 13 August 1940; this time, he was picked up by a German seaplane. By the end of the Battle of Britain, he had shot down thirteen enemy aircraft.

Wilcke took part in the invasion of Russia, and on the first day of the campaign, he shot down five enemy aircraft, but it has to be said they were obsolete biplanes. Then, on 25 June 1941, he collided with another fighter during take-off. Both aircraft burst into flames, but Wilcke escaped with minor injuries. He was awarded the Knight's Cross on 6 August 1941 with twenty-five aircraft to his credit. In December 1941, his unit was moved to Sicily to take part in raids on Malta, but in May 1942, he was back on the Russian Front. His tally increased to 100 victories by 6 September 1942, and he was awarded the Oak Leaves three days later. On 23 December 1942, with his total at 155, Wilcke was awarded the Swords, which also meant he was grounded to avoid his loss.

In the spring of 1943, his unit was transferred to home defence. For almost a year, Wilcke remained on the ground, but in February 1944, he started combat flights again. He shot down four B-17 Flying Fortresses, but on 6 March 1944, he was baldly shot up and had to crash land. On 23 March 1944, Wilcke shot down a P-51 Mustang for his 162nd victory, but shortly afterwards, he was shot down himself and killed. He has no known grave.

748. *Oberleutnant* Hubert MÜTHERICH

Mütherich was born on 12 November 1912 in Lippstadt. He was a squadron leader in Fighter Wing 54 when he was awarded the Knight's Cross on 6 August 1941. Mütherich was killed on landing on 9 September 1941 and is buried at Krasnoje Selo, Russia; his remains are awaiting transfer to a German war cemetery.

749. Leutnant Josef PÖHS—'Joschi'

Pöhs was born on 14 March 1912 in Altkettenhof, Austria-Hungary. He was a pilot in Fighter Wing 54 when he was awarded the Knight's Cross on 6 August 1941. Pöhs is credited with forty-three victories. He was killed when his Me 163 jet crashed near Bad Zwischenahn on 30 December 1943; he has no known grave.

750. Leutnant Herbert SCHRAMM

Schramm was born on 13 October 1913 in Wetzlar. He was a fighter pilot and scored his first but unconfirmed victory on 14 May 1940 over Sedan. Schramm also fought in the Battle of Britain, ending the campaign with eight confirmed victories and the Iron Cross 1st and 2nd Class. He took part in the invasion of Russia and was awarded the Knight's Cross on 6 August 1941 with his tally at twenty-five enemy aircraft shot down.

With thirty-seven victories to his credit, Schramm was sent back to Germany to train new pilots, but he still managed to shot down another two enemy aircraft as an instructor. In August 1943, Schramm was given command of Fighter Wing 27, with which he shot down three B-17 four-engined bombers. On 1 December 1943, he was shot down over Eupen, Belgium. He has no known grave. Schramm was awarded the Oak Leaves on 11 February 1945.

751. Leutnant Hans (or Johannes) THURNER

Thurner was born on 24 October 1918 in Innsbruck. He fought in the Battle of Britain and was awarded the Iron Cross 1st and 2nd Class. Thurner was a group commander in Bomber Wing 55 when he was awarded the Knight's Cross on 6 August 1941. He was shot down on 11 June 1944 and is buried in the German War Cemetery, Block 9, Row 4, Grave 124, La Cambe, Normandy, France. Thurner was awarded the Oak Leaves on 17 September 1944.

752. Oberfeldwebel Alfred TYKIEL

Tykiel was born on 6 July 1911 in Mühlengrund. He was a platoon leader in Rifle Regiment 10 when he was awarded the Knight's Cross on 6 August 1941. Tykiel died on 22 March 1981 and is believed to be buried in Waldfriedhof, Dülmen, North Rhine-Westphalia.

753. Generalleutnant Otto SPONHEIMER

Sponheimer was born on 19 December 1886 in Nuremberg. He fought in the First World War and was awarded the Iron Cross 1st and 2nd Class (1914). Sponheimer was commander of the 21st Infantry Division when he was awarded the Knight's Cross on 8 August 1941. He died on 14 March 1961 in Bad Kötzting, Bavaria.

754. SS-Gruppenführer Paul HAUSSER—'Papa'

Hausser was born on 7 October 1880 in Brandenburg. He served on the staff during the First World War, being awarded the Iron Cross 1st and 2nd Class (1914). Hausser served in Poland, being awarded the Iron Cross 2nd

Class (1939) in September 1939, and France, where he commanded the 2nd SS-Panzer Division and was awarded Iron Cross 1st Class in May 1940. Known as 'Papa' by his men, he was awarded the Knight's Cross on 8 August 1941 for his part in the opening stages of the invasion of Russia.

He remained in Russia, where he withdrew from Kharkov against Hitler's orders only to retake the city in March 1943. For this, he was awarded the Oak Leaves on 28 July 1943. He was wounded in the eye, which he ultimately lost. Hausser was also involved in the great tank battles of Kursk. Sent to Italy for a brief period, Hausser was then sent to Normandy with his 2nd SS-Panzer Corps to fight against the Allied landings there. He took over the VII Army and remained in the Falaise Pocket until wounded by a bullet through the jaw. Hausser was awarded the Swords on 26 August 1944; he ended the war on Kesselring's staff. He is author of *Waffen SS in Action* and *Soldiers Like Any Others*. Hausser died on 21 December 1972 and buried in Waldfriedhof, Munich.

755. Oberst Theodor BOHLMANN-COMBRINCK

Bohlmann-Combrinck was born on 18 November 1891 in Delmenhorst. He fought in the First World War and was awarded the Iron Cross 1st and 2nd Class (1914). Bohlmann-Combrinck was awarded the Iron Cross 1st and 2nd Class (1939) after the fall of Poland. He was commander of Rifle Regiment 111 when he was awarded the Knight's Cross on 8 August 1941. Bohlmann-Combrinck died on 18 November 1956 and is believed to be buried in Alter Friedhof, Menzenberger Strasse, Bad Honnef, North Rhine-Westphalia.

756. Oberst Fritz HERTZSCH

Hertzsch was born on 15 June 1892 in Zittau. He was commander of Infantry Regiment 77. Hertzsch was killed in action on 15 July 1941 and is buried at Wetrino, Belarus; his remains are awaiting transfer to a German war cemetery. Hertzsch was awarded the Knight's Cross on 8 August 1941.

757. Oberstleutnant Carl-Friedrich von der MEDEN

Von der Meden was born on 3 December 1896 in Samplau. He fought in the First World War and was awarded the Iron Cross 1st and 2nd Class (1914). Von der Meden was commander of Bicycle Battalion 12 when he was awarded the Knight's Cross on 8 August 1941. He died on 25 December 1961 and is believed to be buried in Gartenfriedhof, Marienstrasse, Hanover.

758. *Major* Franz (or Erhard) GNADEN

Gnaden was born on 13 February 1905 in Unterneuhausen. He was commander of I Battalion, *Jäger* Regiment 85, when he was awarded the Knight's Cross on 8 August 1941. Gnaden died on 16 November 1967 and is buried in Hauptfriedhof, Friedhofstrasse 1, Landshut, Bavaria.

759. *Major* Martin PÜSCHEL

Püschel was born on 8 September 1899 in Spremberg. He was commander of II Battalion, Rifle Regiment 33, when he was awarded the Knight's Cross on 8 August 1941. Püschel died on 7 July 1989 and is believed to be buried in Südfriedhof, Brühl, North Rhine-Westphalia.

760. *Major* Egon TREECK

Treeck was born on 14 December 1894 in Dortmund. He was commander of II Battalion, *Jäger* Regiment 85, when he was awarded the Knight's Cross on 8 August 1941. Treeck died on 16 December 1966 and is buried in Hauptfriedhof, Am Gottesacker 25, Dortmund, North Rhine-Westphalia.

761. *Oberleutnant* Helmut (or Helmuth) HAUN

Haun was born on 16 October 1915 in Bielefeld. He was adjutant in Infantry Regiment 77 when he was awarded the Knight's Cross on 8 August 1941. Haun died of wounds on 26 November 1941 in Berlin and has no known grave.

762. Leutnant Wilhelm HENZ

Henz was born on 1 October 1915 in Eschhofen. He was a company commander in Motorcycle Battalion 29 when he was awarded the Knight's Cross on 8 August 1941. Henz was killed in action at Stalingrad on 30 January 1943 and has no known grave.

763. Oberst Walter HARTMANN

Hartmann was born on 23 July 1891 in Mülheim. He fought in the First World War and was awarded the Iron Cross 1st and 2nd Class (1914). Hartmann was awarded the Iron Cross 1st and 2nd Class (1939) after the fall of Poland. He was Artillery Commander 140 when he was awarded the Knight's Cross on 10 August 1941. The Oak Leaves followed on 30 November 1943 and the Swords on 18 March 1945. Hartmann died on 11 March 1977 and is buried in Waldfriedhof, Hameln, Lower Saxony.

764. Oberfeldwebel Josef GRETSCHMANN

Gretschmann was born on 13 February 1914 in Leithen. He was a platoon leader in Rifle Regiment 40 when he was awarded the Knight's Cross on 11 August 1941. Gretschmann died on 8 September 1965 and is buried in Alter Friedhof, Herdweg 41, Böblingen, Baden-Württemberg.

765. *Oberleutnant* Max BUCHOLZ (or BUCHHOLZ)

Bucholz was born on 3 November 1912 in Zerbst. He fought in the Battle for France and was awarded the Iron Cross 1st and 2nd Class; he also fought in the Battle of Britain. Bucholz shot down twenty-eight or thirty enemy aircraft and was awarded the Knight's Cross on 12 August 1941. He died on 19 July 1996 in Warnemünde, Mecklenburg-Vorpommern.

766. *Oberleutnant* Helmut MECKEL

Meckel was born on 23 August 1917 in Munich. He fought in the Battle for France, the Battle of Britain, and on the Eastern Front. He shot down twenty-five enemy aircraft and was awarded the Knight's Cross on 12 August 1941. Meckel was killed in a flying accident during the evacuation of Tunis on 8 May 1943 and is buried in the German War Cemetery, Ossario 5, Panel 12, Bordj-Cedria, Tunisia.

767. *Oberleutnant* Kurt SOCHATZY

Sochatzy was born on 5 February 1915 in Schloss Pragerhof, Austria-Hungary. He took part in the Spanish Civil War with the Condor Legion. Sochatzy saw service in Poland but missed the French campaign and the Battle of Britain as he was sent to train new pilot. His first victory was on 7 June 1941 when he shot down an RAF Spitfire over the English Channel. Four days later, his unit was transferred to Poland for the invasion of Russia.

Sochatzy shot down thirty-five enemy aircraft in the first mouth of the campaign. On 16 July, he was shot down; however, he was able to make it back to his own lines. After shooting down three more aircraft and with his total at thirty-eight, Sochatzy was shot down and taken prisoner. He was awarded the Knight's Cross on 12 August 1841. The Russians held him for two years after the end of the war. Sochatzy died on 2 May 1996 and is buried in Zentralfriedhof, Vienna.

768. Leutnant Erwin FLEIG

Fleig was born on 6 December 1912 in Freilburg im Breisgau. During the Battle of Britain, he shot down six Spritfires and one Hurricane. Moved to the Russian Front, he shot down a further fifty-seven aircraft and was awarded the Knight's Cross on 12 August 1941. Fleig was shot down and captured by the Russians on 29 May 1942; he was not released until the 1950s. He died on 1 March 1986 in Freilburg im Breisgau, Baden-Württemberg.

769. Oberfeldwebel Heinrich HOFFMANN

Hoffmann was born on 8 March 1913 in Worms. He shot down his first enemy aircraft during the Battle of Britain on 7 September 1940. On the Russian Front, he was awarded the Iron Crass 1st and 2nd Class in July 1941, having shot down twenty enemy aircraft in July and another twenty-five in August; the Knight's Cross was awarded to him on 12 August 1941. With his total at sixty-three, he was posted missing in Russia on 3 October 1941. Hoffmann was awarded the Oak Leaves on 19 October 1941; he was the first NCO to be awarded them.

770. Generalleutnant Otto-Ernst OTTENBACHER

Ottenbacher was born on 18 November 1888 in Esslingen am Necker. He fought in the First World War and was awarded the Iron Cross 1st and 2nd Class (1914). Ottenbacher was commander of the 36th Infantry Division when he was awarded the Knight's Cross on 13 August 1941. He died on 7 January 1975 and is buried in Hoppenlau Friedhof, Stuttgart, Baden-Württemberg.

771. Generalmajor Walter von BOLTENSTERN

Von Boltenstern was born on 26 November 1889 in Breslau. He fought in the First World War and was awarded the Iron Cross 1st and 2nd Class (1914). Von Boltenstern took part in the Polish campaign and was awarded the Iron Cross 1st and 2nd Class (1939). He also fought in the French campaign.

Von Boltenstern commanded the 29th Infantry Division in Russia and was awarded the Knight's Cross on 13 August 1941. He was retired in 1945, but later that year, he was taken by the Russians and died on 19 January 1952 in their hands. Von Boltenstern is buried in the German War Cemetery, Row 2, Grave 2, Cherntsy, Russia.

772. Generalmajor Josef HARPE

Harpe was born on 21 September 1887 in Buer. He fought in the First World War and was awarded the Iron Cross 1st and 2nd Class (1914). In 1940, Harpe was commandant of the Panzer School at Wünsdorf. He was commander of the 12th Panzer Division when he was awarded the Knight's Cross on 13 August 1941. The Oak Leaves followed on 31 December 1941.

Harpe commanded XXXXI Panzer Corps from July 1942 until October 1943, and he was awarded the Swords during this time, on 15 September 1943. He was relieved of his command due to the inability to stop the Russian Vistula-Oder offensive. Harpe ended the war on the Western Front. He died on 14 March 1968 and is buried in the village cemetery (headstone removed), Eschau, Lower Franconia, Bavaria.

773. Oberst Helmut FRIEBE

Friebe was born on 4 November 1894 in Namslau. He fought in the First World War and was awarded the Iron Cross 1st and 2nd Class (1914). Friebe was commander of Infantry Regiment 164 when he was awarded the Knight's Cross on 13 August 1941. He died on 14 January 1970 and is buried in the village cemetery, Fischbach, Feld 4, Row 2, Grave 22–23, Near Friedrichshafen, Baden-Württemberg. His brother, Werner, was also awarded the Knight's Cross.

774. *Oberleutnant* Gerhard BENACK

Benack was born on 23 June 1915 in Züllichau. He was a company commander in Motorcycle Battalion 38 when he was awarded the Knight's

Cross on 13 August 1941. Benack died on 9 December 1994 and is buried in Hauptfriedhof, Koblenz, Rhineland-Palatinate.

775. *Oberleutnant* Wolfgang SCHENCK—'Bombo'

Schenck was born on 7 February 1913 in Windhoek, German West Africa. A pilot in Heavy Fighter Wing 1, he took part in the Polish (Iron Cross 2nd Class) and Norwegian campaigns, but he shot down his first enemy aircraft on 11 May 1940 over France. He was seriously wounded on the 16th and missed most of the Battle of Britain. Schenck was awarded the Iron Cross 1st Class on 25 May 1940. In Russia, he was awarded the Knight's Cross on 14 August 1941 with nine victories to his credit. By January 1942, he had shot down eighteen enemy aircraft, as well as destroyed numerous shipping, tanks, and transports.

In August, he was moved to the German Air Ministry and awarded the Oak Leaves on 30 October 1942. In January 1943, he was flying a Fw 190 fighter-bomber in the Mediterranean area. Wounded again in December 1943, he was appointed as inspector of combat airman. In June 1944, was evaluating the Me 262 jet fighter. He flew forty missions in the Me 262. Schenck died on 5 March 2010 in Marburg, Hesse.

776. General Carl-Heinrich von STÜLPNAGEL

Von Stülpnagel was born on 2 January 1886 in Berlin. He served on the General Staff in the First World War and was awarded the Iron Cross 1st and 2nd Class (1914). Von Stülpnagel was commander of XVII Army when he was awarded the Knight's Cross on 21 August 1941. In Russia, he ordered reprisals against civilians for partisan attacks and collaborated with the mass killing of Jews.

He was made military commander of France in February 1942, and it was here that he became involved in the plot to kill Hitler. When the 20 July plot failed, he tried to shoot himself, but only succeeded in blinding himself. Von Stülpnagel was arrested and tortured and is said to have screamed the name 'Rommel' while delirious. He was hanged in Berlin on 30 August 1944 and has no known grave.

777. Oberst Walter (or Walther) MELZER

Melzer was born on 7 October 1894 in Leipzig. He fought in the First World War, being awarded the Iron Cross 1st and 2nd Class (1914). Melzer was commander of Infantry Regiment 151 when he was awarded the Knight's Cross on 21 August 1941. The Oak Leaves followed on 23 August 1944. He died on 23 June 1961 in Bremen.

778. Oberst Hermann-Bernhard RAMCKE

Ramcke was born on 24 January 1889 in Schleswig. He fought in the First World War with the Marine Assault Battalion, being awarded the Wound Badge in Gold and the Iron Cross 1st and 2nd Class (1914). He was awarded the Iron Cross 2nd Class (1939) after fighting in Poland. Ramcke passed the parachutist course in 1940, at the age of fifty-one. His first action was at Crete where he commanded *Fallschirmjäger* Assault (Glider) Regiment 1 with the rank of *Oberst*. He was awarded the Iron Cross 1st Class (1939) and the Knight's Cross on 21 August 1941 for his part in the Crete campaign.

In 1942, he commanded the 'Ramcke' Brigade in Africa, and it was while here that his men were cut off and had to fight their way back 80 miles to the German lines. On the way, they captured a British convoy and freed 100 German and Italian POWs from another convoy. For this, Ramcke was awarded the Oak Leaves on 13 November 1942. On 13 February 1943, he was named commander of the 2nd Parachute Division, which he led in Russia and Normandy. While stationed in Auray, France, his men enjoyed good relations with the locals. Ramcke had eight local men released who had been held prisoner since 1940. In Fortress Brest, his division held out until 19 September 1944; he was awarded the Swords and Diamonds on the same day. Ironically, he was tried by the French for war crimes, being found guilty, but he was released in 1951. Ramcke died from cancer on 5 July 1968 and is buried in Domfriedhof, Feld A1 (family plot), Kappeln, Schleswig-Holstein.

779. Oberstleutnant Hans EMIG

Emig was born on 7 December 1902 in Wonsowo (present-day Wąsowo). He was commander of *Kampfgruppe* 806 when he was killed in action at Stalingrad, Russia, on 28 June 1941; he has no known grave. Emig was awarded the Knight's Cross on 21 August 1941.

780. Oberstleutnant Alfred HEMMANN

Hemmann was born on 13 October 1895 in Gleiwitz. He fought in the First World War and was awarded the Iron Cross 2nd Class (1914). Hemmann was commander of Infantry Regiment 426 when he was awarded the Knight's Cross on 21 August 1941. He died on 26 September 1957 in Friedberg, Hesse.

781. Oberstleutnant Hermann HENNICKE

Hennicke was born on 27 December 1896 in Magdeburg. He was commander of Infantry Regiment 37 and was awarded the Knight's Cross on 21 August 1941. Hennicke was killed in action on 27 August 1941 and is buried at Punewo, Russia; his remains are awaiting transfer to a German war cemetery.

782. Fregattenkapitän Kurt WEYHER

Weyher was born on 30 August 1901 in Graudenz. He fought in the last year of the First World War. Weyher was awarded the Iron Cross 1st and 2nd Class in 1940. He was commander of the armed merchant raider *Orion* (HSK1) when he was awarded the Knight's Cross on 21 August 1941. Weyher is author of *The Black Raider*. He died on 17 February 1991 in Wilhelmshaven, Lower Saxony.

783. *Major* Hans KROH

Kroh was born on 13 May 1907 in Heidelberg. He took command of I Battalion, *Fallschirmjäger* Regiment 2, on 1 September 1940. In Crete, he had to take over command of Battle Group 'Sturm' when its commander was captured, their objective being Rethymnon airfield. Near Stavromenos and the oil refinery, he held out against vastly superior forces. It was here that one of his companies stormed the village of Kimari. Following a ten-day struggle, the paratroopers were relieved by mountain troops. For this, he was awarded the Knight's Cross on 21 August 1941.

He saw action in North Africa and in Russia, where he fought near Novo Andreyevka and Novgorodka. His regiment eliminated a Russian bridgehead on the Dnieper. He also fought at Kirovograd, where Russian attacks were repulsed. He was awarded the Oak Leaves on 6 April 1944. Moved to the West, he fought at Brest and was awarded the Swords on 12 September 1944. Kroh was captured on 18 September 1944. He died on 18 July 1967 and is buried in Hauptfriedhof, Feld 40A, Grave 67, Braunschweig, Lower Saxony.

784. *Hauptmann* Albert KAISER

Kaiser was born on 1 March 1910 in Haarbrücken. He was a company commander in Panzer *Jäger* Battalion 44 when he was killed in action on 6 August 1944 and has no known grave. Kaiser was awarded the Knight's Cross on 21 August 1944.

785. Oberstabsarzt Heinrich NEUMANN

Neumann was born on 17 February 1908 in Berlin. He became CO of Parachute First-aid Battalion 7 and, on 15 October 1940, regimental medical officer of Parachute Assault Regiment 1. Neumann took part in the Battle at Wola Gułowska and the assault on 'Fortress Holland', for which he was awarded the Iron Cross 1st and 2nd Class on 20 May 1940. During the invasion of Crete, he took over I Battalion (when Koch was wounded) and led it in action, storming Hill 107, from where the British were firing down on to Maleme airfield. For this action, he was awarded the Knight's Cross on 21 August 1941.

Neumann served in Russia, rescuing 5,000 wounded men from the Juchnov Pocket. He later served as division medical officer with the 6th Parachute Division and corps medical officer with II Parachute Corps—a position he held until the end of the war. He died on 19 May 2005 and is buried in Nordfriedhof, Düsseldorf.

786. *Hauptmann* Johann SCHMID

Schmid was born on 13 January 1911 in Gainfarn, Austria-Hungary. He fought in the Condor Legion in Spain but shot down his first enemy aircraft over France on 14 May 1940. Schmid ended the campaign with seven victories. During the Battle of Britain, he shot down nine aircraft before being sent to train other pilots in August 1940. Schmid returned to the Channel coast in August 1941 and soon started to make up for lost time, shooting down twelve aircraft in two weeks, including three Spitfires on 7, 9, and 10 August.

He was awarded the Knight's Cross on 21 August 1941 with twenty-four victories. Schmid shot down another eleven aircraft in September. Then, on 6 November 1941, he was posted missing after shooting down a Spitfire. It is believed he was circling low to look at the downed plane when his wing hit the water and his Bf 109 sank. Schmid had shot down forty-five enemy aircraft, including thirty-four Spritfires.

787. *Oberleutnant* Georg DÖRFFEL

Dörffel was born on 27 July 1914 in Rengersdorf. He fought in Poland as a close support pilot. During the French campaign, he was shot down on 14 May, but on the 17th, his unit repelled a large tank attack north of Cambrai for which he was awarded the Iron Cross 1st and 2nd Class on 21 May 1940. Dörffel was shot down again in June 1940 near Dunkirk. He took part in the Battle of Britain and the Balkans campaign. Dörffel was awarded the Knight's Cross in Russia on 21 August 1941 after completing 200 combat missions.

Dörffel was shot down again in July 1942 and, in August, carried out his 600th combat mission. He was awarded the Oak Leaves on 14 April 1943 and flew this 1,000th mission on 6 October 1943, the same day he shot down his thirtieth enemy aircraft. After this, he was sent to a training school, but in May 1944, he was recalled to combat in Italy. On 26 May 1944, he was forced to bale out of his Fw 190 after an attack on a formation of heavy bombers. His parachuted failed to open and he was killed. Dörffel is buried in the German War Cemetery (as unknown), Pomezia, Italy.

788. *Oberleutnant* Werner DÖRNBRACK

Dörnbrack was born on 29 February 1916 in Dortmund. He was a pilot and fought in Poland, France, the Battle of Britain, the Balkans, Greece, Russia, Italy, Normandy, and Prague. Dörnbrack was a squadron leader in Training Group 2 when he was awarded the Knight's Cross on 21 August 1941. The Oak Leaves followed on 25 November 1944.

He flew 1,118 missions and was captured by US forces in May 1945. Dörnbrack was handed over to the Russians but escaped. He died on 16 March 1981 and is buried in Stadtfriedhof, Göttingen, Lower Saxony.

789. *Oberleutnant* Alfred DRUSCHEL

Druschel was born on 4 February 1917 in Bindsachen. He was awarded the Iron Cross 2nd Class after the fall of Poland and the 1st Class after the fall of France. He was awarded the Knight's Cross on 21 August 1941 for shooting down seven enemy aircraft and for flying 200 missions as a close support pilot.

The Oak Leaves were awarded on 3 September 1942 for 600 missions and the Swords (the first to a combat pilot) on 19 February 1943 for over 700 missions. Druschel was posted missing on 1 January 1945 over Aachen, North Rhine-Westphalia.

790. *Oberleutnant* Gottfried GEISSLER

Geissler was born on 17 October 1914 in Homberg. He was a company commander in Assault-Gun Battalion 185 when he was awarded the Knight's Cross on 21 August 1941. Geissler died on 21 July 2006 and is buried in Hauptfriedhof, Moers, North Rhine-Westphalia.

791. *Oberleutnant* Bruno MEYER

Meyer was born on 13 November 1914 in Haiti. He was a squadron leader in Close Support Wing 2 when he was awarded the Knight's Cross on 21 August 1941. Meyer died on 16 November 1990 in Australia.

792. Leutnant Hans-Otto BRANDT

Brandt was born on 3 August 1914 in Halberstadt-Wehrstedt. He was a platoon leader in Infantry Regiment 67 when he was awarded the Knight's Cross on 21 August 1941. Brandt was killed in action on 22 July 1943 and is buried in the German War Cemetery, Block 2, Row 14, Grave 1433, Sologubowka, Russia.

793. Leutnant Edwin EWALD

Ewald was born on 29 March 1903 in Mysłowice. He was a platoon leader in Pioneer Battalion 298 when he was awarded the Knight's Cross on 21 August 1941. Ewald died on 26 March 1994 in Stuttgart, Baden-Württemberg.

794. Oberfeldwebel Richard HELLER

Heller was born on 21 December 1913 in Melperts. He was a pilot in Heavy Fighter Wing 26 when he was awarded the Knight's Cross on 21 August 1941. Heller was killed in action over Wülfingerode on 5 April 1945 and has no known grave.

795. Oberfeldwebel Heinz HERZER

Herzer was born on 3 February 1914 in Hohensalza. He was a platoon leader in Rifle Regiment 25 when he was awarded the Knight's Cross on 21 August

1941. Herzer was killed in action at Warsaw on 7 September 1944 and has no known grave.

796. Oberfeldwebel Heindrich WELSKOP—'Heiner'

Welskop was born in Duisburg on 8 August 1916. He joined *Fallschirmjäger* Regiment 1 in April 1939 and was promoted to *Oberjäger* in December. Welskop was awarded the Iron Cross 1st and 2nd Class for action in 'Fortress Holland' and was promoted to *Feldwebel* in June 1940. He fought in Crete with *Fallschirmjäger* Regiment 3, and his company was dropped in the mountains south of Privolia and had to fight its way to I Battalion. With his company commander killed, Welskop acted on his own initiative and stormed a hill near Chania, which his men held against counterattacks by the New Zealanders.

When *Oberst* Heidrich ordered the position abandoned, the order did not get through to Welskop, so he held on alone in the face of overwhelming enemy forces. For this action, he was awarded the Knight's Cross on 21 August 1941. He also saw action in Russia, where he was wounded, and in Italy. Welskop died on 7 May 1981 and is buried in Nordfriedhof, Blütenstrasse 55, Duisburg, North Rhine-Westphalia.

797. Feldwebel Wilhelm KEMPKE

Kempke was born in Lalendorf on 15 November 1920. As part of the 'Koch' Parachute Assault Battalion, he was evolved in the attack on the Albert Canal in 1940. Kempke was awarded the Iron Cross 1st Class on 25 May 1940. In Crete, his battalion was given the mission to eliminate a flak battery south of Chania. Kempke took command of his platoon when his CO was killed and captured the position. For this, he was awarded the Knight's Cross personally by Göring on 21 August 1941 and promoted to *Oberfeldwebel*.

In Russia, he was promoted to *Leutnant* in 1942 and to *Oberleutnant* in 1943. On 22 March 1943, he reported to a special unit which was to investigate the use of gliders against enemy ships. Kempke was killed in a plane crash on 19 December 1944 and is buried in the German War Cemetery, Block III, Row 4, Grave 28, Gustrow-Rostock, Mecklenburg-Vorpommern.

798. Feldwebel Erich SCHUSTER

Schuster was born in Norbach on 6 November 1919. He landed in 'Fortress Holland' with Assault Group Stahl on 10 May 1940, near the Veldwezelt

Bridge. Schuster distinguished himself and was awarded the Iron Cross 1st and 2nd Class. His next action was in Crete on 20 May 1941, where Schuster landed at Maleme airfield. When his platoon leader was put out of action, he took over, eliminating a flak battery and occupying the western end of the airfield. For this, he was awarded the Knight's Cross on 21 August 1941.

Sent to Russia in January 1942 as a platoon leader, he assumed command of the company when *Leutnant* Arpke was killed counterattacking near Mithinka. Promoted to *Leutnant* with *Fallschirmjäger* Regiment 5 and commanding a company, Schuster was killed in action on 11 November 1943. He is buried in the German War Cemetery, Ossario 4A, Panel 4, Bordj-Cedria, Tunisia.

799. General Otto-Wilhelm (or Otto-Hermann) FÖRSTER

Förster was born on 16 March 1885 in Ilmenau. He fought in the First World War, being awarded the Iron Cross 1st and 2nd Class (1914). Förster was commander of the 93rd Infantry Division when he was awarded the Knight's Cross on 23 August 1941. He retired from active duty in January 1944 but was taken prisoner by the Russians, who held him until 1955. Förster died on 24 June 1966 and is buried in Stadtfriedhof, Feld 10, Row 7, Grave 26, Walsrode, Lower Saxony.

800. Generalmajor Kurt FELDT

Feldt was born on 22 November 1887 in Schmentau. He fought in the First World War and was awarded the Iron Cross 1st and 2nd Class (1914). Feldt was commanding the 1st Cavalry Divison when he was awarded the Knight's Cross on 23 August 1941. He died on 11 March 1970 and is buried in Südwest Friedhof, Feld Trinitatis, Grave 34, Stahnsdorf, Bahnhofstarsse, Berlin.

801. Oberst Horst GROSSMANN

Grossmann was born on 19 November 1891 in Sybba. He fought in the First World War and was awarded the Iron Cross 1st and 2nd Class (1914). Grossmann was awarded the Iron Cross 1st and 2nd Class (1939) in May 1940. He was commander of Infantry Regiment 84 when he was awarded the Knight's Cross on 23 August 1941. The Oak Leaves followed on 4 September 1943. Grossman died on 4 May 1972 and is buried in Waldfriedhof, Russelsheim, Rhineland-Palatinate.

802. Oberstleutnant Rudolf LANG

Lang was born on 25 October 1898 in Neustadt. He was commander of Mountain Panzer *Jäger* Battalion 44 when he was awarded the Knight's Cross on 23 August 1941. Lang died on 27 July 1969 in Murnau, Bavaria.

803. *Hauptmann* Robert BORCHARDT

Borchardt was born on 9 January 1912 in Munich. He was a company commander in Reconnaissance Battalion 341 when he was awarded the Knight's Cross on 23 August 1941. Borchardt died on 10 March 1985 and is believed to be buried in Munchener Friedhof, Pullach, Munich.

804. *Hauptmann* Herbert OLL

Oll was born on 5 March 1909 in Berlin. He was commander of I Battalion, Artillery Regiment 78, when he was awarded the Knight's Cross on 23 August 1941. Oll died in an accident near Berlin on 18 April 1944 and is buried in German War Cemetery (Hauptfriedhof), Lübben, Brandenburg.

805. *Hauptmann* Johannes ROHWEDER

Rohweder was born on 19 August 1903 in Lütjenwestedt. He was commander of Motorised Panzer *Jäger* Battalion 670 when he was awarded the Knight's Cross on 23 August 1941. Rohweder died on 6 January 1992 in Bremen.

806. *Oberleutnant* Bruno Freiherr von BRACKEL

Freiherr von Brackel was born on 20 December 1911 in Kassel. He was awarded the Iron Cross 2nd Class after the fall of Poland and the 1st Class after the fall of France. Von Brackel was a company commander in Panzer Regiment 15. He was killed in action on 13 August 1941 at Korsun-Shevchenkivskyi, Ukraine, and has no known grave. Von Brackel was awarded the Knight's Cross on 23 August 1941.

807. *Oberleutnant* Karl HÄNERT

Hänert was born on 25 October 1914 in Flensburg. He was a company commander in Motorised Infantry Regiment 'GD' when he was awarded the Knight's Cross on 23 August 1941. Hänert was killed in action near Brjansk, Russia, on 14 October 1941 and has no known grave.

808. *Oberleutnant* Ernst-Wilhelm IHRIG

Ihrig was born on 27 July 1915 in Darmstadt. He was a squadron leader in Bomber Wing 3 when he was awarded the Knight's Cross on 23 August 1941. Ihrig was killed in action on 30 November 1942 near Zhilinscina, Russia, and has no known grave.

809. *Oberleutnant* Helmut KALBITZ

Kalbitz was born on 3 January 1912 in Wilhelmsburg. He was a company commander in Pioneer Battalion 125 when he was awarded the Knight's Cross on 23 August 1941 and the Oak Leaves on 7 January 1944. Kalbitz was posted missing on 23 August 1944 in Romania.

810. *Oberleutnant* Franz TREFFER

Treffer was born on 22 August 1904 in Beilngries. He was a company commander in Motorised Infantry Regiment 20. Treffer was killed in action at Kliney, Russia, on 10 August 1941 and has no known grave. Treffer was awarded the Knight's Cross 23 August 1944.

811. Oberstleutnant Georg Ritter von HENGL

Ritter von Hengl was born on 21 October 1897 in Lailing. He fought in the First World War in the infantry and the air service shooting down seven aircraft; he was awarded the Iron Cross 1st and 2nd Class (1914). Von Hengl was awarded the Iron Crass 1st and 2nd Class (1939) in September 1939.

He was commander of Mountain *Jäger* Regiment 137 when he was awarded the Knight's Cross on 25 August 1941. He also held the rank of *Obersturmbannführer* in the *Waffen*-SS. Von Hengl died on 19 March 1952 and is buried in Stadtfriedhof, Feld PA-22, Sonthofen, Bavaria.

812. *Major* Fritz Graf von OBERNDORFF

Graf von Oberndorff was born on 20 December 1891 in Neckarhausen. He was commander of Reconnaissance Battalion 34 when he was awarded the Knight's Cross on 25 August 1941. Von Oberndorff died on 27 March 1970 in Weiherhof, Bavaria.

813. *Major* Hyazinth Graf STRACHWITZ von GROSS-ZAUCHE und CAMMINETZ— 'The Panzer Cavalier'

Graf Strachwitz von Gross-Zauche und Camminetz was born on 30 July 1893 in Gross Stein Castle. He fought in the First World War, being awarded the Iron Cross 1st and 2nd Class (1914). A panzer commander, he fought in Poland and France, where on one occasion he came across a single unit in its barracks, he bluffed the commander into surrendering. He took part in the invasion of Russia and saw action in all the major victories and closed the Uman Pocket, for which he was awarded the Knight's Cross on 25 August 1941.

He fought through the Russian winter of 1941–42, and in summer of 1942, he drove his tanks to the Don River in the south. At Kalach, his regiment destroyed over 270 enemy tanks within forty-eight hours. In October 1932, his regiment was the first to reach the Volga, north of Stalingrad. Luckily for Graf Strachwitz von Gross-Zauche und Camminetz, he was wounded and evacuated before the Russian counterattack that encircled the city. While recovering he was awarded the Oak Leaves on 13 November 1942.

Sent back to Russia to command a panzer regiment in the *Grossdeutschland* Division, he fought at Belgorod and Kharkov in February and March 1943. Seeing particularly heavy fighting at Borisovka and Tomarovka, on one occasion, with just four tanks, he ambushed and knocked-out 105 enemy tanks in thirty minutes for no loss to himself, and after his regiment received a battalion of Tiger tanks, they destroyed another 100 Russian tanks in one hour. For this, he was awarded the Swords on 28 March 1943.

He fought at Kursk and in the long retreat after its failure, reaching Kirovgrad with one tank. In April 1944, he personally led an attack to break the encirclement of Riga to rescue the garrison, which included a large number of wounded. For this, he was awarded the Diamonds on 15 April 1944. Almost killed in a traffic accident, he ended the war on the Eastern Front commanding an anti-tank unit before surrendering to US forces in May 1945. Graf Strachwitz von Gross-Zauche und Camminetz died on 25 April 1968 and is buried in the village cemetery, Grabenstätt, Bavaria. His distant nephew, Ernst Strachwitz von Gross-Zauche, was also awarded the Knight's

Cross and his two cousins, Smilo *Freiherr* von Lüttwitz and Heinrich *Freiherr* von Lüttwitz, were awarded the Knight's Cross with Oak Leaves and Swords.

814. *Oberleutnant* Jürgen von FLOTOW

Von Flotow was born on 13 July 1914 in Frankfurt am Main. He was a company commander in Rifle Regiment 8 when he died of wounds on 20 August 1941. He is buried at Wolossowo, Leningrad; his remains are awaiting transfer to a German war cemetery. Von Flotow was awarded the Knight's Cross 25 August 1941.

815. Leutnant Karl-Ludwig KEGEL

Kegel was born on 10 May 1918 in Eisleben. He was a company commander in Panzer Regiment 18 when he was awarded the Knight's Cross on 25 August 1941. Kegel was killed in action on 1 January 1943 and is buried at Chertkovo, Russia; his remains are awaiting transfer to a German war cemetery.

816. Leutnant Manfred SCHWARZ

Schwarz was born on 10 June 1914 in Munich. He was a company commander in Motorised Panzer *Jäger* Battalion 10 when he was awarded the Knight's Cross on 25 August 1941. Schwarz died on 20 April 1980 and is believed to be buried in Waldfriedhof, Munich.

817. Leutnant Werner THOFERN

Thofern was born on 12 October 1920 in Berlin. He was a platoon leader in Motorised Infantry Regiment 5 when he was awarded the Knight's Cross on 25 August 1941. Thofern died on 13 January 1957 and is buried in the village cemetery, Geismar, near Göttingen, Lower Saxony.

818. Oberfeldwebel Fritz AXTMANN

Axtmann was born on 7 December 1914 in Burglengenfeld. He was awarded the Iron Cross 1st and 2^{n+d} Class in September 1939. Axtmann was a section leader in Infantry Regiment 20 when he was awarded the Knight's Cross on

25 August 1941. He died of wounds on 13 September 1943 and is buried at Kiev; Axtmann's remains are awaiting transfer to a German war cemetery.

819. Unteroffizier Arthur BECKER (-NEETZ added later)

Becker was born in Danzig on 31 December 1920. He fought in Poland and France, where he was awarded the Iron Cross 2nd Class. Becker took part in the invasion of Russia and was awarded the Iron Cross 1st Class in July 1941.

During an attack on his unit's flank near Mogilev, Becker took command when all the other officers had been killed or wounded. He led the men in counterattacks even after receiving a head wound; for this and subsequent actions, he was awarded the Knight's Cross on 25 August 1941. After recovery, he was posted to a sniper training school in Denmark, where he remained for the rest of the war. Becker died on 12 October 2016.

820. SS-Unterscharführer Erich ROSSNER

Rossner was born on 26 May 1918 in Helmbrechts. He was a gun commander in SS Panzer *Jäger* Battalion 'Reich' when he was awarded the Iron Cross 2nd Class on 25 July 1941. Rossner knocked-out thirteen Russian tanks before being fatally wounded. For this, he was awarded the Iron Cross 1st Class on 3 August and the Knight's Cross on 25 August 1941. He has no known grave. Rossner was the first *Waffen*-SS NCO to be awarded the Knight's Cross.

821. Marshal Baron Carl Gustaf Emil MANNERHEIM (Commander-in-Chief, Finnish Defence Forces)—'The Father of Finland'

Mannerheim was born on 4 June 1867 in Askainen, Grand Duchy of Finland, part of the Russian Empire. He fought in the Russo-Japanese War of 1904–05 and the First World War. After the Bolshevik revolution, Finland declared independence and was soon involved in civil war between the pro-Bolshevik 'Reds' and the 'Whites' of the Senate of Finland. Mannerheim was made commander of the Finnish troops in January 1918. During the 1939–40 Russo-Finnish or Winter War, Mannerheim was again made commander-in-chief of Finnish forces.

After the 1941 German invasion of Russian, Finland entered into an uneasy partnership with Germany, and Mannerheim was awarded the Knight's Cross on 30 August 1941. The Oak Leaves followed on 5 August 1944. In August

1944, as the war dragged on and it was becoming clear Germany was losing, parliament passed a special act making Mannerheim president of Finland. He set about making peace with Russia and the UK. Although militarily successful, Finland lost much in the peace treaty. Mannerheim resigned as president on 4 March 1946. He died on 27 January 1951 and is buried in the German War Cemetery (Hietaniemi Cemetery), Helsinki, Finland.

822. *Oberleutnant* Franz BEYER

Beyer was born on 22 April 1918 in Berlin. He was a squadron leader in Fighter Wing 3 when he was awarded the Knight's Cross on 30 August 1941. Beyer had shot down eighty-one enemy aircraft when he was killed in action on 11 February 1944. He is buried in the German War Cemetery, Block L, Row 11, Grave 263, Timmermansweg, Ysselsteyn, the Netherlands.

823. *Oberleutnant* Reinhold ECKARDT

Eckardt was born on 26 March 1918 in Bamberg. He was a night fighter pilot when he was awarded the Knight's Cross on 30 August 1941. Eckardt was credited with twenty-two victories when, on 30 July 1942, his parachute caught on his aircraft as he baled out, killing him. He is buried in the German War Cemetery, Block 45, Grave 495, Kattenbos N746, Lommel, Belgium.

824. *Oberleutnant* Helmut LENT

Lent was born in Neumark on 13 June 1918. Serving in Heavy Fighter Wing 76, he shot down his first enemy aircraft on 2 September 1939 flying a Bf 110 twin-engined heavy fighter over Poland. Then, in December, he shot down two Wellington bombers, and during the Norwegian campaign, he scored five more victories. Lent switched to a night-fighter unit and, on 30 August 1941, was awarded the Knight's Cross, having shot down fourteen bombers during night sorties.

Now flying the Do 215, Lent was awarded the Oak Leaves on 6 June 1942 with thirty-five night victories—all bombers. In January 1943, his score reached fifty, and on 2 August 1943, with his tally at sixty-six, Lent was awarded the Swords. He was now the highest-scoring night fighter pilot in Germany. On the night of 15 June 1944, he became the first night fighter pilot to shoot down 100 enemy bombers. For this, he was awarded the Diamonds on 31 July 1944. The first night fighter pilot to be awarded them.

On 5 October 1944, Lent was flying to Nordborchen with Walter Kubisch (also a Knight's Cross holder); on arrival, they found the main runway bombed-out, and as Lent brought the aircraft in to land on an emergency runway, one of his engines failed and the aircraft burst into flames. Both of Lent's legs were badly burned. The surgeon delayed operating for two days, fearing the shock would kill him, by which time gangrene set in and Lent died while undergoing amputation of both legs. Kubisch died the day after the crash. Lent is buried in German War Cemetery (Alter Garnison Friedhof), Plot 1042, Grave 37, Stade, Lower Saxony. Kubisch is buried in the same cemetery. Lent's final score was 102 enemy bombers.

825. *Oberleutnant* Hartmut SCHAIRER

Schairer was born on 16 September 1916 in Nagold. He saw action over France and England as a Stuka pilot in 1940. In Crete, he flew in support of the paratroops, sinking a destroyer, four transports, and damaging several other ships. Following this, he flew in support of the Africa Corps by bombing Tobruk. Schairer was awarded the Knight's Cross on 30 August 1941.

He saw action in Russia during the 1941–42 winter, but he was shot down and killed with Heinz Bevernis on 19 July 1942; they are buried at Solzy, Russia, and their remains are awaiting transfer to a German war cemetery. Heinz Bevernis was posthumously awarded the Knight's Cross.

826. *Oberleutnant* zur See Adalbert SCHNEE

Schnee was born in Berlin on 31 December 1913. He served as watch officer on *U-23* and took command of *U-6* in December 1939. Then, in July 1940, he took over command of *U-60* from Schewe. In August and September, he sank two ships and torpedoed the 15,434-ton *Volendam*. On 25 January 1941, Schnee commissioned *U-201* and, with his boat, finished off a crippled tanker, torpedoed by *U-552*. He sank two ships and damaged another from convoy OB318. In August, he attacked convoy OG71, sinking two and torpedoing another. He was awarded the Knight's Cross on 30 August 1941. In September, Schnee sank seven ships from convoy OG64. Then, in April 1942, *U-201* was ordered to the US coast, sinking four ships.

From 27 June to 8 August 1942, he sank six ships, including the 14,443-ton *Avila Star* between Rio and Freetown. During this patrol, the Oak Leaves were awarded to him on 15 July. On 29 September 1944, Schnee commissioned *U-2511* and sailed on 30 April 1945. He was at sea when the war ended. He died on 4 November 1982 and is buried in Ohlsdorf Friedhof, Plot P07, Grave 6–16, Manshardstrasse, Hamburg.

827. *Oberleutnant* Johannes STEINHOFF—'Macky'

Steinhoff was born on 15 September 1913 at Bottendorf. He fought in the Battle of Britain, but with limited success. In Russia, however, he was able to shoot down thirty-five enemy aircraft, for which he was awarded the Knight's Cross on 30 August 1941. By August 1942, he had raised his score to 100 and was awarded the Oak Leaves on 2 September 1942.

Transferred to North Africa in March 1943, Steinhoff was himself shot down more than once. He fought on from Sicily, Italy, after the end of the war in Africa and was awarded the Swords on 28 July 1944, with his total at 167 enemy aircraft. Steinhoff was post as CO to a Me 262 jet fighter unit in November 1944, with which he scored a number of victories. Then, on 18 April 1945, he crashed on take-off; Steinhoff was badly burned in the crash. He spent two years in hospital undergoing skin grafts, and he would carry the scars for the rest of his life. Steinhoff flew 993 sorties, shot down 176 aircraft, and was shot down himself twelve times, but he never baled out, always choosing to crash land his fighter. He is the author of *Straits of Messina*. Steinhoff died on 21 February 1994 and is buried in Niederbachem Friedhof, Mehlemer Stresse, Wachtberg, North Rhine-Westphalia.

828. *Oberleutnant* Kurt von WITZENDORFF

Von Witztendorff was born on 26 September 1916 in Berlin. He was a company commander in Infantry Regiment 178 when he was awarded the Knight's Cross on 30 August 1941. Von Witztendorff died on 10 February 1994 in Neustadt am Rübenberge.

829. Leutnant Friedrich GEISSHARDT—'Fritz'

Geisshardt was born on 22 January 1919 in Sonnefeld. He shot down his first enemy aircraft over Poland but was shot down and captured the next day. He managed to escape during an air raid and spent five days walking back to German lines. Geisshardt seems to have missed the French campaign but shot down six aircraft during the Battle of Britain, followed by six more in early 1941. In the Balkans campaign, he shot down four and added two RAF fighters over Crete.

Geisshardt brought down his twentieth opponent on 23 June 1941 and was awarded the Knight's Cross on 30 August 1941. In Russia, his score rapidly increased until he reached seventy-nine and was awarded the Oak Leaves on 23 June 1942. Geisshardt added eighteen enemy aircraft to his credit over Malta and North Africa. He came over as arrogant towards fellow pilots who had not yet earned the Knight's Cross. With his total at 103, Geisshardt was wounded by return fire from a B-17 bomber on 5 April 1944. He died the following day and is buried in the German War Cemetery, Block 32, Row 8, Grave 304, Bourdon, Picardy, France.

830. Leutnant Herbert HUPPERTZ

Huppertz was born on 3 June 1919 in Rheydt. He took part in the Battle for France as a fighter pilot and was awarded the Iron Cross 2nd Class in May 1940. Huppertz also fought in the Battle of Britain and was awarded the Iron Cross 1st Class in October 1940. He was a group commander in Fighter Wing 2 when he was awarded the Knight's Cross on 30 August 1941.

With sixty-eight enemy aircraft to his credit, Huppertz was killed in action on 8 June 1944. He is buried in the German War Cemetery, Block 48, Row 9, Grave 360A, La Cambe, Normandy, France. He was awarded Oak Leaves on 24 June 1944.

831. Oberfeldwebel Erdmann GABRIEL

Gabriel was born on 7 November 1911 in Olbersdorf. He was awarded the Iron Cross 2nd Class after the fall of Poland and the 1st Class after the fall of France. Gabriel was a platoon leader in II Battalion, Panzer Regiment 35, when he was awarded the Knight's Cross 30 August 1941. He died on 28 January 1996 in Essenbach, Bavaria.

832. Oberfeldwebel Franz SCHLUND

Schlund was born on 10 August 1913 in Leimen. He was a radio operator in Close Support Wing 1 when he was awarded the Knight's Cross on 30 August 1941. Schlund died on 15 September 1995 and is buried in German War Cemetery, Heidelberg, Baden-Württemberg.

833. Feldwebel Johann JUNGKUNST

Jungkunst was born on 24 October 1917 in Vohenstrauss. He was a platoon leader in Motorised Infantry Regiment 41 when he was awarded the Knight's Cross on 30 August 1941. Jungkunst died on 21 March 1988 and buried in Vohenstrauss Friedhof, Bavaria.

834. Feldwebel Rudolf SCHMIDT

Schmidt was born on 17 October 1918 in Wölfershausen. He was a pilot in Fighter Wing 77 when he was awarded the Knight's Cross on 30 August 1941. Schmidt was killed in action at Jevpatorija on 6 April 1942 and has no known grave.

835. General Werner KIENITZ

Kienitz was born on 3 June 1885 in Kisslegg. He fought in the First World War and was awarded the Iron Cross 1st and 2nd Class (1914). Kienitz was commander of XVII Army Corps when he was awarded the Knight's Cross on 31 August 1941. He died on 31 December 1959 and is believed to be buried in Ohlsdorf Friedhof, Fuhlsbüttler Strasse, Hamburg.

836. Generalleutnant Otto STAPF

Stapf was born on 13 November 1890 in Hellmitzheim. He fought in the First World War and was awarded the Iron Cross 1st and 2nd Class (1914). Stapf was commander of the 111th Infantry Division when he was awarded the Knight's Cross on 31 August 1941. Stapf died on 30 March 1963 and is buried in Alter Friedhof, Kitzingen, Bavaria.

837. Oberstleutnant Wilhelm von LENGERKE

Von Lengerke was born on 17 June 1894 in Salchow. He fought in the First World War and was awarded the Iron Cross 1st and 2nd Class (1914). Von Lengerke was commander of I Battalion, Cavalry Regiment 1, when he was awarded the Knight's Cross on 31 August 1941. He was killed in action near Stalingrad on 26 August 1942 and is buried in Waldfriedhof, Lüneburg, Lower Saxony.

838. *Hauptmann* Josef SALMINGER

Salminger was born on 5 March 1903 in Munich. He was commander of III Battalion, Mountain *Jäger* Regiment 98, when he was awarded the Knight's Cross on 31 August 1941. Salminger was killed by partisans on 1 October 1943 and is buried in the German War Cemetery, Crypt 2, Row 1, Plate 2, Dionyssos-Rapendoza, Greece.

839. *Hauptmann* Kilian WEIMER

Weimer was born on 12 May 1904 in Kembach. He was awarded the Iron Cross 1st and 2nd Class soon after the start of the Russian campaign. Weimer was commander of I Battalion, Infantry Regiment 109, when he was awarded the Knight's Cross on 31 August 1941. The Oak Leaves followed on 14 May 1944. Weimer was captured by the Russians in March 1945 and was held until 1949. He died on 21 September 1979 and is believed to be buried in Trunkelsberg Friedhof, Bavaria.

840. Leutnant Claus von LUCKE

Von Lucke was born on 22 January 1916 in Mückenhain. He was a platoon leader in Panzer Regiment 18 when he was awarded the Knight's Cross on 31 August 1941. Von Lucke died on 18 April 2006 in Gut Martinsbüttel, Lower Saxony.

841. General Erik HANSEN

Hansen was born on 27 May 1889 in Hamburg. He fought in the First World War and was awarded the Iron Cross 1st and 2nd Class (1914). Hansen was commander of LIV Corps when he was awarded the Knight's Cross on 4 September 1941. He was captured by the Russians in August 1944 and held until 1955. Hansen died on 20 March 1967 in Hamburg.

842. Generalleutnant Hans-Jürgen von ARNIM

Von Arnim, the son of General Hans von Arnim, was born on 4 April 1889 in Ernsdorf, Silesia. He fought in the First World War, being wounded three times, and he was awarded the Iron Cross 1st and 2nd Class (1914). At the start of the Second World War, von Arnim was commanding the 52nd Infantry Divison; he led this unit in Poland and France with the rank of *Generalleutnant*. He was awarded the Iron Cross 1st and 2nd Class in 1939. In Russia, he commanded the 17th Panzer Division, taking part in the battles of Brest-Litovisk, the encirclement of Smolensk, Kiev, and the Briansk, which led him to be awarded the Knight's Cross on 4 September 1941.

Promoted to *General*, he commanded the XXXIX Panzer Corps in Russia until he was named commander-in-chief of V Panzer Army in Tunisia on 3 December 1942. From 9 March 1943, he led Army Group Africa until his capture on 12 May 1943. Von Arnim died on 1 September 1962 in Bad Wildungen, Hesse.

843. Generalmajor Walther von AXTHELM

Von Axthelm was born on 23 December 1893 in Hersbruck. He fought in the First World War and was awarded the Iron Cross 1st and 2nd Class (1914). Von Axthelm was awarded the Iron Cross 1st and 2nd Class (1939) after the fall of France. He was commander of I Flak Corps when he was awarded the Knight's Cross on 4 September 1941. Von Axthelm died on 6 January 1972 and is buried in Waldfriedhof, Traunstein, Bavaria.

844. Oberst Paul CONRATH

Conrath was born on 22 November 1896 in Rudow. He fought in the First World War and was awarded the Iron Cross 1st and 2nd Class (1914). Conrath was commander of Motorised Flak Regiment 'HG' when he was awarded the Knight's Cross on 4 September 1941. The Oak Leaves followed on 21 August 1943. He was responsible for removing many treasures to the Vatican from the Abbey at Monte Cassino for safekeeping, for which he was honoured by the Pope after the war. Conrath died on 15 January 1979 and is believed to be buried in Ohlsdorf Friedhof, Fuhlsbüttler Strasse, Hamburg.

845. Oberst Fritz LINDEMANN

Lindemann was born on 11 April 1894 in Berlin. He fought in the First World War and was awarded the Iron Cross 1st and 2nd Class (1914). Lindemann was Artillery Commander 138 when he was awarded the Knight's Cross on 4 September 1941. He was involved in the plot to kill Hitler and was seriously wounded by the Gestapo during his arrest. Lindemann died from his injuries on 22 September 1944 in Berlin. He has no known grave.

846. Oberstleutnant Helmuth von PANNWITZ

Von Pannwitz was born on 14 October 1898 in Botzanwitz. He fought in the First World War and was awarded the Iron Cross 1st and 2nd Class (1914). He fought in Poland and was awarded the Iron Cross 1st and 2nd Class (1939). In August 1941, his reconnaissance battalion wiped out a Russian cavalry brigade and an infantry division. For this, he was awarded the Knight's Cross on 4 September 1941.

Pannwitz was instrumental in setting up a volunteer Cossack force. He was awarded the Oak Leaves on 23 December 1942 at which time he personally told Hitler that treating the Slavs as sub-humans was totally wrong. Pannwitz commanded a Cossack force against partisans in Russia and later Yugoslavia. It was there that Cossacks under his command committed atrocities against civilians, including rape and executions. In an order dated 20 October 1943, Pannwitz made it clear to all under his command that any crime of that kind would result in the death penalty for those involved. He surrendered to the British in May 1945 but was handed over to the Russians with many of his men. Pannwitz was tried for war crimes and shot in Moscow on 16 January 1947; he has no known grave. In 1996, his conviction was overturned by a Russian court as it was felt he was a victim of Stalin's repression, but the conviction was reinstated for military war crimes in 2001.

847. *Major* Kurt BOETTCHER

Boettcher was born on 3 March 1905 in Brandenburg. He was a commander of I Battalion, Artillery Regiment 27. Boettcher died of wounds on 4 September 1941 and is buried in the German War Cemetery, Block 8, Row 23, Grave 2026, Kiev, Ukraine. He was awarded the Knight's Cross 4 September 1941.

848. *Kapitänleutnant* Werner DOBBERSTEIN

Dobberstein was born on 4 April 1911 in Roggenhausen. He was awarded the Iron Cross 2nd Class in July and the 1st Class in September 1940. Dobberstein was commander of R-Boat Flotilla 1 when he was awarded the Knight's Cross on 4 September 1941. He died on 25 February 1993 and is buried in Evangel Friedhof, Ahrensburg, Schleswig-Holstein.

849. *Major* Franz WELLER

Weller was born on 5 December 1901 in Berlin. He was awarded the Iron Cross 2nd Class after the fall of Poland and the 1st Class after the fall of France. Weller was commander of Infantry Regiment 54 when he was awarded the Knight's Cross on 4 September 1941. The Oak Leaves followed on 23 October 1944. Weller died on 14 August 1994 in Cologne, North Rhine-Westphalia.

850. *Hauptmann* Arnulf BLASIG

Blasig was born on 30 December 1913 in Berlin. He was a group commander in Dive Bomber Wing 1 when he was awarded the Knight's Cross on 4

September 1941. Blasig died on 13 November 1998 and is buried in Herborn Friedhof, Hesse.

851. *Hauptmann* Helmut BRUCK

Bruck was born on 16 February 1913 in Kittlitztreben. He was awarded the Iron Cross 2nd Class after the fall of Poland and the 1st Class after the fall of France. Bruck was a squadron leader in Dive Bomber Wing 77 when he was awarded the Knight's Cross on 4 September 1941. The Oak Leaves followed on 19 February 1943. He died on 25 August 2001 and is buried in Veitlahm Friedhof, Mainleus, Bavaria.

852. *Hauptmann* Heinz UNGER

Unger was born on 21 August 1912 in Chemnitz. He was a company commander in Rifle Regiment 10 when he was awarded the Knight's Cross on 4 September 1941. Unger died on 19 August 1998 in Bad Boll, Baden-Württemberg.

853. *Oberleutnant* Hartmann GRASSER

Grasser was born on 23 August 1914 in Graz, Austria-Hungary. He shot down an observation balloon on 16 September 1939 for his first 'kill' and his second was a French fighter on 24 September. During the Battle of Britain, Grasser flew a Bf 110 heavy fighter and ended the battle with seven victories. On the Russian Front, Grasser shot down his twentieth enemy aircraft on 29 July and was awarded the Knight's Cross on 4 September 1941; he raised his score to thirty four days later.

On 24 January 1942, with his tally at forty-five, Grasser was shot down, and despite a severe eye wound, he was able to bale out. He landed behind enemy lines but managed to get back to his own. Grasser spent several mouths recovering before returning to combat. He shot down his fiftieth enemy aircraft on 23 June 1942. On 5 July 1942, he shot down six aircraft, including three Sturmoviks. Grasser scored his seventieth victory on 13 August and his eightieth on 29 August 1942. With his tally at ninety-one, Grasser was transferred to the African campaign. There he added another twelve aircraft, bringing his total to 103 and the award of the Oak Leaves on 31 August 1943. At the end of the war, he was handed over to the Russians who held him until 1949. Grasser died on 2 June 1986 and is buried in Zentralfriedhof (family vault), Graz, Austria.

854. *Oberleutnant* Kurt UBBEN—'Kuddel'

Ubben was born on 18 November 1911 in Dorstadt. He shot down his first enemy aircraft on 10 May 1940, the very first day of the war in the west, being awarded the Iron Cross 1st and 2nd Class in May and August 1940. Ubben shot down a number of enemy aircraft in the Balkans and hit the British battleship *Warspite* with bombs. In Russia, he scored his twenty-eighth victory and was awarded the Knight's Cross on 4 September 1941. The Oak Leaves followed on 12 March 1942.

Moved to Africa, he shot down his first enemy aircraft there on 3 November 1942. On 14 January 1943, he brought down his 100th and 101st enemy aircraft. Two Mitchell bombers followed on 8 February. With his total at 110 enemy aircraft, Ubben was killed on 27 April 1944 over Fére-en-Tardenois, France, when his parachute failed to open. He is buried in the German War Cemetery, Block 3, Row 40, Grave 1239, St Desiré-de-Lisieux, Normandy, France.

855. Leutnant Max-Hellmuth OSTERMANN

Ostermann was born on 11 December 1917 in Hamburg. In Poland, he flew the Bf 110 heavy fighter. But in the French campaign, he flew the Bf 109 fighter, shooting down two enemy aircraft. By the end of the Battle of Britain, Ostermann had shot down eight enemy aircraft. He briefly saw action in the Balkans before taking part in the invasion of Russia. It was here that his tally increased rapidly, being awarded the Knight's Cross on 4 September 1941 with his score at thirty.

By the time of the award of the Oak Leaves on 12 March 1942, Ostermann had shot down sixty enemy aircraft. He was shot down himself on 10 May 1942, and on the 12th, Ostermann shot down his 100th enemy aircraft but was wounded in the process. The award of the Swords followed on 17 May 1942. After a short leave, he returned to the front in August 1942 and brought down one enemy aircraft on the 8th. The next day, he shot down his 102nd but Ostermann was shot down near Lake Ilmen the same day; he has no known grave.

856. Stabsfeldwebel Albert BOCK

Bock was born on 14 December 1911 in Flensburg. He was an observer in Dive Bomber Wing 2 when he was awarded the Knight's Cross on 4 September 1941. Bock died on 21 December 1964 and is believed to be buried in Mühlenfriedhof, Flensburg, Schleswig-Holstein.

857. Oberfeldwebel Kurt BÜHLIGEN

Bühligen was born in Granschütz on 13 December 1917. He joined JG2 'Richthofen' in 1942 and stayed with this unit throughout his career. Bühligen flew his first combat mission in July 1940 and shot down his first enemy aircraft over England on 4 September. In the period that followed, he distinguished himself on numerous occasions; he was awarded Iron Cross 1st and 2nd Class in 1940 and the Knight's Cross on 4 September 1941 after shooting down twenty-one enemy aircraft. His greatest success, however, came in Tunisia when, between December 1942 and March 1943, Bühligen shot down over forty British and American aircraft.

He was awarded the Oak Leaves on 2 March 1944 for shooting down ninety-six enemy aircraft and the Swords on 14 August 1944 as *Kommodore* in JG2. Bühligen shot down 112 Allied planes, including twenty-four four-engined bombers. He was captured by the Russians and not released until 1950. Bühligen died on 11 August 1985 and is buried in Nidda Friedhof, Section D, Grave 42, Hesse.

858. Oberfeldwebel Georg SCHENTKE—'Peterle'

Schentke was born on 23 November 1919 in Kriescht. He shot down one enemy aircraft during the Battle for France and three during the Battle of Britain. Schentke took part in the invasion of Russia and was awarded the Knight's Cross on 4 September 1941 with his tally at thirty-four victories. After his seventy-first victory in late July 1942, he was sent home as an instructor. Schentke returned to the front in November 1942 where he flew in support of the air left for Stalingrad. He shot down twenty-nine enemy aircraft, including three on 10 December and six on the 12th. On Christmas Day 1942, he shot down a Sturmovik, but debris damaged his fighter, forcing him to bale out; he was never seen again. Schentke is credited with ninety victories, of which fifteen were Sturmoviks.

859. Oberfeldwebel Hans STECHMANN

Stechmann was born on 14 May 1918 in Buxtehude. He was a pilot in Fighter Wing 3 when he was awarded the Knight's Cross on 4 September 1941. Stechmann died on 27 June 1994 in Neustadt.

860. Oberfeldwebel Josef WURMHELLER—'Sepp'

Wurmheller was born on 4 May 1917 in Hausham. He shot down his first enemy aircraft on 30 September 1939 and was awarded the Iron Cross 2nd Class in October 1939. Between November 1939 and June 1940, Wurmheller was an instructor before returning to action in the Battle of Britain. He was awarded the Iron Cross 1st Class in October 1940 but had to ditch in the English Channel twice. The second time, in November, put him in hospital until March 1941.

By the end of May, he had shot down ten aircraft. A short tour of the Russian Front saw him shoot down nine more before returning to the West in July 1941. August saw him shoot down thirteen Spitfires, and he was awarded the Knight's Cross on 4 September 1941. More instructing followed, which kept him away from the front until May 1942. Wurmheller shot down ten in May and eleven June, but his best day came during the Dieppe Raid on 19 August 1942, when, despite a broken leg, he shot down six Spitfires and a Blenheim. With his score at sixty, he was awarded the Oak Leaves on 13 November 1942. Then, with his total at 102, including twenty four-engined bombers and fifty-six Spitfires, Wurmheller was killed on 22 June 1944 when he collided with his wingman. He was awarded the Swords on 24 October 1944. Wurmheller is buried in the German War Cemetery, Block 9, Grave 1704, Champigny-St André, Normandy, France.

861. Feldwebel Hans HOFFRITZ

Hoffritz was born on 29 April 1914 in Schweinfurt. He was a platoon leader in Infantry Regiment 268 when he was awarded the Knight's Cross on 4 September 1941. Hoffritz died on 24 October 1971 in Hollerath, North Rhine-Westphalia.

862. General Kuno-Hans von BOTH

Von Both was born on 9 April 1884 in Saverne, Alsace-Lorraine. He fought in the First World War and was awarded the Iron Cross 1st and 2nd Class (1914), as well as the *Pour le Mérite*. Von Both was awarded the Iron Cross 1st and 2nd Class (1939) after the fall of Poland. He was commander of I Army Corps when he was awarded the Knight's Cross on 7 September 1941. Von Both died on 22 May 1955 and is buried in Miliair Friedhof, Feld A, Kassel, Hesse.

863. Generalleutnant Karl-Adolf HOLLIDT

Hollidt was born on 28 April 1891 in Speyer. He fought in the First World War and was awarded the Iron Cross 1st and 2nd Class (1914). Hollidt was awarded the Iron Cross 1st and 2nd Class (1939) after the fall of France. He was commander of the 50th Infantry Division when he was awarded the Knight's Cross on 8 September 1941.

The Oak Leaves followed on 15 May 1943 as commander of the VI Army. His formation suffered heavy losses in 1944 and Hollidt was dismissed. He was taken prisoner by US forces in May 1945 and tried for unlawful use of prisoners and the mass deportation and enslavement of civilians. Hollidt was sentenced to five years' imprisonment, but he was released after fourteen months. He died on 22 May 1985 and is buried in Stadtfriedhof, Abt 37, Main Path (Hauptweg), Grave 45–46, Speyer, Rhineland-Palatinate.

864. Oberst Karl-Albrecht von GRODDECK

Von Groddeck was born on 18 February 1894 in Berlin. He fought in the First World War and was awarded the Iron Cross 1st and 2nd Class (1914). Von Groddeck was commander of Motorised Infantry Regiment 120 when he was awarded the Knight's Cross on 8 September 1941. He was killed in action at Breslau on 10 January 1944 and has no known grave.

865. Oberst Karl-Wilhelm SPECHT

Specht was born on 22 May 1894 in Herdecke. He fought in the First World War and was awarded the Iron Cross 1st and 2nd Class (1914). Specht was awarded the Iron Cross 2nd Class (1939) after the fall of Poland and the 1st Class after (1939) the fall of France. He was commander of Infantry Regiment 55 when he was awarded the Knight's Cross on 8 September 1941. The Oak Leaves followed on 16 January 1942. Specht was taken prisoner at the end of the war and died in Russian hands on 3 December 1953. He is buried in the German War Cemetery, Row 2, Grave 4, Cherntsy, Russia.

866. *Major* Meinrad von LAUCHERT

Lauchert was born on 29 August 1905 in Potsdam. He fought in Poland, for which he was awarded the Iron Cross 1st and 2nd Class and France. Lauchert fought in Russia and was awarded the Knight's Cross on 8 September 1941.

He trained and commanded the first unit of Panther tanks to be used at Kursk in 1943. Lauchert was awarded the Oak Leaves on 12 February 1944.

In the Battle of the Bulge, Lauchert commanded the 2nd Panzer Division and achieved the deepest penetration into enemy territory. Later, his division fought a continuous rear-guard, and during February and March 1945, his division ceased to exist. Fed up, he quit the war and walked home to Bamberg. Charged with war crimes, he was found not guilty. Lauchert was an advisor for the Film *Battle of the Bulge*. He died on 4 December 1987 and is buried in Möhringen Friedhof, Stuttgart, Baden-Württemberg.

867. *Major* Herbert MÜLLER

Müller was born on 16 August 1896 in Altenburg. He was commander of II Battalion, Rifle Regiment 394, when he was awarded the Knight's Cross on 8 September 1941. Müller was killed in action on the Don River, Millerovo, Russia, on 14 July 1942 and has no known grave.

868. *Major* Heinrich ROECKL

Rodeckl was born on 21 August 1897 in Munich. He was commander of Bicycle Battalion 402 when he was awarded the Knight's Cross on 8 September 1941. Rodeckl died on 21 October 1996 in Munich.

869. *Hauptmann* Erich SCHRÖTER

Schröter was born on 25 June 1904 in Schönburg. He was awarded the Iron Cross 1st and 2nd Class after the fall of Poland. Schröter was commander of I Battalion, Motorised Infantry Regiment 120, when he was awarded the Knight's Cross on 8 September 1941. Schröter was killed in action at Losowenka, Russia, on 26 May 1942 and has no known grave.

870. *Oberleutnant* Hans-Detloff von COSSEL

Von Cossel was born on 1 July 1916 in Swakopmund, German South West Africa. He was awarded the Iron Cross 1st and 2nd Class in 1939. Von Cossel was a platoon leader in Panzer Regiment 35 when he was awarded the Knight's Cross on 8 September 1941. He was killed in action on 22 July 1943 near Orel, Russia, and has no known grave. Von Cossel was awarded the Oak Leaves on 29 August 1943.

871. *Oberleutnant* Hermann HOGEBACK

Hogeback was born on 25 August 1914 in Idar-Oberstein. He flew over 100 missions in a He 111 with the Condor Legion in Spain. Hogeback took part in the Polish and French campaigns, and the Battle of Britain, during which time he was awarded the Iron Cross 1st and 2nd Class. After Yugoslavia, he was moved to Sicily, from where he flew in support of the Africa Corps. In one attack, he sank a 10,000-ton ship. Reconnaissance sorties and dive-bombing attacks on enemy troops followed. In one action, he was jumped by enemy fighters; his radio operator, Franz Lehner, shot down two of them. Hogeback was awarded the Knight's Cross on 8 September 1941 after his 163rd mission. Hogeback's crew was unique in that all members were all awarded the Knight's Cross. The crew comprised Wilhelm Dipberger, Willy Lehnert, and Günter Glasner.

Hogeback subsequently served in Russia and was awarded the Oak Leaves on 19 February 1943 after his 416th mission. The Swords followed on 26 January 1945. Hogeback died on 15 February 2004 and is buried in Alter Friedhof, Dötlingen, Lower Saxony.

872. *Oberleutnant* Thilo Freiherr von WERTHERN

Freiherr von Werthern was born on 24 July 1912 in Coburg. He was commander of Rifle Regiment 394 when he was awarded the Knight's Cross on 8 September 1941. Von Werthern died on 10 January 2004 in Hamburg.

873. Oberfeldwebel Hans-Wilhelm BENDER

Bender was born on 20 March 1916 in Oberschefflenz. He was a pilot in Bomber Wing 3 when he was awarded the Knight's Cross on 8 September 1941. Bender died on 20 January 1982 and is buried in Mosbach Friedhof, Baden-Württemberg.

874. Oberfeldwebel Otto SAWATZKI

Sawatzki was born on 1 April 1910 in Harburg. He was a platoon leader in Infantry Regiment 505 when he was awarded the Knight's Cross on 8 September 1944. Sawatzki KIA on 22 September 1941 and is buried in the German War Cemetery (Forest Cemetery, Waldfriedhof) (as unknown), Riga, Latvia.

875. Admiral Nikolaus HORTHY de NAGYBÁNYA (Commander-in-Chief Hungarian Army)

Horthy de Nagybánya was born on 18 June 1868 in Kenderes, Austria-Hungary. He fought in the navy during the First World War, being awarded the Iron Cross 1st and 2nd Class (1914); he ended the war as C-in-C of the navy. On 1 March 1920, after a series of short revolutions and interventions, the National Assembly of Hungary re-established the Kingdom of Hungary and voted Horthy de Nagybánya as regent.

Allied to Germany, Hungary sent units to fight in the Finnish Winter War of 1940–41 and to take part in the invasions of Yugoslavia and Russia in 1941. Horthy de Nagybánya was awarded the Knight's Cross on 10 September 1941. However, by early 1942, he was already seeking to distance himself from Hitler's regime. He was reluctant to contribute to the German war effort and to the deportation of Hungarian Jaws, together with secret attempts to make deals with the Allies, ensured that the German took over the country in March 1944. In October 1944, he withdrew from the Axis and resigned as regent. He was arrested and taken to Germany. Horthy de Nagybánya's memoirs are called *A Life for Hungary*. He died on 9 February 1957 in Estoril, Portugal. He was reburied in 1993 in the Horthy family vault, Municipal Cemetery, Kenderes, Hungary, as he wished not to be returned to Hungary until the last Russian soldier left.

876. SS-Standartenführer Hans-Christian SCHULZE

Schulze was born on 15 July 1893 in Schwarzenbeck. He fought in the First World War and was awarded the Iron Cross 1st and 2nd Class (1914). Schulze was commander of SS-Police Rifle Regiment 2 when he was awarded the Knight's Cross on 11 September 1941. He died of wounds on 13 September 1941 and is buried in the German War Cemetery (as unknown), Sologubowka, Russia.

877. Generalmajor Walter WEISS

Weiss was born on 5 September 1890 in Tilsit. He fought in the First World War and was awarded the Iron Cross 1st and 2nd Class (1914). Weiss was awarded the Iron Cross 1st and 2nd Class (1939) after the fall of Poland. He was commander of the 26th Infantry Division when he was awarded the Knight's Cross on 12 September 1941. The Oak Leaves followed on 5 November 1944. Weiss died on 21 December 1967 and is believed to be buried in Stadtfriedhof, Aschaffenburg, Bavaria.

878. Oberst Franz BEYER

Beyer was born on 27 May 1892 in Bautzen. He fought in the First World War and was awarded the Iron Cross 1st and 2nd Class (1914). Beyer was awarded the Iron Cross 1st and 2nd Class after the fall of Poland. He also fought in France, Russia, Italy, and the Battle of the Budge. Beyer was commander of Infantry Regiment 131 when he was awarded the Knight's Cross on 12 September 1941. Beyer died on 15 October 1968 and is buried in Bergfriedhof, Bad Wiessee, Bavaria.

879. Oberst Paul GURRAN

Gurran was born on 11 January 1893 in Zauche. He fought in the First World War and was awarded the Iron Cross 1st and 2nd Class (1914). Gurran was commander of Infantry Regiment 506 when he was awarded the Knight's Cross on 12 September 1941. He died of wounds at Majewo, Russia, on 22 February 1944 and has no known grave.

880. Oberst Harry (born Arthur) HOPPE—'Stan Laurel'

Hoppe was born on 11 February 1894 in Braunschweig. He fought in the First World War and was awarded the Iron Cross 1st and 2nd Class (1914). Hoppe was commander of Infantry Regiment 424 when he was awarded the Knight's Cross on 12 September 1941. He was awarded the Oak Leaves on 18 December 1944. Hoppe died on 23 August 1969 and is buried in Bergstrasse Friedhof (old part of the cemetery), Block 23, Grave 62, Wetzlar, Hesse.

881. Oberst Ernst SIELER

Sieler was born on 22 August 1893 in Altenburg. He fought in the First World War and was awarded the Iron Cross 1st and 2nd Class (1914). Sieler was commander of Infantry Regiment 46 when he was awarded the Knight's Cross on 12 September 1941. The Oak Leaves followed on 24 June 1944. Captured by the Russians in 1945, he was held for ten years. Sieler died on 6 October 1983 and is buried in Alter Friedhof, Bernau, Brandenburg.

882. Oberst Theodor Graf von SPONECK

Graf von Sponeck was born on 24 January 1896 in Offenburg. He fought in the First World War and was awarded the Iron Cross 1st and 2nd Class (1914). Graf von Sponeck was chief-of-staff of XV Army Corps during the Polish campaign, and he commanded Rifle Regiment 11 in France. He also severed with this unit in Russia, being awarded the Knight's Cross on 12 September 1941.

Graf von Sponeck was badly wounded in Russia and, on his recovery, was sent to Africa in late 1941. He commanded the 90th Light Africa Division, and at El Alamein, he personally took part in the fighting. In Tunisia, he was one of the last to surrender to US forces. He died on 13 July 1982 in Bächingen, Bavaria.

883. Oberstleutnant Albrecht ERDMANN

Erdmann was born on 8 October 1894 in Frankfurt an der Order. He was commander of Motorcycle Battalion 53 when he was awarded the Knight's Cross on 12 September 1941. Erdmann was killed in action on 15 April 1942; he is believed to be buried in the German War Cemetery (as unknown), Duchowschitschina, Russia.

884. *Hauptmann* Albert BRUX

Brux was born on 11 November 1907 in Lauban. He was awarded the Iron Cross 2nd Class after the fall of Poland and the 1st Class after the Fall of France. Brux was commander of Rifle Regiment 40 when he was awarded the Knight's Cross on 12 September 1941. The Oak Leaves followed on 24 June 1944. He was captured by the Russians in 1945 and held until 1956. Brux died on 16 December 2001 and is buried in Hauptfriedhof, Mainz, Rhineland-Palatinate.

885. *Hauptmann* Günter ZUGEHÖR

Zugehör was born on 28 December 1909 in Posen. He was commander of II Battalion, Motorised Artillery Regiment 19, when he was awarded the Knight's Cross on 12 September 1941. Zugehör died on 1 July 1966 and is buried in Stadtfriedhof, Kassel, Hesse.

886. *Oberleutnant* Heinz-Jürgen ISSBRÜCKER

Issbrücker was born on 15 July 1917 in Erlau. He was commander of Panzer Reconnaissance Battalion 7 when he was awarded the Knight's Cross on 12 September 1941. Issbrücker died on 28 February 1983 in Wörthsee, Bavaria.

887. Oberfeldwebel Friedrich HENGSTLER

Hengstler was born on 11 July 1913 in Öfingen. Hengstler was a platoon leader in *Jäger* Regiment 98 when he was awarded the Knight's Cross on 12 September 1941. Hengstler died on 8 February 1998 and is believed to be buried in Kirche St Nikolaus, Murnau, Bavaria.

888. Oberst Conrad-Oskar HEINRICHS

Heinrichs was born on 5 May 1890 in Wallstawe. He fought in the First World War and was awarded the Iron Cross 1st and 2nd Class (1914). Heinrichs was commander of Infantry Regiment 24 when he was awarded the Knight's Cross on 13 September 1941. He was killed in action on 8 September 1944 and is buried in the German War Cemetery, Block 58, Grave 40, Kattenbos N746, Lommel, Belgium.

889. Oberst Johannes MAYER

Mayer was born on 6 September 1893 in Stepenitz. He fought in the First World War and was awarded the Iron Cross 1st and 2nd Class (1914). Mayer was commander of Infantry Regiment 50 when he was awarded the Knight's Cross on 13 September 1941. The Oak Leaves followed on 13 April 1944 and the Swords on 23 August 1944. Mayer died on 7 August 1963 and is buried in Ohlsdorf Friedhof, Fuhlsbüttler Strasse, Hamburg.

890. SS-Sturmbannführer Werner OSTENDORFF (or OSTENDORF)

Ostendorff was born on 15 August 1903 in Königsberg. He was awarded the Iron Cross 1st and 2nd Class after the fall of France. Ostendorf was operation officer of the SS-Division 'Reich' (later 2nd SS-Panzer Division) when he was awarded the Knight's Cross on 13 September 1941.

He was badly wounded in Normandy on 16 June 1944. For a short time, Ostendorff was chief-of-staff of Army Group '*Oberrhein*' before commandeering the 2nd SS-Panzer Division in Hungary. He died of wounds on 1 May 1945 and is believed to be buried in Bad Aussee Friedhof. Ostendorff was awarded the Oak Leaves on 6 May 1945. This award was unlawfully presented by Sepp Dietrich.

891. *Oberleutnant* Friedrich-Karl MÜLLER—'Tutti'

Müller was born on 25 December 1916 in Berlin. He shot down eight enemy aircraft during the Battle for France and two more during the Battle of Britain. In Russia, Müller added twelve more enemy aircraft to his score and was awarded the Knight's Cross on 14 September 1941. He was transferred to the Mediterranean area in early 1942 and shot down three RAF Hurricanes over Malta.

By May 1942, he was back on the Russian Front and shot down twenty-five aircraft in August and another thirty-five in September. Müller was awarded the Oak Leaves on 23 September 1942. After a short spell in Tunisia, where he shot down three enemy aircraft, Müller was sent on enforced leave due to combat stress. Back in action in February 1944, he shot down three US four-engined bombers on 8 March 1944. With his total at 140 (including seventeen heavy bombers), Müller was killed in a landing accident at Salzwedel on 29 May 1944; he has no known grave.

892. SS-Sturmbannführer Theodor WISCH—'Teddi'

Wisch was born on 13 December 1907 in Wesselburenerkoog. He fought in Poland, being awarded the Iron Cross 1st and 2nd Class. Wisch also fought in France and the Balkans. He took part in the invasion of Russia as a battalion commander and was instrumental during an attack to free an encircled unit against overwhelming odds. For this, Wisch was awarded the Knight's Cross on 15 September 1941.

After a brief spell in Italy, the division was back on the Eastern Front and thrown into the battles for Tarnopol and the Dnieper. Encircled at Kamenez, the 1st SS Panzer Division only broke-out with heavy losses. For his command of the division, Wisch was awarded the Oak Leaves on 12 February 1944.

Withdrawn to Belgium for rest and refit, the division was thrown into the battle of Normandy in June 1944, fighting around Caen and in the Falaise Pocket. For his command of the division, Wisch was awarded the Swords on 30 August 1944. He died on 11 January 1995 and is buried in Stadtfriedhof, Barsbuttel, Schleswig-Holstein.

893. Leutnant Wilhelm WESTERMANN

Westermann was born on 21 June 1914 in Recklinghausen. He was a company commander in Motorcycle Battalion 25 when he was awarded the Knight's Cross on 15 September 1941. Westermann died on 19 November 1972 and is buried in Stadtmitte Friedhof, Grevenbroich, North Rhine-Westphalia.

894. General Hans-Gustav FELBER

Felber was born on 8 July 1889 in Wiesbaden. He fought in the First World War and was awarded the Iron Cross 1st and 2nd Class (1914). Felber was awarded the Iron Cross 1st and 2nd Class (1939) after the Fall of Poland. He was commander of XIII Army Corps when he was awarded the Knight's Cross on 17 September 1941. Felber died on 7 March 1962 and is buried in Hauptfriedhof, Block G, Grave 1014, Frankfurt am Main.

895. General Albrecht SCHUBERT

Schubert was born on 23 June 1886 in Marienwerder. He fought in the First World War and was awarded the Iron Cross 1st and 2nd Class (1914). Schubert was commander of XXIII Army Corps when he was awarded the Knight's Cross on 17 September 1941. Schubert died on 26 November 1966 and is buried in Sennefriedhof, Bielefeld, North Rhine-Westphalia.

896. Generalleutnant Siegfried HAENICKE

Haenicke was born on 8 September 1878 in Konstanz. He fought in the First World War and was awarded the Iron Cross 1st and 2nd Class (1914), as well as the *Pour le Mérite*. Haenicke was commander of the 61st Infantry Division when he was awarded the Knight's Cross on 17 September 1941. Haenicke was captured by the Russians in 1945 and died on 19 February 1946; he is buried in Camp Cemetery, Mühlberg, Brandenburg.

897. Generalleutnant Otto von KNOBELSDORFF

Von Knobelsdorff was born on 31 March 1886 in Berlin. He fought in the First World War and was awarded the Iron Cross 1st and 2nd Class (1914).

Von Knobelsdorff was awarded the Iron Cross 2nd Class (1939) after the fall of Poland and the 1st Class (1939) after the fall of France.

He was commander of the 19th Panzer Division when he was awarded the Knight's Cross on 17 September 1941. The Oak Leaves followed on 12 November 1943 and the Swords on 21 September 1944. Von Knobelsdorff died on 21 October 1966 in Hanover.

898. Oberst Maximilian JAIS

Jais was born on 4 March 1891 in Munich. He fought in the First World War and was awarded the Iron Cross 1st and 2nd Class (1914). Jais was awarded the Iron Cross 1st and 2nd Class (1939) in April 1941. He was commander of *Jäger* Regiment 141 when he was awarded the Knight's Cross on 17 September 1941. Jais died on 24 January 1957 and is buried in Engeshode Friedhof, Abt 5, Grave M152–153, Hanover.

899. Oberstleutnant Rudolf SIECKENIUS

Sieckenius was born on 18 August 1896 in Ludwigsthal. He fought in the First World War. He fought in Poland and France, where it was said his panzer battalion was the only one that could keep up with Rommel. In Russia, Sieckenius commanded the Panzer Regiment 2, and between 26 and 29 June 1941, during a Russian counterattack involving over a 1,000 tanks, his regiment knocked-out over 240 tanks; for this, he was awarded the Knight's Cross on 17 September 1941.

At Salerno, he commanded the 16th Panzer Division and almost succeed in throwing the Allies back into the sea. Despite this, he was blamed for the failure and side-lined. Sieckenius was killed in action on 28 April 1945 and is buried in the German War Cemetery, Block 1, Grave 98, Buchholzer Strasse, Teupitz, Brandenburg.

900. *Major* Felix HANNIG

Hannig was born on 15 March 1891 in Durr-Arndorf. He was commander of I Battalion, Infantry Regiment 9, when he was killed in action on 23 July 1941. He is buried at Mogilev, Belarus; his remains are awaiting transfer to a German war cemetery. Hannig was awarded the Knight's Cross on 17 September 1941.

901. *Hauptmann* Hans-Henning Freiherr von BEUST

Freiherr von Beust was born on 17 April 1913 in Karlsruhe. He fought in the Spanish Civil War with the Condor Legion. Von Beust was awarded the Iron Cross 2nd Class after the fall of Poland and the 1st Class after the fall of France. He was a group commander in Fighter Wing 27 when he was awarded the Knight's Cross on 17 September 1941. The Oak Leaves followed on 25 November 1943. Von Beust died on 27 March 1991 and is believed to be buried in Waldfriedhof, Munich.

902. *Hauptmann* Walter BRADEL

Bradel was born on 31 July 1911 in Breslau. He took part in the Spanish Civil War. Bradel was a squadron leader in Bomber Wing 2 when he was awarded the Knight's Cross on 17 September 1941. He was killed in action after a raid on Norwich, when his bomber crash landed near Landsmeer on 5 May 1943. Bradel is buried in the German War Cemetery, Block CX, Row 4, Grave 85, Timmermansweg, Ysselsteyn, the Netherlands.

903. *Hauptmann* Reinhard GÜNZEL

Günzel was born on 2 February 1907 in Posen. He was awarded the Iron Cross 2nd Class after the fall of Poland and the 1st Class after the fall of France. Günzel was a group commander in Bomber Wing 27 when he was awarded the Knight's Cross on 17 September 1941. The Oak Leaves followed on 21 January 1943. He died on 5 December 1970 in Plön, Schleswig-Holstein.

904. *Hauptmann* Richard LINKE

Linke was born on 3 April 1909 in Queissen. He was a group commander in Bomber Wing 54 when he was awarded the Knight's Cross on 17 September 1941. Linke died on 31 December 1995 and is believed to be buried in Nordfriedhof, Siegburg, North Rhine-Westphalia.

905. *Oberleutnant* Jürgen Freiherr von MAERCKEN zu GEERATH

Freiherr von Maercken zu Geerath was born 14 August 1915 in Berlin. He was a company commander in Panzer Regiment 36 when he was awarded the

Knight's Cross on 17 September 1941. Von Maercken zu Geerath was killed in action at Grünberg, Silesia, on 14 February 1945. He has no known grave.

906. *Oberleutnant* Ernst PETZOLD

Petzold was born on 6 August 1914 in Rammenau. He was a pilot in Bomber Wing 54 when he was awarded the Knight's Cross on 17 September 1941. Petzold died on 20 April 1999 in Überlingen, Baden-Württemberg.

907. *Oberleutnant* Werner RODE

Rode was born on 6 November 1912 in Dortmund. He was a company commander in Motorcycle Battalion 34 when he was awarded the Knight's Cross on 17 September 1941. Rode died on 2 November 2002 and is buried in Hauptfriedhof, Am Gottesacker 25, Dortmund, North Rhine-Westphalia.

908. *Oberleutnant* Wolfgang SKORCZEWSKI

Skorczewski was born on 3 July 1913 in Berlin. He was a squadron leader in Bomber Wing 27 when he was awarded the Knight's Cross on 17 September 1941. Skorczewski died on 30 November 2005 in Auckland, New Zealand.

909. Leutnant Theodor NORDMANN—'Theo'

Nordmann was born on 18 December 1918 in Dorsten. He was a reconnaissance pilot until March 1940 when he transferred to a Dive Bomber Wing. Nordmann was awarded the Iron Cross 2nd Class in May and the 1st Class in August 1940. In 1941, he was in action over Malta and sank a 5,000-ton merchant ship. In Russia, after knocking out twenty tanks during 200 missions, he was awarded the Knight's Cross on 17 September 1941. During the summer of 1942, he became the first Stuka pilot to complete 600 missions.

Nordmann was awarded the Oak Leaves on 17 March 1943 and the Swords on 17 September 1944. He knocked-out eighty tanks and sank 43,000 tons of shipping in 1,300 missions. Nordmann was killed near Insterburg, Russia, on 19 January 1945 when he collided with his wingman in bad weather; he has no known grave.

910. Oberwachtmeister Ernst THIEM

Thiem was born on 11 October 1909 in Gross-Tinz. He was a platoon leader in Reconnaissance Battalion 298 when he was awarded the Knight's Cross on 17 September 1941. Thiem was killed in action at Sinjavino, Russia, on 19 September 1943. He has no known grave.

911. Feldwebel Jakob GOLDBRUNNER

Goldbrunner was born on 12 August 1920 in Freising. He was a platoon leader in Infantry Regiment 19 when he was awarded the Knight's Cross on 17 September 1941. Goldbrunner died on 13 April 1978 and is buried in Friedhof St Jakob, Freising, Bavaria.

912. Gefreiter Heinz BERGER

Berger was born on 1 December 1914 in Wahren. He was a gunner in Infantry Regiment 187 when he was awarded the Knight's Cross on 17 September 1941. Berger died on 16 April 1983 in Leipzig.

913. *Generaloberst* Hans-Jürgen STUMPFF

Stumpff was born on 15 June 1889 in Kolberg. He served in the First World War and was awarded the Iron Cross 1st and 2nd Class (1914). Stumpff was commander of *Luftflotte* 5 when he was awarded the Knight's Cross on 18 September 1941. He was one of the signatories of the surrender in 1945. Stumpff died on 9 March 1968 and is buried in Zentralfriedhof, Abt V, Grave 199–200, Bonn.

914. General Gotthard HEINRICI—'Our Poison Dwarf'

Heinrici was born on 25 December 1886 in Gumbinnen. He fought in the First World War and was awarded the Iron Cross 1st and 2nd Class (1914). Heinrici fought in France, for which he was awarded the Iron Cross 1st and 2nd Class (1939), and Russia, for which he was awarded the Knight's Cross on 18 September 1941 for his command of XXXXIII Army Corps. He was a noted defensive commander, and his nickname *Unser Giftzwerg*, literally 'Our Poison Dwarf', basically meaning 'our tough little bastard', was very much meant as a compliment.

He was awarded the Oak Leaves on 24 November 1943 but was dismissed from his command due to 'ill health' for refusing to burn Smolensk. In the summer of 1944, he was sent to Hungary where he fought so well he was awarded the Swords on 3 March 1945. His last command was the defence of Berlin, but he was again dismissed for retreating without orders. Heinrici died on 10 December 1971 and is buried in Bergacker Friedhof, Freiburg im Breisgau, Baden-Württemberg.

915. Generalleutnant Walter LICHEL

Lichel was born on 1 May 1885 in Stolp. He fought in the First World War and was awarded the Iron Cross 1st and 2nd Class (1914). Lichel was commander of the 123rd Infantry Division when he was awarded the Knight's Cross on 18 September 1941. Lichel died on 10 December 1969 in Bernau, Brandenburg.

916. Generalmajor Ernst von LEYSER

Von Leyser was born on 18 November 1889 in Berlin. He fought in the First World War and was awarded the Iron Cross 2nd Class (1914). Von Leyser missed the Polish campaign but fought in France and Russia, where he was awarded the Knight's Cross on 18 September 1941. In December 1942, he was sent to fight against Yugoslav partisans in Croatia.

He was relieved of his command on 29 April 1945 and captured by US forces on 8 May 1945. Von Leyser was tried for mistreatment of POWs and partisans, as well as reprisals against civilians. Found guilty, he was sentenced to ten years but was pardoned in February 1951. He died on 23 September 1962 in Garstedt, Lower Saxony.

917. Oberstleutnant Paul WEITKUS

Weitkus was born on 17 October 1898 in Miswalde. He was a *Kommodore* in Bomber Wing 53 when he was awarded the Knight's Cross on 18 September 1941. Weitkus died on 9 November 1974 and is buried in Eichholzstrasse Friedhof, Feld 1, Grave 13–14, Arnsberg, North Rhine-Westphalia.

918. *Major* Friedrich BECKH

Beckh was born on 17 January 1908 in Nuremberg. He was commander of Fighter Wing 51 when he was awarded the Knight's Cross on 18 September

1941, with twenty-seven victories to his credit. Although his eyesight was poor, he shot down forty-eight enemy aircraft, but he was posted missing at Kharkov, Russia, on 21 June 1942.

919. *Hauptmann* Franz ECKERLE

Eckerle was born on 24 April 1912 in Baden Baden. He was awarded the Iron Cross 2nd Class after the fall of Poland and the 1st Class after the fall of France. Eckerle was a squadron leader in Fighter Wing 54 when he was awarded the Knight's Cross on 18 September 1941. With fifty-nine victories to his credit, he was posted missing near Velikiye Kuki, Russia, on 14 February 1942. Eckerle was awarded the Oak Leaves on 12 March 1942.

920. *Hauptmann* Gordon M. GOLLOB (born MacGOLLOB)—'Mac'

Gollob was born in Vienna on 16 June 1912; he changed his name in 1938 when he joined the Luftwaffe, but he kept the 'M' as a middle initial and was always known by his nickname Mac. He fought over Poland, for which he was awarded the Iron Cross 2nd Class; Norway, for which he was awarded the Iron Cross 1st Class; and in the West, where he flew the Bf 110 twin-engined heavy fighter. During the Battle of Britain, he flew the Bf 109, shooting down five enemy aircraft. Moved east for the invasion of Russia, Gollob had found his calling; he would often use only twenty rounds to shoot down an enemy aircraft, and more often than not, he would return low on fuel rather an ammunition.

With his tally at forty-two, he was awarded the Knight's Cross on 18 September 1941. In October, he shot down thirty-seven enemy aircraft, including nine in one day, and on 26 October, with his score at eighty-five, he was awarded the Oak Leaves. In November, Gollob was sent to a test centre to trial new weapons but returned to the Russian Front in May 1942.

By 20 May 1942, he had shot down 100 enemy aircraft, and with his score at 107, he was awarded the Swords on 23 June 1942. In August 1942, he shot down forty aircraft, and on the 29th, he became the first pilot to be credited with 150 victories. Gollob was awarded the Diamonds the next day.

Following this award, he was given a staff posting on the Channel coast. Gollob went to the test unit at Rechlin in September 1944 and was on the staff controlling fighter operations for the Ardennes offensive. When Adolf Galland was dismissed in January 1945, Gollob took his place as general of fighters—a post he held until the end of the war. Gollob died on 7 September 1987 and is buried in the village cemetery, Sulingen, Lower Saxony.

921. *Oberleutnant* Rudolf MONS

Mons was born on 2 October 1914 in Vienna. He was a pilot in Bomber Wing 40 when he was awarded the Knight's Cross on 18 September 1941. Mons was killed in action over the Mediterranean Sea on 26 November 1943 and has no known grave.

922. *Oberleutnant* Heinrich SCHLOSSER

Schlosser was born on 1 August 1908 in Chemnitz. He was a pilot in Bomber Wing 40 when he was awarded the Knight's Cross on 18 September 1941. Schlosser died on 17 December 1990 in Penzing, Bavaria.

923. *Oberleutnant* Winfried SCHMIDT

Schmidt was born on 28 February 1915 in Cologne. He was a squadron leader in Fighter Wing 3 when he was awarded the Knight's Cross on 18 September 1941. Schmidt died on 3 August 2009.

924. *Hauptmann* Werner PANKOW

Pankow was born on 2 February 1897 in Königsberg. He was commander of II Battalion, Infantry Regiment 151, when he was awarded the Knight's Cross on 20 September 1941. Pankow died on 6 September 1980 in Helsdorf, Saxony.

925. *Hauptmann* Konrad HUPFER

Hupfer was born on 27 October 1911 in Altdorf. He was awarded the Iron Cross 2nd Class after the fall of Poland and the 1st Class after the fall of France. Hupfer was a company commander in Infantry Regiment 72 when he was awarded the Knight's Cross on 21 September 1941. The Oak Leaves followed on 28 October 1942. He was killed in action on 10 April 1944 and is buried in the German War Cemetery (as unknown), Chisinau. Moldova.

926. *Hauptmann* Erich RING

Ring was born on 9 February 1909 in Güsterbiese. He was commander of II Battalion, Infantry Regiment 84, when he was awarded the Knight's Cross on 21 September 1941. Ring was killed in action on 3 September 1942 and is buried in the German War Cemetery (as unknown), Rzhev, Russia.

927. *Oberleutnant* Theodor HOPF

Hopf was born on 23 September 1918 in Schwarzenberg. He was a company commander in Infantry Regiment 170 when he was awarded the Knight's Cross on 21 September 1941. Hopf died on 23 January 2008 in Prien am Chiemsee, Bavaria.

928. Leutnant Viktor LINDEMANN

Lindemann was born on 23 November 1916 in Koblenz. He was adjutant in III Battalion, Infantry Regiment 124, when he was awarded the Knight's Cross on 21 September 1941. Lindemann was killed in action on 9 September 1942 and is buried in the German War Cemetery, Dubakino, Russia.

929. General Hans-Wolfgang REINHARD

Reinhard was born on 11 December 1888 in Hohenstein-Ernstthal. He fought in the First World War and was awarded the Iron Cross 1st and 2nd Class (1914). Reinhard was commander of LI Army Corps when he was awarded the Knight's Cross on 22 September 1941. He died on 18 January 1950 (some references say 6 October). He is buried in Hauptfriedhof, Feld P3, Grave 58, Karlsruhe, Baden-Württemberg.

930. Generalleutnant Hans SCHMIDT

Schmidt was born on 28 April 1877 in Ulm. He fought in the First World War and was awarded the Iron Cross 1st and 2nd Class (1914). Schmidt was commander of the 260th Infantry Division when he was awarded the Knight's Cross on 22 September 1941. The Oak Leaves followed on 24 November 1943. He died on 5 June 1948 and is buried in Alten Friedhof, Abt 3, Row 3, Grave 18–19, Stuttgart, Baden-Württemberg.

931. Generalleutnant Hans-Heinrich von SIXT von ARMIN

Von Sixt von Armin was born on 6 November 1890 in Stettin. He fought in the First World War and was awarded the Iron Cross 1st and 2nd Class (1914). Von Sixt von Armin was commander of the 95t+h Infantry Division when he was awarded the Knight's Cross on 22 September 1941. He was captured at Stalingrad and died as a POW on 1 April 1952. He has no known grave.

932. Generalmajor Friedrich HERRLEIN

Herrlein was born on 27 April 1889 in Ehrenbreitstein. He fought in the First World War and was awarded the Iron Cross 1st and 2nd Class (1914). Herrlein was commander of the 18th Infantry Division when he was awarded the Knight's Cross on 22 September 1941. He died on 28 July 1974 and is buried in Alter Friedhof, Giessen, Hesse.

933. Oberst Carl CASPER

Casper was born on 22 February 1893 in Rehden. He fought in the First World War and was awarded the Iron Cross 1st and 2nd Class (1914). Casper was awarded the Iron Cross 1st and 2nd Class (1939) in May 1940. He was commander of Motorised Infantry Regiment 118 when he was awarded the Knight's Cross on 24 September 1941. Casper died on 25 August 1970 and is buried in Stadtfriedhof, Feld 44, Rastatt, Baden-Württemberg.

934. Oberst Heinrich (aka Heinz) GREINER—'The Lion of Yelnya'

Greiner was born on 12 August 1895 in Amberg. He fought in the First World War and was awarded the Iron Cross 1st and 2nd Class (1914). Greiner was awarded the Iron Cross 1st and 2nd Class after the fall of Poland. He was in a staff position during the French campaign but was commander of Infantry Regiment 499 during the invasion of Russia. He was awarded the Knight's Cross on 22 September 1941 for preventing a Russian encirclement at Yelnya.

Transferred to Italy, he led a number of counterattacks to slow down the Allied advance towards Rome. For this, he was awarded the Oak Leaves on 5 September 1944. Greiner was also wounded and did not return to the front until April 1945. He died on 19 November 1977 and is buried in Katholisher Friedhof, Rottach-Egern, Bavaria.

935. Oberst Georg von NEUFVILLE

Von Neufville was born on 27 October 1883 in Frankfurt am Main. He fought in the First World War and was awarded the Iron Cross 1st and 2nd Class (1914). Von Neufville was commander of Infantry Regiment 195 when he was awarded the Knight's Cross on 22 September 1941. He died of wounds on 26 November 1941 and is buried at Panowo, Russia; Von Neufville's remains are awaiting transfer to a German war cemetery.

936. Oberst Walther RISSE

Risse was born on 13 December 1892 in Geithain. He fought in the First World War and was awarded the Iron Cross 1st and 2nd Class (1914). Risse was commander of Infantry Regiment 474 when he was awarded the Knight's Cross on 22 September 1941. The Oak Leaves followed on 18 January 1945. He died on 21 June 1965 and is believed to be buried in Ohlsdorf Friedhof, Fuhlsbüttler Strasse, Hamburg.

937. Oberstleutnant Friedrich-Wilhelm MÜLLER—'The Butcher of Crete'

Müller was born on 29 August 1897 in Barmen. He fought in the First World War and was awarded the Iron Cross 1st and 2nd Class (1914). Müller was awarded the Iron Cross 2nd Class (1939) after the fall of Poland and the 1st Class after the fall of France. He was commander of Infantry Regiment 105 when he was awarded the Oak Leaves for action on the Russian Front. Müller was sent to Crete in August 1942 and was responsible for the massacre at Viannos and the destruction of the villages of Anogia and Kedros.

In the autumn of 1943, he led the Germans in their victory over the Italo-British forces in the Dodecanese campaign. On 6 October, he ordered the execution of over 100 Italian POWs who had surrendered after the fall of Kos because they refused to join their former allies. By 1945, he was back on the Russian Front, where, on 27 January 1945, he was awarded the Swords. Captured by the Russians, he was handed over to the Greeks, tried for war crimes, and shot on 20 May 1947. Müller is buried in the German War Cemetery, Crypt 3, Row 10, Plate 10, Dionyssos-Rapendoza, Greece.

938. *Major* Rudolf GERHARDT

Gerhardt was born on 26 March 1896 in Greiz. He fought in the First World War and was awarded the Iron Cross 1st and 2nd Class (1914). Gerhardt was awarded the Iron Cross 1st and 2nd Class (1939) after the fall of Poland. He was commander of II Battalion, Panzer Regiment 7, when he was awarded the Knight's Cross on 22 September 1941. Gerhardt died on 10 November 1964 and is believed to be buried in Zentralfriedhof, Münster.

939. *Oberleutnant* Gotthard ESSBACH

Essbach was born on 29 March 1917 in Falkenstein. He was a company commander in Infantry Regiment 31 when he was awarded the Knight's Cross on 22 September 1941. Essbach died on 19 April 2001 in Marburg, Hesse.

940. *Oberleutnant* Hans-Joachim KÜNZEL

Künzel was born on 6 November 1914 in Schwarzenberg. He was a company commander in Rifle Regiment 10 when he was awarded the Knight's Cross on 22 September 1941. Künzel died on 25 November 2000 in Ettlingen, Baden-Württemberg.

941. *Oberleutnant* Günther MÖLLER

Möller was born in Berlin on 12 June 1917. He was a company commander in Assault-Gun Battalion 191 when he was killed in action near Kiev, Russia, on 22 September 1941. He has no known grave. Möller was awarded the Knight's Cross the same day.

942. *Oberleutnant* Eberhard PASTERNACK

Pasterneck was born on 25 November 1914 in Wiltschin. He was a company commander in Infantry Regiment 506 when he was awarded the Knight's Cross on 22 September 1941. Pasterneck died on 15 December 1996 in Brauneberg, Rhineland-Palatinate.

943. *Oberleutnant* Heinz SCHNEIDER

Schneider was born on 13 May 1915 in Berlin. He was a company commander in Panzer Pioneer Battalion 59 when he was awarded the Knight's Cross on 22 September 1941. Schneider died on 1 September 1996 in Meckenheim, North Rhine-Westphalia.

944. *Oberleutnant* Kurt SPEIDEL

Speidel was born on 4 March 1917 in Düsseldorf. He was a company commander in Panzer Pioneer Battalion 86 when he was awarded the Knight's Cross on 22 September 1941. Speidel died on 5 November 1976 and is buried in Ostfriedhof, Cologne, North Rhine-Westphalia.

945. Leutnant Ulrich KRESS

Kress was born on 20 March 1919 in Canstatt. He was a platoon leader in Reconnaissance Battalion 20 when he was awarded the Knight's Cross on 22 September 1941. Kress was killed in action at Dubenskaja, Russia, on 15 January 1943; he has no known grave.

946. Leutnant Georg STÖRCK

Störck was born on 1 April 1917 in Misdroy. He was a platoon leader in Rifle Regiment 394 when he was awarded the Knight's Cross on 22 September 1941. The Oak Leaves followed on 9 May 1945 (this award was made in accordance with the Dönitz-Decree). Störck died on 20 December 2011.

947. Oberwachtmeister Adolf HAINLE

Hainle was born on 15 March 1914 in Neckarweihingen. He was leader of a machine-gun section in Reconnaissance Battalion 5 when he was awarded the Knight's Cross on 22 September 1941. Hainle died of wounds on 22 May 1942 and is buried at Novo Swinuchowo, Russia; his remains are awaiting transfer to a German war cemetery.

948. Oberfeldwebel Kurt SCHÖNFELD

Schönfeld was born on 14 December 1913 in Heiligenbeil. He was a platoon leader in Panzer Regiment 10 when he was awarded the Knight's Cross on 22 September 1941. Schönfeld died on 9 March 2004 in Suhl, Thuringia.

949. *Oberleutnant* Horst CARGANICO

Carganico was born on 27 September 1917 in Breslau. He shot down his first four enemy aircraft in June 1940 while stationed in Norway. Carganico was transferred to France in November 1940 and shot down two more aircraft. By January 1941, he was back in Norway. On the Eastern Front, he raised his score to twenty-seven aerial victories and was awarded the Knight's Cross on 25 September 1941.

In the summer of 1942, he shot down twenty-three enemy aircraft in six weeks. Then, on 12 August, he was shot down behind enemy lines, but he managed to make his way back to his unit. In March 1944, he was deployed in the defence of the Reich and raised his total to sixty enemy aircraft. On 27 May 1944, his fighter was damaged by return fire from a US bomber; Carganico hit high-tension cables while attempting a forced landing and was killed. He is buried in German War Cemetery (Waldfriedhof), Wasgenensteig, Zehlendorf, Berlin.

950. Oberfeldwebel Georg DONHAUSER

Donhauser was born in Amberg on 22 August 1909. He was a platoon leader in Infantry Regiment 501 when he was awarded the Knight's Cross on 26 September 1941. Donhauser died on 1 October 1982 in Edenstetten, Bavaria.

951. SS-Sturmbannführer Walter BESTMANN

Bestmann was born on 2 October 1907 in Lubeck. He fought in Poland, for which he was awarded the Iron Cross 2nd Class in September 1939, and France, for which he was awarded the Iron Cross 1st Class in June 1940. Bestmann was commander of SS-Reconnaissance Battalion 3 when he was awarded the Knight's Cross on 28 September 1941 for action in Russia.

In September 1942, he was given commanded of SS-Panzer Regiment 10, but in September 1943, he was sent to train new recruits at Klagenfurt. Bestmann died (as a result of his wartime wounds) on 17 June 1958 and is buried in Burgtor Friedhof, Lubeck, Schleswig-Holstein.

952. Generalleutnant Friedrich-Wilhelm von LOEPER

Von Loeper was born on 3 August 1888 in Prieborn. He fought in the First World War and was awarded the Iron Cross 1st and 2nd Class (1914). Von Loeper was commander of the 10th Infantry Division when he was awarded the Knight's Cross on 29 September 1941. He died on 7 October 1983 and is believed to be buried in Stadtfriedhof, Bückeburg, Lower Saxony.

953. Generalleutnant Horst STUMPFF

Stumpff was born on 20 November 1887 in Giessen. He fought in the First World War and was awarded the Iron Cross 1st and 2nd Class (1914). Stumpff fought in Poland and France. He was commander of the 20th Panzer Division when he was awarded the Knight's Cross on 29 September 1941, but he moved to the reserve list shortly after.

In April 1942, he was appointed military inspector of the Königsberg recruiting area, and in July 1944, he became inspector general of panzer troops. Stumpff died on 25 November 1958 and is buried in Ohlsdorf Friedhof, Plot T20, Grave 260, Fuhlsbüttler Strasse, Hamburg.

954. Oberst Wilhelm BURGDORF

Burgdorf was born on 15 February 1895 in Fürstenwalde. He fought in the First World War and was awarded the Iron Cross 1st and 2nd Class (1914). Burgdorf was awarded the Iron Cross 1st and 2nd Class in June 1940 and the Knight's Cross on 29 September 1941. He spent almost the entire war on the staff, and after the 20 July bomb plot to kill Hitler, he, with General Maisel, was sent to inform Rommel that he had a choice of suicide and a state funeral or face trial for treason.

Burgdorf joined Hitler in the *Führerbunker* on 28 April 1945 and killed himself on 2 May 1945. His body was cremated.

955. Oberst Heinrich WITTKOPF

Wittkopf was born on 15 August 1892 in Hildesheim. He was commander of Infantry Regiment 530 when he was awarded the Knight's Cross on 29 September 1941. Wittkopf died on 12 February 1946 while in British hands and is buried in the German War Cemetery, Block 62, Grave 197, Kattenbos N746, Lommel, Belgium.

956. *Major* Willi WIESNER

Wiesner was born on 2 October 1900 in Oschersleben. He was commander of I Battalion, Artillery Regiment 257, when he was awarded the Knight's Cross on 29 September 1941. Wiesner died on 19 June 1960 in Hanover.

957. *Hauptmann* Willi WELSCH

Welsch was born on 21 December 1910 in Nieder-Scheld. He was a company commander in Rifle Regiment 110 when he was awarded the Knight's Cross on 29 September 1941. Welsch was killed in action on 27 July 1944 and is buried in the German War Cemetery, Block 49, Row 6, Grave 215, La Cambe, Normandy, France.

958. *Oberleutnant* Ernst BORCHERT

Borchert was born on 14 December 1918 in Wormditt. He was awarded the Iron Cross 2nd Class after the fall of Poland and the 1st Class after the fall of France. Borchert was a company commander in Motorised Infantry Regiment 29 when he was awarded the Knight's Cross on 29 September 1941. He was killed in action on 1 May 1945 and is buried in Drolshagen Catholic Cemetery, Feld 3, Grave 11, North Rhine-Westphalia.

959. *Oberleutnant* Horst KRAFFT

Krafft was born 6 November 1911 in Königsberg. He was a company commander in Assault-Gun Battalion 185 when he was awarded the Knight's Cross on 29 September 1941. Krafft died on 28 July 2002 and is believed to be buried in Kirchfriedhof, Achim, Lower Saxony.

960. *Oberleutnant* Adolf-Hilmar von TIPPELSKIRCH

Von Tippelskirch was born on 3 October 1914 in Berlin. He was a company commander in Motorised Artillery Regiment 3 when he was awarded the Knight's Cross on 29 September 1941. Von Tippelskirch was killed in action near Mogilev, Russia, on 28 June 1944 and has no known grave. His father, Kurt, and his uncle, Curt Gallenkamp, were also awarded the Knight's Cross.

961. Leutnant Rolf FROMME

Fromme was born on 5 September 1914 in Hanover. He was a company commander in Panzer Regiment 3 when he was awarded the Knight's Cross on 29 September 1941. Fromme died on 29 June 1992 in Bad Pyrmont, Lower Saxony.

962. Leutnant Heinz KIRCHNER

Kirchner was born on 23 April 1916 in Eisenberg. He was a platoon leader in Rifle Regiment 113 when he was awarded the Knight's Cross on 29 September 1941. Kirchner was killed in action on 27 November 1942 and is buried at Lenino, Bely, Russia; his remains are awaiting transfer to a German war cemetery.

963. Leutnant Eugen METZGER

Metzger was born on 1 August 1914 in Feuerbach. He was a platoon leader in Assault-Gun Battalion 203 when he was awarded the Knight's Cross on 29 September 1941. Metzger died on 6 February 2004 and is buried in Brackenheim Friedhof, Baden-Württemberg.

964. Oberfeldwebel Emil SACK

Sack was born on 25 June 1913 in Prostken. He was a platoon leader in Infantry Regiment 445 when he was awarded the Knight's Cross on 29 September 1941. Sack was killed in action on 18 August 1942 and is buried in the German War Cemetery, Grave 119, Krassny, Russia.

965. Oberst Traugott HERR

Herr was born on 16 September 1890 in Weferlingen. He fought in the First World War and was awarded the Iron Cross 1st and 2nd Class (1914). Herr was awarded the Iron Cross 2nd Class (1939) after the fall of Poland and the 1st Class in May 1940. He was commander of the 13th Rifle Brigade when he was awarded the Knight's Cross on 2 October 1941. Herr was awarded the Oak Leaves on 9 August 1942 and wounded on 25 September.

In June 1943, he was appointed as acting commander of LXXVI Army Corps, but one month later, he was redesignated to LXXVI Panzer Corps and sent to Italy. Herr was awarded the Swords on 18 December 1944, and after a short time in the reserve, he was back in Italy commanding X Army. Herr was taken prisoner by the British on 2 May 1945. He died on 13 April 1976 in Achterwehr, Schleswig-Holstein.

966. Oberst Helmuth SCHLÖMER

Schlömer was born on 30 May 1893 in Hausberge. He fought in the First World War and was awarded the Iron Cross 1st and 2nd Class (1914). Schlömer was commander of Rifle Regiment 5 when he was awarded the Knight's Cross on 2 October 1941. The Oak Leaves followed on 23 December 1942. He was captured at Stalingrad but released in 1949. Schlömer died on 18 August 1995 and is buried in Bolhorst Friedhof, Minden, North Rhine-Westphalia.

967. Oberstleutnant Oskar von BODDIEN

Von Boddien was born on 19 April 1900 in Neuruppin. He fought in the First World War and was awarded the Iron Cross 1st and 2nd Class (1914). Von Boddien was awarded the Iron Cross 1st and 2nd Class (1939) in July 1941.

He was commander of Reconnaissance Battalion 22 when he was awarded the Knight's Cross on 2 October 1941. Von Boddien was killed in action on 6 January 1942 and is buried in the German War Cemetery, Block 10 (as unknown), Sebastopol, Ukraine. He was awarded the Oak Leaves on 8 January 1942.

968. *Hauptmann* Karl KOETZ

Koetz was born on 8 February 1908 in Berlin. He was awarded the Iron Cross 2nd Class in June 1940 and the 1st Class in July 1941. Koetz was commander of II Battalion, Infantry Regiment 46, when he was awarded the Knight's Cross on 2 October 1941. The Oak Leaves followed on 24 January 1944. He died on 11 June 1977 in Meran, Italy.

969. *Oberleutnant* Franz BUCHNER

Buchner was born on 9 September 1918 in Kaschau. He was a company commander in Motorised Infantry Regiment 30 when he was awarded the Knight's Cross on 2 October 1941. Buchner was killed on 27 November 1941 and is buried at Tikhvin, Russia; his remains are awaiting transfer to a German war cemetery.

970. *Oberleutnant* Benno SALWEY

Salwey was born on 17 July 1912 in Trunz. He was *aide-de-camp* in Infantry Regiment 270 when he was awarded the Knight's Cross on 2 October 1941. Salwey died on 15 March 1976 in Oberrottweil, Baden-Württemberg.

971. Oberst Friedrich FRANEK—'Fritz'

Franek was born on 16 July 1891 in Vienna. He fought in the First World War and was awarded the Iron Cross 2nd Class (1914). Franek was commander of Infantry Regiment 405 when he was awarded the Knight's Cross on 4 October 1941. He was captured by the Russians in 1945 but only held until 1948. Franek died on 8 April 1976 and is buried in Zentralfriedhof, Vienna.

972. Generalleutnant Johann PFLUGBEIL

Pflugbeil was born on 24 August 1882 in Hütten. He fought in the First World War and was awarded the Iron Cross 1st and 2nd Class (1914). Pflugbeil was commandant of Milau when he was awarded the Knight's Cross on 5 October 1941.

He was partly responsible for the massacre of Jews in Bialystok, Poland, on 27 June 1941 when the 221 Security Battalion started to round up Jews—some were shot. The leaders of the Jewish community went to see Pflugbeil in his office and begged him to stop the killing, but Pflugbeil turned his back on them and the killing increased. A synagogue with 700 Jews in it was set on fire. Pflugbeil asked Mayor Weis of the security division what had started the fire and Weis filed a false report. He died on 21 October 1951 and is believed to be buried in Waldfriedhof, Stuttgart, Baden-Württemberg. His brother, Kurt, was also awarded the Knight's Cross on the same day.

973. Generalleutnant Kurt PFLUGBEIL

Pflugbeil was born on 9 May 1890 in Hütten. He fought in the First World War and was awarded the Iron Cross 1st and 2nd Class (1914). Pflugbeil was awarded the Iron Cross 2nd Class (1939) after the fall of Poland and the 1st Class after the fall of France. He fought in the Battle of Britain and the Balkans, but he is most noted for commanding *Fliegerkorps* VI during the Second Battle of Kharkov, Stalingrad, and the Siege of Sebastopol.

Pflugbeil was awarded the Knight's Cross on 5 October 1941 and the Oak Leaves on 27 August 1944. He was captured in 1945 and sentenced by the

Russians to twenty-five years' hard labour, but he was released in 1950 due to bad health. Pflugbeil died on 31 May 1955 in Weende, Schleswig-Holstein. His brother, Johann, was also awarded the Knight's Cross on the same day.

974. *Oberleutnant* Alwin BOERST

Boerst was born on 20 October 1910 in Osterode. He served in Poland and the West, making over 150 sorties as a Stuka pilot, and was awarded the Iron Cross 1st and 2nd Class. Boerst also saw action over the Balkans and at Crete where he sank one British destroyer and damaged another. In Russia, he made some notable success, including a bridge over the Dnieper, eighty enemy vehicles, six tanks, a train, and several gun emplacements. On 5 October 1941, with 300 sorties completed, Boerst was awarded the Knight's Cross.

In September 1942, with 600 sorties to his credit, Boerst was sent home to train new pilots, and on 28 November, he was awarded the Oak Leaves. After some home leave, he was posted back to Russia in early 1943. By 29 January 1944, Boerst had made 1,000 sorties. On 30 March 1944, he took off for his first sortie with the 37-mm anti-tanks guns, and during an attack on enemy tanks near Iaşi, Romania, he was shot down and killed; he has no known grave. Boerst was awarded the Swords on 6 April 1944.

975. *Oberleutnant* Bruno FREITAG

Freitag was born on 21 July 1918 in Potsdam. He was a squadron leader in Dive Bomber Wing 2 when he was awarded the Knight's Cross on 5 October 1941. Freitag died on 16 February 1990 in Malente, Schleswig-Holstein.

976. *Oberleutnant* Erich HOHAGEN

Hohagen was born on 9 January 1915 in Velbert. He shot down twelve enemy aircraft during the Battle of Britain before being transferred to the East for the invasion of Russia. Hohagen was awarded the Knight's Cross on 5 October 1941 with more than thirty aircraft to his credit. In January 1943, he was back on the Western Front, where he was accidently shot down by one of his own men. Hohagen baled out safely. Now taking part in the defence of the Reich, he was shot down while attacking a bomber on 16 September 1943 and crashed landed near Rennes, France. Hohagen was passed fit for flying despite suffering from headaches.

In January 1944, his unit was sent to Italy, but it returned to France in April due to heavy losses. On D-Day, Hohagen was over the front and shot down an RAF fighter. He was declared unfit for flying due to his headaches and sent to a fighter pilots' hospital near Berlin, from where he was recruited by Adolf Galland to train pilots to fly the Me 262 jet fighter. He would remain in his post until the end of the war. Hohagen is credited with fifty-six victories, including thirteen four-engined bombers. He died on 8 March 1990 in Jever, Lower Saxony.

977. *Oberleutnant* Wolfgang SPÄTE

Späte was born on 8 September 1911 in Dresden. He started the war as a Reconnaissance pilot and was awarded the Iron Cross 2nd Class after the fall of Poland and the 1st Class in September 1940, before transferring to fighters. His first combat patrol was over the Balkans, where he shot down his first enemy aircraft on 7 April 1941. Späte took part in the invasion of Russia and, with his tally at forty-five victories, was awarded the Knight's Cross on 5 October 1941.

After a refit, his unit returned to Russia and Späte was awarded the Oak Leaves on 23 April 1942 with his score at seventy-two enemy aircraft shot down. However, he was withdrawn from the front to test fly the Me 163 jet fighter. Späte also flew the Me 262 jet, becoming one of the few pilots to fly both. In May 1944, he returned to combat in Romania, but in June, he was recalled to the Reich after the Allied landings in Normandy. His unit was then sent to Poland in time for the Russian Summer Offensive, where it was almost wiped out. The unit was pulled back for refit and fought into the battles over the Netherlands in September 1944, where it was destroyed in less than a fortnight. He ended the war flying the Me 262 and was credited with ninety-nine victories, including five in jets. Späte died on 30 April 1997 and is buried in Edewecht Friedhof, Lower Saxony.

978. *Oberleutnant* Günther TONNE

Tonne was born on 21 May 1916 in Frankfurt an der Oder. He was a Bf 110 twin-engined heavy fighter pilot. Tonne fought in the Polish campaign and was awarded the Iron Cross 2nd Class in March 1940. The 1st Class followed in June 1940. He shot down about seven enemy aircraft over the English Channel during 1940. Tonne took part in the invasion of Russia and was awarded the Knight's Cross on 5 October 1941. Transferred to Italy and with his total at fifteen enemy aircraft, Tonne was killed in a crash on 15 July 1943 and is buried in the German War Cemetery, Block 8, Grave 788, Cassino, Italy. He was awarded the Oak Leaves on 24 October 1944.

979. Leutnant Peter KIESGEN

Kiesgen was born on 22 November 1915 in Lieser. He was a company commander in Infantry Regiment 239 when he was awarded the Knight's Cross on 5 October 1941. Kiesgen had knocked-out five tanks with handheld weapons, for which he was awarded the Tank Destruction Badge in Gold. He died on 22 March 1946 in Lieser, Rhineland-Palatinate.

980. Leutnant Detlev ROHWER

Rohwer was born on 14 November 1917 in Kiel. He was a pilot in Fighter Wing 3 when he was awarded the Knight's Cross on 5 October 1941. Rohwer was credited with thirty-eight victories. He died on 30 March 1944 following the amputation of his leg at Ibbenburen, North Rhine-Westphalia, and has no known grave.

981. Oberfeldwebel Rudolf KRÜGER

Krüger was born on 4 November 1911 in Leipzig. He was a platoon leader in Infantry Regiment 32 when he was awarded the Knight's Cross on 5 October 1941. Krüger died on 28 October 1972 and is buried in German War Cemetery, Eilenburg, Lower Saxony.

982. Oberfeldwebel Johannes LUTTER—'Hanns'

Lutter was born on 17 December 1912 in Düsseldorf. He was a pilot in Fast (Rapid Response) Fighter Wing 210 when he was awarded the Knight's Cross on 5 October 1941. Lutter is credited with twelve aerial victories, fifteen tanks, and thirty aircraft destroyed on the ground. He died on 13 March 2004 and is believed to be buried in Stadtfriedhof, Bückeburg, Lower Saxony.

983. Oberfeldwebel Christian ROSSFELD

Rossfeld was born on 6 August 1914 in Maikammer. He was a platoon leader in Infantry Regiment 62 when he was awarded the Knight's Cross on 5 October 1941. Rossfeld died on 12 May 1998 in Ergolding, Bavaria.

984. Unteroffizier Wilhelm BRÜCKNER

Brückner was born on 27 April 1915 in Weis. He was serving in Infantry Regiment 253 when he was awarded the Knight's Cross on 5 October 1941. Brückner was killed in action on 15 November 1941 and is buried at Tarutino, Kaluga, Russia; his remains are awaiting transfer to a German war cemetery.

985. *Major* Johannes SCHULZ

Schulz was born on 3 February 1902 in Althütte. He was commander of I Battalion, Infantry Regiment 49, when he was awarded the Knight's Cross on 6 October 1941. Schulz died on 12 September 1991 in Goslar, Lower Saxony.

986. *Oberleutnant* Rudolf GRAF

Graf was born on 25 February 1915 in Halle. He was commander of I Battalion, Motorised Flak Regiment 'General Göring', when he was awarded the Knight's Cross on 6 October 1941. Graf was killed in action on 21 January 1945 and is buried at Ksiazki, Poland; his remains are awaiting transfer to a German war cemetery.

987. Leutnant Georg SEELMANN

Seelmann was born on 4 February 1917 in Bamberg. He shot down his first two enemy aircraft over France in 1940 and took part in the Battle of Britain. In Russia, his score increased, reaching thirty on 9 August. However, on 30 August 1941, Seelaman's fighter was rammed by a Russian bomber and he was forced down behind enemy lines. He managed to make his way back to his unit on foot. With thirty-seven victories to his credit, he was awarded the Knight's Cross on 6 October 1941.

During the winter, he was sent to train new pilots and did not return to the front until August 1942. On 3 August, he was shot down by return fire from a bomber and he was wounded. Seelmann spent a month in hospital before returning in October 1942 to another unit. He fought in North Africa against the Allied landings; however, his wounds were not healing and he was home for further rest. With his total at thirty-nine victories, Seelmann ended the war training new units. He died on 18 September 1987 in Lichtenfels, Bavaria.

988. Unteroffizier Franz-Josef BEERENBROCK

Beerenbrock was born on 9 April 1920 in Datteln. He shot down his first enemy aircraft on 24 June 1941 and was awarded the Iron Cross 1st and 2nd Class in July 1941. Beerenbrock was awarded the Knight's Cross on 6 October 1941 and the Oak Leaves on 3 August 1942. With 117 victories (including twelve Sturmoviks) to his credit, he was shot down on 9 November 1942 and taken prisoner by the Russians. He was released in 1949. Beerenbrock died on 13 December 2004 in Olfen, North Rhine-Westphalia.

989. Leutnant zur See Rudolf PORATH

Porath was born on 22 March 1914 in Berlin. He was commander of patrol boat *VP-1806* in VP-Boat Flotilla 18 when he was awarded the Knight's Cross on 8 October 1941. Porath died on 9 September 1995 and is buried in Neuer Friedhof, Rostock, Mecklenburg-Vorpommern.

990. Oberst Horst von WOLFF

Von Wolff was born on 26 July 1886 in Rosenberg. He was commander of Infantry Regiment 478 when he was killed in action on 10 October 1941 at Woroniski, Russia, and he has no known grave. Wolff was awarded the Knight's Cross the same day.

991. *Hauptmann* Helmut BODE

Bode was born on 15 October 1907 in Metz. He took part in the Campaign in the West and the Battle of Britain as a Stuka pilot. Bode also fought in the Balkans and Russia. He was awarded the Knight's Cross on 10 October 1941.

In September 1942, he was sent to work on the *Graf Zeppelin* project, after which Bode was sent to train new pilots. From August 1944 to January 1945, he was appointed liaison officer with the Bulgarian Army. Bode died on 13 April 1985 in Bielefeld, North Rhine-Westphalia.

992. *Oberleutnant* Johannes PFEIFFER

Pfeiffer was born on 8 December 1916 in Babst. He fought in Poland, France, the Battle of Britain, and in Russia. Pfeiffer was a squadron leader in (Stuka) Training Wing 1 when he was awarded the Knight's Cross on 10 October 1941. He died on 26 December 1994 and is believed to be buried in Waldfriedhof, Timmendorfer Strand, Schleswig-Holstein.

993. *Oberleutnant* Werner THIERFELDER

Thierfelder was born on 24 December 1915 in Berlin. He was a squadron leader in Heavy Fighter Wing 26 when he was awarded the Knight's Cross on 10 October 1941. Thierfelder was killed when his Me 262 jet fighter was shot down over Landsberg am Lech on 18 July 1944. He has no known grave. Allied records show no victories to match this, so it is possible his aircraft suffered engine or structural failure. Thierfelder is credited with twenty-seven victories.

994. Oberfeldwebel Wilhelm BEIER

Beier was born on 18 November 1913 in Homberg. He was a pilot in Night Fighter Wing 2 when he was awarded the Knight's Cross on 10 October 1941. Beier is credited with thirty-eight enemy aircraft shot down—all at night. He died on 12 July 1977 and is buried in Repelen Friedhof, Moers, Rhineland-Palatinate.

995. Gefreiter Herbert STÖCKERT

Stöckert was born on 19 January 1920 in Neuzelle. He was a machine-gunner in Motorised Infantry Regiment 156 when he died of wounds on 4 October 1941 and is buried in the German War Cemetery, Block 8, Row 40, Grave 3915, Kharkov, Ukraine. Stöckert was awarded the Knight's Cross on 10 October 1941.

996. Generalleutnant Hans BEHLENDORFF

Behlendorff was born on 13 August 1889 in Allenstein. He fought in the First World War and was awarded the Iron Cross 1st and 2nd Class (1914). Behlendorff was awarded the Iron Cross 1st and 2nd Class (1939) after the fall of Poland. He was commander of the 34th Infantry Division when he was awarded the Knight's Cross on 11 October 1941. Behlendorff died on 16 March 1961 and is buried in Hauptfriedhof, Baden Baden, Baden-Württemberg.

997. Oberst Curt BADINSKI

Badinski was born on 17 May 1890 in Grebenstein. He fought in the First World War and was awarded the Iron Cross 1st and 2nd Class (1914). Badinski was awarded the Iron Cross 1st and 2nd Class (1939) after the fall of France. He was commander of Infantry Regiment 489 when he was awarded the Knight's Cross on 11 October 1941. Badinski was captured in the Falaise Pocket in August 1944. He died on 27 February 1966 and is buried in Parkfriedhof, Dept. 4, Feld E/R 15, Grave 9–10, Sandkrugerstrasse 26, Oldenburg, Lower Saxony.

998. Oberst Erhard RAUS

Raus was born on 8 January 1889 in Wolframitz, Austria-Hungary. He fought in the First World War. Raus was on the staff during the Polish and French campaigns. He commanded the 6th Motorised Infantry Brigade for the invasion of Russia, breaking through the Stalin Line and fighting alone for several days after capturing a bridgehead over the Luga Riverm for which he was awarded the Knight's Cross on 11 October 1941. He fought all through the winter ballets as commander of the 6th Panzer Division, and he was sent to France for rest and refit in April 1942.

Back on the Russian Front in November 1942, his division was heading for Stalingrad; during this time, with other units, his division smacked the Russian 2nd Guards Army. In 1943, he fought at Kharkov and Kursk, where his unit formed the rear guard. For his fighting during his time, he was awarded the Oak Leaves on 22 August 1943. He continued to fight until released of his command by Hitler when the Russians crossed the German border. Raus died from lung disease on 3 April 1956 and is buried Zentralfriedhof, Vienna.

999. Oberst Rudolf Freiherr von WALDENFELS

Freiherr von Waldenfels was born on 23 September 1895 in Ingolstadt. He fought in the First World War and was awarded the Iron Cross 1st and 2nd Class (1914). Von Waldenfels was awarded the Iron Cross 1st and 2nd Class (1939) after the fall of Poland.

He was commander of Rifle Regiment 4 when he was awarded the Knight's Cross on 11 October 1941. The Oak Leaves followed on 14 May 1944 when he was commanding the 6th Panzer Division. Von Waldenfels died on 14 August 1969 in Rottach-Egern, Bavaria.

1000. *Major* Willi BUNZEL

Bunzel was born on 13 November 1899 in Leignitz. He was commander of III Battalion, Infantry Regiment 426, when he was awarded the Knight's Cross on 11 October 1941. Bunzel died of wounds on 25 October 1941 and is buried at Malaja Wischera, Russia; his remains are awaiting transfer to a German war cemetery.

1001. *Hauptmann* Fritz RÄTZEL

Rätzel was born on 5 June 1895 in Rödlitz. He was a company commander in Rifle Regiment 86 when he was awarded the Knight's Cross on 11 October 1941. Rätzel died of wounds in Gagarin, Russia, on 26 October 1941. He has no known grave.

1002. *Hauptmann* Adolf WOLF

Wolf was born on 27 April 1904 in Schladen. He was commander of I Battalion, Infantry Regiment 431, when he was awarded the Knight's Cross on 11 October 1941. Wolf was killed in action on 25 December 1944 and is buried in the German War Cemetery, Block O, Row 26, Grave 1141, Saldus, Latvia.

1003. Leutnant Hans KÜRSTEN

Kürsten was born on 29 March 1917 in Pegau. He was a platoon leader in Panzer Regiment 7 when he was awarded the Knight's Cross on 11 October 1941. Kürsten was killed in action on 6 December 1942 and is buried in the German War Cemetery, Court NAS Ossario 11, Panel 19, Bordj-Cedria, Tunisia.

1004. Gefreiter Sebastian REISER

Reiser was born on 14 August 1918 in Kutzenhausen. He was a gunner in Artillery Regiment 297 when he was awarded the Knight's Cross on 11 October 1941. Reiser died of wounds on 1 February 1943 at Stalingrad and has no known grave.

1005. General Friedrich KOCH

Koch was born on 15 January 1879 in Odenkirchen. He fought in the First World War and was awarded the Iron Cross 1st and 2nd Class (1914). Koch was commander of XXXXIV Army Corps when he was awarded the Knight's Cross on 13 October 1941. He died on 3 November 1961 and is buried in Kessenich Friedhof, Feld A16, Grave 78–80, Bonn.

1006. Generalleutnant Sigfrid HENRICI

Henrici was born on 10 May 1889 in Soest. He fought in the First World War and was awarded the Iron Cross 1st and 2nd Class (1914). Henrici was awarded the Iron Cross 2nd Class (1939) after the fall of Poland and the 1st Class in May 1940. He was commander of the 16th Motorised Infantry Division when he was awarded the Knight's Cross on 13 October 1941.

Henrici spent a short time on the reserve due to illness during October and November 1943 but was awarded the Oak Leaves on 9 December 1943. He was captured by the Russians in May 1945 and not released until 1955. Henrici died on 8 November 1964 and is buried in Bad Nauheim Friedhof, Hesse.

1007. Generalmajor Wilhelm BOHNSTEDT

Bohnstedt was born on 5 October 1888 in Schmarsow. He fought in the First World War and was awarded the Iron Cross 1st and 2nd Class (1914). Bohnstedt was awarded the Iron Cross 1st and 2nd Class (1939) after the fall of Poland. He was commander of the 32nd Infantry Divison when he was awarded the Knight's Cross on 13 October 1941. Bohnstedt died on 11 August 1947 in Hamelin, Lower Saxony.

1008. Oberst Ulrich KLEEMANN

Kleemann was born on 23 March 1892 in Langensalza. He fought in the First World War, being awarded the Iron Cross 1st and 2nd Class (1914). Kleemann took part in the Polish and French campaigns and was awarded the Iron Cross 1st and 2nd Class (1939). In Russia, he was awarded the Knight's Cross on 13 October 1941 and was promoted to *Generalmajor* in November.

In April 1942, Kleemann was sent to Africa where he showed that he was an aggressive commander. Wounded during the advance to El Alamein,

Rommel recommended him for the Oak Leaves, which was awarded on 16 September 1943. Kleemann was back in action in Rhodes and played a major part in defeating the Italians rebels. On 1 April 1944, he assumed command of IV Panzer Corps and led it until the end of the war. Kleemann died on 1 January 1963 and is buried in Stadtfriedhof, Feld 23, Grave 14–15, Oberursel, Hesse.

1009. Oberst Wilhelm THOMAS

Thomas was born on 8 October 1892 in Minden. He fought in the First World War and was awarded the Iron Cross 1st and 2nd Class (1914). Thomas was commander of Infantry Regiment 71 when he was awarded the Knight's Cross on 13 October 1941. He died on 24 August 1976 and is believed to be buried in Waldfriedhof, Hamelin, Lower Saxony.

1010. Oberstleutnant Walter HEROLD

Herold was born on 10 August 1897 in Weiden in der Oberpfalz. He fought in the First World War and was awarded the Iron Cross 1st and 2nd Class (1914). Herold was commander of Motorised Artillery Regiment 10 when he was awarded the Knight's Cross on 13 October 1941. He was killed in action by partisans at Bochnia, Poland, on 28 November 1944 and has no known grave.

1011. Oberstleutnant Heinrich KREIPE

Kreipe was born on 5 June 1895 in Niederspier. He fought in the First World War and was awarded the Iron Cross 1st and 2nd Class (1914). Kreipe was commander of Infantry Regiment 209 when he was awarded the Knight's Cross on 13 October 1941.

Sent to Crete in March 1944, he was kidnapped on 26 April by British Major Patrick Leigh Fermor and Captain Bill Stanley Moss, aided by Greek SOE agents and resistance fighters. In an epic journey lasting over two weeks, and with German soldiers searching the island, he was moved across the mountains and taken to Egypt. In 1950, Moss wrote a bestselling book about the operation called *Ill Met by Moonlight*, which was made into a film of the same name, starring Dirk Bogarde, in 1957. Kreipe met his kidnappers again in a 1972 Greek TV show. He died on 14 June 1976 and is buried in Ricklinger Friedhof, Hanover.

1012. *Major* Gottfried WEBER

Weber was born on 31 January 1899 in Breslau. He fought in the latter part of the First World War. Weber was awarded the Iron Cross 1st and 2nd Class after the fall of Poland in 1939. He was commander of I Battalion, Infantry Regiment 162, when he was awarded the Knight's Cross on 13 October 1941. The Oak Leaves followed on 9 June 1944. Weber was captured by the Russians in May 1945 and held for ten years. He died in a car crash on 16 August 1958 in Villach, Austria.

1013. *Hauptmann* Otto FONDERMANN

Fondermann was born on 31 December 1905 in Mülheim. He was commander of II Battalion, Rifle Regiment 79, when he was awarded the Knight's Cross on 13 October 1941. Fondermann died on 5 April 1980 in Düsseldorf.

1014. SS-Obersturmführer Fritz RENTROP

Rentrop was born on 19 November 1917 in Münster. He was a company commander in SS-Flak Battalion 2 when he was awarded the Knight's Cross on 13 October 1941. Rentrop was posted missing in Hungary on 2 February 1945 and is believed to have been executed by the Russians.

1015. *Oberleutnant* Wolfgang RYLL

Ryll was born on 24 January 1915 in Marienwerder. He was a company commander in Panzer Regiment 7 when he was awarded the Knight's Cross on 13 October 1941. Ryll was killed in action on 21 January 1942 and has no known grave.

1016. *Oberleutnant* Werner TENNHARDT

Tennhardt was born on 26 November 1915 in Deuben. He was adjutant of Infantry Regiment 446 when he was killed in action near Livny, Russia, on 11 October 1941. He has no known grave. Tennhardt was awarded the Knight's Cross two days later.

1017. *Oberleutnant* Hermann WULF

Wulf was born in Eichede on 25 July 1915. He fought in Poland, being awarded the Iron Cross 2nd Class, and in the West, for which he was awarded the Iron Cross 1st Class. Next Wulf took part in the invasion of Russia, on the northern front, where his regiment was able to relieve an encircled battalion. For this, he was awarded the Knight's Cross on 13 October 1941.

Badly wounded in January 1942, Wulf did not return to the front until April 1943. He fought at Kursk during the summer and was again badly wounded, this time in the knee, but he refused to leave his men on this occasion. In early 1944, his regiment was nearly cut off, but by skilful manoeuvring, Wulf managed to get this men back to the German lines. For this, he was awarded the Oak Leaves on 3 July 1944. He was also awarded the Close Combat Clasp in Gold and the Wound badge in Gold. In the Ardennes Offensive, he commanded a *Kampfgruppe* in Panzer Brigade 150. This unit was equipped with American vehicles and German vehicles modified to look American. Their mission was to work behind the Allied lines. After the failure of the attack, Wulf was moved back to the Eastern Front in Pomerania. Badly wounded yet again—although reports that he lost a leg proved untrue—Wulf was captured by the Russians; he soon escaped, however. He died on 19 May 1990 and is believed to be buried in Friedhof Friedrichsgabe, Norderstedt, Schleswig-Holstein.

1018. Leutnant Gustav-Adolf BURSCHE

Bursche was born on 27 September 1918 in Eberswalde. He was a company commander in Infantry Regiment 90 when he was awarded the Knight's Cross on 13 October 1941. He died on 4 July 2005 and is buried in Ohlsdorf Friedhof, Fuhlsbüttler Strasse, Hamburg.

1019. Oberwachtmeister Paul GOLBACH

Golbach was born on 14 July 1915 in Kirchhasel. He was a platoon leader in Artillery Regiment 263 when he was awarded the Knight's Cross on 13 October 1941. Golbach died on 15 October 2004 and is buried in Zentralfriedhof, Fulda, Hesse.

1020. Oberfeldwebel Ernst SANDER

Sander was born on 22 September 1913 in Schliestedt. He was a platoon leader in Rifle Regiment 79 when he was awarded the Knight's Cross on 13

October 1941. Sander was killed in action near Mius, Russia, on 16 February 1942 and has no known grave.

1021. Unteroffizier Walter WEBER

Weber was born on 23 December 1908 in Hemstedt. He was a platoon leader in Infantry Regiment 211 when he was awarded the Knight's Cross on 13 October 1941. Weber was posted missing near Soborowje, Russia, on 19 July 1944.

1022. *Oberleutnant* Richard GRÜNERT

Grünert was born on 8 October 1899 in Ströbel. He was a company commander in Motorcycle Battalion 7 when he was awarded the Knight's Cross on 14 October 1941. Grünert was killed in action on 13 March 1943 and is buried in the German War Cemetery, Block 5, Row 12, Grave 983, Kharkov, Ukraine. He was awarded the Oak Leaves on 17 May 1943.

1023. Oberst Johann RAITHEL

Raithel was born on 11 March 1897 in Munich. He fought in the First World War and was awarded the Iron Cross 1st and 2nd Class (1914). Raithel was a *Kommodore* in Bomber Wing 77 when he was awarded the Knight's Cross on 17 October 1941. He died on 29 January 1961 in Hamburg.

1024. *Major* Viktor von LOSSBERG

Von Lossberg was born in Posen on 14 March 1904. He was a group commander in Bomber Wing 26 when he was awarded the Knight's Cross on 17 October 1941. Von Lossberg died on 24 May 1983 and is buried in Stadtfriedhof, Garmisch-Partenkirchen, Bavaria.

1025. *Hauptmann* Josef PIZALA

Pazala was born on 28 May 1911 in Kleinenberg. He was a company commander in Motorised Flak Regiment 111 when he died of wounds on 14 October 1941 and is buried in the German War Cemetery, Block 11, Row 43,

Grave 4856, Sologubowka, Russia. Pazala was awarded the Knight's Cross on 17 October 1941.

1026. *Hauptmann* Ernst-Siegfried STEEN

Steen was born on 25 September 1912 in Kiel. He was a Stuka pilot when he was awarded the Iron Cross 2nd Class after the fall of Poland and the 1st Class after the fall of France. Steen also took part in the Battle of Britain. He was killed in action by anti-aircraft fire over Kronstadt harbour on 23 September 1941 and has no known grave. Steen was awarded the Knight's Cross on 17 October 1941.

1027. Leutnant Franz EVERS

Evers was born on 17 January 1911 in Cologne. He was a pilot in Long Range Reconnaissance Group 121 when he was awarded the Knight's Cross on 17 October 1941. Evers died on 19 April 1991 in Cologne, North Rhine-Westphalia.

1028. General Walter KUNTZE

Kuntze was born on 23 February 1883 in Pritzerbe. He fought in the First World War and was awarded the Iron Cross 1st and 2nd Class (1914). Kuntze was commander of XXXXII Army Corps when he was awarded the Knight's Cross on 18 October 1941. Captured by the Allies at the end of the war, he was triad for war crimes and sentenced to life, but he was released in 1953 due to bad health. Kuntze died on 1 April 1960 and is buried in Waldfriedhof, Detmold, North Rhine-Westphalia.

1029. Generalleutnant Kurt HERZOG

Herzog was born on 27 March 1889 in Quedlinburg. He fought in the First World War and was awarded the Iron Cross 1st and 2nd Class (1914). Herzog was awarded the Iron Cross 1st and 2nd Class (1939) after the fall of Poland. He was commander of the 291st Infantry Division when he was awarded the Knight's Cross on 18 October 1941. The Oak Leaves followed on 12 January 1945. Herzog was captured by the Russians in May 1945 and died at Workuta on 8 May 1948 while still a POW; he has no known grave.

1030. Generalmajor Ernst DEHNER

Dehner was born on 5 March 1889 in Hersbruck. He fought in the First World War and was awarded the Iron Cross 1st and 2nd Class (1914). Dehner was awarded the Iron Cross 1st and 2nd Class after the fall of Poland.

He was commander of the 106th Infantry Division when he was awarded the Knight's Cross on 18 October 1941. Dehner was sentenced to seven years' imprisonment for war crimes but was released after serving three years. He died on 13 September 1970 and is buried in Nordfriedhof, Feld A 06, North Side, Grave 9–10, Wiesbaden, Hesse.

1031. Oberst Martin GRASE

Grase was born on 3 May 1891 in Schlochau. He fought in the First World War and was awarded the Iron Cross 1st and 2nd Class (1914). Grase was awarded the Iron Cross 2nd Class (1939) after the fall of Poland and the 1st Class after the fall of France.

He was commander of Infantry Regiment 1 when he was awarded the Knight's Cross on 18 October 1941. The Oak Leaves followed on 23 May 1943. Grase died on 4 August 1963 in Freilburg im Breisgau, Baden-Württemberg.

1032. *Major* Richard LAUKAT

Laukat was born on 3 August 1902 in Alt-Ballupönen. He was commander of II Battalion, Artillery Regiment 103, when he was awarded the Knight's Cross on 18 October 1941. Laukat was killed in action near Beresina, Russia, on 5 July 1944 and has no known grave.

1033. *Major* Max LEMKE

Lemke was born on 7 April 1895 in Schwedt. He fought in the First World War and was awarded the Iron Cross 1st and 2nd Class (1914). Lemke was commander of Reconnaissance Battalion 7 when he was awarded the Knight's Cross on 18 October 1941. He died on 29 May 1985 and is buried in Stadtfriedhof, Feld A20, Grave 162–163 (headstone removed), Seelhorst, Hanover.

1034. *Major* Hans REINHARDT

Reinhardt was born on 10 July 1905 in Hameln. He was commander of I Battalion, Artillery Regiment 241, when he died of wounds on 4 September 1941 and is buried in the German War Cemetery, Block 24, Row 15, Grave 886, Duchowschitschina, Russia. Reinhardt was awarded the Knight's Cross on 18 October 1941.

1035. *Oberleutnant* Günter GOEBEL

Goebel was born on 14 November 1917 in Hagen. He first saw action in 1939 against French troops on the Saar Front and was awarded the Iron Cross 2nd Class in November. In May 1940, Goebel took part in the campaign in the West and was awarded the Iron Cross 1st Class. He also fought in the Balkans and the invasion of Russia.

He was awarded the Knight's Cross on 18 October 1941 for his part in capturing/cutting off a supply route for the Russian Army. Severely wounded in February 1942, he was away from the front for two months. In May 1942, he was appointed to the staff in the Stalingrad area, but in December, he commanded a *Kampfgruppe* in the Don bridgehead. For this, he was awarded the Oak Leaves on 18 January 1943. Wounded again just two weeks later, Goebel returned to the front in time for the Kursk offensive. He spent most of the remainder of the war in staff or quartermaster posts, but he did command a regiment near the end of the war and was captured by the Russians, who held him for two years. Goebel died on 4 September 1993 and is buried in Stadtfriedhof, Kuhlestrasse, Hagen, North Rhine-Westphalia.

1036. *Oberleutnant* Franz MILLONIG

Millonig was born on 2 October 1914 in Villach. He was a company commander in Panzer Pioneer Battalion 57 when he was awarded the Knight's Cross on 18 October 1941. Millonig was posted missing near Ržev, Russia, on 12 January 1942.

1037. Leutnant Wilhelm HÜMMERICH—'Willi'

Hümmerich was born 22 July 1917 in Ehlscheid. He was a platoon leader in Infantry Regiment 80 when he was awarded the Knight's Cross on 18 October 1941. Hümmerich died on 17 July 2008 and is believed to be buried in Hauptfriedhof, Am Gottesacker 25, Dortmund, North Rhine-Westphalia.

1038. Leutnant Heinz-Jürgen LÜTJE

Lütje was born on 21 June 1918 in Hamburg. He was a company commander in Motorised Infantry Regiment 76 when he was awarded the Knight's Cross on 18 October 1941. Lütje was killed in action near Leningrad on 14 November 1941 and has no known grave.

1039. Oberfeldwebel Wilhelm-August (aka Erich) VIELWERTH

Vielwerth was born on 10 February 1912 in Büdingen. He fought in France, for which he was awarded Iron Cross 2nd Class for destroying enemy bunkers. Vielwerth was a platoon leader in Motorised Infantry Regiment 87 when he was awarded the Knight's Cross on 18 October 1941 for personally destroying several enemy bunkers. He died on 13 August 1997 in Büdingen, Hesse.

1040. Feldwebel Karl HIRSCH

Hirsch was born on 16 September 1914 in Dortmund. He was a platoon leader in Rifle Regiment 4 when he was awarded the Knight's Cross on 18 October 1941. Hirsch was killed in action on 3 December 1941 and is buried at Jasikowo, Klin, Russia; his remains are awaiting transfer to a German war cemetery.

1041. Unteroffizier Heinz FRITSCH

Fritsch was born on 22 December 1920 in Luckenau. He was serving in Panzer Pioneer Battalion 37 when he was awarded the Knight's Cross on 18 October 1941. Fritsch died of wounds on 5 July 1945 and is buried in the German War Cemetery, Grave 17, St Johann, Kitzbuhel, Austria.

1042. Unteroffizier Alois ZMUGG

Zmugg was born on 5 August 1905 in Graz, Austria-Hungary. He was serving in Rifle Regiment 114 when he was awarded the Knight's Cross on 18 October 1941. Zmugg died on 10 December 1975 and is buried in Zentralfriedhof, Graz, Austria.

1043. Gefreiter Heinrich SCHULZ (or SCHULTZ)

Schulz was born on 9 November 1919 in Josefow. He was a flamethrower operator in Pioneer Battalion 161 when he was awarded the Knight's Cross on 18 October 1941. Schulz was posted missing at Konin on 18 January 1945.

1044. SS-Oberführer Max SIMON

Simon was born on 16 January 1899 in Breslau. He fought in the First World War and was awarded the Iron Cross 2nd Class (1914). Simon was awarded the Iron Cross 1st and 2nd Class (1939) after the fall of Poland. He fought in France and Russia. Simon was awarded the Knight's Cross on 20 October 1941 for his part in capturing large numbers of prisoners and equipment south of Lake Ilmen.

In 1944, his division was moved to Italy and fought at Anzio and later Arno. The division also fought partisans in the Rückraum area, where men under his command carried out massacre of civilians at St Anna di Stazzema and Marzabotto. Simon was awarded the Oak Leaves on 28 October 1944. He was captured by US forces in May 1945 and tried for the Italian massacre. Simon was sentenced to death but this was changed to life. However, he was pardoned in 1954. Simon died on 1 February 1961 in Lünen, North Rhine-Westphalia.

1045. *Hauptmann* Jürgen von GOERNE-PLAUE

Von Goerne-Plaue was born on 12 February 1908 in Allenstein. He was commander of Motorised Reconnaissance Battalion 29 when he was awarded the Knight's Cross on 20 October 1941. Von Goerne-Plaue died on 3 March 2001 and is buried in Stadtfriedhof, Rottach-Egern, Bavaria.

1046. *Oberleutnant* Peter-Paul PLINZNER

Plinzner was born on 19 December 1915 in Berlin. He was a company commander in Panzer Regiment 27 when he died of wounds near Moscow on 17 October 1941 and has no known grave. Plinzner was awarded the Knight's Cross on 20 October 1941.

1047. Leutnant Ekkehard KYLLING-SCHMIDT

Kylling-Schmidt was born in Flensburg on 21 June 1918. He fought in Poland and France. Kylling-Schmidt also took part in the invasion of Russia. He was awarded the Knight's Cross on 20 October 1941 for his command of a company in the early part of the invasion.

His regiment was encircled at Demjansk and remained in the pocket for over a year before breaking-out. It was for this that he was awarded the Oak Leaves on 4 December 1942. Seriously wounded in October 1943, he was sent home. On recovery, he was posted to a staff training school in Berlin. He was taken prisoner in 1945 by the Western Allies but soon released. Kylling-Schmidt died on 28 August 2000 and is buried in Hauptfriedhof, Koblenz, Rhineland-Palatinate.

1048. SS-Sturmmann Fritz CHRISTEN

Christen was born on 29 June 1921 in Wredenhagen. He saw action in the invasion of Russia and was awarded the Iron Cross 2nd Class in July 1941. On 24 September 1941, when all the other members of his unit had been killed or wounded, Christen knocked-out thirteen Russian tanks while manning his anti-tank gun alone. He held this position for three days; he is also credited with killing nearly 100 enemy soldiers. For this action, Christen was immediately awarded the Iron Cross 1st Class; the Knight's Cross followed on 20 October 1941.

He served with distinction throughout the remainder of the war and surrendered to US forces in the spring of 1945, but he was handed over to the Russians. He was released in 1955. Christen died on 23 September 1995 and is buried in Neusorg Friedhof, Bavaria.

1049. *Major* Oskar BAUER

Bauer was born on 13 March 1900 in Mannheim. He fought in the First World War and was awarded the Iron Cross 2nd Class (1914). Bauer was awarded the Iron Cross 2nd Class (1939) after the fall of Poland and the 1st Class after the fall of France.

He was commander of II Battalion, Flak Regiment 4, when he was awarded the Knight's Cross on 22 October 1941. Bauer died on 20 January 1975 and is buried in Südwest Friedhof, Essen, North Rhine-Westphalia.

1050. *Oberleutnant* Joseph BISPING

Bisping was born on 22 March 1913 in Emsdetten. He was an observer in Reconnaissance Group 4 when he was awarded the Knight's Cross on 22 October 1941. Bisping was killed in a flying accident on 13 February 1945 near Oranienburg, Brandenburg, and has no known grave.

1051. *Oberleutnant* Cornelius NOËLL

Noëll was born on 29 March 1909 in Berlin. He was a pilot in Reconnaissance Group 4 when he was awarded the Knight's Cross on 22 October 1941. Noëll died on 8 July 1985 in Berlin.

1052. Generalleutnant Kurt von der CHEVALLERIE

Von der Chevallerie was born on 23 December 1891 in Berlin. He fought in the First World War and was awarded the Iron Cross 1st and 2nd Class (1914). Von der Chevallerie was awarded the Iron Cross 1st and 2nd Class (1939) after the fall of France. He was commander of the 99th Light Infantry Division when he was awarded the Knight's Cross on 23 October 1941. The Oak Leaves followed on 19 December 1943 as commander of LIX Army Corps. Von der Chevallerie was placed on the reserve list in January 1945 and disappeared near Kolberg on 18 April 1945. His brother, Hellmut, was also awarded the Knight's Cross. Kurt's only son, Hans-Rudolf, was killed in action in 1940.

1053. Generalmajor Karl EGLSEER

Eglseer was born on 5 July 1890 in Bad Ischl, Austria-Hungary. He fought in the First World War. Eglseer was commander of the 4th *Jäger* Division when he was awarded the Knight's Cross on 23 October 1941. He was killed along with Eduard Dietl, Thomas-Emil Von Wickede, and Franz Rossi when his aircraft crashed near Hartberg, Austria, on 23 June 1944. Eglseer is buried in St Ruprecht Friedhof, Klagenfurt, Austria.

1054. Oberstleutnant Ludwig RUEDERER

Ruederer was born on 31 May 1894 in Munich. He was commander of Infantry Regiment 332 when he was awarded the Knight's Cross on

23 October 1941. Ruederer died on 12 September 1960 in Siggenham, Bavaria.

1055. *Hauptmann* Hans WACK

Wack was born on 19 March 1905 in Kusel. He was commander of II Battalion, Infantry Regiment 485, when he was awarded the Knight's Cross on 23 October 1941. Wack was killed in action near Mogilev, Russia, on 28 June 1944 and has no known grave.

1056. *Oberleutnant* Karl-Otto LEUKEFELD

Leukefeld was born on 1 May 1913 in Wiesbaden. He was a company commander in Infantry Regiment 123 when he was awarded the Knight's Cross on 23 October 1941. Leukefeld died on 24 May 2008 and is buried in Stadtfriedhof, Celle, Lower Saxony.

1057. Leutnant Paul BRUCHER

Brucher was born on 11 September 1916 in Villingen. He was awarded the Iron Cross 2nd Class in December 1939 and the 1st Class in August 1941. Brucher was a platoon leader in Infantry Regiment 447 when he was awarded the Knight's Cross on 23 October 1941. He died on 18 March 1977 and is buried in Waldfriedhof, Singen, Baden-Württemberg.

1058. Leutnant Hans-Ulrich FISCHER

Fischer was born on 26 March 1914 in Hameln. He was a company commander in Infantry Regiment 431 when he was awarded the Knight's Cross on 23 October 1941. Fischer was killed in action on 14 November 1941 near Kaluga, Russia, and has no known grave.

1059. Leutnant Hans-Hermann SASSENBERG

Sassenberg was born on 20 March 1919 in Osnabrück. He was a platoon leader in Panzer Reconnaissance Battalion 13 when he was awarded the Knight's Cross on 23 October 1941. Sassenberg was killed in action near Zhdanov, Russia, on 25 October 1943 and has no known grave.

1060. Oberfeldwebel Rudolf SCHLEE

Schlee was born on 10 November 1913 in Ludwigshafen. He was awarded the Iron Cross 1st and 2nd Class after the fall of France. Schlee was a platoon leader in Mountain *Jäger* Regiment 13 when he awarded the Knight's Cross on 23 October 1941. The Oak Leaves followed on 6 April 1943. He was taken prisoner by the Russians in 1945 but released in 1947. Schlee died on 19 June 1979 and is buried in Hauptfriedhof, Ludwigshafen, Rhineland-Palatinate.

1061. Unteroffizier Willi BLUMENROTH

Blumenroth was born on 19 July 1919 in Langerfeld. He was awarded the Iron Cross 2nd Class on 15 June 1940 and the 1st Class on 21 September 1941. Blumenroth was a section leader in Infantry Regiment 124 when he was awarded the Knight's Cross on 23 October 1941. He was killed in action on 17 June 1942 and is believed to be buried in the German War Cemetery (as unknown), Sebastopol, Ukraine.

1062. Generalleutnant Bruno BIELER

Bieler was born on 18 June 1888 in Gumbinnen. He fought in the First World War and was awarded the Iron Cross 1st and 2nd Class (1914). Bieler was awarded the Iron Cross 1st and 2nd Class (1939) after the fall of Poland. Bieler was commander of the 73rd Infantry Division when he was awarded the Knight's Cross on 26 October 1941. He died on 22 March 1966 and is buried in Dorfmark Friedhof, Bad Fallingbostel, Lower Saxony.

1063. Generalleutnant Willi MOSER

Moser was born on 2 November 1887 in Breslau. He fought in the First World War and was awarded the Iron Cross 1st and 2nd Class (1914). Moser was commander of the 299th Infantry Division when he was awarded the Knight's Cross on 26 October 1941. He was captured by the Russians in 1945 and died while a POW near Kalinin on 16 October 1946 and has no known grave.

1064. Generalleutnant Karl STRECKER

Strecker was born on 20 September 1884 in Radmannsdorf. He fought in the First World War and was awarded the Iron Cross 1st and 2nd Class (1914). Strecker was awarded the Knight's Cross on 26 October 1941. He was captured at Stalingrad in February 1943 and held until 1955. Strecker died on 10 April 1973 in Riezlern, Austria.

1065. Generalleutnant Walther GRAESSNER

Graessner was born on 31 January 1891 in Magdeburg. He fought in the First World War and was awarded the Iron Cross 1st and 2nd Class (1914). Graessner was commander of the 298th Infantry Division when he was awarded the Knight's Cross on 27 October 1941. He was killed in action at Opava, Czechoslovakia, on 16 July 1943 and has no known grave.

1066. Generalmajor Heinrich THOMA

Thoma was born on 26 April 1891 in Nuremberg. He fought in the First World War and was awarded the Iron Cross 1st and 2nd Class (1914). Thoma was commander of Infantry Regiment 519 when he was awarded the Knight's Cross on 27 October 1941. He died while still in Russian hands on 30 October 1948 and is buried in the German War Cemetery, Row 5, Grave 2, Cherntsy, Russia.

1067. Oberst Wilhelm WEGENER

Wegener was born on 29 April 1895 in Trebatsch. He fought in the First World War and was awarded the Iron Cross 1st and 2nd Class (1914). Wegener was awarded the Iron Cross 2nd Class (1939) after the fall of Poland and the 1st Class after the fall of France. He was commander of Infantry Regiment 94 when he was awarded the Knight's Cross on 27 October 1941. The Oak Leaves followed on 19 January 1942 and the Swords on 17 September 1944. Wegener was killed in action on 24 September 1944 and is buried in the German War Cemetery (Forest Cemetery, Waldfriedhof) (as unknown), Riga, Latvia.

1068. *Hauptmann* Kurt LEUSCHNER

Leuschner was born on 11 August 1906 in Alt-Wohlau. He was commander of III Battalion, Rifle Regiment 25, when he was awarded the Knight's Cross on 27 October 1941. Leuschner died on 9 August 1970 in Kelkheim, Hesse.

1069. Leutnant Fritz FESSMANN

Fessmann was born on 25 December 1913 in Urbach. He was awarded the Iron Cross 2nd Class in May 1940 and the 1st Class in July 1941. Fessmann was a platoon leader in Panzer Reconnaissance Battalion 1 when he was awarded the Knight's Cross on 27 October 1941. The Oak Leaves followed on 4 January 1943. Fessmann was killed in action near Tilsit, Russia, on 11 October 1944 and has no known grave. He was awarded the Swords on 23 October 1944.

1070. Oberfeldwebel Hans LIMMER

Limmer was born on 7 October 1914 in Pilsting. He was a section leader in Panzer Reconnaissance Battalion 7 when he was awarded the Knight's Cross on 27 October 1941. Limmer was killed in action on 1 February 1945 and is buried at Debina, Poland; his remains are awaiting transfer to a German war cemetery.

1071. Oberst Karl GÜMBEL

Gümbel was born on 24 June 1888 in Finstingen. He fought in the First World War and was awarded the Iron Cross 1st and 2nd Class (1914). Gümbel was commander of Infantry Regiment 516 when he was awarded the Knight's Cross on 30 October 1941. He died on 28 October 1970 and is buried in Bergfriedhof, Heidelberg, Baden-Württemberg.

1072. Oberstleutnant Otto HITZFELD—'The Lion of Sebastopol'

Hitzfeld was born on 7 May 1898 in Schluchsee. He fought in the First World War and was awarded the Iron Cross 1st and 2nd Class (1914). Hitzfeld was awarded the Iron Cross 2nd Class (1939) in August 1940 and the 1st Class in August 1941. He was commander of Infantry Regiment 213 when he was awarded the Knight's Cross on 30 October 1941. The Oak Leaves followed on 17 January 1942. Hitzfeld was wounded for the fifth time in August 1942 and received the Wound Badge in Gold.

He was taken prisoner by the US Army in April 1945 and awarded the Swords on 9 May 1945 (this award was made in accordance with the Dönitz-Decree). Hitzfeld only learnt of the award of the Swords after the war. He died on 6 December 1990 and is buried in Stadtfriedhof, Feld 5, Border Row, Grave 99–100, Dossenheim, Baden-Württemberg.

1073. *Hauptmann* Walter KÖSTER

Köster was born on 2 December 1906 in Gelsenkirchen. He was commander of III Battalion, Motorised Infantry Regiment 156, when he was awarded the Knight's Cross on 30 October 1941. Köster was killed in action on the Don River, Russia, on 31 July 1942 and has no known grave.

1074. SS-Obersturmführer Gerhard (aka Gerd) BREMER

Bremer was born on 25 July 1917 in Düsternthal. He fought in Poland, for which he was awarded the Iron Cross 2nd Class in October 1939, and France, for which he was awarded the Iron Cross 1st Class in June 1940. Bremer took part in the invasion of Russia with his motorcycle company. During the early phase, his company captured 500 prisoners and a great deal of equipment. For this, he was awarded the Knight's Cross on 30 October 1941.

He stayed on the Russian Front until given command of a reconnaissance unit in the 12th SS-Panzer Division in Normandy. During the fighting, his unit fought its way out of the Falaise Pocket and Bremer was awarded the Oak Leaves on 26 November 1944. He also fought in the Ardennes Offensive, but ended the war in Hungary, surrendering to US forces. He was held by the French until 1947. Bremer died on 29 October 1989 and is buried in Cemiterio de Alicante, Spain.

1075. *Oberleutnant* Otto SCHMALZRIED

Schmalzried was born on 6 June 1914 in Wangen im Allgäu. He was a company commander in Infantry Regiment 419 when he was awarded the Knight's Cross on 30 October 1941. Schmalzried died on 22 February 1970 and is buried in Hoppenlau Friedhof, Stuttgart, Baden-Württemberg.

1076. *Oberleutnant* Jürgen NEUMANN

Neumann was born on 14 October 1915 in Gollnow. He was a company commander in Motorised Infantry Regiment 5 when he was awarded the Knight's Cross on 1 November 1941. Neumann was killed in action on 19 July 1943 and is buried in the German War Cemetery (as unknown), Kursk-Besedino, Russia.

1077. Generalmajor Stephan RITTAU

Rittau was born on 27 December 1891 in Wongrowitz. He fought in the First World War and was awarded the Iron Cross 1st and 2nd Class (1914). Rittau was commander of the 129th Infantry Division when he was awarded the Knight's Cross on 2 November 1941. Rittau was killed in action at Rzhev, Russia, on 22 August 1942 and has no known grave.

1078. Oberst Erwin JOLLASSE

Jollasse was born on 8 December 1892 in Hamburg. He fought in the First World War in the infantry and as a pilot observer, being awarded the Iron Cross 1st and 2nd Class (1914). Jollasse took part in the Campaign in the West and was awarded the Iron Cross 1st and 2nd Class (1939) in June 1940. At Kiev in Russia, he closed the pocket on the enemy forces and for this was awarded the Knight's Cross on 2 November 1941.

Jollasse was wounded a number of times and received the Wound Badge in Gold. He was declared unfit for front-line duty in late 1944 and was given a desk job at the inspectorate of panzer troops. In March 1945, he was given command of the 244th *Volksgrenadier* Division in Czechoslovakia—a command he held until the end of the war. Jollasse died on 14 March 1987 in Tutzing, Bavaria.

1079. Oberst Karl PHILIPPI

Philippi was born on 22 April 1894 in Saargemünd. He was commander of Infantry Regiment 207 when he was killed in action at Artemowsk, Russia, on 30 October 1941; he has no known grave. Philippi was awarded the Knight's Cross on 2 November 1941.

1080. *Hauptmann* Gerhard PICK

Pick was born on 17 November 1910 in Graudenz. He was awarded the Iron Cross 1st and 2nd Class in June and July 1941. Pick was commander of II Battalion, Infantry Regiment 490, when he was awarded the Knight's Cross on 2 November 1941. The Oak Leaves followed on 19 August 1944. Pick died on 11 May 1987 in Dortmund, North Rhine-Westphalia.

1081. *Oberleutnant* Walter BIRK

Birk was born on 31 October 1913 in Nagold. He was a company commander in Divisions Reconnaissance Battalion 44 when he was awarded the Knight's Cross on 2 November 1941. Birk died on 24 July 1967 and is buried in Tamm Friedhof, Baden-Württemberg.

1082. Oberstleutnant Botho von FRANTZIUS

Von Frantzius was born on 9 August 1898 in Sawdin. He was commander of Reconnaissance Battalion 161 when he was awarded the Knight's Cross on 4 November 1941. Von Frantzius was killed in action on 11 December 1942 and is buried at Nevel, Russia; his remains are awaiting transfer to a German war cemetery.

1083. Oberstleutnant Fritz KÖHLER

Köhler was born on 14 November 1897 in Derby, England. He was commander of Long Range Reconnaissance Group 122 when he was awarded the Knight's Cross on 4 November 1941. Köhler died on 20 February 1949 in Ulm, Baden-Württemberg.

1084. *Major* Alexander LESCHKE

Leschke was born on 5 February 1889 in Strasbourg. He fought in the First World War and was awarded the Iron Cross 1st and 2nd Class (1914). Leschke was commander of II Battalion, Motorised Infantry Regiment 11, when he was awarded the Knight's Cross on 4 November 1941. He was killed in action on 7 December 1942 and is buried in the German War Cemetery (Südfriedhof), Dept. XXV, Group II, Grave 7–8, Friedhofsweg 3, Leipzig.

1085. Rittmeister Adolf WEITKUNAT

Weitkunat was born on 7 February 1895 in Grünfliess. He fought in the First World War and was awarded the Iron Cross 1st and 2nd Class (1914). Weitkunat was commander of Reconnaissance Squadron 206 when he was awarded the Knight's Cross on 4 November 1941. The Oak Leaves followed on 5 December 1943. He died on 28 June 1988 in Buchholz, Thuringia.

1086. *Oberleutnant* Horst KRÜGER

Krüger was born on 23 May 1916 in Altona. He was an observer in Night Reconnaissance Squadron 3 when he was awarded the Knight's Cross on 4 November 1941. Krüger died on 7 April 1989 and is buried in Hauptfriedhof, Friedhofstrasse 8, Freilburg im Breisgau, Baden-Württemberg.

1087. *Oberleutnant* Joachim LÜTZOW

Lützow was born on 8 November 1913 in Bautzen. He was commander of Assault-Gun Battery 667 when he was awarded the Knight's Cross on 4 November 1941. Lützow died on 18 August 1998 in Remagen, Rhineland-Palatinate.

1088. *Oberleutnant* Georg MICHALEK

Michalek was born on 17 June 1913 in Vienna. He was a squadron leader in Fighter Wing 3 when he was awarded the Knight's Cross on 4 November 1941. Michalek is credited with shooting down between fifty-nine and sixty-two enemy aircraft. He died on 2 September 1992 and is believed to be buried in San Paulo Cemiterio, Brazil.

1089. *Oberleutnant* Hans-Joachim SCHIBAU

Schibau was born on 17 November 1915 in Marienwerder. He took part in the Spanish Civil War. Schibau was awarded Iron Cross 2nd Class in December 1940 and the 1st Class in August 1941. He was a company commander in Flak Regiment 36 when he was awarded the Knight's Cross on 4 November 1941. Schibau died on 22 July 1985 in Burgdorf, Hanover.

1090. Feldwebel Walter OHLROGGE

Ohlrogge was born on 15 January 1909 in Bochum. He was a pilot in Fighter Wing 3 when he was awarded the Knight's Cross on 4 November 1941. Ohlrogge died on 30 April 2003 in Bochum, North Rhine-Westphalia.

1091. Oberst Hermann LICHTENBERGER

Lichtenberger was born on 20 August 1892 in Germersheim. He fought in the First World War and was awarded the Iron Cross 2nd Class (1914). Lichtenberger was awarded the Iron Cross 2nd Class (1939) in June 1940 and the 1st Class in May 1941. He was commander of Motorised Flak Regiment 104 when he was awarded the Knight's Cross on 12 November 1941. Lichtenberger died on 15 January 1959 and is buried in Stadtfriedhof, Germersheim, Rhineland-Palatinate.

1092. *Major* Richard KOLB

Kolb was born on 29 June 1891 in Bamberg. He was commander of Motorised Light Flak Battalion 91 when he was awarded the Knight's Cross on 12 November 1941. Kolb died on 16 September 1945 in Salzburg, Austria.

1093. *Hauptmann* Heinrich WITTMER

Wittmer was born on 28 February 1910 in Bordeaux. He was a group commander in Bomber Wing 55 when he was awarded the Knight's Cross on 12 November 1941. Wittmer died on 27 June 1992 in Neuhaus, Bavaria.

1094. *Oberleutnant* Adalbert KARBE

Karbe was born on 28 December 1913 in Barenwinkel. He was a squadron leader in Bomber Wing 55 when he was awarded the Knight's Cross on 12 November 1941. Karbe was killed in action over England on 31 July 1942 and is buried in the German War Cemetery, Block 7, Row 9, Grave 215, Camp Road, Cannock Chase, Staffordshire, England.

1095. *Oberleutnant* Heinz KLIEN

Klien was born on 5 November 1914 in Dresden. He was a squadron leader in Bomber Wing 27 when he was awarded the Knight's Cross on 12 November 1941. Klien died on 1 May 1998 and is believed to be buried in Hauptfriedhof, Heidelberg, Baden-Württemberg.

1096. *Oberleutnant* Karl ROSSMANN

Rossmann was born on 23 November 1916 in Kempten. He was awarded the Iron Cross 2nd Class in June and the 1st Class in July 1940. Rossmann was a company commander in Motorised Flak Regiment 'GG' when he was awarded the Knight's Cross on 12 November 1941. The Oak Leaves followed on 1 February 1945. Rossmann died on 1 April 2002 in Bad Kreuznach, Rhineland-Palatinate.

1097. Leutnant Waldemar STADERMANN

Stadermann was born on 3 January 1916 in Gotha-Siebleben. He was a pilot in Bomber Wing 77 when he was awarded the Knight's Cross on 12 November 1941. Stadermann was killed in action on 15 February 1942 and is buried in the German War Cemetery, Block 1, Grave 48, Cagliari, Sardinia, Italy.

1098. General Erwin VIEROW

Vierow was born on 1 May 1890 in Berlin. He fought in the First World War and was awarded the Iron Cross 1st and 2nd Class (1914). Vierow commanded the 9th Infantry Division in Russia and was appointed commandant of Kharkov in October 1941. He was awarded the Knight's Cross on 15 November 1941.

On 1 July 1943, he took command of an army in the northwest France, which he held until September 1944 when he took over the 'General Command Somme', an *ad hoc* formation. Vierow died on 1 February 1982 in Tecklenburg, North Rhine-Westphalia.

1099. Generalleutnant Heinrich MEYER-BUERDORF

Meyer-Buerdorf was born on 13 December 1888 in Kassel. He fought in the First World War and was awarded the Iron Cross 1st and 2nd Class (1914).

Meyer-Buerdorf was commander of the 131st Infantry Division when he was awarded the Knight's Cross on 15 November 1941. He died on 1 May 1971 and is buried in Hauptfriedhof, Tannenkeckerweg 6, Kassel, Hesse.

1100. Oberst Walther HAHM

Hahm was born on 21 December 1894 in Neudorf-Sulau. He fought in the First World War and was awarded the Iron Cross 1st and 2nd Class (1914). Hahm was awarded the Iron Cross 1st and 2nd Class (1939) in May and June 1940. He was commander of Infantry Regiment 480 when he was awarded the Knight's Cross on 15 November 1941. The Oak Leaves followed on 9 December 1944. Hahm died on 11 August 1951 and is buried in Südfriedhof, Heide, Schleswig-Holstein.

1101. Oberst Helwig LUZ

Luz was born on 28 June 1892 in Buttenheim. He fought in the First World War and was awarded the Iron Cross 1st and 2nd Class (1914). Luz was commander of Rifle Regiment 110 when he was awarded the Knight's Cross on 15 November 1941. He died on 28 April 1980 in Kruen, Bavaria.

1102. SS-Standartenführer Alfred WÜNNENBERG

Wünnenberg was born on 20 July 1891 in Saarburg. He fought in the First World War in the infantry and as a reconnaissance pilot, being awarded the Iron Cross 1st and 2nd Class (1914). He was awarded the Iron Cross 2nd Class (1939) in June 1940 and the 1st Class in August 1941.

Wünnenberg was commander of Police Rifle Regiment 3 when he was awarded the Knight's Cross on 15 November 1941. The Oak Leaves followed on 23 April 1942. He died on 30 December 1963 and is buried in Hauptfriedhof, Feld 56, Grave 200, Krefeld, North Rhine-Westphalia.

1103. Oberstleutnant Heinrich TROMM

Tromm was born on 2 June 1896 in Leba. He was commander of Infantry Regiment 411 when he was awarded the Knight's Cross on 15 November 1941. Tromm was killed in action on 19 June 1942 and is buried in the German War Cemetery, Block 16, Row 3, Grave 127, Korpowo, Russia.

1104. *Major* Hans GRADL

Gradl was born on 8 December 1903 in Nuremberg. He was commander of I Battalion, Panzer Regiment 39, when he was awarded the Knight's Cross on 15 November 1941. Gradl died on 10 March 1980 and is buried in Neuhaus Friedhof, Bavaria.

1105. *Major* Georg RITTER

Ritter was born on 22 December 1897 in Dachau. He was commander of II Battalion, Infantry Regiment 62, when he was killed in action near Moscow on 17 October 1941. He has no known grave. *Ritter* was awarded the Knight's Cross on 15 November 1941.

1106. *Hauptmann* Joachim von HARBOU

Von Harbou was born on 5 November 1910 in Magdeburg. He was commander of I Battalion, Rifle Regiment 5, when he was awarded the Knight's Cross on 15 November 1941. Von Harbou was killed in action on 24 February 1944 and is buried in the German War Cemetery, Block E, Grave 961, Pomezia, Italy.

1107. Kapitän zur See Karl WENIGER

Weniger was born on 24 May 1899 in Dassel. He fought in the First World War. Weniger was awarded the Iron Cross 2nd Class on 17 September 1939 and the 1st Class on 21 May 1940. He was commander of the 2nd Security Division when he was awarded the Knight's Cross on 15 November 1941. Weniger killed in action in the English Channel, near Dieppe on 1 October 1941, and he is buried in the German War Cemetery, Block 17, Grave 1240, Champigny-St André, Normandy, France.

1108. *Oberleutnant* Harald von HIRSCHFELD

Von Hirschfeld was born on 10 July 1912 in Weimar. He was awarded the Iron Cross 2nd Class on 1 November 1939 and the 1st Class on 28 June 1941. Von Hirschfeld was a company commander in Mountain *Jäger* Regiment 98 when he was awarded the Knight's Cross on 15 November 1941. The Oak

Leaves followed on 23 December 1942. In September 1943, he played a *major* part in the defeat and subsequent massacre of the Italian 'Acqui' Division in Cephallonia. Von Hirschfeld was killed in action on 18 January 1945 and is buried at Tarnów, Poland; his remains are awaiting transfer to a German war cemetery.

1109. *Oberleutnant* Adolf HOFMANN

Hofmann was born on 11 February 1912 in Oberstdorf. He was a company commander in Mountain *Jäger* Regiment 100 when he was awarded the Knight's Cross on 15 November 1941. Hofmann was killed in action on 18 January 1943 and is buried at Possjolok, Russia; his remains are awaiting transfer to a German war cemetery.

1110. *Oberleutnant* Hans-Heinrich MACH

Mach was born on 3 August 1916 in Hamburg. He was a company commander in Infantry Regiment 220 when he was awarded the Knight's Cross on 15 November 1941. Mach was killed in action on 10 November 1943 and is buried at Niwje, Russia; his remains are awaiting transfer to a German war cemetery.

1111. *Oberleutnant* Hans-Gotthard PESTKE

Pestke was born on 17 June 1914 in Preussisch-Stargard. He was awarded the Iron Crass 2nd Class after the fall of Poland and the 1st Class after the fall of France. Pestke was a company commander in Infantry Regiment 176 when he was awarded the Knight's Cross on 15 November 1941. The Oak Leaves followed on 14 October 1943. Pestke died on 17 April 2001 and is believed to be buried in Stadtfriedhof, Celle, Lower Saxony.

1112. *Oberleutnant* Gerhard PETER

Peter was born on 12 February 1915 in Berlin. He was a company commander in Panzer Pioneer Battalion 16 when he was awarded the Knight's Cross on 15 November 1941. Peter died on 4 June 1998 in Lehrte, Lower Saxony.

1113. Oberfeldwebel Fritz MEUSGEIER

Meusgeier was born 8 March 1913 in Scheuerfeld. He was a mechanic in Panzer *Jäger* Battalion 13 when he was awarded the Knight's Cross on 15 November 1941. Meusgeier died as a POW on 30 August 1945 and is buried in the German War Cemetery (as unknown), Meziřiči Valašské, Czech Republic.

1114. Feldwebel Karl KOPP

Kopp was born on 18 December 1914 in Böblingen. He was a platoon leader in Infantry Regiment 512 when he was awarded the Knight's Cross on 15 November 1941. Kopp died on 17 July 1997 and is believed to be buried in Weinsberg Friedhof, Baden-Württemberg.

1115. *Kapitänleutnant* Rolf MÜTZELBURG

Mützelburg was born in Kiel on 23 June 1913. He commissioned *U-203* in February and sailed on his first patrol on 5 June 1941, sinking three ships. Sailing into the North Sea on his next patrol, he came across the British ship *Canadian Star*, which was adrift. He shelled the ship, but it did not sink. Three ships were sunk on this patrol. His third patrol took him back to the Atlantic and once again he sank three ships. Mützelburg sank two steamers on the Newfoundland route before the boat was bombed so badly that it had to return to base. Off Cape Hatteras, he torpedoed three tankers and a steamer, but two of the tankers were towed to port. He was awarded the Knight's Cross on 17 November 1941. A patrol in the Caribbean Sea in the summer of 1942 resulted in six ships sunk, including the Panamanian tanker *Stanvac Palembang*. The Oak Leaves were awarded to him on 15 July 1942.

On 11 September 1942, during a patrol south-west of the Azores, Mützelburg took advantage of the good summer weather to take a swim. He dived from the conning tower, striking the deck and breaking his neck; he was buried at sea the next day.

1116. Oberfeldwebel Edmund WAGNER

Wagner was born on 5 December 1914 in Neuhäusel. He was a pilot in Fighter Wing 51 when he was killed in action near Pawmutowka, Russia, on 13 November 1941; he has no known grave. Credited with shooting down fifty-six enemy aircraft, Wagner was awarded the Knight's Cross on 17 November 1941.

1117. Generalleutnant Friedrich Maximilian SIEBERT

Siebert was born on 6 July 1888 in Ludwigshafen. He fought in the First World War and was awarded the Iron Cross 1st and 2nd Class (1914). Siebert was commander of the 44th Infantry Division when he was awarded Knight's Cross on 18 November 1941. He died on 13 March 1950 and is buried in Hauptfriedhof, Feld 9, Row 1, Grave 658, Würzburg, Bavaria.

1118. Oberst Ludwig MERKER

Merker was born on 1 September 1894 in Künzelsau. He fought in the First World War and was awarded the Iron Cross 1st and 2nd Class (1914). Merker was commander of Infantry Regiment 215 when he was awarded the Knight's Cross on 18 November 1941. He died on 14 March 1964 and is buried in Stadtfriedhof, Gmelinstrasse 20, Tübingen, Baden-Württemberg.

1119. Oberst Egbert PICKER

Picker was born on 15 February 1895 in Nuremberg. He fought in the First World War and was awarded the Iron Cross 1st and 2nd Class (1914). Picker was awarded the Iron Cross 1st and 2nd Class (1939) after the fall of Poland. He was commander of Mountain *Jäger* Regiment 98 when he was awarded the Knight's Cross on 18 November 1941. Picker died on 27 March 1960 in Ingolstadt, Bavaria.

1120. Oberst Arnold SZELINSKI

Szelinski was born on 30 August 1891 in Hohenstein. He was commander of Infantry Regiment 525 when he was awarded the Knight's Cross on 18 November 1941. Szelinski was killed in action on 9 December 1943 and is buried in the German War Cemetery, Block 5, Row 17, Grave 1428, Kiev, Ukraine.

1121. Oberstleutnant Hans FAASCH

Faasch was born on 2 January 1897 in Bad Schwartau. He was commander of II Battalion, Infantry Regiment 164, when he was awarded the Knight's Cross on 18 November 1941. Faasch died on 16 February 1983 and is buried in the village cemetery, Oberaudorf, Bavaria.

1122. *Kapitänleutnant* Ernst MENGERSEN

Mengersen was born on 30 June 1912 in Bremke. When the war broke out, he was commander of *U-18*. As well as laying mines, he sank the British trawler *Wigmore*, the Norwegian ship *Bisp*, and torpedoed the destroyer *Inglefield*. After taking over command of *U-101*, he sank the *Aracataca* at the end of November 1940. On 1 December, he sighted convoy HX90. On his first attack, he sank the tanker *Appalachee* and the *Lady Glannely*, while his second attack sent the *Kavak* to the bottom. An hour later, Mengersen sank the 6,022-ton *Stirlingshire*.

He sank two ships each in February and June 1941, and then on 18 October, he sank the destroyer *Broadwater*. He was awarded the Knight's Cross on 18 November 1941. At the request of Dönitz, he took over the 15th U-Boat Flotilla, which he commanded until the end of the war. He died on 6 November 1995 and is buried in Waldfriedhof, Detmold, North Rhine-Westphalia.

1123. *Oberleutnant* Thilo Freiherr und Herr von WERTHERN-BEICLINGEN

Freiherr und Herr von Werther-Beiclingen was born on 28 December 1914 in Hoppenrade. He was a company commander in Panzer Regiment 27 when he was awarded the Knight's Cross on 18 November 1941. Von Werther-Beiclingen died on 7 June 1987 in Hammersbach, Hesse.

1124. Leutnant Gerhard MOKROS

Mokros was born on 18 March 1909 in Dresden. He was a company commander in Infantry Regiment 331 when he was awarded the Knight's Cross on 18 November 1941. The Oak Leaves followed on 3 May 1945. Mokros died on 3 April 1996 in Sonthofen, Bavaria.

1125. Oberfeldwebel Josef HÄFELE

Häfele was born on 26 December 1910 in Stockheim. He was a platoon leader in *Jäger* Regiment 99 when he was awarded the Knight's Cross on 18 November 1941. Häfele was killed in action on 17 May 1942 and is buried at Grigorjewka, Barwenkowo, Ukraine; his remains are awaiting transfer to a German war cemetery.

1126. Oberfeldwebel Hans KÖCKERBAUER

Köckerbauer was born on 1 October 1914 in Simbach am Inn. He was a platoon leader in Mountain *Jäger* Regiment 91 when he was awarded the Knight's Cross on 18 November 1941. Köckerbauer was killed in action on the Don River, near Batask, Russia, on 28 July 1942 and has no known grave.

1127. Feldwebel Josef GOLLAS

Gollas was born on 15 December 1914 in Mömlingen. He was a platoon leader in Infantry Regiment 106 when he was awarded the Knight's Cross on 18 November 1941. Gollas died on 12 December 1980 and is buried in Alter Friedhof, Niedernberg, Bavaria.

1128. Unteroffizier Paul SPEICH

Speich was born on 22 August 1914 in Oberglogau. He was a section leader in Pioneer Battalion 162 when he was awarded the Knight's Cross on 18 November 1941. Speich died on 1 July 2005 in Wedemark, Lower Saxony.

1129. Generalleutnant Curt GALLENKAMP

Gallenkamp was born on 17 February 1890 in Wessel. He fought in the First World War and was awarded the Iron Cross 1st and 2nd Class (1914). Gallenkamp was commander of the 78th Infantry Division when he was awarded the Knight's Cross on 19 November 1941. He was captured by the British in May 1945 and tried for the deaths of British paratroopers and commandos, as well as one US airman. Gallenkamp was sentenced to death, but this was commuted to life imprisonment; he was released in 1952. Gallenkamp died on 13 April 1958 and is believed to be buried in Südfriedhof, Wiesbaden, Hesse. His brother-in-law, Kurt, and his nephew, Adolf-Hilmar von Tippelskirch, were also awarded the Knight's Cross.

1130. *Major* Otto SCHELL

Schell was born on 9 July 1895 in Altendorf. He fought in the First World War and was awarded the Iron Cross 1st and 2nd Class (1914). Schell was commander of III Battalion, Infantry Regiment 39, when he was awarded the

Knight's Cross on 19 November 1941. He was killed in action on 2 September 1944 and is buried in the German War Cemetery (Eternitatea Cemetery) (as unknown), Strada Eternitate, Iaşi, Romania.

1131. *Oberleutnant* Klaus DÜWELL

Düwell was born on 3 March 1917 in Munich. He was a company commander in Mountain *Jäger* Regiment 137 when he was awarded the Knight's Cross on 19 November 1941. Düwell died on 15 February 1998 and is buried in Waldfriedhof, Oberstdorf, Bavaria.

1132. Oberfeldwebel Adam EBNER

Ebner was born on 24 December 1911 in Eben-Schattbach. He was a platoon leader in Mountain *Jäger* Regiment 137 when he was awarded the Knight's Cross on 19 November 1941. Ebner died on 17 October 1975 in Eben i Pongau, Austria.

1133. *Oberleutnant* Helmut ADAM

Adam was born on 1 October 1916 in Bobersberg. He was awarded the Iron Cross 2nd Class in May 1940 and the 1st Class in August 1941. Adam was a company commander in Assault-Gun Battalion 192 when he was awarded the Knight's Cross on 21 November 1941. He was killed in action on 1 December 1942 and is believed to be buried in the German War Cemetery (as unknown), Rzhev, Russia.

1134. Generalleutnant Oskar BLÜMM

Blümm was born on 26 June 1884 in Zwiesel. He fought in the First World War and was awarded the Iron Cross 1st and 2nd Class (1914). Blümm was awarded the Iron Cross 1st and 2nd Class (1939) after the fall of Poland. He was commander of the 57th Infantry Division when he was awarded the Knight's Cross on 23 November 1941. Blümm died on 12 December 1951 and is buried in Klosterfriedhof, Ursberg, Bavaria.

1135. Generalleutnant Franz MATTENKLOTT

Mattenklott was born on 19 November 1884 in Grünberg. He fought in the First World War and was awarded the Iron Cross 1st and 2nd Class (1914). Mattenklott was awarded the Iron Cross 1st and 2nd Class (1939) in December 1939. He took part in the French and Balkans campaigns and the invasion of Russia. On 6 November 1941, Mattenklott was placed on the reserve list and awarded the Knight's Cross on 23 November 1941.

On Christmas Day 1941, he had delivered to all the men of his division a card reading: 'In remembrance of the struggle on the Westwall, in France, in Greece and Russia. I thank you for your bravery and loyalty'. In January 1942, he took command of XXXXII Army Corps, and between August 1942 and April 1943, he was commander of the Crimea. In June 1944, he was moved to VI Army Corps in Münster. Arrested for war crimes by the Allies in 1945, Mattenklott was released without charge. He died on 28 June 1954 and is buried in the village cemetery, Braunlage, Lower Saxony.

1136. Generalleutnant Kurt von TIPPELSKIRCH

Von Tippelskirch was born on 9 October 1891 in Berlin. He fought in the First World War and was awarded the Iron Cross 1st and 2nd Class (1914); he was also captured by the French. Von Tippelskirch was awarded the Iron Cross 2nd Class (1939) after the fall of Poland and the 1st Class after the fall of France.

He was commander of the 30th Infantry Divison when he was awarded the Knight's Cross on 23 November 1941. The Oak Leaves followed on 30 July 1944. Von Tippelskirch wrote a number of works on the war years, including the *History of the Second World War*. He died on 10 May 1957 and is buried in Zentralfriedhof, Feld 14, Grave 12A–12B, Lüneburg, Lower Saxony. His son, Adolf-Hilmar, and his brother-in-law, Curt Gallenkamp, were also awarded the Knight's Cross.

1137. Generalmajor Martin WANDEL

Wandel was born on 15 April 1892 in Berlin. He fought in the First World War and was awarded the Iron Cross 1st and 2nd Class (1914). Wandel was commander of the 121st Infantry Division when he was awarded the Knight's Cross on 23 November 1941. He was posted missing near Stalingrad, Russia, on 14 January 1943.

1138. *Major* Walter MECKE

Mecke was born on 26 August 1896 in Hanover. He was commander of I Battalion, Panzer Regiment 27, when he was awarded the Knight's Cross on 23 November 1941. Mecke was killed in action on the Narwa River, Russia, on 1 December 1941 and has no known grave.

1139. *Hauptmann* Gerhard BALL

Ball was born on 29 October 1908 in Graudenz. He was commander of Motorised Reconnaissance Battalion 53 when he was killed in action on 9 October 1941. He is buried at Woronki, Russia; Ball's remains are awaiting transfer to a German war cemetery.

1140. *Hauptmann* Herbert ENGBRECHT

Engbrecht was born on 23 August 1910 in Nickelswalde. He was commander of III Battalion, Infantry Regiment 3, when he was awarded the Knight's Cross on 23 November 1941. Engbrecht was killed in action on 7 August 1942 and is buried at Kirischi, Russia; his remains are awaiting transfer to a German war cemetery.

1141. *Hauptmann* Heinz-Martin EWERT

Ewert was born on 12 May 1915 in Preussisch. He was awarded the Iron Cross 2nd Class in June 1940 and the 1st Class in August 1941. Ewert was commander of II Battalion, Infantry Regiment 2, when he was awarded the Knight's Cross on 23 November 1941. The Oak Leaves followed on 22 February 1945. Ewert was captured by the Russians in February 1945 and released in 1949. He died on 24 February 1995 and is buried in Waldfriedhof, Krefeld, North Rhine-Westphalia.

1142. *Hauptmann* Ernst KUPFER

Kupfer was born on 2 July 1907 in Coburg. He took part in the Battle of Britain and the Battle for Crete, where he was instrumental in sinking the cruiser HMS *Gloucester*. In Russia, he hit the battleship *October Revolution* with a 2,200-lb bomb. For this, he was awarded the Knight's Cross on 23

November 1941. The Oak Leaves followed on 8 January 1943. Kupfer fought in the Crimea and at Kursk during 1943.

In September 1943, he was appointed inspector of attack aircraft and handled the procurement of the Fw 190 to replace the outdated Ju 87s and Hs 123s. Kupfer was killed on 6 November 1943 when his aircraft crashed in bad weather and he is buried in the German War Cemetery, Crypt 1, Row 4, Plate 7, Dionyssos-Rapendoza, Greece. He was awarded the Swords on 11 April 1944.

1143. *Hauptmann* Otto MARTENS

Martens was born on 9 July 1897 in Warwerort. He was commander of Panzer *Jäger* Battalion 72 when he was awarded the Knight's Cross on 23 November 1941. Martens died on 3 February 1977 in Wilhelminenhof, Brandenburg.

1144. *Hauptmann* Alfons ORTHOFER

Orthofer was born on 7 December 1909 in Neustadt. He was a group commander in Dive Bomber Wing 77 when he was awarded the Knight's Cross on 23 November 1941. Orthofer died of wounds on 12 October 1944 at Maikop, Russia, and has no known grave.

1145. *Hauptmann* Herbert WITTMANN

Wittmann was born on 3 January 1914 in Döllnitz. He fought in Spain with the Condor Legion. Wittmann was awarded the Iron Cross 2nd Class in May and the 1st Class in June 1940 during the Battle of Britain. He was a squadron leader in Bomber Wing 53 when he was awarded the Knight's Cross on 23 November 1941. The Oak Leaves followed on 11 February 1945. Wittmann died on 26 July 2007 and is buried in Munchener Strasse Friedhof, Pullach, Bavaria.

1146. *Oberleutnant* Horst BEEGER

Beeger was born on 8 June 1913 in Bautzen. He was a squadron leader in Close Support Wing 1 when he was awarded the Knight's Cross on 23 November 1941. Beeger died on 3 March 1998 in Wahnbek, Lower Saxony.

1147. *Oberleutnant* Friedrich LANG

Lang was born on 12 January 1915 in Mährisch-Trübau, Austria-Hungary. He was awarded the Iron Cross 2nd Class after the fall of Poland and the 1st Class after the fall of France. Lang was a pilot in Dive Bomber Wing 2 when he was awarded the Knight's Cross on 23 November 1941. The Oak Leaves followed on 21 November 1942 and the Swords on 2 July 1944. Lang flew 1,008 combat missions from the first day of the war until the very last day. He was never shot down, never crash landed, and never had to bale out. He died on 29 December 2003 and is believed to be buried in Gartenfriedhof, Marienstrasse, Hanover.

1148. *Oberleutnant* Hans-Joachim LEHMANN

Lehmann was born on 18 August 1912 in Treuenbrietzen. He was a squadron leader in Dive Bomber Wing 2 when he was awarded the Knight's Cross on 23 November 1941. Lehmann died on 7 April 1982 and is believed to be buried in Waldfriedhof, Seeheim-Jugenheim, Hesse.

1149. *Oberleutnant* Werner PAULS

Pauls was born on 12 January 1902 in Preussisch. He was a company commander in Infantry Regiment 45 when he was awarded the Knight's Cross on 23 November 1941. Pauls was killed in action near Bonn on 15 April 1945 and has no known grave.

1150. *Oberleutnant* Hermann RUPPERT

Ruppert was born on 8 August 1915 in Irbit. He was a squadron leader in Dive Bomber Wing 77 when he was awarded the Knight's Cross on 23 November 1941. Ruppert was killed in action on 2 March 1942 and is buried in the German War Cemetery (as unknown), Kharkov, Ukraine.

1151. *Oberleutnant* Karl TORLEY

Torley was born on 16 October 1913 in Iserlohn. He was a company commander in Motorised Infantry Regiment 60 when he was awarded the Knight's Cross on 23 November 1941. The Oak Leaves followed on 11

October 1942. Torley was killed in action on 19 July 1943 near Kalinovka, Russia, and has no known grave.

1152. Leutnant Dirk ITZEN

Itzen was born on 16 October 1919 in Klein Schulenburger Polder. He was a reconnaissance officer in Motorised Flak Regiment 'GG'. Itzen died of wounds at Berditschew, Russia, on 13 July 1941 and has no known grave. He was awarded the Knight's Cross on 23 November 1941.

1153. Leutnant Georg LOOS

Loos was born on 24 January 1914 in Windecken. He was a platoon leader in Pioneer Battalion 152 when he was awarded the Knight's Cross on 23 November 1941. Loos died on 11 May 1992 in Riedstadt-Goddelau, Hesse.

1154. Oberfeldwebel Josef ABEL

Abel was born on 3 January 1914 in Bad Kissingen. He was awarded the Iron Cross 2nd Class in June 1940 and the 1st Class in July 1941. Abel was a platoon leader in Infantry Regiment 217 when he was awarded the Knight's Cross on 23 November 1941. He died on 30 November 1984 and is buried in Stadtfriedhof, Donauwörth, Bavaria.

1155. Oberst Bruno Ritter von HAUENSCHILD

Ritter von Hauenschild was born on 7 June 1896 in Würzburg. He fought in the First World War and was awarded the Iron Cross 1st and 2nd Class (1914), as well as the Wound Badge in Gold. Von Hauenschild was commander of the 4th Panzer Brigade when he was awarded the Knight's Cross on 25 November 1941. The Oak Leaves followed on 27 September 1942.

In 1943, he was appointed to command the schools for panzer troops. On 26 January 1945, von Hauenschild was given command of the III Military District HQ in Berlin. As the Russians neared Berlin, he was also given command of the Berlin Defence Area, but he was relieved from his post on 6 March. Von Hauenschild died on 10 March 1953 and is buried in Stadtfriedhof, Feld 1, Grave 135, Würzburg, Bavaria.

1156. *Oberleutnant* Georg GRÜNER

Grüner was born on 9 August 1915 in Windhoek, German South West Africa. He was awarded the Iron Cross 2nd Class in October 1939 and the 1st Class in July 1941. Grüner was a company commander in I Battalion, Panzer Regiment 33, when he was awarded the Knight's Cross on 25 November 1941. He was killed in action on 11 March 1944 and is buried at Khmelnitsky, Ukraine; Grüner's remains are awaiting transfer to a German war cemetery. He was awarded the Oak Leaves on 26 March 1944.

1157. Oberstleutnant Wilhelm FALLEY

Falley was born on 25 September 1897 in Metz. He fought in the First World War and was awarded the Iron Cross 1st and 2nd Class (1914). Falley was awarded the Iron Cross 2nd Class (1939) in July 1940 and the 1st Class in June 1941. He was commander of Infantry Regiment 4 when he was awarded the Knight's Cross on 26 November 1941.

Falley was killed in action on 6 June 1944 and is buried in the German War Cemetery, Block 10, Row 2, Grave 207, Orglandes, Normandy, France. He was the first German general to be killed in Normandy.

1158. Oberstleutnant Karl MAUSS

Mauss was born in Plön on 17 May 1898. He fought in the First World War and was awarded the Iron Cross 1st and 2nd Class (1914). Mauss also fought in Poland, for which he was awarded the Iron Cross 2nd Class (1939), and in the campaign in West, for which he was awarded the Iron Cross 1st Class (1939). He took part in the invasion of Russia and was awarded the Knight's Cross 26 November 1941.

In 1942, he briefly commanded the 4th Panzer Division during the push into the Caucasus. Mauss also fought at Kursk in July 1943 and was awarded the Oak Leaves on 24 November 1943 for fighting his way out of an encirclement. In January 1944, he was appointed commander of the 7th Panzer Division and fought in the defensive battles throughout the year. Mauss was awarded the Swords on 23 October 1944. In 1945, the division was involved in heavy fighting, during which Mauss was wounded; he was evacuated and had his leg amputated. He was awarded the Diamonds on 15 April 1945. Mauss died following a heart attack on 9 February 1959 and is buried in Ohlsdorf Friedhof, Fuhlsbüttler Strasse, Hamburg.

1159. Oberstleutnant Hellmuth PFEIFER

Pfeifer was born on 18 February 1894 in Altenburg. He fought in the First World War and was awarded the Iron Cross 1st and 2nd Class (1914). Pfeifer was awarded the Iron Cross 2nd Class (1939) on 8 June and the 1st Class on 16 June 1940. He was commander of Infantry Regiment 185 when he was awarded the Knight's Cross on 26 November 1941. The Oak Leaves followed on 5 September 1944. Pfeifer was killed in action on 22 April 1945 and is buried in the German War Cemetery, Block 49, Grave 177, Futa Pass, near Bologna, Italy.

1160. *Major* Alois WEBER

Weber was born on 26 July 1903 in Kastl. He was awarded the Iron Cross 1st and 2nd Class after the fall of Poland. Weber was commander of I Battalion, Infantry Regiment 19, when he was awarded the Knight's Cross on 26 November 1941. The Oak Leaves followed on 10 September 1944. He died on 19 June 1976 in Freising, Bavaria.

1161. *Oberleutnant* Wilhelm BOOK

Book was born on 12 September 1916 in Lubeck. He was a company commander in Infantry Regiment 6 when he was awarded the Knight's Cross on 26 November 1941. Book was posted missing near Lake Ilmen, Russia, on 21 December 1941.

1162. Oberstleutnant Werner MARIENFELD

Marienfeld was born on 10 August 1904 in Alt-Sussmilken. He was a group commander in Bomber Wing 54 when he was awarded the Knight's Cross on 27 November 1941. Marienfeld was accidently killed on 23 October 1944 at Flugplatz Giebelstadt and has no known grave.

1163. Konteradmiral Robert EYSSEN

Eyssen was born on 2 April 1892 in Frankfurt am Main. He fought in the First World War and was awarded the Iron Cross 1st and 2nd Class (1914). Eyssen was commander of the auxiliary cruiser *Komet* when he was awarded the Knight's Cross on 29 November 1941. He died on 30 April 1960 and is buried in Hauptfriedhof, Baden Baden, Baden-Württemberg.

1164. Colonel-General Béla Vitéz MIKLÓS DE DÁLNOK (Hungarian Army)

Miklós De Dálnok was born on 11 June 1890 in Budapest. He fought in the First World War. Miklós De Dálnok was awarded the Knight's Cross on 4 December 1941 while commanding a regiment of the Hungarian Army. He became military director of the office of Admiral Miklós Horthy, regent of Hungary, in October 1942. Miklós De Dálnok was appointed commander of the Hungarian 1st Army in August 1944 and supported leaving the Axis powers to join the Russians. On 16 October 1944, he was ordered to report to General Heinrici, but, fearing arrest, he defected to the Russians. Miklós De Dálnok tried to get others to follow, but this was unsuccessful. He was appointed prime minster of the Kingdom of Hungary (with Russian approval) on 22 December 1944, but he only held this post until 15 November 1945. Miklós De Dálnok died on 21 November 1948 and is buried in an unmarked grave at Kerepesi Cemetery, Budapest, Hungary.

1165. Generalleutnant Herbert von BÖCKMANN

Von Böckmann was born on 24 July 1886 in Bremen. He fought in the First World War and was awarded the Iron Cross 1st and 2nd Class (1914). Von Böckmann was awarded the Iron Cross 1st and 2nd Class (1939) after the fall of Poland.

He was commander of the 11th Infantry Division when he was awarded the Knight's Cross on 4 December 1941. Von Böckmann was discharged from the army on 31 March 1943 due to his age; he took no further part in the war. He died on 10 March 1974 and is buried in Lichtenthal Friedhof, Feld B, Grave 183–184, Baden Baden, Baden-Württemberg.

1166. Generalleutnant Hugo HÖFL

Höfl was born on 16 June 1878 in Regensburg. He fought in the First World War and was awarded the Iron Cross 1st and 2nd Class (1914). Höfl was commander of the 206th Infantry Division when he was awarded the Knight's Cross on 4 December 1941. He retired from active service in April 1943. Höfl died on 13 April 1957 in Weipertshausen, Bavaria.

1167. Generalleutnant Max PFEFFER

Pfeffer was born on 12 June 1883 in Geldern. He fought in the First World War and was awarded the Iron Cross 1st and 2nd Class (1914). Pfeffer was commander of the

297th Infantry Division when he was awarded the Knight's Cross on 4 December 1941. He was captured at Stalingrad and died in Russian hands on 3 January 1956; Pfeffer is buried in the German War Cemetery, Row 5, Grave 6, Cherntsy, Russia.

1168. *Generalmajor* Gerhard BERTHOLD

Berthold was born on 12 March 1891 in Schneeberg. He fought in the First World War and was awarded the Iron Cross 1st and 2nd Class (1914). Berthold was awarded the Iron Cross 1st and 2nd Class (1939) after the fall of Poland. He was commander of the 31st Infantry Division when he was awarded the Knight's Cross on 4 December 1941. Berthold was killed in action on 14 April 1942 and is believed to be buried at Korolewka, Juchnow, Russia; his remains are awaiting transfer to a German war cemetery.

1169. *Oberst* Eduard HAUSER

Hauser was born on 22 June 1895 in Erlangen. He fought in the First World War and was awarded the Iron Cross 1st and 2nd Class (1914). Hauser was awarded the Iron Cross 2nd Class (1939) after the fall of Poland and the 1st Class after the fall of France. He was commander of Panzer Regiment 25 when he was awarded the Knight's Cross on 4 December 1941. The Oak Leaves followed on 26 January 1944. Hauser died on 16 July 1961 and is buried in Stadtfriedhof, Abt II, Feld 2, Row 1, Grave 20–21, Garmisch-Partenkirchen, Bavaria.

1170. *Oberst* Erich JASCHKE

Jaschke was born on 11 May 1890 in Danzig. He fought in the First World War and was awarded the Iron Cross 1st and 2nd Class (1914). Jaschke was awarded the Iron Cross 2nd Class (1939) in May 1940 and the 1st Class in July 1941. He was commander of Infantry Regiment 90 when he was awarded the Knight's Cross on 4 December 1941. The Oak Leaves followed on 7 September 1943. Jaschke died on 18 October 1961 and is buried in Ohlsdorf Friedhof, Plot Z12, Grave 278–279, Fuhlsbüttler Strasse, Hamburg.

1171. *Oberstleutnant* Jobst-Hilmar von BOSE

Von Bose was born on 21 September 1897 in Berlin. He fought in the First World War and was awarded the Iron Cross 1st and 2nd Class (1914). Von

Bose was awarded the Iron Cross 2nd Class (1939) in March and the 1st Class in July 1940. He was commander of I Battalion, Infantry Regiment 289, on 4 December 1941. Von Bose died on 26 March 1949 and is buried in Bamberg Friedhof, Bavaria.

1172. *Fregattenkapitän* Theodor DETMERS

Detmers was born on 22 August 1902 in Witten. He was awarded the Iron Cross 2nd Class in November 1939 and the 1st Class in June 1940 as captain of the destroyer *Hermann Schoemann*. In July 1940, Detmers was made captain of the auxiliary cruiser *Kormoran* and sank or captured eleven enemy merchant ships. On 19 November 1941, the *Kormoran* was intercepted by the cruiser HMAS *Sydney*. Detmers tried to pose as a Dutch merchant ship but lacked the necessary codes, and he was forced to engage the *Sydney*, which he sank in the waters off Western Australia. However, his own ship was severely damaged and had to be scuttled. Detmers and his crew were taken prisoners.

He was awarded the Knight's Cross on 4 December 1941 while a POW. Detmers and some of his men tried to dig a tunnel to escape the POW camp, but this was unsuccessful. He also suffered a stroke while in Australia. Detmers died on 4 November 1976 and is buried in Rahlstedt Friedhof, Pogfreedweg, Hamburg.

1173. *Oberstleutnant* Walter DIETLEN

Dietlen was born on 7 February 1897 in Hemmingen. He was commander of Motorcycle Battalion 54 when he was awarded the Knight's Cross on 4 December 1941. Dietlen died 15 March 1982 and is buried in Hauptfriedhof, Schweinfurt, Bavaria.

1174. *Oberstleutnant* Alfred-Hermann REINHARDT

Reinhardt was born on 15 November 1897 in Affalterbach. He fought in the First World War and was awarded the Iron Cross 1st and 2nd Class (1914). Reinhardt was awarded the Iron Cross 1st and 2nd Class (1939) after the fall off France. He was commander of Infantry Regiment 421 when he was awarded the Knight's Cross on 4 December 1941. The Oak Leaves followed on 28 September 1943 and the Swords on 24 December 1944. Reinhardt died on 14 January 1973 and is buried in Öhringen Friedhof, Baden-Württemberg.

1175. *Hauptmann* Franz-Josef KOHOUT

Kohout was born on 16 August 1908 in Waidhofen. He was commander of II Battalion, Panzer Regiment 33, when he was awarded the Knight's Cross on 4 December 1941. Kohout died on 21 November 1980 in Waidhofen, Bavaria.

1176. *Oberleutnant* Georg FEIG

Feig was born on 27 February 1899 in Annaberg. He fought in the First World War and was awarded the Iron Cross 2nd Class (1914). Feig fought in France and Belgium, being awarded the Iron Cross 1st and 2nd Class (1939). He was a company commander in Rifle Regiment 113 when he was awarded the Knight's Cross on 4 December 1941. Feig was also awarded the Wound Badge in Gold for multiple wounds. He died on 12 February 1970 in Wiesbaden, Hesse.

1177. *Oberleutnant* Heinrich MONDABON

Mondabon was born on 25 April 1911 in Attendorn. He was a company commander in II Battalion, Rifle Regiment 114, when he was awarded the Knight's Cross on 4 December 1941. Mondabon was killed in action on 12 December 1941 and is buried at Borissowglebskaja, Russia; his remains are awaiting transfer to a German war cemetery.

1178. *Oberleutnant* Theodor TOLSDORFF—'The Lion of Vilnius' or 'Tolsdorff the Mad'

Tolsdorff was born on 3 November 1909 in Lehnarten. He fought in Poland with an anti-tank company, being awarded the Iron Cross 1st and 2nd Class. Tolsdorff missed the campaign in the West but did take part in the invasion of Russia. Wounded in action during the advance on Leningrad, he returned to his men before his wounds had healed.

He was awarded the Knight's Cross on 4 December 1941 while still in hospital. He returned to the front in April 1942 badly wounded; shortly after, he lost his right foot. However, he was back at the front with a prosthetic as *Hauptmann* and commanding a battalion in June 1942. Wounded again, this time he did not return to the front until September 1942. Promoted to *Major* in 1943, he now commanded a regiment and was awarded the Oak Leaves on 15 September 1943 for his outstanding leadership at Lake Ladoga. Moved to the southern front, Tolsdorff was wounded in the stomach. He was posted as a tactics instructor on his recovery. Tolsdorff was sent back to Russia at his own request in March 1944, commanding a regiment. Tasked with defending Vilnius in Lithuania, he first had to break into the city. On the way, he freed a hospital with 3,000 German wounded. He held on until a Panzer Army broke through. For this, he was awarded the Swords on 18 July 1944.

Tolsdorff commanded the 340th *Volksgrenadier* Division for the Ardennes Offensive, capturing a vital bridge. For this, he was awarded the Diamonds on 18 March 1945. His last command was LXXXII Army in the Balkans, where he surrendered to US forces. Tolsdorff died following a car crash on 25 May 1978 and is buried in Heckinghauserstrasse Friedhof, Section 8, Grave 210–204, Wuppertal, North Rhine-Westphalia.

1179. *Oberleutnant* Gerhard ZONEWITZ

Zonewitz was born on 6 June 1910 in Hohenstein. He was a company commander in Infantry Regiment 151 when he was awarded the Knight's Cross on 4 December 1941. Zonewitz died on 5 December 1996 in Neustadt am Rübenberge, Lower Saxony.

1180. *Leutnant* Walter EVERS

Evers was born on 3 August 1912 in Hamburg. He was a company commander in Infantry Regiment 271 when he was awarded the Knight's Cross on 4 December 1941. Evers was killed in action on 28 December 1943 and is believed to be buried in the German War Cemetery (as unknown), Schatkowo, Belarus.

1181. *Unteroffizier* Hans-Erwin SCHRÖDER

Schröder was born on 30 April 1916 in Brunshausen. He was serving in Panzer *Jäger* Battalion 20 when he was awarded the Knight's Cross on 4 December 1941. Schröder was killed in action near Orel, Russia, on 10 August 1943 and has no known grave.

1182. *Kapitänleutnant* Friedrich GUGGENBERGER

Guggenberger was born in Munich on 6 March 1915. He joined the U-boat service in 1939 and commissioned *U-81* on 26 April 1941. On 9 September, he torpedoed a 5,000-ton ship in the Atlantic, which exploded in a pillar of fire.

He sank a ship from convoy SC 42 before being ordered to the Mediterranean Sea. On 13 November, he fired a spread of torpedoes at the aircraft carrier *Ark Royal*, which was badly damaged and later sank. In December, he torpedoed several steamers and a destroyer. Guggenberger was awarded the Knight's Cross on 10 December 1941. He sank the tanker *Caspia* off the coast of Beirut, and in April 1942, he sank eight sailing ships with gunfire. In November 1942, he sank two more ships. On 8 January 1943, he was awarded the Oak Leaves.

He took over command of *U-513* and sank the US *Elihu Washburne*, followed in July by another US ship. Then, on 19 July 1943, *U-513* was sunk by aircraft off the coast of Brazil. Only seven men survived, including Guggenberger, and they were taken to the USA as prisoners. He made several escapes attempts but was recaptured each time. After the war, he became an architect, before joining the *Bundesmarine* in 1956, ending as a *Konteradmiral*. He retired to Erlenbach am Main in 1972. On 13 May 1988, he went for a walk in the forest and never returned. His body was found two years later and is buried in Erlenbach Friedhof, Bavaria.

1183. *Generalmajor* Karl Heinrich BÖTTCHER

Böttcher was born in Thorn on 25 October 1889. He fought in the First World War as a *Leutnant* in the artillery and was awarded the Iron Cross 1st and 2nd Class (1914). He initially served on the home front as an artillery officer. Böttcher was awarded the Iron Cross 1st and 2nd Class (1939) in 1940. He was posted to the Africa Corps on 1 February 1941 as CO of the 21st Panzer Division.

Between 24 and 28 November 1941, his battle group prevented far superior enemy armoured forces from breaking through to Tobruk. Rommel said that he was 'tireless in preparing for the attack on Tobruk, fearless and circumspect in command of an independent battle group'. He was awarded the Knight's Cross on 13 December 1941. Sent home due to illness, he spent some time on the staff but also commanded the 326th and 347th Infantry Regiments as well as the 305th Army Artillery Command, before becoming general of Artillery Special Duties No. 4. This was a position he held until the end of the war. Böttcher died on 9 February 1975 and is buried in Bad Wimpfen Friedhof, Baden-Württemberg.

1184. *Generalmajor* Alfred GAUSE

Gause was born in Königsberg on 14 February 1896. He fought in the First World War, was wounded several times, and was awarded the Iron Cross 1st and 2nd Class (1914). During the campaign in the West in 1940, he severed as chief-of-staff of X Corps and soon held the same position at von Manstein's XXXVIII Corps. Subsequently, he became liaison officer to the Italian High Command. He was awarded the Iron Cross 1st and 2nd Class (1939). In June 1941, Gause was promoted to *Generalmajor*, and in July, he was named chief-of-staff of Panzer Group Africa. Rommel thought highly of Gause and he was awarded the Knight's Cross on 13 December 1941.

Wounded near Tobruk, Gause was sent home, but he was back in the winter of 1942–43. On 23 February 1943, he was named chief-of-staff of Army Group Africa, a post he held until 13 May 1943. Gause was flown out of Tunisia before the surrender and served under Rommel in Italy. On 14 January 1945, he began a course for commanding generals and subsequently took command of II Army Group, which he held until the end of the war. Gause was held as a POW by the Russians until 1955. He died on 30 September 1967 and is buried in Poppelsdorf Friedhof, Abt XXVIII, Grave 300–301, Bonn.

1185. *SS-Brigadeführer* Walter KRÜGER

Krüger was born on 27 February 1890 in Strasbourg. He fought in the First World War and was awarded the Iron Cross 1st and 2nd Class (1914). Krüger was commander of the SS-*Polizei* Division when he was awarded the Knight's Cross on 13 December 1941. He was awarded the Oak Leaves on 31 August 1943 and the Swords on 11 January 1945. Krüger killed himself in Lithuania on 22 May 1945 and has no known grave.

1186. *Oberst* Johann MICKL

Mickl was born on 18 April 1893 in Zelting. He fought in the First World War and was wounded seven times. Mickl fought in Poland, for which he was awarded the Iron Cross 2nd Class, and France, for which he was awarded the Iron Cross 1st Class. Sent to Africa in September 1941 as CO of the 155th Rifle Regiment, Mickl took part in the British defeat at Tobruk; he also fought at Sidi Rezegh, El Duda, and Belhamed. Captured by the British on 26 November 1941, he managed to escape two days later and led 800 prisoners back to the German lines.

At the end of December, he was wounded in the head and hand, but took over command of the division. Mickl was awarded the Knight's Cross on 13 December 1941. By the end of March 1942, he was in Russia and was awarded the Oak Leaves on 6 March 1943. Mickl was shot by partisans and died of his wounds on 10 April 1945. He is buried in the German War Cemetery, Block 82, Feld 6, Row 10, Grave 297, Zagreb-Mirogoi, Croatia.

1187. *Oberstleutnant* Hans-Levin von BARBY

Von Barby was born on 25 July 1899 in Berlin. He fought in the latter part of the First World War, being awarded the Iron Cross 1st and 2nd Class (1914). Von Barby fought in France as a battalion commander in 1940 and was awarded the Iron Cross 1st and 2nd Class (1939). Promoted to *Oberstleutnant* and sent to North Africa in April 1941, he fought in a number of defensive battles at Marmarica during the winter. Finally, in November 1941, he achieved a major success in the attack on Sidi Rezegh. Advancing at the head of his battalion, von Barby prevented the British from linking up with the defenders of Tobruk. For this action, he was awarded the Knight's Cross on 13 December 1941.

With the German Spring Offensive, von Barby and his battalion once again went on the attack. On 26 May 1942, he was badly wounded and died the next day at Derna hospital; he is buried in the German War Cemetery, Tobruk, Libya.

1188. *General* Joachim WITTHÖFT

Witthöft was born on 23 September 1887 in Marienwerder. He fought in the First World War and was awarded the Iron Cross 1st and 2nd Class (1914). Witthöft was commander of the 86th Infantry Division when he was awarded the Knight's Cross on 14 December 1941. He died on 7 July 1966 and is buried in Dalheim-Rodgen Friedhof, North Rhine-Westphalia.

1189. *Generalleutnant* Paul LAUX

Laux was born on 11 November 1887 in Weimar. He fought in the First World War and was awarded the Iron Cross 1st and 2nd Class (1914). Laux was awarded the Iron Cross 1st and 2nd Class (1939) in January and July 1940. He was commander of the 126th Infantry Division when he was awarded the Knight's Cross on 14 December 1941. The Oak Leaves followed on 17 May 1943. Laux died of wounds on 2 September 1944 following a crashing landing and is buried in the German War Cemetery, Ogre, Latvia.

1190. *SS-Oberführer* Wilhelm BITTRICH—'Willi'

Bittrich was born on 26 February 1894 in Wernigerode. He fought in the infantry and as a pilot during First World War and was awarded the Iron Cross 1st and 2nd Class (1914). Bittrich was awarded the Iron Cross 2nd Class (1939) in September 1939 and the 1st Class in June 1940 as commander of the *Deutschland* Regiment. Later, he commanded the 2nd SS-Panzer Division. He was awarded the Knight's Cross on 14 December 1941. The Oak Leaves followed on 28 August 1944. At Arnhem in September 1944, he commanded the II SS-Panzer Corps, with which he was largely responsible for the only Allied defeat in Northwest Europe.

Bittrich was tasked with defending Vienna in the spring of 1945, but he immediately pulled his men out of the city to save them from destruction despite the order to hold Vienna 'to the last breath'. He was awarded the Swords on 6 May 1945; it was unlawfully presented by Sepp Dietrich. Bittrich was very critical of the High Command and Hitler, saying that he was convinced of large parts of the Nazi ideology, but felt disdain for the 'incompetent' leaders and thought the regime's crimes would violate an officer's sense of honour.

He was arrested and tried in France for ordering the execution of seventeen resistance members. The trial revealed that Bittrich had not given the order and had, in fact, opened proceedings against those responsible. However, as their commander, he was sentenced to five years' imprisonment. He was released immediately due to the long pre-trial detention. In 1953, he was arrested again and sentenced to five years for countenancing hangings, pillage, and arson, but he was acquitted by the French court. Bittrich died on 19 April 1979 and is buried in the village cemetery, Munsing, Bavaria.

1191. *Oberst* Alfons HITTER

Hitter was born on 4 June 1892 in Hochstatt, Alsace-Lorraine. He fought in the First World War and was awarded the Iron Cross 1st and 2nd Class (1914). Hitter was awarded the Iron Cross 2nd Class (1939) in May and the 1st Class in July 1940. He was commander of Artillery Regiment 178 when he was awarded the Knight's Cross on 14 December 1941. The Oak Leaves followed on 4 June 1944. Hitter was captured by the Russians in 1944 and held until 1955. He died on 11 March 1968 and is buried in Königswinter Friedhof, Logebachstrasse, Königswinter-Ittenbach, North Rhine-Westphalia.

1192. *Oberst* Gustav WAGNER—'Iron Guatav'

Wagner was born on 23 September 1890 in Bischofsburg. He fought in the First World War and was awarded the Iron Cross 1st and 2nd Class (1914). Wagner was commander of Infantry Regiment 44 when he was awarded the Knight's Cross on 14 December 1941. He died on 26 May 1951 and is buried in German War Cemetery (Stadtfriedhof), Hildesheimerstrasse, Goslar, Lower Saxony.

1193. *Oberstleutnant* Eugen-Heinrich BLEYER

Bleyer was born on 20 November 1896 in Mainz. He fought in the First World War and was awarded the Iron Cross 1st and 2nd Class (1914), as well as the Wound Badge in Gold. Bleyer was awarded the Iron Cross 2nd Class in January and the 1st Class in June 1940. He was commander of Infantry Regiment 379 when he was awarded the Knight's Cross on 14 December 1941. Bleyer died on 18 March 1979 and is buried in Waldfriedhof, Bad Tölz, Bavaria.

1194. *Major* Werner NEBE

Nebe was born on 3 March 1904 in Oberrossbach. He was commander of Rifle Regiment 59 when he was awarded the Knight's Cross on 14 December 1941. Nebe was posted missing near Baranoviči, Russia, on 1 July 1944.

1195. *Hauptmann* Arthur JÜTTNER

Jüttner was born on 18 August 1908 in Kattowitz. He was awarded the Iron Cross 1st and 2nd Class after the fall of Poland. Jüttner was commander of III Battalion, Infantry Regiment 38, when he was awarded the Knight's Cross on 14 December 1941. The Oak Leaves followed on 18 October 1944 and the Swords on 5 April 1945. He died on 1 December 2003 in Bramstedt, Schleswig-Holstein.

1196. *Hauptmann* Werner KLEINSCHMIDT

Kleinschmidt was born on 2 February 1908 in Wittenberg. He was a company commander in Motorised Reconnaissance Battalion 341 when he was awarded the Knight's Cross on 14 December 1941. Kleinschmidt was killed in action near Lago di Como, Italy, on 15 March 1945 and has no known grave.

1197. *Rittmeister* Hans-Hermann SACHENBACHER

Sachenbacher was born on 2 August 1910 in Munich. He was commander of Bicycle Squadron 219 when he was awarded the Knight's Cross on 14 December 1941. Sachenbacher was killed in action on 27 November 1943 and is buried in the German War Cemetery, Block 8 (as unknown), Kiev, Ukraine.

1198. *Oberleutnant* Erich DIENENTHAL

Dienenthal was born on 17 December 1915 in Siegen. He was awarded the Iron Cross 2nd Class after the fall of Poland and the 1st Class in August 1941. Dienenthal was a company commander in Reconnaissance Battalion 45 when he was awarded the Knight's Cross on 14 December 1941. He died on 26 July 1990 and is buried in Lindenberg Friedhof, Siegen, North Rhine-Westphalia.

1199. *Oberleutnant* Hermann KRENZER

Krenzer was born on 1 March 1907 in Niederroden. He was a company commander in Infantry Regiment 379 when he was awarded the Knight's Cross on 14 December 1941. Krenzer died on 22 December 1988 and is buried in Alter Friedhof, Darmstadt, Hesse.

1200. *Oberleutnant* Heinrich SEIDEL

Seidel was born on 1 April 1913 in Dietrichswalde. He was commander of II Battalion, Infantry Regiment 422, when he was awarded the Knight's Cross on 14 December 1943. Seidel died on 16 December 2000 and is buried in Südfriedhof, Wiesbaden, Hesse.

1201. *Oberleutnant* Hans VOHBURGER

Vohburger was born on 11 February 1910 in Aham. He was a company commander in Infantry Regiment 19 when he was awarded the Knight's Cross on 14 December 1941. Vohburger was killed in action at Upolosy, Russia, on 18 August 1942 and has no known grave.

1202. *Oberfeldwebel* Ernst ZIEMER

Ziemer was born on 9 December 1911 in Schwirsen. He was awarded the Iron Cross 1st and 2nd Class after the fall of France. Ziemer was a platoon leader in Infantry Regiment 94 when he was awarded the Knight's Cross on 14 December 1941. The Oak Leaves followed on 2 November 1943. Ziemer died on 8 August 1986 in Lüneburg, Lower Saxony.

1203. *Feldwebel* Robert SIEGER

Sieger was born on 19 May 1914 in Binjay. He was a platoon leader in Infantry Regiment 133 when he was awarded the Knight's Cross on 14 December 1941. Sieger was killed in action on 1 April 1945 and is buried in the German War Cemetery, Hünfeld-Sargenzell, Hesse.

1204. *Hauptmann* Theodor TRIEBE

Triebe was born on 11 February 1904 in Churschütz. He was a company commander in Motorised Flak Regiment 7 when he was awarded the Knight's Cross on 18 December 1941. Triebe was killed in action in Küstrin, Poland, on 28 March 1945 and has no known grave.

1205. *Oberleutnant* Matthias SCHWEGLER

Schwegler was born 18 February 1916 in Augsburg. He was a squadron leader in Bomber Wing 51 when he was awarded the Knight's Cross on 18 December 1941. Schwegler was killed in action at Neuses on 18 April 1945 and has no known grave.

1206. *Feldwebel* Gerhard KÖPPEN

Köppen was born on 17 May 1918 in Holzendorf. He was a pilot in Fighter Wing 52 when he was awarded the Knight's Cross on 18 December 1941 with forty victories to his credit. On 27 February 1942, Köppen claimed four victories, bringing his tally to seventy-two; he was awarded the Oak Leaves the same day. With his total at eighty-five victories, Köppen was posted missing over the Sea of Azov on 5 May 1942.

1207. *Generalleutnant* Ernst HAMMER

Hammer was born on 20 October 1884 in Falkenau, Austria-Hungary. He fought in the First World War and was awarded the Iron Cross 1st and 2nd Class (1914). Hammer was commander of the 75th Infantry Division when he was awarded the Knight's Cross on 20 December 1941. He died on 2 December 1957 and is believed to be buried in Zentralfriedhof, Vienna.

1208. *Oberst* Norbert HOLM

Holm was born on 16 December 1895 in Hamburg. He fought in the First World War and was awarded the Iron Cross 1st and 2nd Class (1914). Holm was commander of Infantry Regiment 156 when he was awarded the Knight's Cross on 20 December 1941.

After the 20 July plot to kill Hitler, Holm was arrested due to his association with Rommel, and on 16 October 1944, he was demoted to private. As such, he fought in the 19th Panzer Division and, in January 1945, was prompted to *Unteroffizier* and to *Feldwebel* before the end of the war. His rank was restored in 1956. Holm died on 3 June 1962 in Hamburg.

1209. *Oberst* Hermann KRESS

Kress was born on 23 July 1895 in Hassfurt. He fought in the First World War and was awarded the Iron Cross 1st and 2nd Class (1914). Kress awarded the Iron Cross 1st and 2nd Class (1939) after the fall of Poland. He was commander of Mountain *Jäger* Regiment 99 when he was awarded the Knight's Cross on 20 December 1941. Kress was killed in action on 11 August 1943 at Myzako, Russia, and has no known grave.

1210. *Oberst* Karl (or Carl) PÜCHLER

Püchler was born on 13 May 1894 in Bad Warmbrunn. He fought in the First World War and was awarded the Iron Cross 1st and 2nd Class (1914). Püchler was commander of Infantry Regiment 228 when he was awarded the Knight's Cross on 20 December 1941. He died on 5 February 1949 and is believed to be buried in Hauptfriedhof, Heilbronn, Baden-Württemberg.

1211. *Oberst* Siegfried RUNGE

Runge was born on 8 June 1884 in Breslau. He was commander of Infantry Regiment 219 when he was awarded the Knight's Cross on 20 December 1941. Runge was killed in action on 24 March 1945 and is buried in the German War Cemetery, Block K, Grave 23, Viborg, Denmark.

1212. *Oberst* Otto SCHÜNEMANN

Schünemann was born on 6 October 1891 in Bad Doberan. He fought in the First World War and was awarded the Iron Cross 1st and 2nd Class (1914). Schünemann was commander of Infantry Regiment 184 when he was awarded the Knight's Cross on 20 December 1941. The Oak Leaves followed on 28 November 1943. He was killed in action at Pagost, Belarus, on 29 June 1944 and has no known grave.

1213. *Hauptmann* Rudolf KIEL

Kiel was born on 25 October 1911 in Sondershausen. He was a group commander in Bomber Wing 55 when he was awarded the Knight's Cross on 20 December 1941. Kiel died on 1 July 2003 in Murnau, Bavaria.

1214. *Hauptmann* Reinhard SEILER

Seiler was born on 30 August 1909 in Rawitsch. He fought in the Spanish Civil War and shot down nine enemy aircraft. Seiler shot down his first enemy aircraft of the war on 10 January 1940, south-west of Freilburg, and he was awarded the Iron Cross 2nd Class. He would shoot down only one more before the Battle of Britain. In July, Seiler was awarded the Iron Cross 1st Class, and in August 1940, Seiler shot down a Spitfire over Dover but was himself shot down shortly afterward and was out of action for next six months.

On 22 June 1941, the first day of the attack on Russia, Seiler shot down three enemy aircraft. On the Leningrad front, his tally started to rise, even shooting down sixteen aircraft at night. Seiler was awarded the Knight's Cross on 20 December 1941. His unit was sent to the West in early 1943 and he shot down one four-engined bomber before being sent back to Russia. On the first day of the Battle of Kursk, Seiler shot down five aircraft, bringing his tally to ninety-seven. In his aim to hit 100 aerial victories, he shot down two aircraft the next day and, after shooting down an Air Cobra, was shot down himself; this time Seiler was wounded and landed behind enemy lines. Rescued by German soldiers, he was sent home for treatment and declared unfit for combat duties. Sieler was awarded the Oak Leaves on 2 March 1944 with his total at 109 enemy aircraft. He died on 4 October 1989 in Grafengehaig, Bavaria.

1215. *Oberleutnant* Peter FLIESSBACH

Fliessbach was born on 28 February 1917 in Kurow. He was a company commander in Artillery Regiment 23 when he was awarded the Knight's Cross on 20 December 1941. Fliessbach was killed in action on 21 March 1944 and is buried at Gaje Dytkowieckie, Ukraine; his remains are awaiting transfer to a German war cemetery.

1216. *Oberleutnant* Ulrich GUNZERT

Gunzert was born on 8 July 1915 in Muansa. He was a company commander in Pioneer Battalion 258 when he was awarded the Knight's Cross on 20 December 1941. Gunzert died on 12 October 2000 and is buried in Parkfriedhof, Ottobrunn, Bavaria.

1217. *Oberleutnant* Erich WEYEL

Weyel was born on 17 December 1909 in Becherbach. He was a company commander in Infantry Regiment 506 when he was awarded the Knight's Cross on 20 December 1941. Weyel died on 22 November 1992 in Bad Kreuznach, Rhineland-Palatinate.

1218. *Leutnant* Fritz BLIESENER

Bliesener was born on 24 January 1920 in Stettin. He was a pilot in Bomber Wing 55 when he was awarded the Knight's Cross on 20 December 1941. Bliesener was killed in action on 25 November 1942 and is buried at Kadijewka, Ukraine; his remains are awaiting transfer to a German war cemetery.

1219. *Leutnant* Dieter (or Diether) LUKESCH

Lukesch was born on 15 July 1918 in Vienna. He was awarded the Iron Cross 1st and 2nd Class in June and July 1941. Lukesch was a pilot in Bomber Wing 76 when he was awarded the Knight's Cross on 20 December 1941. The Oak Leaves followed on 10 October 1944 while he was training to fly the Arado Ar 234 jet bomber. He was one of the first pilots to carry out jet bombing missions flying the Ar 234, supporting the attack in the Ardennes during December 1944. Lukesch was also the first pilot to carry out a night bombing raid. He died on 28 February 2004 and is believed to be buried in Henstedt Friedhof, Schleswig-Holstein.

1220. *Leutnant* Heinz MARTIN

Martin was born on 15 July 1916 in Schwarzenberg. He was an *aide-de-camp* in Infantry Regiment 520 when he was awarded the Knight's Cross on 20 December 1941. Martin was killed in action on 27 September 1942 and is buried at Posdnjakowo, Bolkhov, Russia; his remains are awaiting transfer to a German war cemetery

1221. *Leutnant* Eduard MEYER

Meyer was born on 8 December 1919 in Detmold. He was a pilot in Heavy Fighter Wing 26 when he was awarded the Knight's Cross on 20 December 1941. Meyer was killed in action near Welish, Russia, on 31 March 1942 and has no known grave. He is credited with twenty-two aerial victories, forty-eight aircraft destroyed on the ground, and two tanks knocked-out.

1222. *Leutnant* Jürgen STEPUTAT

Steputat was born on 20 January 1912 in Danzig. He was a pilot in Bomber Wing 30 when he was killed in action on 8 September 1941 and is buried in the German War Cemetery, Block 9, Row 53, Grave 1315, Route de Kerivoal, Ploudaniel-Lesneven, Bretagne, France. Steputat was awarded the Knight's Cross on 20 December 1941.

1223. *Obergefreiter* Peter GRÜBL

Grübl was born on 27 December 1917 in Pötzing. He was a section leader in *Jäger* Regiment 98 when he was awarded the Knight's Cross on 20 December 1941. Grübl died on 19 May 1980 in Peikertsham, near Triftern, Bavaria.

1224. *Generalmajor* Fritz SCHLIEPER

Schlieper was born on 4 August 1892 in Koldromb. He fought in the First World War. Schlieper was commander of the 45th Infantry Division when he was awarded the Knight's Cross on 27 December 1941 for his part in the victory at the Brest Fortress. Schlieper died on 4 June 1977 and is believed to be buried in Westfriedhof, Nuremberg. His brother, Franz, was also awarded the Knight's Cross.

1225. *Generalmajor* Erwin RAUCH

Rauch was born on 19 October 1889 in Berlin. He fought in the First World War and was awarded the Iron Cross 1st and 2nd Class (1914). Rauch was commander of the 123rd Infantry Division when he was awarded the Knight's Cross on 22 December 1941. He died on 26 February 1969 in Kirchenlamitz, Bavaria, although there is also a reference to him dying in Austria.

1226. *Oberst* Johannes BLOCH (or BLOCK)

Bloch was born on 17 November 1894 in Büschdorf. He fought in the First World War and was awarded the Iron Cross 1st and 2nd Class (1914). Bloch was commander of Infantry Regiment 202 when he was awarded the Knight's Cross on 22 December 1941. The Oak Leaves followed on 22 November 1943. He was killed in action on 26 January 1945. He is buried at Baranov Sandomierz, Poland; his remains are awaiting transfer to a German war cemetery.

1227. *Oberst* Ehrenfried-Oskar BOEGE

Boege was born on 11 November 1889 in Ostrowo. He fought in the First World War and was awarded the Iron Cross 1st and 2nd Class (1914). Boege was awarded the Iron Cross 1st and 2nd Class (1939) on 16 June 1940. He was commander of Infantry Regiment 7 when he was awarded the Knight's Cross on 22 December 1941. The Oak Leaves followed on 21 September 1944. Boege was captured by the Russians at the end of the war and was held until 1955. He died on 31 December 1965 and is buried in Rosenthal Friedhof, Hesse.

1228. *Oberst* Alexander RATCLIFFE

Ratcliffe was born on 17 August 1890 in Munich. He was commander of Infantry Regiment 192 when he was awarded the Knight's Cross on 22 December 1941. Ratcliffe died on 30 April 1979 and is buried in Gauting Friedhof, Bavaria.

1229. *Oberleutnant* Ernst-Martin RHEIN

Rhein was born on 6 April 1917 in Birkholz. He was a company commander in Infantry Regiment 18 when he was awarded the Knight's Cross on 22 December 1941. Rhein died on 20 April 2016 and is buried in Zehlendorf Friedhof, Berlin.

1230. *Oberleutnant* Heinrich STENZEL

Stenzel was born on 1 July 1915 in Wusterwitz. He was a company commander in Reconnaissance Battalion 12 when he was awarded the Knight's Cross on 22 December 1941. Stenzel was killed in action at Demjansk, Russia, on 19 January 1942 and has no known grave.

1231. *Leutnant* Wido TILMANN

Tilmann was born on 16 September 1917 in Bonn. He was a platoon leader in Pioneer Battalion 297 when he was awarded the Knight's Cross on 22 December 1941. Tilmann died on 15 February 1987 and is buried in Ostfriedhof, Cologne, North Rhine-Westphalia.

1232. *SS-Gruppenführer* Theodor EICKE—'Papa'

Eicke was born on 17 October 1892 in Hudingen. He fought in the First World War and was awarded the Iron Cross 2nd Class (1914). Eicke was commandant of Dachau Concentration Camp and later concentration camp inspector. After the 'Night of the Long Knives', Eicke, along with Michael Lippert, shot Ernst Röhm. In 1940, he commanded the SS-*Totenkopf* Division in France, where his men murdered ninety-seven British POWs at Le Paradis. Eicke was awarded the Iron Cross 1st and 2nd Class in May 1940.

He was awarded Knight's Cross on 26 December 1941 and the Oak Leaves followed on 20 April 1942. Eicke was killed in action when his light aircraft was shot down near Kharkov, Russia, on 26 February 1943. He was buried in a field near Orelka, Russia. Later, he was moved to the Hegewald German Military Cemetery at Zhitomir, but his cemetery was destroyed by the Russians and his grave is now lost.

1233. *Generalmajor* Maximilian FRETTER-PICO

Fretter-Pico was born on 6 February 1892 in Karlsruhe. He fought in the First World War and was awarded the Iron Cross 1st and 2nd Class (1914). Fretter-Pico missed the campaigns in Poland and France as he was recalled from Turkey. However, he was awarded the Iron Cross 2nd Class (1939) in October 1939 and the 1st Class in June 1940.

Fretter-Pico was commander of the 97th Infantry Division when he was awarded the Knight's Cross on 26 December 1941. The Oak Leaves followed on 16 January 1944. He died on 4 April 1984 and is buried in Friedhof der Jerusalem, Bergmannstrasse, Kreuzberg, Berlin. His brother, Otto, was also awarded the Knight's Cross.

1234. *Generalmajor* Robert MARTINEK

Martinek was born on 2 February 1889 in Gratzen, Austria-Hungary. He fought in the First World War and was regarded as one of the most skilled artillerymen of his generation. Martinek was commander of the 267th Infantry Division when he was awarded the Knight's Cross on 26 December 1941. The Oak Leaves followed on 10 February 1944. Martinek was killed in action on 28 June 1944 and is buried at Tscherwen, Belarus; his remains are awaiting transfer to a German war cemetery.

1235. *Oberst* Erwin MENNY

Menny was born on 10 August 1893 in Saarburg. He fought in the First World War and was awarded the Iron Cross 1st and 2nd Class (1914). During the French campaign, he commanded the 69th Rifle Regiment. Menny arrived in Africa in April 1941 where he took command of the 15th Rifle Regiment. His regiment fought at all the hotspots of Africa, as well as during the withdrawal. It was for this that he was awarded the Knight's Cross on 26 December 1941.

In the new offensive in January 1942, Manny helped to retake Cyrenaica in just seventeen days and subsequently fought at Tobruk. Forced to leave Africa, he took command of the 84th Infantry Divison in February 1944. He was captured on 21 August 1944 during the Russian onslaught that was Operation Bagration. Menny died on 6 December 1949 and is buried in Hauptfriedhof, Friedhofstrasse 8, Freilburg im Breisgau, Baden-Württemberg.

1236. *Oberstleutnant* Fritz BAYERLEIN

Bayerlein was born on 14 January 1899 in Würzburg. He was awarded the Iron Cross 2nd Class (1914) during the First World War. He served in Poland and France on Guderian's Staff and was awarded the Iron Cross 1st and 2nd Class (1939). Still under Guderian, he served in Russia and was transferred to the Africa Corps, taking temporary command at Alam-el-Halfa, being forced to fight at short notice as Nehring had been wounded. Bayerlein was awarded the Knight's Cross on 26 December 1941. The Oak Leaves followed on 6 July 1943. When von Thoma was captured, he was again forced to take command of the Africa Corps. Bayerlein was withdrawn to Europe before the final surrender in Tunisia. Sent back to Russia, he commanded the 3rd Panzer Division, with which he broke-out of an encirclement at Kirovograd. He spent a short time in Hungary with the Panzer *Lehr* Division before being moved to France in May 1944.

The Panzer *Lehr* Division, which had been earmarked for an anti-invasion role, went to the Russian Front in March 1944, but it was back in Normandy by the end of May. At the end of July, the division was all but wiped out by the ferocious bombing along the Saint-Lô–Perriers road during Operation Cobra. It took part in the counterattack at Avranches and was almost lost in the Falaise Pocket. He was awarded the Swords on 20 July 1944. The Panzer *Lehr* Division took part in the Ardennes offensive. Again, the division suffered badly. In January 1945, Bayerlein was placed in command of LIII Corps and fought on until trapped in the Rühr Pocket. He is the author of *War Without Hate*. Bayerlein died on 30 January 1970 and is buried in Hauptfriedhof, Abt 1, Feld 2, Grave 32, Würzburg, Bavaria.

1237. *Oberstleutnant* Eduard CRASEMANN

Crasemann was born on 5 March 1891 in Hamburg. He fought in the First World War and was awarded the Iron Cross 1st and 2nd Class (1914). At the start of the Second World War, he commanded an artillery battery and, by 1940, was CO of the battalion. On 10 May 1941, he took command of the 33rd Armoured Artillery Regiment, with which he went to Africa. He fought with great *élan* and demonstrated a high level of ability, for which he was awarded the Knight's Cross on 26 December 1941.

During July and August 1942, Crasemann commanded the 15th Panzer Division before being wounded and returning to Germany. He became CO of the artillery of XXIV Panzer Corps and later held the same post in XXXIV Army Corps. Crasemann was awarded the Oak Leaves on 18 December 1944 while CO of 26th Panzer Division, and in January 1945, he assumed command of XII SS-Panzer Corps. At the end of the war, he was taken prisoner by the British and sentenced to ten years' imprisonment for wars crimes; he died in Prison on 29 April 1950. Crasemann is buried in Parkfriedhof, Werl, North Rhine-Westphalia.

1238. *Kapitänleutnant* Gerhard BIGALK

Bigalk was born in Berlin on 26 November 1908. He spent some time in the merchant marine before joining the *Kriegsmarine* in April 1934. After several patrols on *U-14*, Bigalk took command of *U-751* on 31 January 1941. He began his first patrol in June and torpedoed the *St Lindsay*, which was carrying munitions. In December, Bigalk took part in attacks on convoy HG 76, during which *U-131* and *U-434* were sunk. While aircraft from the carrier *Audacity* were engaged in shooting down two German Fw 200 long-range bombers, *U-751* was able to creep up on the carrier in the falling darkness and fire a spread of torpedoes; the 11,000-ton carrier sank, taking its aircraft with it.

Bigalk continued his success, sinking two ships each in February and May 1942. Then, on 17 July 1942, *U-751* was attacked and sunk with all hands by aircraft from 502 and 61 Squadrons RAF, off Cape Ortegal, Spain.

1239. *Major* Fritz HERRMANN

Herrmann was born on 29 May 1895 in Adelsheim. He was commander of I Battalion, Infantry Regiment 36, when he was awarded the Knight's Cross on 26 December 1941. Herrmann died on 13 March 1971 in Rheinberg, North Rhine-Westphalia.

1240. *Kapitänleutnant* Klaus SCHOLTZ

Scholtz was born on 22 March 1908 in Magdeburg. He reported to the U-boat arm in April 1940 and commissioned *U-108* on 22 October 1940. On his first patrol, he sank two ships. On his second patrol in the Strait of Denmark on 13 April 1941, he sank the 16,444-ton armed merchant cruiser *Rajputana* after a forty-eight-hour chase. In June, he sank six ships, including three from convoy HG76 in the 'Long Hunt', during which Scholtz spent ninety-six hours in the conning tower. He was awarded the Knight's Cross on 26 December 1941. At the end of January 1942, *U-108* sailed to the East Coast of the USA, sinking four ships. His next patrol was to the same area he was resupplied by *U-459*, enabling him to extend his patrol. Scholtz sunk eight ships, including the 9,925-ton *Mobiloil*. The award of the Oak Leaves came on 10 September 1942. He sank twenty-five ships—a total of 123,990 tons.

On 1 October 1942, he took command of the 12th U-Boat Flotilla in Bordeaux. After the Allied invasion of Europe, Bordeaux became a fortress. They were overtaken by the enemy advance and surrendered on 11 September 1944. Scholtz died on 1 May 1987 in Bad Schwartau, Schleswig-Holstein.

1241. *Hauptmann* Ludwig BACHMAIER

Bachmaier was born on 24 August 1895 in St Wolfgang. He fought in the First World War and was awarded the Iron Cross 1st and 2nd Class (1914). Bachmaier was commander of I Battalion, Infantry Regiment 179, when he was awarded the Knight's Cross on 26 December 1941. He died on 19 December 1957 and is buried in Hauptfriedhof, Friedhofstrasse 1, Landshut, Bavaria.

1242. *Oberfeldwebel* Gerhard HENSEL

Hensel was born on 24 May 1889 in Soest. He was a platoon leader in Panzer Regiment 15 when he was awarded the Knight's Cross on 26 December 1941. Hensel died of wounds on 26 January 1943 near Rostov, Russia, He has no known grave.

1243. *Korvettenkapitän* Karl-Friedrich BRILL

Brill was born on 18 July 1898 in Stolzenau. He fought in the First World War, being awarded the Iron Cross 2nd Class (1914). Brill was awarded the Iron Cross 2nd Class (1939) in April 1940 and the 1st Class in November 1941. He was commander of the minelayer *Cobra* when he was awarded the Knight's Cross on 27 December 1941. Brill was killed in action on 22 October 1943 when his ship the *Juminda* was sunk. He is buried in the German War Cemetery, Block S, Grave 1068, Pomezia, Italy. He was awarded the Oak Leaves on 18 November 1943.

1244. *Kapitän* zur See Otto (aka Ernst) LINDEMANN

Lindemann was born on 28 March 1894 in Altenkirchen. He fought in the First World War and was awarded the Iron Cross 1st and 2nd Class (1914). Lindemann also served in the Spanish Civil War. He was awarded the Iron

Cross 1st and 2nd Class (1939) in May 1940. Lindemann was given command of the battleship *Bismarck* on 24 August 1940. The *Bismarck* and the heavy cruiser *Prinz Eugen* set sail on 19 May 1941, and on 21 May, they engaged two British heavy cruisers, HMS *Suffolk* and *Norfolk*; no hits were scored, but the British ships withdrew.

In the early hours of 24 May, the Germans spotted the heavy battlecruiser HMS *Hood* and the battleship *Prince of Wales*. After just five salvos, the *Hood* was hit by the *Bismarck* and exploded, sinking in just three minutes—there were only three survivors. The *Prince of Wales* disengaged after receiving seven direct hits, four from the *Bismarck* and three from the *Prinz Eugen*. After this action, the two German ships split up and the *Bismarck* was later attacked by Swordfish torpedo bombers from the aircraft carrier HMS *Victorious* under the command of Eugene Esmonde (who was awarded the Victoria Cross). One hit was scored, but no real damage was done.

The *Bismarck* was again attacked by Swordfish bombers in the evening of 26 May, this time from the carrier HMS *Ark Royal*. One torpedo damaged the *Bismarck*'s rudder. Throughout the night, the *Bismarck* was under torpedo attack by the destroyers HMS *Cossack*, *Sikh*, *Maori*, *Zulu*, and ORP *Piorun*. At 8.30 a.m. on 28 May 1941, the battleships HMS *Rodney* and *King George V*, with the cruisers HMS *Norfolk* and *Dorsetshire*, opened fire on the *Bismarck*. With her rudder damaged, the *Bismarck* could not manoeuvre as she wished. Outgunned and outnumbered, the *Bismarck* was sunk at 10.36 a.m.; only 115 men survived. Lindemann went down with his ship. He was awarded the Knight's Cross on 27 December 1941. His cousin, Georg Lindemann, was also awarded the Knight's Cross.

1245. *Oberleutnant* Georg MÜGGE

Mügge was born on 11 March 1916 in Berlin. He was commander of II Battalion, Infantry Regiment 203, when he was awarded the Knight's Cross on 27 December 1941. Mügge died on 24 August 1953 and is believed to be buried in Tellingstedt Friedhof, Schleswig-Holstein.

1246. *Leutnant* zur See Axel GOETZKE

Goetzke was born on 2 January 1904 in Stettin-Frauendorf. He was commander of a minesweeper in R-Boat Flotilla 5 when he was killed in action on 14 September 1941 and is buried in the German War Cemetery (Hietaniemi Cemetery), Block 39, Row 10, Grave 135, Helsinki, Finland. Goetzke was awarded the Knight's Cross on 27 December 1941.

1247. *Obergefreiter* Michael SCHROEPFER

Schroepfer was born on 16 January 1915 in Nim-Vorgut. He was a gunner in Infantry Regiment 111 when he was awarded the Knight's Cross on 27 December 1941. Schroepfer died on 27 December 1980 and is buried in Bergfriedhof, Lahr, Baden-Württemberg.

1248. *Generalleutnant* Friedrich-Georg EBERHARDT

Eberhardt was born on 15 January 1892 in Strasbourg. He fought in the First World War, being awarded the Iron Cross 1st and 2nd Class (1914). Eberhardt was awarded the Iron Cross 1st and 2nd Class (1939) after the fall of Poland. He was commander of the 60th Infantry Division when he was awarded the Knight's Cross on 31 December 1941. Eberhardt died on 9 September 1964 and is buried in Nordfriedhof, Feld 39B, Grave 4, Wiesbaden, Hesse.

1249. *Generalmajor* Wilhelm Ritter von THOMA

Ritter von Thoma was born on 11 September 1891 in Dachau. He fought in the First World War and was awarded the Iron Cross 1st and 2nd Class (1914), as well as the Wound Badge in Silver for being wounded four times. Von Thoma also fought in the Spanish Civil War. He was awarded the Iron Cross 1st and 2nd Class (1939) after the fall of Poland. Von Thoma was commander of the 20th Panzer Division when he was awarded the Knight's Cross on 31 December 1941.

After Russia, he was sent to North Africa where he was captured by the British on 4 November 1942. Von Thoma had both legs amputated while a POW. He died from a heart attack on 30 April 1948 and is buried in Waldfriedhof (headstone removed), Weblingerweg, Dachau, Bavaria.

1250. *Oberst* Hasso von MANTEUFFEL—'The Hero of Zhitomir'

Von Manteuffel was born on 14 January 1897 in Potsdam. He served in the First World War, being awarded the Iron Cross 1st and 2nd Class (1914). At the start of the Second World War, von Manteuffel was a training instructor at a panzer school. He took command of a motorised infantry battalion in 7th Panzer Division and fought with it in Russia. With his unit, he fought in the advance to Moscow and winter battles. He was awarded the Knight's

Cross on 31 December 1941. He was moved to Africa in February 1943 to commanded *ad hoc* units thrown together in a vain attempt to stop the Allies in Tunisia. Von Manteuffel was awarded the Oak Leaves on 23 November 1943 and was sent home ill; on his recovery, he was sent back to Russia. He received the Swords on 22 February 1944. Later, von Manteuffel took over the *Grossdeutschland* Panzer Division in Russia as an expert in manoeuvring large tank units. He was to suffer from Hitler's insistence on holding territory at all costs.

Still only a divisional general, he was moved to the West in September 1944 to command the 5th Panzer Army with which he was ordered to stop Patton's advance into Lorraine. Knowing his forces were not up to the job, he attacked with misgivings, and in a four-day battle, he suffered considerable losses. In the Ardennes offensive that followed, his army was in the centre and aimed to cross the Meuse and capture Antwerp. His army actually had the greatest success in the early stages; some of his units reached the Meuse near Dinant. However, he was severely defeated, although he was not to blame for this. Moved back to the East in Poland, where the Russians had broken through, von Manteuffel was no longer able to stop the Russian tidal wave. He was awarded the Diamonds on 18 February 1945. He was sent to trial after the war over the ordering of a sentry to be shot for dereliction of duty, but he only served two months in prison. Manteuffel died from a heart attack on 24 September 1978 and is buried in St Johann Friedhof, Diessen am Ammersee, Bavaria.

1251. *Korvettenkapitän* Hans REHM

Rehm was born on 22 December 1903 in Regensburg. He was awarded the Iron Cross 2nd Class in October 1939 and the 1st Class in May 1940. Rehm was commander of M-Boat Flotilla 2 when he was awarded the Knight's Cross on 31 December 1941. He died on 7 October 1986 in Flensburg, Schleswig-Holstein.

1252. *Major* Günther FENSKI

Fenski was born on 2 January 1907 in Pestlin. He took part in the Polish and French campaigns, being awarded the Iron Cross 1st and 2nd Class. In Africa, during British Operation Crusader, Fenski took command of his battalion and rolled over the Trigh Capuzzo to Sidi Rezegh. The pursuit of the enemy continued until 22 November 1941, when he ran into the British 4th Armoured Bridge. Fenski, in the first tank, sighted the British armour and surrounded the tanks; following a brief exchange of fire, the enemy surrendered.

He captured a brigadier-general, seventeen officers, 150 men, thirty-five tanks, and a number of guns and radio vehicles. Fenski was killed in action on 23 November 1941 and is buried in the German War Cemetery, Tobruk, Libya. He was awarded the Knight's Cross on 31 December 1941.

1253. *Kapitänleutnant* Robert GYSAE

Gysae was born on 14 January 1911 in Berlin. He commissioned *U-98* on 12 October 1940, and on his first patrol in March, he sank a large steamer and three other merchant ships. On 13 May, he sank the 10,549-ton British armed merchant cruiser *Salopian.* Two more ships followed in July. In September, he fired at convoy SC 42, sinking one ship. On 31 December 1941, he was awarded the Knight's Cross. Gysae sank his last ship with *U-98* in February 1942. Now commanding *U-177*, Gysae sailed into southern waters in November 1942 where he sank several large ships, including the 10,799-ton *Llandaff Castle*. He returned to port, flying eight sinking pennants. He was awarded the Oak Leaves on 31 May 1943.

His last patrol took him to southern waters again, where he sank the 6,679-ton *Agwimonte*, followed by the 7,886-ton tanker *Storaas* and two US ships, the *Jasper Park* and the *Alice F. Palmer*, both over 7,000 tons. Two more steamers completed his record before he handed over *U-177* to Buchholz. From December 1943 until April 1945, Gysae commanded the 25th U-Boat Flotilla. His last command was an anti-tank regiment and his final rank was *Korvettenkapitän*. He sank a total of twenty-four ships—a total of 139,413 tons. Gysae died on 26 April 1989 and is buried in Wilhelmshaven Friedhof, Lower Saxony.

1254. *Major* Georg HESSE

Hesse was born on 30 September 1907 in Oberschönbrunn. He was commander of III Battalion, Motorised Infantry Regiment 120, when he was awarded the Knight's Cross on 31 December 1941. Hesse was killed in action near Stalingrad on 22 September 1942 and has no known grave.

1255. *Kapitänleutnant* Eitel-Friedrich KENTRAT

Kentrat was born on 11 September 1906 in Stahlheim. With the outbreak of war, he volunteered for the U-boat service and served on board *U-25* as watch officer. His first command was *U-8*, but on 31 October 1940, he commissioned *U-74*. Kentrat sank his first ship on 3 April 1941 and torpedoed the merchant cruiser *Worcestershire*, which was part of the SC26 convoy. During his next patrol in May, he, along with all other U-boats, was ordered to assist with picking up survivors from the *Bismarck*. *U-74* only found three men.

On his third patrol, he sank a ship from convoy SL81. Kentrat then commissioned *U-196* and took her into the Indian Ocean on what was to become the longest U-boat combat patrol in history—225 days. He sank four ships on this patrol. In February 1944, he sailed into the Arabian Sea but no ships were sighted, and after 150 days at sea, *U-196* sailed into Penang. His last command was the support base at Kobe, Japan. He died on 9 January 1974 in Bad Schwartau, Schleswig-Holstein.

1256. *Major* Johann MOSHAMMER

Moshammer was born on 9 January 1903 in Judenburg. He was commander of II Battalion, Infantry Regiment 50, when he was awarded the Knight's Cross on 31 December 1941. Moshammer was killed in action at Terek, Russia, on 27 September 1942 and has no known grave.

1257. *Major* Horst von USEDOM

Von Usedom was born on 9 March 1906 in Celle. He was awarded the Iron Cross 2nd Class after the fall of Poland and the 1st Class after the fall of France. He was commander of Motorcycle Battalion 61 when he was awarded the Knight's Cross on 31 December 1941. The Oak Leaves followed on 28 March 1945. Von Usedom died on 14 October 1970 and is believed to be buried in Waldfriedhof, Munich.

1258. *Hauptmann* Edgar DÜNKER

Dünker was born on 22 August 1902 in Posen. He was commander of I Battalion, Infantry Regiment 336, when he died of wounds at Kalinin, Russia, on 29 December 1941 and has no known grave. Dünker was awarded the Knight's Cross on 31 December 1941.

1259. *Hauptmann* Erich LABRENZ

Labrenz was born on 6 December 1903 in Jeschkendorf. He was commander of III Battalion, Infantry Regiment 480, when he was awarded the Knight's Cross on 31 December 1941. Labrenz died as a POW during July 1949 and is buried at Vorkuta, Russia; his remains are awaiting transfer to a German war cemetery.

1260. *Oberleutnant* Otto BENZIN

Benzin was born on 23 November 1910 in Pritzwalk. He was awarded the Iron Cross 2nd Class in May 1940 and the 1st Class in July 1941. Benzin was a company commander in Infantry Regiment 89 when he was awarded the Knight's Cross on 31 December 1941. The Oak Leaves followed on 22 February 1944. He was also awarded the Wound Badge in Gold for multiple wounds. Benzin was killed in action at Babruysk, Belarus, on 3 July 1944 and has no known grave.

1261. *Oberleutnant* Klaus von BISMARCK

Von Bismarck was born on 6 March 1912 in Jarchlin. He was awarded the Iron Cross 2nd Class after the fall of Poland and the 1st Class after the fall of France. Von Bismarck was commander of II Battalion, Infantry Regiment 4, when he was awarded the Knight's Cross on 31 December 1941. The Oak Leaves followed on 26 November 1944. Von Bismarck died on 22 May 1997 and is buried in Ohlsdorf Friedhof, Plot AA17, Grave 150–155, Fuhlsbüttler Strasse, Hamburg. He is related to Otto von Bismarck.

1262. *Oberleutnant* Ernst EMMERT

Emmert was born on 26 February 1900 in Kitzingen. He was a company commander in Infantry Regiment 282 when he was awarded the Knight's Cross on 31 December 1941. Emmert died of wounds on 22 January 1945 and is buried the Gross Nädlitz German War Cemetery, Block 2, Row 17, Grave 401–425, Nadolice Wielkie, near Wroclaw, Poland.

1263. *Oberleutnant* Wilhelm FAHLBUSCH

Fahlbusch was born on 8 November 1914 in Hanover. He was a company commander in Motorised Flak Regiment 11 when he was awarded the Knight's Cross on 31 December 1941. Fahlbusch died on 12 June 2006 in Bonn.

1264. *Oberleutnant* Alfred MUES

Mues was born on 3 July 1913 in Warstein. He was a company commander in Rifle Regiment 64 when he was awarded the Knight's Cross on 31 December 1941. Mues died of wounds on 26 November 1942 and is buried in the German War Cemetery (as unknown), Rossoschka, Volgograd, Russia.

1265. *Oberleutnant* Heinrich SETZ

Setz was born on 12 March 1915 in Gundelsdorf. He was a pilot in Fighter Wing 77 when he shot down his first enemy aircraft off the coast of Norway on 27 August 1940; two more followed shortly afterwards. Setz was awarded the Iron Cross 2nd Class in September and the 1st Class in October 1940. He was awarded the Knight's Cross on 31 December 1941 with forty-five victories to his credit.

During 1942, his score raised rapidly when he shot down his forty-sixth to fiftieth victories on 19 March, his fifty-eighth to sixtieth on 21 April, his sixty-eighth to seventieth on 13 May, and his eighty-first on 23 June 1942, just one year after arriving in Russia. Setz was awarded the Oak Leaves on 23 June 1942. He scored his 100th victory on 24 July 1942. In October, with his tally at 135, Setz was wounded forcing him to spend time away from the front. In November, he was given command of I Group, Fighter Wing 27, which he took to France for the defence of the Reich, becoming operational on 20 February 1943. Setz first flight was also his last when, on 13 March 1943, he shot down two Spritfires (victories 136 and 137) in five minutes, but was killed when he collided with a third. He is buried in the German War Cemetery, Block 32, Row 11, Grave 427, Bourdon, Picardy, France. His cousin, Franz Ruhl, was also awarded the Knight's Cross.

1266. *Oberleutnant* Hermann VALLE

Valle was born on 3 January 1910 in Posen. He was a company commander in Rifle Regiment 112 when he was awarded the Knight's Cross on 31 December 1941. Valle was killed in action near Kursk on 13 February 1943 and has no known grave.

1267. *Leutnant* Werner ZIEGLER

Ziegler was born on 30 April 1916 in Hausach. He was awarded the Iron Cross 2nd Class in July 1940 and the 1st Class in April 1941. Ziegler was a company commander in Infantry Regiment 186 when he was awarded the Knight's Cross on 31 December 1941. The Oak Leaves followed on 8 September 1942 and the Swords on 23 October 1944. Ziegler died on 15 April 2001 and is believed to be buried in Oftersheim Friedhof, Baden-Württemberg.

Bibliography

Ailsby, C., *Combat Medals of the Third Reich* (UK, Patrick Stephen Limited, 1987)

Bender, R. J., *Organization, Uniforms and History of the Afrika Korps* (San Jose, R. James Bender Publishing 1973)

Bender, R. J., & Taylor, H. P., *Uniforms, Organization and History of the Waffen-SS Volumes 1-5* (San Jose, R. James Bender Publishing 1969)

Berger, F., *The Face of Courage,* (USA, Stackpole Books, 2011)

Brinkmann, J., *Orden Und Ehrenzeichen des Dritten Reiches* (Germany, Jürgen Brinkmann)

Caddick-Adams, P., *Monty and Rommel; Parallel Lives,* (UK, Preface Publishing, 2011)

Carius, O., *Tigers in the Mud,* (USA, Stackpole Books, 1992)

Carell, P., *Invasion; They're Coming* (London, Corgi Books, 1963); *Operation Barbarossa* (London, Corgi Books, 1976)

Cremer, P., *U333: The story of a U-Boat Ace,* (UK, The Bodley Head, 1984)

Davis, B. L., *German Army Uniforms and Insignia 1933-1945,* (UK, Arms and Armour Press, 1971)

Deighton, L., *Fighter,* (UK, Vintage Books, 1977)

Editors of WE Inc., *German Military Uniforms and Insignia 1933-1945,* (USA, WE Inc, 1967)

Franks, N., Bailey, F., & Guest, R., *Above the Lines,* (UK, Grub Street, 1993)

Fellgiebel, W.-P., *Elite of the Third Reich,* (UK, Helion and Company Limited, 2003)

Gerritsen, B., & Revell, S., *Retake Arnhem Bridge,* (The Netherlands, R.N. Sigmond Publishing 2010)

Guderian, H., *Achtung Panzer,* (UK, Brockhampton Press 1999)

Günther, F., *Knight's of the Reich,* (USA, Schiffer Publishing, 2004)

Hastings, M., *Overlord, D-Day and the Battle for Normandy* (UK, Michael Joseph Ltd 1984)

Jones, G., *U-Boat Aces,* (UK, William Kimber & Company Limited, 1988)

Kemp, A., *German Commanders of World War II* (UK, Osprey, 1982)

Kershaw, R., *'It Never Snows in September'* (UK, The Crowood Press 1990)

Kurowski, F., *Knight's Cross Holders of the Afrikakorps,* (USA, Schiffer Publishing, 1996); *Knight's Cross Holders of the Fallschirmjäger,* (USA, Schiffer Publishing, 1995); *Knight's Cross Holders of the U-boat Service,* (USA, Schiffer Publishing, 1995); *Infantry Aces,* (USA, Stackpole Books, 2005); *Luftwaffe Aces,* (USA, Stackpole Books, 2004); *Panzer Aces,* (USA, Stackpole Books, 2004); *Panzer Aces II,* (USA, Stackpole Books, 2004); *Panzer Aces III,* (USA, Stackpole Books, 2010)

Macksey, K., *Guderian: Panzer General,* (UK, Greenhill Books, 2003)
Miller, M., *Knight's Cross Holders of the SS and German Police 1940-45 Volume 1,* (USA, Helion & Company, 2016)
Pallud, J. P., *Battle of the Bulge, Then and Now* (UK, After the Battle 1984); *Blitzkrieg in the West, Then and Now* (UK, After the Battle 1991)
Paul, W., *Hermann Göring; Hitler Paladin or Puppet,* (UK, Brockhampton Press, 1999)
Rommel, E., *Infantry Attacks,* (USA, Echo Point Books & Media 2015)
Rudel, H.-U., *Stuka Pilot,* (UK, George Mann, 1973)
Ryan, C., *The Last Battle* (UK, New English Library 1966)
Scherzer, V., *The Knight's Cross 1939 – 1945,* (Germany, Scherzers Military-Verlag, 2007)
Seemen, G. von, *The Knight's Cross Bearers 1939-1945,* (1955 & 1976)
Taylor, D., *Villers-Bocage through the Lens,* (UK, After the Battle, 1999)
Wacker, A., *Sniper on the Eastern Front,* (UK, Pen & Sword 2005)
Williamson, G., *Infantry Aces of the Reich,* (BCA, 1991); *Knight's Cross and Oak-Leaves Recipients 1939-40,* (UK, Osprey, 2004); *Knight's Cross and Oak-Leaves Recipients 1941-45,* (UK, Osprey, 2005); *Knight's Cross, Oak-Leaves and Swords Recipients 1941-45,* (UK, Osprey, 2005); *Knight's Cross with Diamonds Recipients 1941-45,* (UK, Osprey, 2006); *Knights of the Iron Cross,* (UK, Blandford Press, 1989); *The Iron Cross: A History 1813-1957,* (UK, Blandford Press, 1984)

Index of Knight's Cross Holders

Each entry starts with the recipient's surname, in CAPITALS, followed by their rank (at time of the award), then their first name or names. If there are two or more men with the same name, then they are listed in the order they were awarded the Knight's Cross. Then their numbered position in the chronological list (in brackets) and finally the page number in the text. Where more than one page number is used their main entry in the text will be in **bold**.

Z